Merchants,
Landlords,
Magistrates

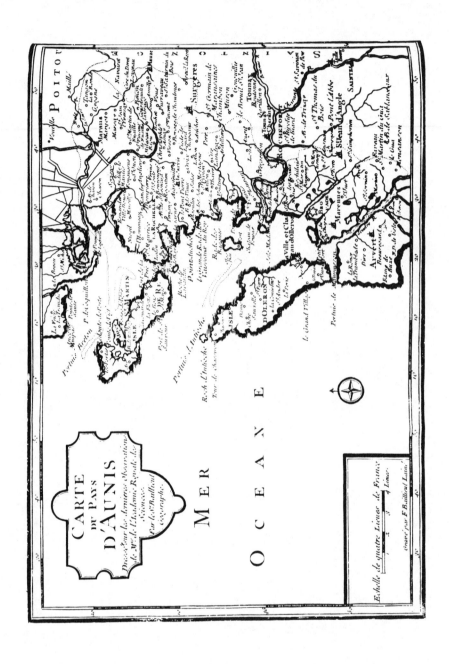

Merchants, Landlords, Magistrates

The Depont Family in Eighteenth-Century France

Robert Forster

THE JOHNS HOPKINS UNIVERSITY PRESS : **BALTIMORE AND LONDON**

The Johns Hopkins University Press, Baltimore, Maryland 21218
The Johns Hopkins Press Ltd., London

Forster, Robert, 1926-
  Merchants, landlords, magistrates.
  Includes index.
  1. Depont family.   2. Social mobility—France—
  Case studies.   I. Title.
CT1017.D46F67   305.5 ′0944   80-14944
ISBN 0-8018-2406-0

frontispiece: Map 1. The Province of Aunis in 1750. *Source:*
Pagniol de la Force, *Nouvelle Déscription de la France* (Paris,
1754), VII, 384.

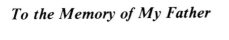
To the Memory of My Father

Contents

Preface

"No amount of scientific analysis or synthesis can take the place of that crucial act of human empathy by which the historian identifies with another time and place, reenacting the thoughts and reliving the experience of people remote from himself."[1] Family biography is one of the most promising avenues to empathetic recreation of the past, since it must stress the concrete and the circumstantial.[2] Flesh-and-blood personalities make day-to-day decisions, cope with the routine operation of institutions around them, and respond to economic pressures, social imperatives, and cultural norms. Properly described, the responses of a limited group or clan over several generations to these pressures and norms can throw light on the wider society—its structure and its values.

This book is intended to illuminate the process of "coping" with the issues and challenges the eighteenth century presented to one socially mobile French family, the Depont of La Rochelle. Fortunately, the sources and the experiences of the Depont family were sufficiently rich and varied to make it possible to treat a whole range of issues in French and early modern European history. What were the approved avenues of social ascent? How and why did a mercantile, Protestant family abandon the Atlantic slave and sugar trade to enter office, buy land and *rentes,* and convert to Catholicism? What were the psychological effects of this metamorphosis? What was the "mentality" of an *anobli,* a social hybrid like Paul-François Depont? What kind of landlords did newcomers make? Were they more businesslike, more entrepreneurial than the older landed families, or does land management seem to have rules of its own, unaffected by the temperaments of individual landlords? What kind of public administrators did parvenus like Jean-Samuel Depont make? Was "new blood" a sure road to innovation and reform or was the newcomer likely to enjoy the emoluments of his new-found status even more than the Old Guard? What was the impact of a Parisian culture on a young provincial raised by an economy-minded *rentier* and a Catholic convert? If Paul-François Depont was ambivalent and even anxious about his recently acquired status, and if Jean-Samuel, his son, paid for his prodigious capacity to adapt to Parisian standards of behavior with a kind of professional lassitude, Charles-François, his grandson, could turn to politics in the next generation of family ascent. This young "DePont" worried less about land and annuities, status and life-style, and much more about law and politics, constitutional reform and "*la Nation*" as the century drew to a dramatic close.

One of the purposes of the book is to trace the emergence by 1800 of a new elite, a social amalgam of landlords, administrators, and professional men, capped by political liberalism and a national awareness. These families would govern France for another century. The history of the Depont family in the eighteenth century is a case study in the making of a nineteenth-century Notable. Yet, at the same time, it is a story about real people who responded, not as a "class" or a sociological category, but as human beings laden with ambiguity and inconsistency who could not see the larger "trends" and "forces" the historian identifies in retrospect. I attempt to capture these ambiguities and nuances in human behavior as well as to identify the major challenges and constraints French society presented to the Deponts over a century. I make no apology for a narrative format; the issues in the field are interwoven into the story.

Within the limits imposed by the sources and common sense, I have tried to allow the Deponts of La Rochelle, Metz, and Paris to reveal their attitudes and values: not only *what* they experienced, but also, where possible, *how* they experienced it. Tone and texture are as much my concern as What and Why.[3] At the very least, I hope the reader will enjoy having lived *chez* the Depont family as much as I have.

Acknowledgments

I wish to express my appreciation to the Social Science Research Council, which provided me with funds to go to La Rochelle for six months in 1962. I also wish to thank the National Endowment for the Humanities, which helped support my year at the Institute for Advanced Study in Princeton in 1975–76 and the publication of this book.

My obligations to friends and colleagues are great, for although the monograph is modest in size, it has been long in gestation. First, I wish to thank those who helped me while I was searching for materials on the Depont family. At the departmental archives at La Rochelle in 1962 I was treated with warm hospitality by Marcel Delafosse and his staff, by Camille Gabet, and especially by Father Bernard Coutant, who guided me through the villages of Saintonge every Thursday afternoon. I also want to thank Yves de Rautlin de La Roy, who made it possible for me and my family to live in La Rochelle, invaluable to any local historian, but indispensable to a foreigner. Many French colleagues provided me with copies of documents, especially from the *Minutier Central* of the National Archives in Paris. They include Michel Antoine, Louis Bergeron, Fernand Braudel, Roger Chartier, Françoise Giteau, and Jacques Godechot. Michel Leymarie provided me with all the information he could find on the Fontages family in Auvergne, and Yves Camus very kindly sent me his law thesis on Jean-Samuel Depont as intendant of Moulins. Finally, Thomas W. Copeland sent me a copy of Charles-Jean-François Depont's reply to Edmund Burke, which he obtained in the Bodleian Library, Oxford.

After an interruption of almost ten years, I resumed work on the Depont family at the Institute for Advanced Study at Princeton in 1975–76. Here I received the invaluable criticism of the informal seminars organized by John H. Elliott and Albert O. Hirschman and of individual colleagues who halted their own research long enough to read my chapters with care. Among these individuals, I am especially indebted to Robert A. Ackerman, Robert Darnton, Lawrence Stone, and Ralph E. Giesey. Four of my colleagues at Johns Hopkins also made many invaluable marginal notations, queries, and comments on my chapter drafts: Louis Galambos, J.G.A. Pocock, Orest Ranum, and Mack Walker. I also thank James C. Davis, Frederick C. Lane, Lewis P. Lipsitt, R. Burr Litchfield, Lynn Lees, F. David Roberts, David Spring, Martin Wolfe, and the late Alfred Cobban and Arthur Wilson, all of whom read earlier versions of chapters of the manuscript. I thank the Center for Advanced Study in the Behavioral Sciences at Stanford, where I was a Fellow in 1979–80, for providing the funds for the preparation of the maps, graphs, and index. My special appreciation goes to Catherine Ingraham, who typed the whole manuscript with care and good humor. Most of all, I thank Elborg Forster, not only for her research in Paris in 1970 for part 3, but for her constant encouragement and optimism, without which the book might never have been completed.

I

First Ascent

La médiocrité en tout genre assure le bonheur et des succès à la longue. L'homme d'esprit connoît à peu près ses limites, il se compare, et n'est pas toujours par conséquent content de lui-même. Le sot est trop souvent averti de son impuissance, pour ne pas se sentir humilié. L'homme médiocre est le seul mortel heureux, soit qu'il descende en lui-même, soit qu'il se répande au dehors: l'imagination ne l'entraîne jamais, et il se glorifie d'être exempt de ses écarts. Il cite avec satisfaction les erreurs, les fautes des gens d'esprit. La froideur, la lenteur du sien sont à ses yeux du jugement, de la sagesse, de la raison. C'est un pilote sur une petite barque, qui ne quitte pas la côte, et qui est plus occupé de compter les naufrages des vaisseaux qui voguent en pleine mer, que les succès de ceux qui arrivent à bon port.

—*Sénac de Meilhan*
"Avantages de la Médiocrité"

THE DEPONT FAMILY IN THE EIGHTEENTH CENTURY

Paul Depont (1661-1744) m. (ca 1690) Sara Bernon (1668-1753)
Merchant-Banker ●42,000 (Father: Trésorier de France at Poitiers)

(ca. 1722) *Paul-François m. Suzanne-Henriette Bernon
(1700-1774) | (1703-1725)
Trésorier de France, 1721, Echévin, 1753.

(1710) Françoise m. Pierre Moreau
■55,000 Banker

Marie-Anne-Sara
■55,000 (1694-1759)

(1719) m. Charles-Xavier Sauvestre Comte de Clisson
— son, military
— Alexis m. Marquis de Lescure (son m. 1765, Durfort)
— Pauline, nun
— Agathe, nun

(1751) *Paul-Charles m. Marie-Henriette Sonnet d'Auzon
(1723-1800) | (d. 1789)
Trésorier de France, 1744, Maire, 1765

Paul-François (Virson)
(1753-1801)
Lieutenant in the French Guards (unmarried)

Charles-Louis-Marie (1768-1841)
m. Louise-Clémentine Carré de Ste-Gemme
(no posterity)

(1776) Pauline m. Froger de l'Equille (d. 1795)
(1760-1808)
■60,000 émigré
(7 children)

(1780) Elizabeth m. Aubert de Boumois
(1762-)
■60,000
(4 children)

3 other children died before 1795.

(1766) *Jean-Samuel m. Marie-Madeleine-Sophie
(1725-1806) | L'Escureul de la Touche (1749-1787)
Intendant, 1765 ●240,000

(1796) Charles-François m. Avoye-Marie Michel de Grilleau
(1767-1797)
Avocat—Général, Parlement of Metz, 1784
Councilor, Parlement of Paris 1789, Minister-Plenipotentiary at Cologne, 1792

Charles-François (1797-1874) Garde de Corps de
Louis XVIII (3 children)

(1788) Marie-Madel-Pauline m. Justin, Marquis de
(1768-1838) | Fontanges, Officer,
■250,000 (1 child) | Regiment du Roi

m married; d. died; ●dowries received; ■dowries paid
Source: E. Garnault, Livre d'Or de la Chambre de Commerce de La Rochelle (La Rochelle, 1902), 13f; L. de La Morinérie, La Noblesse de l'Aunis et de Saintonge aux Etats Généraux de 1789 (Paris, 1861), 283-284; A.D., E-472-475.

CHAPTER ONE

Paul-François Depont: Ennobled Merchant

La Rochelle has lost little of its eighteenth-century character. The sardine boats and small fishing craft still flit between the massive stone towers of Saint-Nicolas and La Chaine at the entrance to the inner harbor. Looking seaward from the nearby tower of La Lanterne, one can still see the bare outline of Cardinal Richelieu's famous dike, a thin line of white-caps before the island of Ré a few miles beyond. Closer at hand are the city ramparts, reminders of La Rochelle's medieval privileges lost forever after the prolonged and desperate siege of 1628. Today the sunny calm of this French resort is broken only by ice cream hawkers and running children, a middle-class vacation spot not yet discovered by American and German tourists. Yet two centuries ago the outer harbor was filled with merchantmen and slave ships. Silt forced them to remain outside the twin towers, and their cargoes of indigo, sugar, cotton, and beaver skins from the Antilles and Canada had to be transferred to shallow-draft vessels, or *barques*, for landing at the wharves.[1] If La Rochelle lacked the proverbial forest of masts hugging the *quais*, it lacked none of the commercial vitality of its sister ports, Nantes and Bordeaux.

Turning toward the inner harbor, one was confronted with a façade of stone buildings pierced by the Porte de la Grosse Horloge, a massive clock tower, typical of port cities of the Old Regime, and perhaps in-dicative of a style of life in which time was important. Through the stone arch of this clock tower one entered the principal artery of La Rochelle. The rue du Palais curved gently eastward from the fish market, where the fishmongers still shout *"sans sels"* (fresh sardines) along the arcades, or *porches,* past the law courts to the cathedral facing the Place du Château. On the rue du Palais and on the narrow adjoining streets—the core of the "Old City"—lived the *officiers* and the mer-

3

chants, perhaps a hundred families in this tight city of seventeen thousand people. Within sight of the clock tower the merchants and shipowners were building a new Chamber of Commerce, which, when finished in 1785, would surpass in beauty if not size the Bourse at Bordeaux.[2] The building was designed to face inward on a flagstone court divided by a Doric colonnade and reflecting the sunlight from stately French windows. The sober elegance of the building was broken by two sculptured bas-reliefs appropriately representing nautical instruments and the high poop decks of the cargo vessels that had made the whole project possible. Much more than the Renaissance *hôtel de ville* where the Huguenot mayor, Jean Guiton, was reputed to have expressed municipal independence by plunging a dagger into the council table, the new Chamber of Commerce represented the focus of local energies in eighteenth-century La Rochelle.[3]

There are few episodes in the economic history of France that evoke more myths than the Atlantic trade in the eighteenth century. Contrasted with the slow development of agriculture and cottage industry, overseas trade, as evidenced by the ad valorem trade statistics, seemed to grow by leaps and bounds.[4] It was an economy entirely apart from the hinterland. The Atlantic ports of Nantes, Bordeaux, and La Rochelle, as well as Marseilles and Le Havre, were regarded as fabulous sources of quick profit by contemporaries, "growth sectors" in the words of more recent economic historians.[5] The Atlantic trade, and that meant the "Islands" for the French merchants, suggested a number of romantic myths as well. It evoked images of cargo ships off the Guinea and Senegalese coasts, the exotic lure of a tropical island, the shipments of sugar, coffee, and indigo, quasi-luxuries that made six-digit sales for the merchant partners. If one could forget the distant horrors of the slave trade, the predominant impression seemed to be one of adventure, exoticism, and wealth, far from the world of the provincial *rentier*. The Chamber of Commerce at La Rochelle knew how to evoke these images when the occasion demanded. Even after the loss of Canada and Louisiana in 1763, the chamber could proclaim: "There are no mines of gold and silver in the French colonies as in those of Spain and Portugal; they yield only sugar, coffee, indigo, and cotton, but these products are more precious than the gold of Peru or Mexico because they are the source of an immense trade for France."[6]

But the greatest myth of all was that of fabulous profits. Only recently have historians begun to measure profits more precisely.[7] Although merchants have a way of hiding their balance sheets from posterity, there are a number of indications that suggest a more sobre picture.

First, it required considerable capital to build and outfit a sailing vessel for the Atlantic trade. Second, it was a long trip from La Rochelle or Nantes to the Guinea coast and then to Saint-Domingue before the return to France, from eighteen months to two years depending on the prevailing winds and, above all, the time required to negotiate and liquidate the cargoes. It is for these reasons that an overseas venture required substantial capital accumulation and a willingness to wait for returns. Moreover, few vessels lasted more than three or four Atlantic voyages so that the rate of amortization of each ship was high. In 1722 a partnership of four merchant families at La Rochelle invested the following sums for the voyage of the *Saint-Paul* bound for the West Indies to sell slaves and bring back sugar and indigo.[8]

Cost of the ship (ca. 300 tons)	20,000 livres
Fitting out the ship (food for the crew, ship supplies, etc.)	16,951
Cargo (brandy, guns, cheap cloth, etc.)	97,805
Total	134,756 livres

In 1729 the *Perle* was purchased, outfitted, and stocked with a cargo for 138,888 livres.[9] Vessels of larger tonnage, five hundred tons, for example, might require as much as 200,000 livres as an initial investment.[10] Nor did costs end there. Consider the third and last voyage of the *Saint-Louis* which left La Rochelle in early 1741 near the peak of the slave trade at La Rochelle. The entire account of this *campagne* is worth inspection for what it reveals not only about profitability, but also about the human dimensions of the trade in "black ivory" (table 1.1).

If one assumes that the cost of the ship had been amortized, there is still the cost of the initial cargo and outfitting. If the evaluation for the purpose of insurance is a reasonable approximation, there were 130,000 livres in expenses still to be liquidated. True, 79,543 livres were in "accounts receivable" at Saint-Domingue.[11] If this sum is added to the income side of the ledger, the bookkeeping profit amounted to 10,000 livres, or about 10 percent of the value of merchandise sold at La Rochelle at the end of the voyage. Unfortunately, the planters on Saint-Domingue were notoriously poor payers.

The six merchants that divided the proceeds of the voyage of the *Saint-Louis* represented a group of Protestant families that had invested in common shipping ventures for more than a decade before 1740. They were almost all related by marriage. Jacques Rasteau had married a Seignette and their daughter had married a Carayon; the widow Carayon was sister-in-law of Paul Depont, and Jean Vivier's mother was a Depont. This family group was typical of the merchant community of

Table 1.1. General Account of the Third Voyage of the Vessel Saint-Louis, 16 February 1743 (Captain Seignette du Jardin)

Destination: the Guinea coast and Saint-Louis, coast of Saint-Domingue
Résumé of operations and management, including the sale of "captives" and return cargo, and claims left in the hands of MM. Mirandes and Mende (agents on the island).

Purchased on the Guinea coast (March 1741):

Negro males	229
Negro females	71
Negro boys	9
Negro girls	2
Total "captives"	311

Cost:
    84 *pièces Indiennes* (cotton cloth)
    37 *pièces Lemenais* (cloth)
    29 *ancres* Brandy

Sale at Saint-Louis, coast of Saint-Domingue:

238 Negroes sold	255,850 livres
71 Negroes died before the sale	
1 musician (*pianiste*) left at Cormanti (Gold Coast) where he died	
1 blind man left at Saint-Louis and can be considered lost	
311 Total	

Merchandise for the return can be considered a pure loss except for guns, pistols, 2 horses, etc. 5,386 livres

Total 261,236 livres

Employment of the said sum at Saint-Domingue:
    25,748 livres for 146 *barriques* (barrels) of unrefined sugar
    101,591 livres for 42 *futailles* (casks) of indigo
    79,543 livres in bills (*billets*) in hands of agents to collect
    54,354 livres in separate itemized account including bonuses for ship's surgeon, local taxes, *droits,* fines, and other expenses at Saint-Domingue.

261,236 livres, total

Receipts
Sales at La Rochelle (23 July 1742)
    Indigo sold to eleven buyers for transshipment including:
        M. Alexandre at Bordeaux
        M. E. Weiss and Co.
        M. E. Vivier of La Rochelle
        M. Schellebeck and Sons

Sale price	67,384 livres
Freight charges	5,579
Net	61,805

La Rochelle, or more precisely of those two dozen Protestant families of *armateurs*, outfitters and associates whose close family bonds greatly facilitated the amassing of capital and maintained the mutual trust so necessary in overseas ventures of such complexity and risk.[12] One senses a certain toughness in this tight community evidenced by a terse *"Moy Rasteau* for 12/32" in the accounts or by Paul Depont's note in the margin of his journal: "It has pleased God to have given me a loss on this voyage." These marginal notations were formulas to be sure, but austere ones all the same.[13] Overseas merchants could be found

Table 1.1. (*continued*)

Sugar sold to five buyers for transshipment including:
M. Allard-Belin of La Rochelle
M. E. Vivier and Co.
Madame Seignette

Sale price:	31,051	
Freight charges	10,206	
Net	20,845	

Diverse merchandise sold locally:

Sugar	11,127	livres
Indigo	4,822	
Cocoa	2,829	
Other (tobacco, coffee, cotton)	223	
Total	19,001	

Other (8 dozen hats for blacks, 15 oz. gold, etc.) merchandise sold locally, acquired on the
Guinea coast   2,028
Ship inspected and found in need of extensive repairs. The partners have decided to abandon
it and sell the dismantled items (anchors, mast, cables, cannon, etc.).

Total	5,115
Total receipts	108,794

Expenses:
Commission due Captain Seignette du Jardin by contract of 16 August 1740: 4.5% of the

value of the return cargo			3,616
Owed to Captain Seignette			6,667
Wages of the crew			20,478
Tax (*Droit*) due to the "*Compagnie*" [*des Indes*] on			
254 "Captives" @ 10 livres			2,540
First insurance policy:	Outfitting	35,000	
	Cargo	45,000	
		80,000 at 12.00% at Nantes	9,600
Second insurance policy:	Outfitting	14,000	
	Cargo	36,000	
		50,000 at 11.75% at Bordeaux	5,875
	Total expenses		48,776
	Net receipts		60,018

Division of net receipts (16 Feb. 1743) to:

M. Paul Depont, for 6/48	7,503
Madame Carayon, widow, for 8/48	10,003
M. Jean Vivier, for 7/48	8,752
M. Elie Vivier, for 4/48	5,001
M. Seignette du Jardin for 6/48	7,503
*The ship (Jacques Rasteau) for 17/48	21,256
Total	60,018

Source: Archives Départementales, E-486, "*Troisième Voyage du V^{au} Le Saint-Louis*," 16
Feb. 1743. Complete balance-sheets are very hard to come by. See Henri Robert, *Les Trafics
coloniaux du port de La Rochelle au XVIIIe siècle* (Poitiers, 1960), p. 40 and passim.

*Jacques Rasteau owned the ship; his share presumably included amortization of the cost of
the ship and perhaps part of the outfitting as well.

among Catholic families as well—the Pascaud, Goguet, Rodrique—but
they were less numerous and invested less frequently in the triangular
trade. It took firm family alliances to sustain a series of *campagnes*, and

those who could outfit only one or two ventures to the "Islands" usually ended in failure. No doubt special stamina was required of those younger members of the family who served as captains on the slavers until they earned their way to full partnership. The stories that Captain Seignette could have told of his two years at the helm of the *Saint-Louis* would surely have exploded many a romantic myth.

Paul-François Depont did not serve as a captain on any of his father's ships. Paul Depont, who had been in the trade himself for more than thirty years,[14] preferred to initiate his son by assigning him a share of his own investments. In 1720 Paul-François began to keep ledgers recording his shares in various shipping ventures and continued to do so until 1734. These accounts reveal that the Depont family knew how to diversify its investments and spread the risks. For example, Paul-François and his father invested an average of 33,000 livres in eight ships in the decade, 1723 to 1734, each ship averaging six voyages. Although precise profits are impossible to determine, this was an investment of about 270,000 livres, and the returns on each voyage must have been sufficient to keep this substantial capital in operation for over a decade.[15] In addition to voyages to the West Indies, at least four of these ships reexported colonial produce, principally indigo, to Amsterdam. Paul-François also invested in smaller lots of merchandise called *pacotilles* which were consigned to the special care of the captain with whom the profits were often divided. Young Depont's journal for 6 March 1721 reads: "Credit: Captain Chauveau for the sale made at Amsterdam of two barrels [*barriques*] of indigo sent on the vessel, *Les Trois Rois* from the *pacotille* divided among M. Belin, Captain Chauveau, and myself."[16] Paul-François made 5,154 livres (1,909 florins) *net* on this transaction and his profit was deposited in the Bank of Amsterdam. He also shared *pacotilles* with his sister and brother-in-law and with his father, and kept a strict accounting with all of them. Close family relations were reflected in exact bookkeeping, not in any careless "generosity." Beside a journal item stipulating a sum owed by his father from the proceeds of indigo sold "during my absence," Paul-François entered: "Owed by M. Depont, my father, for one wig (sent from Paris)—eighty livres."[17] Given this early training, Paul-François's attitudes about money in later life should not seem surprising.

At the age of sixty Paul Depont showed no sign of flagging energy. In addition to investments in ship cargoes and *pacotilles*, he handled sales of merchandise sent in other ships to La Rochelle. During the Law Boom of 1719 and 1720 he was particularly astute. La Rochelle had been chosen in 1718 for one of the five branches of the new National Bank, thus providing merchants in the port not only with prompt information of the latest royal edicts affecting the new paper money, but also with easy access to the bank for making deposits of paper in the accounts of their creditors. This was a great advantage when the Law Boom began to collapse and the government recalled all its *billets*, reducing their nominal value by three-fourths and eventually converting the paper into *rentes* at only 2 percent. The summer of 1720 was a time when all over France debtors were attempting to transfer their paper to their creditors' accounts. In Saint-Domingue, where news took months to arrive from Paris, planters who had sent indigo and sugar to La Rochelle learned only too late that the payments they received were worth but a tiny fraction of the real value of the merchandise. Paul Depont was sales agent for more than one Saint-Domingue exporter in 1720. One Arnauld Lalande sold his indigo for 12,324 livres in paper, only to find it worth no more than 3,081 a year later, subsequently transformed into a *rente* at 2 percent or 61 livres per annum. It was the same with a consignment of sugar from one Sieur Merinville which sold for 1,982 livres *anciennes écritures*, but ended as a *rente* of only 13 livres, 10 sous per annum. This is not to suggest that Depont had acted illegally or that he had even sold the merchandise on his own account for hard silver. But he was not going to be caught with any near-worthless paper. In September 1720, just before the total collapse of Law's paper money, Paul Depont deposited 45,000 livres in paper in his creditors' accounts, and retained a token 412 in his own.

When news of the debacle finally reached Saint-Domingue, it was too late for the exporters to change the contracts of sale and require payment *en espèces*. M. Lassel was wasting words when he wrote, in August 1722, that he had asked Depont to sell his indigo in coin and that "consequently, these banknotes must remain in your account." Another exporter, M. Lalande, was more resigned. "I beg you to regard all this as your business . . . in a word, my banknotes will end up like yours [i.e., worthless]." In fact, the planters on Saint-Domingue had little choice. The terms of trade were against them, and they needed the merchants of La Rochelle not only to handle their exports but also to respond to personal requests often involving their relatives in the motherland. Moreover, the planters were not without means of retribution over the long run. Such an episode made it easier to delay payments for slave imports in the future.[18]

For Depont, this activity was only one among many. In 1718 he had been named manager of the *Compagnie des Indes* at La Rochelle, managing its depots, warehouses, and merchandise, purchasing ships, consigning goods to Québec and Louisiana and maintaining correspondence with its affiliate, the Louisiana Company. He also made substantial advances on his own account to the company, claiming 277,938 livres from the directors in Paris in 1722.[19] No wonder Paul

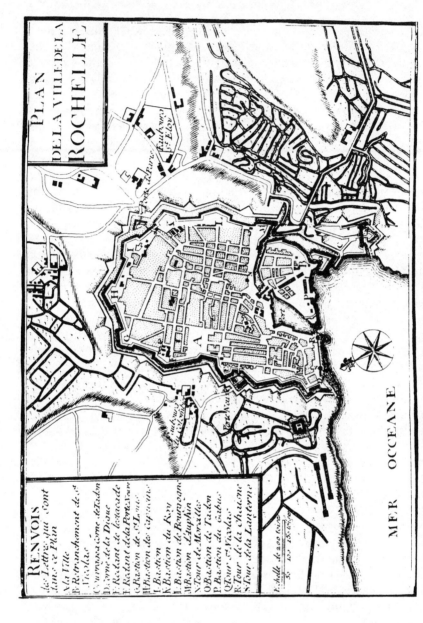

Map 2
The City of
La Rochelle
in 1750

Source: Pagniol de la Force, *Nouvelle Déscription de la France* (Paris, 1754), VII, 400.

Depont was addressed as *"marchand-banquier."* He knew how to keep his capital working.

Paul Depont's role in the *Compagnie des Indes* gave him a quasi-public function and increased his notoriety outside of the province. When La Rochelle was awarded its Chamber of Commerce in 1719, he would play a major role there as well. Among some thirty important merchants, he was chosen by the intendant to be one of the five syndics of the chamber. Even his formal Protestantism was no obstacle. The *juges-consuls* who had represented the city's merchants in the past supported the participation of Protestants and *nouveaux convertis*. "We have here such a large number of *nouveaux convertis* who are the best merchants [*négociants*] and of such acknowledged probity that, far from having any objection to admitting these *Messieurs* to the Chamber of Commerce, all the former judges will be delighted to have them."[20] The consuls added, however, that they thought the director of the new chamber should always be a Catholic. But even this limitation could not be enforced. In 1725 and again in 1727 Paul Depont was elected director with a majority of the thirty votes in the chamber. The Catholic minority felt it necessary to protest to Cardinal Fleury himself in 1730: "Contrary to the provisions of the edict prohibiting Protestants from holding any public office, those of La Rochelle have found a way to enter the Chamber of Commerce established in 1719. Not content with two offices of syndic accorded them, they have gained control of the directorship and after M. Depont ..., have elected M. Vivier, a Protestant, claiming that they have twenty-six ships and the Catholics only eleven. ... The nomination of M. Vivier has been sustained."[21]

The twenty years from 1720 to 1740 were unquestionably the best years of the Atlantic trade for the Rochelais, as they were for the other French ports, Nantes, Bordeaux, and Saint-Malo. Not that the volume of trade was less at other times—in the late 1780s, for example. But the sustained prosperity of the Fleury period would never again be equaled. La Rochelle fitted out an average of thirty ships a year in the early 1730s and forty per year in the 1740s. From 1737 to 1741 the slave trade showed a marked increase, and La Rochelle "delivered" over 12,000 slaves to Saint-Domingue in these years, making it second to Nantes with 21,000.[22] The losses among the human cargo almost always exceeded those among the crews, though complete figures are lacking. The losses given on four of Depont's ventures between 1738 and 1743 totaled 286 on a cargo of 1,402 slaves or 20.3 percent. These compare with 16.4 percent for Rochelais slavers in 1786–88 (1,521 lost in a total of 9,323). Of course, the losses varied enormously from ship to ship. The *Victoire*, for example, lost 111 of 382 on its second voyage in 1740, and 137 of 424 on another voyage![23]

In 1738 there were two disasters on the Atlantic passage that drove home the perils of the trade. The *Phoenix* ran short of water off the Guinea coast, was obliged to land forty-eight slaves, lost twenty more who escaped as the ship was loading supplies, and then underwent a mutiny, a fire, and finally ran aground off Saint-Domingue. The most dramatic incident occurred when fifteen slave women committed mass suicide by hurling themselves overboard, one devoured by sharks within sight of Captain Champeau. The *Galatée* had been outfitted by one of Depont's closest associates, Jacques Rasteau. In the middle of the night off Cape Sainte-Apollonie the slaves mutinied and took over the ship except for the officers' quarters at the stern. The slaves then broke into the arms and powder supply and set fire to the mizzenmast, while the crew and officers literally threw themselves into the sea. From his sloop, the captain witnessed the explosion of the entire ship. The remains of the crew rowed back to the African coast, where they were picked up by an English merchantman. There were no more entries for the *Galatée* in Rasteau's journal.[24]

Such disasters were risks of the trade. More ominous over the long run was the increase in English and Dutch interlopers off Saint-Domingue which the local governor and intendant seemed unable (or unwilling) to halt.[25] La Rochelle merchants had to pay a certain price for Cardinal Fleury's policy of *détente* with the English. There were increasing difficulties with the English off Guinea as well.[26] With first rumors of hostilities in 1741, insurance rates began to climb from the customary 11 to 17 percent at Bordeaux and 25 percent at La Rochelle. Even before the formal declaration of war in March 1744, the English frigates seized thirteen ships belonging to La Rochelle merchants.[27] In the first twenty months of the war they captured another thirty valued at over eight million livres. The Chamber of Commerce, representing the principal mercantile houses at La Rochelle, made no effort to hide the desperate situation of the trade in a letter to the Navy Department in Paris. "The *négociants* and *armateurs* expose with great insistence the deplorable state of their maritime commerce, which is totally ruined by continual seizures by English warships. There is no mail which does not bring disastrous news. ... All expeditions have been stopped because no one in the whole kingdom will insure the ships, nor anyone abroad for that matter."[28]

Until recently, historians have emphasized the rapid recovery of the French ports after each successive war with England. But it is becoming increasingly clear that the wars had a permanent debilitating effect upon French overseas trade. Between 1744 and 1763 there were only eight years of peace. How many merchants like Depont, Rasteau, or Vivier, not to mention smaller ones like Goguet, Rodrigue, or Pascaud could afford to keep their capital immobilized for so long, even assuming they could replace their lost ships and cargoes? And how many English, Dutch, and other interlopers had used the period of French absence from the trade to replace them permanently? Jean Tarrade writes: "All local studies of the port-cities show that the great fortunes, the great families dominating the commercial activity . . ., and the great urban enterprises all date from *before* the Seven Years' War. . . . This [prosperous] phase lasted until 1743."[29]

But even without the constant menace of war and blockade by the greatest naval power of the century, there were other warnings of difficult times ahead for merchants like Depont. As the detailed account of the *Saint-Louis* demonstrated, even in its heyday the Atlantic slave trade was not a source of certain, much less "fabulous," profits for the French merchant. True, by an astute diversification of investments, by adapting quickly to new opportunities, a Paul Depont could do better than survive. But Henri Robert was probably correct when he attributed commercial success, not to the single "*coup à la Volpone*," but rather to the long-run accumulation of small profits, mustered by careful management, and reinvested not only in major shipping ventures but also in *pacotilles* for Amsterdam, consignments from Cap-Français, maritime insurance, outright loans at interest, and real estate, urban and rural.[30]

Moreover, the daily accounts reminded the Deponts of those unrecovered debts in Saint-Domingue from the voyages of the *Saint-Paul* (18,200 livres), the *Saint-Philippe* (27,672), the *Perle* (33,494), the *Saint-Louis* (79,543), and no doubt many more.[31] When Paul Depont died in 1744 there were 218,315 livres in his inheritance noted as "doubtful," most of it representing the unpaid obligations of West Indian planters for Depont's shipments of supplies and slaves.[32] The imbalance would grow worse with time. At La Rochelle after 1750 the planters' debts averaged over 100,000 livres *per shipment* of slaves to reach a total of eight million livres by 1762.[33] But by then the Deponts were no longer in the slave trade. Their name no longer appears on the *armateurs'* almanac after 1748.[34] Twenty years later, in a letter to his own son, Paul-François alluded to the *traite* (slave trade) as if it had been long forgotten. "My father gave me some shipping interests as a marriage portion [in 1723] which I lost in large part three or four years later, when some of his ships were judged unfit for further voyage."[35]

Paul Depont died in 1744 at the age of eighty-three. His long life spanned a full cycle of the Atlantic trade at La Rochelle. His death coincided with a new phase in the history of his family as well. Paul-François spent the years from 1744 to 1746 reinvesting his father's fortune before the worst ravages of the English fleet or the full impact of planter resistance were felt. If his decision to leave trade may have been prompted by his father's death and the outbreak of the war, his decision to invest in land and *rentes* was not unprecedented. Nor was the possibility of a different style of life based on public service and landed income something completely foreign to a son who was already in middle age.

Paul Depont, after all, had been investing in land as early as 1687 when he bought the seigneury of Les Granges in the vineyard country some twenty kilometers east of La Rochelle.[36] He added new seigneuries, domains, and farms (*cabanes*) in 1707, 1711, 1716, 1718, 1726, and 1735, another proof of his investment acumen and unwillingness to leave any capital idle.[37] It was common practice among the shipowners of La Rochelle to buy land in the hinterland, partly to insure their credit as merchants. But surely the economic motive was not the only one at play. Paul Depont was too wise in the ways of the world—he was already sixty in 1720—not to appreciate the prestige only land could bring. Public service was not foreign to him either. In 1718 and again in 1721 he was agent of the *Compagnie des Indes,* in 1719 he became syndic, and in 1726–27, director of the Chamber of Commerce with the blessing of the intendant. In 1722 he was among the notables of the city who offered to raise sixty thousand livres to dredge the harbor, and he himself subscribed one thousand.[38] No doubt this public service was not entirely disinterested, but it did give him a status somewhat above most of his fellow merchants. In any case, in 1721 Paul Depont purchased the office of *Trésorier de France* in the Bureau of Finances of La Rochelle for his son.[39]

Each of the thirty *généralités* that made up the kingdom had a Bureau of Finances, a fiscal administration that varied in size depending on the importance of the district. There were thirty-five *trésoriers* at Montauban and thirty-three at Toulouse, but only six at Nantes. La Rochelle was among the smallest with only ten.[40] The bureaus were originally intended to administer the Royal Domain, supervise the public highways (*voirie*), assess the royal taille, receive formal declarations of seigneurial rights (*aveux*), and register letters of nobility. Important as these functions appear, they were shared by other officials and institutions even from the inception of the office in the sixteenth century. By the seventeenth century, and especially after the Fronde, the most powerful rivals of the bureaus were the thirty intendants whose fiscal and judicial powers gradually sapped the *trésoriers* of all substantive power, leaving the façade of emoluments and privileges. In addition, despite the efforts of Colbert in 1672 to reduce their number to twelve per bureau, the number of *trésoriers* increased, spreading the diminishing functions more thinly. La Bruyère and Racine were both *trésoriers* who never exercised their functions. In short, the Bureau of Finances was increasing in size but diminishing in power at the time Paul-François entered the office.[41]

Despite its increasingly perfunctory role in public finance, the office remained part of the hierarchy of "sovereign courts," albeit at the lower end, and conferred *noblesse graduelle* on its owner. That is, hereditary nobility was acquired if a father exercised the office for twenty years (or died in office) *and* if his son followed in the same office for another twenty years (or died in office).[42] Thus, Paul-François acquired *noblesse personnelle* and *his* son, when he followed him in office in 1744, acquired *noblesse transmissible* or hereditary nobility. Here was one of those many ennobling offices of the Old Regime which, along with that of *Secrétaire du Roi*, maintained an avenue of social mobility for those who had some legal training, sufficient capital, some "connections" with the public powers either through local notoriety or past services to the Crown, and who belonged to the state religion. Paul-François could meet all of these criteria in 1721.[43]

La Rochelle had its share of administrative institutions in the eighteenth century. The *capitation* for 1764 listed the following "privileged *officiers*":

Présidial (district court)	29	Receivers of Tailles	2
Bureau of Finances	5	Admiralty	4
Eaux et Forêts	6	*Traites* (wine taxes)	4
Siège royal	7	*Monaye* (Mint)	5
Election (taxes)	8	Other	13
		Total	83

But since it was a port city of only seventeen thousand people, the intendance (new in 1694) was the only major judicial or administrative institution. Unlike Bordeaux or even Poitiers, La Rochelle could not claim a parlement, a *chambre des comptes*, or a *cour des aides*. It did not possess those bodies or *compagnies* which spawned a "high robe" nobility. Very few nobles of any kind lived in La Rochelle. The *capitation* for 1764 lists only thirty-five in residence; most of the *noblesse*—a modest gentry—lived in the bourgs of the hinterland—Saintes, Surgères, Mauzé. Consequently, there remained only two elites at La Rochelle, the *officiers* in the courts and tax bureaus, and the *négociants* of the port.[44]

Paul-François Depont had simply exchanged one elite for another. Leaving the shadow of the clock tower at the entrance to the harbor he had moved up the rue du Palais closer to the Place du Château and the cathedral, exchanging the mercantile quarter for the "canton" of the *gens de basoche*. But while the new office marked a change of function and status for the young Depont, it did not lead to a rupture with the merchant community of his father. Financial interest tied both communities together in a network of loans and *rentes*.[45] Moreover, such a modest provincial town could provide only a limited *bonne société*. It would not do in the wet winter months to separate the families of some eighty magistrates from those of thirty wealthy *négociants*; together they could attend the receptions of the intendant and whatever other *réunions* and *soupers* the city could muster. Finally there was no "high society" at La Rochelle comparable to what Arthur Young, the famous English traveler, encountered at Nantes or Bordeaux—not to mention Paris—which would further accentuate invidious distinctions.

Access to office and ennoblement in the Ancien Régime did not mean that even the educated and "skilled" were highly mobile. Achievement, ambition, drive are nineteenth-century traits which, to the extent they existed a century earlier, were contained and circumscribed by a profound sense of rank and differential function. Roland Mousnier concludes for the eighteenth as well as the seventeenth century that "most often" families kept their offices in the *bailliages* and *présidiaux* jurisdictions for many generations, sometimes eight or nine. Stability at this level of the hierarchy was the norm. This was especially true in middling provincial towns.[46] La Rochelle in the early eighteenth century was a far cry from Boston in the late nineteenth.[47] The Deponts, father and son, had no expectations of rapid upward mobility in 1721. Even a generation later, Paul-François was to evince uneasiness, even dismay, when *his* younger son did not follow paternal advice to marry the daughter of a *trésorier de France* in the neighboring *généralité* of Angoulême.[48] The acquisition of the office was regarded as an end in itself, a reward for public service and a mark of acceptance into the local notability, not a way-station to bigger things. Were not the Deponts already at the top of their world—the only one they knew—La Rochelle and the Pays d' Aunis?

Whatever the social potentialities of the office for future generations of Deponts, the immediate rewards were palpable enough. The office of *trésorier* was a *dignité*, an honor that signaled admission into a distinct *corps* of the social hierarchy, the *officiers*.[49] Paul-François would take his place beside the magistrates of his *bailliage*—the *élus, conseillers* and *prévôts*. He would become part of their world professionally, socially, and even culturally. Of course, some adaptation would be necessary. The younger Depont would slowly abandon warehouse and bourse for a less active life. The economic role of the family would change from shipowning and local banking to the life of the *rentier* and landlord. Because Paul-François had more leisure at his disposal, it is probable that his library with its complement of religious literature represented a part of his own acquired "general culture" and not that of his father.[50] But a wider cultural horizon did not mean that Paul-François would welcome the literature of the *lumières*; in fact, he was deeply suspicious of it along with many other dubious fashions he saw coming from the capital. Indeed, Paul-François Depont's departure from international trade made him more sedentary and "provincial" than his father and socially more conservative as well. His views on marriage, for example, would suggest that he opposed "alliances" above one's station and outside of the *corps* of *officiers*.[51] His own father had been somewhat more adventuresome in this matter.

The first departure from the family custom of marriage within the Protestant merchant community of La Rochelle had occurred early in the century. In 1719 Paul Depont's younger daughter married Charles-Bernard-Xavier Sauvestre, comte de Clisson, Grand Seneschal of Aunis, a country nobleman of some importance. The seigneury of Clisson was a considerable distance from La Rochelle, much closer to Nantes and near the heart of the Catholic Vendée. Marie-Anne-Sara Depont's dowry of 55,000 livres and the expectation of much more no doubt lessened any hesitancy the count may have had toward a *mésalliance*.[52] Clisson's own financial situation had been rapidly deteriorating. In 1717 he had borrowed 35,000 livres in silver from Paul Depont in order to make a payment on a much larger obligation of 180,000 livres to one Antoine Daraznes, *Bourgeois de Paris*, contracted three years before.[53] Apparently Clisson's financial obligations to Depont did not end here. Even after the marriage portion had been paid, Paul Depont held a mortgage on the Clisson estate in the amount of 70,000 livres. This obligation was never liquidated by the count and even the arrears in interest were finally given to the new countess as a legacy from her father.[54] To say that Depont "bought" a noble son-in-law would be unkind, but Clisson's financial woes were considerably eased by the match.

Within four years of the marriage the Clissons had four children, one son and three daughters. Paul Depont's provisions for these grandchildren in 1723 suggest a man willing to write off bad debts in exchange for the promotion of this branch of his family. To his newborn grandson he bequeathed a farm in Poitou, a town house in La Rochelle, and 8,000 livres to purchase a lieutenancy in the "guards." The importance of a military career for his grandson was underlined by the stipulation that the legacy would be reduced by half if the army grade was not acquired.[55] To his granddaughters, he bequeathed modest life annuities of 100 livres if they became nuns, or annuities of 120 livres if they married. Paul Depont, Protestant merchant, was providing for granddaughters who might enter Catholic convents. In fact, two of the Clisson girls, Pauline and Agathe, later did become nuns.

Marie-Anne-Sara Depont, comtesse de Clisson, apparently adapted quickly to her new status as a member of the Poitevin nobility and converted to Catholicism between 1710 and 1720. She later expressed deep regret that her father, Paul Depont, had died in the "miserable error of Calvinism."[56] Her eldest daughter, Alexis, eventually married Comte de Lescure, also Poitevin nobility and apparently of more means and higher status than the Clissons.[57] To the son of this marriage Madame de Clisson bequeathed 100,000 livres for the purchase of a military grade, a substantial sum by provincial standards.[58] By contrast, she added only 50 livres to the pensions of her two daughters in orders. Had she lived into the 1760s, Madame Depont-Clisson would have proudly witnessed the marriage of her grandson to a Durfort, high court nobility, and at the very top of D'Hozier's heraldic almanac.[59] Yet Madame de Clisson's last will in 1753 bore traces of a certain austerity, possibly attributable to her provincial origins in La Rochelle. One passage in the will read: "Having lost all that I hold most dear, I wish to be buried without any ceremony other than that of a *bourgeoise.*"[60]

Paul-François also converted to Catholicism. The exact date is unknown, but it must have been before 1721, the date of his reception into office. After 1685 no one could be a *trésorier de France* who did not belong to the state religion. His eldest sister, Françoise, had probably converted in 1710 at the time of her marriage to the banker, Pierre Moreau, also a *nouveau converti.*[61] In a letter to the intendant, written in 1730, even the Catholic faction of the Chamber of Commerce had to admit that "the children of M. [Paul] Depont are good Catholics and have edified the city by examples of piety unknown among Protestants."[62]

It would be only too easy to see the conversion of Paul-François Depont to Catholicism as one more "adaptation" in a consciously planned strategy for ennoblement and social ascent. But just as the motives for the purchase of the office of *trésorier* should not be regarded in the light of the status of later generations of Deponts, so the motives for conversion to a new faith must not be interpreted too simply and too cynically. There is good reason to believe that the conversion of Paul-François was sincere, whatever its practical conveniences for his professional career and social esteem. It can be argued that his newfound Catholicism had a profound influence on his entire outlook, shaping his views toward trade and banking, spending and consumption, as well as inculcating a very austere, even chilling set of moral imperatives by which he judged his own and the behavior of others. In the long run, the highly pietistic Catholicism that Paul-François imbibed worked against further social ascent, for it reinforced his latent provincialism, his distrust of Paris and its corrupting influence, especially on his own younger son. Far better to accept one's station—*état* or *vocation* were his words—than to risk one's soul in that modern Babylon where unrestrained ambition was bound to lead. On a very simple level, we see the dual, even conflicting consequences of conversion to the state religion for a mercantile provincial family: on the one hand, conversion was a sine qua non for office and ennoblement; at the same time it also increased doubts about certain forms of money-making, thus contributing to socially approved forms of wealth such as the land and public *rentes*. On the other hand, conversion, especially in this pietistic form, could contribute to a suspicion of all forms of ambition and reinforce a belief in functional hierarchy (to each his own *état* or "calling"), keeping evil contamination at arm's length and avoiding, perhaps unconsciously, the anxieties of an uncertain status.

Paul-François's conversion came at a very special moment, not only in the history of the Counter-Reformation in France, but in that of La Rochelle in particular.[63] The diocese of La Rochelle presented special problems for the Church, given its reputation as a Huguenot stronghold in the early seventeenth century. The efforts of the Church, not only to convert Protestants, but also to discipline Catholics and enforce the spirit, if not the letter, of the Tridentine decrees, began in earnest in 1648 and continued until 1724. The "offensive" had many phases and contained various packages of techniques, including a new training program for the parish priests, pastoral visits, special missions, the creation of new teaching brotherhoods and sisterhoods, the construction of churches, shrines and sanctuaries, the organization of religious processions, and the planting of crosses, as well as more systematic efforts at charity, aid to the sick, and education, from the *petites écoles* in the villages to colleges and seminaries in the towns. No Protestant, whether La Rochelle merchant or artisan, could have been unaware of this sustained effort on the part of the Church under the direction of the bishops of La Rochelle, backed by the intendants, and encouraged by such eminent churchmen as Fénelon himself, who led special missions to La Rochelle in 1685 and in 1686.[64]

What was most striking about this campaign was its apparent lack of success in converting many Protestants before 1690. Protestants numbered about 5,200 in a population of 17,500 in 1679. The *dragonnades*—armed raids on Protestant gatherings—in 1685 provoked some emigration, but even this grim episode did not seem to shake the hard core of Protestantism, especially the groups in the city of La Rochelle itself. But from the arrival of Etienne de Champflour as bishop of La Rochelle in 1702 the situation began to change. Already in 1690 a few important Protestant notables were converted, including Baron de Châtelaillon, Marquis de Culant, Doctor Seignette, and significantly for the merchant community, the *négociant* Massiot. With Bishop Champflour in the first quarter of the eighteenth century Protestant "resistance" began to crumble, and by 1765 there were only 835 Protestants left in the port.[65] The Depont family was among the *négociants* who converted.

Although the Depont correspondence does not acknowledge it specifically, one can detect an affinity between the particular approach of the bishop to "Catholic piety" and the later religious outlook of Paul-François Depont. First, Bishop Champflour was more concerned about Jansenists than Protestants when he first came to La Rochelle. He was less zealous than his predecessor and there was no question of using blunt force. He placed great emphasis on education, not only for the villagers, but for the sons and daughters of the well-to-do in La Rochelle. He organized charities, increased the distribution of alms, and expanded the *hôpitaux* in La Rochelle and in the smaller towns of the diocese. He also appealed to the general public with massive processions on the rue du Palais and with a dramatic planting of the cross in the Place du Château. But what gave Champflour his special stamp was his movement away from liturgy and Christology in general to an emphasis on meditation from prescribed books such as the *Journal des Saints*. It was not by whim that he encouraged the Jesuit mission to the city in 1704 and the increased activity of the Society of Jesus in the following years; the *Spiritual Exercises* of Loyola were his obvious model. But as Champflour's new catechism of 1716 would demonstrate, it was Loyola with a special flavor. There would be less emphasis on the sacerdotal ideal and more on "the limits beyond which evil begins." Using the logical pattern of simple questions and answers, the bishop's new catechism stressed "the duties of the Christian Religion" and the "means" to fulfill them—prayer, meditation, the sacraments, and acts of piety. The identification of evil was fundamental. Faith must be protected from heresy and novelty, by inculcating a horror of mortal sin, especially of blasphemy, impurity, drunkenness, and avarice; love of God and of one's neighbor was not stressed. One sometimes forgets that Catholicism can have a Calvinist austerity; it may appear ironic that Bishop Champflour welcomed the papal bull *Unigenitus* anathematizing Jansenism in the same years he wrote his catechism.[66]

The awareness of sin and the moral earnestness evoked in the letters of Paul-François to his son in Paris are not mere carryovers from a Protestant tradition. They are the moral armament of a convert. They not only harp on the themes of "death and hellfire" or on such ubiquitous temptations of the flesh as dancing and gambling; they constantly refer to prescribed reading, recommending the texts of the casuists to determine which acts are "evil" and the meditations of the saints to fortify body and soul against them. Paul-François spent many of his long leisure hours in the 1750s and 1760s reading these books which he stocked in his library. He quoted and prescribed them often to his son.

Whatever the inner springs of his own actions, he clearly believed that these were the ideas that should guide Jean-Samuel, and not any others the young man might imbibe in Paris.

Paul-François was partial to the Jesuits and perhaps had been converted by them during their mission to La Rochelle in the first two decades of the century. Later in his life he was much distressed by the expulsion of the Society in 1762. In 1764 he wrote to his son, Jean-Samuel, a *maître des requêtes* in Paris: "I cannot understand how you can imagine that religion will not suffer from the absence of the Jesuits. Here we have already seen proof to the contrary. It is very difficult to find a zealous and assiduous confessor." Paul-François much regretted the departure of Abbé Vazeilles, Jesuit tutor of his grandchildren at La Rochelle. He was upset with the attitude of Jean-Samuel who seemed to "applaud" the exile of the archbishop of Paris. You are "as *parlementaire* as the others," he wrote, a reference to the avowed Jansenist persuasion of the Parlement of Paris in the 1760s.[67] No doubt Paul-François as a *trésorier* had good reason to be jealous of the parlements as "sovereign courts," but their doctrinal deviance counted for something too.

At Christmas 1765 he commiserated with Duc de La Vauguyon, tutor to the royal princes and a mainstay of the pious circle around the Dauphin (the *dévots*). It was an occasion for one of his frequent lamentations about "God's punishment upon this evil land." "But how can this surprise us, when we see that contempt for religion and moral corruption hold sway everywhere. ... [Many] think that the end of the world is not too far off, but as for me, I am happy that I am rapidly approaching the moment when I shall leave a world where God is so grievously offended, for the contempt for religion has become so powerful that those who speak of God or for Him are almost looked upon as people from another world."[68]

The beleaguered quality in this passage—not to speak of its wordiness— was characteristic of Paul-François's letters to his son in Paris, from where all "Godlessness" emanated.

That Paul-François took his conversion seriously is also indicated by his public charities. In the twenty years from 1751 to 1771 he established a series of Catholic foundations on which he spent over forty thousand livres, about 10 percent of his income over that period. These charities included hospital beds for the *hôpital général* at La Rochelle, a charity school on one of his properties in Aunis, and a number of perpetual masses for himself and his family.[69] The charities were clustered in two periods, one a few years after the death of his father and the other a few years before his own.

Paul-François showed a particular interest in the charity school at

Aigrefeuille. In front of the parish church in the spring of 1754, in the presence of the priest, the syndic, the head of the vestry (*fabrique*), the *huissier*, and an assortment of carpenters, caskmakers, small wine merchants, and *laboureurs* that made up this local winegrowing community, Paul-François formally opened his school. Intended for girls only, the stated purpose of the school was to teach reading and writing, prayer and catechism, and "instruction in the Catholic Religion." It would also provide one meal a day. The building plans described a house 75 by 40 feet, including a classroom, dining room, kitchen, garden, latrine, and shed. It was to be run by two sisters from the Order of *Sagesse*. Depont provided a *rente* of 315 livres "assigned" on his land of Chagnées in the parish. In the 1750s this was enough money not only to provide meals and clothing for the schoolgirls, but also to establish a small medical center (*une petite pharmacie*) for the parish sick. Paul Depont's widow approved of her son's *bonne oeuvre de charité* and contributed 200 livres income "in perpetuity" from her *rentes* on the Clergy as well as a house in La Rochelle. The payments were made to the sisters even during the most anticlerical moments of the Revolution. In 1814 the Order of *Sagesse* was replaced by agreement between the bishop and the prefect by the Ursulines, but a *maison de charité* "founded by M. Paul-François De Pont, 1754" was still there. In 1840 when the sisters left the parish, the 315 livres (311 francs, 11 centimes, new currency) were still enough to support one indigent patient from the village in the general hospital of La Rochelle. The domain of Chagnées no longer belonged to the family, but Charles-Louis-Marie Depont, Paul-François' grandson, mortgaged some of his mother's property in the Vendée to continue the annual payments and pay the arrears accumulated since 1835.[70] After almost a century, the charity school and the "pharmacy" were gone, but for some parishioners the name of Depont recalled something besides seigneurial dues.

Paul-François contributed twenty-five thousand livres to support five sick people and one orphan in perpetuity at various convents and hospitals. In most cases, Depont reserved the right to choose them. He gave eleven thousand more for daily masses in both the cathedral and at the church of Saint-Barthélémie on the rue du Palais. He also donated a perpetual lamp in the parish churches in his villages of Aigrefeuille, Forges, and Virson. Perhaps he was moved by the remains of the old sanctuary at the crossroads at Forges—Notre Dame de Manderoux, a pilgrimage stop in the seventeenth century.[71]

One of the perpetual masses has a special interest. It was established "in order to obtain the conversion of Madame, his mother, to the Catholic Church." Apparently his wish was fulfilled. A list of pew assignments in the Church of Saint-Barthélémie notes that number 37 was occupied by Madame, the widow Depont, adjoining those of M. Depont des Granges, her son, Sieur Moreau, her son-in-law, M. Paul-Charles Depont des Granges, her grandson, and Dame Henriette-Lucie Sonnet d'Auzon, his wife. Like the Clisson branch of the family in the heart of the Vendée, the Deponts of La Rochelle had "rallied" en masse to Catholicism.[72] Only Paul-François's younger son, Jean-Samuel, a councilor at the Parlement of Paris since 1748, seemed absent spiritually as well as physically from the family ranks at Sunday mass in La Rochelle. All the more necessary that Paul-François write often to his son. As he said many times, he was convinced that he had been chosen by God to be the instrument of his son's salvation.

There is no question that Paul-François was deeply concerned about sin, moral corruption, and salvation. He believed that one must prepare for the Day of Judgment, and that as head of the family he had a duty to warn those members who had been careless or lax. His admonitions stressed more than the faithful partaking of the sacraments of the Church; they touched economic practice as well. In early 1766 he wrote to his niece, comtesse de Lescure, of the Clisson branch of the family:

We have a much greater obligation than others to give abundantly to charity. I discovered long ago, after studying my parents' account books, that we were heirs to a fortune that included more than 100,000 livres in ill-gotten interest [*d'intérêts mal acquis*], not counting those sums about which I do not know, and which may amount to an equal sum. I have every reason to believe that my sister [Comtesse de Clisson] has not done what she should have about this, since she appeared rather indifferent to what I told her—thinking perhaps that such interest was permitted—and then she fell ill too soon afterward to put her affairs in order. Judge for yourself, dear niece, what your duties are. As for me, I believe I have satisfied mine after consulting the Sorbonne and the best casuists . . . in order to discern exactly which [investments] were usurious [*usuriaires*] and to conform accordingly.[73]

The slaves who died by the scores on the *Saint-Louis* or the *Victoire* in the 1730s and 1740s did not trouble Paul-François's conscience; his father's "usury" did. It was not simply a matter of engaging in trade; Paul-François was not ashamed of the fact that his father had been a *négociant*. But his father had acted contrary to the canon law, which a good Catholic like Paul-François must obey. The sight drafts and other obligations in his father's portfolio no doubt included a time limit and interest. There was no equivocation for a convert like Paul-François. Only *rentes constituées* and *rentes perpétuelles*, where capital was alienated, were approved by the Sorbonne.[74] Paul-François had satisfied his conscience as well as his sense of respectability and security when he reinvested 135,000 livres in *rentes* in the two years after his father's death. Almost half of this capital—60,000 livres—was "placed" in the bonds of the Clergy of France.[75] Surely the fortune of the Depont des Granges, Catholic notables of La Rochelle, was above reproach.

How complex and ambiguous—not to say fortuitous—were the circumstances that led the Depont family gradually to adopt a new style of life. The purchase of land had begun long before the Deponts thought of leaving overseas commerce. It was part of an effort to diversify investment and secure loans. The purchase of office in 1721 was a badge of local public esteem, not a steppingstone toward nobility. What eventually turned out to be a move "upward" was originally only a mutation in the social hierarchy. The conversion of the family to Catholicism was the consequence of a subtle and intense effort of the Catholic Counter-Reformation which happened to bear fruit at La Rochelle in the early eighteenth century. In 1744 the family left commerce more as a consequence of economic conditions and the approach of war than because of any conscious decision to live *noblement*. At this juncture the death of Paul Depont consolidated changes that were already in motion. Only in retrospect do these developments appear to be part of a concerted strategy of social ascent, a quest for nobility. To a very large degree, these choices were determined by the immediate situation, so that each had its own distinct origin. Nonetheless the cumulative effects of these decisions, however determined by larger and apparently separate developments in French society—the declining opportunities in overseas trade, the relative security of land and *rentes*, the marks of status in a provincial town, the growth of bureaucracy, the success of the Counter-Reformation—were significant. One can understand how more than one merchant family became *bourgeois vivant noblement*, particularly in the middle years of the eighteenth century.

CHAPTER TWO

The Mentality of a Provincial Notable

If the style of life of the head of the Depont family had changed from bourse to treasury court, from ship cargoes to tax assessments, one thing had not changed—meticulous bookkeeping. The ledgers that had recorded ships and *pacotilles* now itemized land leases and *rentes* without any obvious transition but the turn of a page.[1] In fact, the family records improved, for Paul-François had more time after 1744 to put his quill to paper; one can picture him writing his letters and adding his accounts in the relatively cramped quarters of his town house over the arcades.[2] We have this recording mania to thank for the existence of about a hundred of Paul-François's private letters written in the years between 1758 and his death in 1774. He kept the drafts of these letters in several bound notebooks. No doubt they appear particularly terse, since he abbreviated those phrases he used most often, such as *"ce Malx siècle"* or *"mon ppal Bien."* The style is at once pontifical and businesslike. Turgid passages are followed by crisp reminders, the trivial interspersed with the significant, the logic at times impaired by a desire to compress every detail onto the page before sealing it. In rapid succession Paul-François would discuss *rentes* on the Clergy, courting a well-placed nobleman at Paris, the health of his daughter-in-law, the sale of a property, the necessity of the sacraments, and English ships blockading the coast.[3] The handwriting is small, and while we cannot be sure it is Paul-François's, the run-on sentences, the absence of paragraphing, and the need to treat every item of possible interest to the correspondent suggest a person who is anxious and even profoundly fearful. This impression is borne out by the substance of the letters.

I believe these letters justify rather extensive quotation, not only because of the variety of topics they treat, but also because of what they say about the values and attitudes of an ennobled merchant.[4] To call Paul-François an example of the "upwardly mobile" is to incur the risk of history by hindsight, for he could not know even in 1774 how far the family would "rise" in the social order. True, his eldest son, Paul-Charles had become a *trésorier de France* in 1744 and would normally attain hereditary nobility after twenty years of service. In 1773, one year before his father's death, he was confirmed *noble d'ancienne extraction* and would vote in the Second Estate of La Rochelle for the delegates to the Estates-General in 1789.[5] But this was no great step beyond his father, and Paul-François did not consider his eldest son much different from himself. More important, he could not have foreseen how far his younger son would go in the High Robe. In fact, the emerging career of Jean-Samuel Depont was the cause of much of his anxiety, forcing him to reflect on his own place in society and on the value of ambition, mobility, and careers or *états* distant in status and space from his own. Fortunately, the great majority of the letters of Paul-François are addressed to his younger son, Jean-Samuel, in Paris. The fact that Jean-Samuel's mother died only twelve days after his birth in 1725 meant that his widowed father had a special parental responsibility for his son's care and education. Naturally, one is occasionally reminded of a Polonius or a Chesterfield; the letters have their timeless quality. Yet beyond the *père de famille,* even beyond the religious ascetic, is the provincial notable of eighteenth-century France. It is his world we wish to recapture.

A first reading of the letters of Paul-François Depont would suggest a person racked by status anxieties, incapable of reconciling provincial with Parisian standards of behavior, economy with *éclat,* and Christian principles with social ambition. The confusion of ideas, the lack of proportion and measure, and the constant preaching tempt one to interpret the man as either a hypocrite or a crank, one minute thundering of hellfire, at another offering pietistic homilies, all interspersed with specific caveats about the cost of linens, the low return on *rentes,* the dangers of the theater, and the weakness of the flesh. Can any case be made for a basic consistency in the man's outlook, where religion played a fundamental guiding role, rather than simply that of rationalization or cliché? What was the relation between Paul-François's religion, his provincialism, and his attitude toward a more fluid, mobile society? One must not be too quick to categorize Depont of La Rochelle as one more "social hybrid" or "Weberian type" without first looking more closely at his personal correspondence. In so doing perhaps we can come closer to those nuances of human behavior and motivation— within the context of long-run constraints described earlier—which surely characterized more than one *officier* in a provincial capital.[6]

Recall that the pietistic Catholicism of Paul-François was *not* the religion of his fathers, as familiar to him as the arcades of La Rochelle.

He was a convert and a very earnest one. Paul-François's pietism was, above all, a bulwark against the "passions," by which he meant much more than the sensual pleasures. It included the ubiquitous temptations of this world, those that played upon vanity and ambition on the one hand and those which produced sloth and indulgence on the other. "*L'esprit du monde* and piety will always be incompatible," he wrote.[7] Suffering is part of the human condition, and austerity, if not the *sign* of salvation, at least the safest path to attain it. Paul-François was constantly reminding his son at Paris of these somber truths. "There are few people who put up more resistance to suffering than you do." In the 1750s Jean-Samuel apparently tried to debate some of these issues on his father's terms. Paul-François replied: "You tell me that you have been born with passions too strong to be abandoned all at once, and also that God can never ask the impossible. ... You can at least avail yourself of the means that ordinarily procure the conversion of the heart such as going every day to mass, reading a passage on the final goal of man, reciting your rosary as you used to do, or offering a prayer to the Holy Virgin or some other prayer that appeals to you ... and avoid bad company" (23 Oct. 1758).

But Jean-Samuel's career in Paris only drew him further from the religion of his father. Paul-François continually warned his son about ascribing his worldly accomplishments to his own merit. "I thank you for the news and I congratulate you on your success. But one must attribute everything to God and never forget the words of Saint Paul that one can have nothing which is not received from God and that often humiliation is more efficacious for the salvation of those who are too easily seduced by vanity" (18 Oct. 1763).

In 1765, when Jean-Samuel was appointed intendant of Moulins, his father hoped the new post would end his "ten years of impiety" (2 Mar. 1765). In a letter to his niece at the Palais de Luxembourg, he thanked her for complimenting him on his son's new promotion and added: "This may contribute to his salvation and deliver him from the dangerous whirlpool of the life of Paris and force him to set a good example by a truly Christian life, for there are no rewards more sure than those which procure a happy eternity" (to Madame Lescure, 8 June 1765).[8]

In a discussion with Jean-Samuel regarding a career for his grandson at La Rochelle, Paul-François criticized his son for considering "God's role as indifferent to the calling [*vocation*]" of the boy. "You place all emphasis on attraction [*attrait*] and taste [*goût*]. If that were always the case, my nieces [de Clisson] would not be the excellent nuns that they are, since they have absolutely no personal attraction to their calling. Madame Alexis [his other niece] has told me many times that it was only her excessive love for pleasure and the dangers that she found in the world that made her decide to retire from it" (18 June 1765). There is no doubt that more than one member of the Depont family had kept the temptations of this world at bay. It serves to remind us that not all of France was undergoing "de-Christianization" in the last half of the eighteenth century.[9]

The step from fear of worldly contamination to the conservation of resources was a short one. Paul-François had been brought up by his merchant father to account for every livre, but there is no doubt that his religion reinforced his view that every advantage in this world had its price. Quoting Saint-François de Sales, he wrote: "Quickly flee a house where there appear to be no costs" (May 1769). A modest pattern of consumption and display befitted a good Christian; it was the badge of a certain respectability (*honnêteté*) that separated *officiers* like the Deponts from the self-indulgent at one end of the social hierarchy and the slothful at the other. The year in which Jean-Samuel became intendant held a promise of fresh beginnings and was especially replete with paternal advice.

I strongly urge you not to buy the very best quality furnishings, but to confine yourself to an *honnête milieu*. I am afraid of your natural tendency toward vanity. But it is much better to be modest and keep expenses within the bounds of one's resources. Although Monsieur Le Peletier [intendant of La Rochelle] might have behaved differently, he was the first to agree with me on this principle. Messrs. Amelot, Bignon, and Boisemont [previous intendants] gave, at the most, two dinners a week, and no one blamed them, knowing that they were not rich. M. Le Peletier even told me that he was not going to give any more than that, at least not before the winter season (18 June 1765).

The term *honnête milieu* appears more than once in Paul-François's correspondence. It caused special problems when he was buying gifts appropriate for the occasion. When his grandnephew married into the Durfort family, Paul-François told his son in Paris to buy a jewel box as a wedding gift. "Go up to nine hundred or even a thousand livres. I think this will be *honnête*" (4 May 1765).

The elder Depont's rapid transitions from principle to practice and his indefatigable eye for detail and sensitivity to social protocol may make it difficult at times to repress a smile. But one should not conclude from this that his principles were mere rationalizations for family economy or a narrow provincialism. Depont was no Tartuffe.

The failure to heed the precepts of moderation could be disastrous and Paul-François invariably ascribed financial failure to moral laxity. About one of his son's acquaintances, he wrote: "I am not surprised about the sad condition of the individual to whom you refer, since he has abandoned all of his property in order to pay his debts and he is still in debt ... *Voilà* the extremity to which the passions lead, due to the abandonment of the sacraments, because I knew him when he was a pious man" (3 Dec. 1765). For others, like one Sieur Giraud who had evaded prison by sailing for "the Islands," there was even less hope. "*Libertinage* will seal his downfall with all the negresses there."[10]

It comes as no surprise that Paul-François had a horror of gambling. Yet it was one of the requisite social graces of Parisian high society. Condemned by the Church in the towns and villages, it had always been permitted (or overlooked) at Court. A father-son encounter was inevitable on this issue. Paul-François made his case on three levels: gambling was a sin; it was a threat to financial solvency; and it was not a social or professional requirement. "I am very angry that you still continue to lose rather heavily. If you continue to lose five *louis* [120 livres] a week, you will spent almost your entire annual revenue. Therefore, if you find yourself in tight circumstances, you must suffer it as God's punishment for an evil act and for having departed from God's narrow way which you have regarded with contempt because *le monde* appears to offer you more flattery for your pride" (26 Sept. 1758). Paul-François footnoted this letter with the comment that "surely it is a mortal sin to gamble heavily (*trop gros jeu*); it is not permissible to risk in a single game for one's amusement enough money to keep a poor deserving family [*pauvre famille honteuse*] alive for a year." Here Depont's religious convictions extended to social example, even to a certain humanitarianism.

The need to set an example was also contained in the following observation: "I know very well that the kind of gaming [*gros jeu*] played at Paris is often the cause of your financial difficulties [*v. misère*]. But it is not my fault if you are unhappy about it and if you do not know how to deny yourself anything. I have had a Monsieur Turgaud [Turgot] visiting here, a *maître des requêtes* like yourself, who circulates in as good company as you do, and who almost never gambles. You should follow his example" (20 July 1758). This last argument was best contrived to have some effect on Jean-Samuel, for Turgot's career closely paralleled the young Depont's at this time. Jean-Samuel must have met the future minister at the *Conseil du Roi*, if not at one of the dozens of salons springing up all over Paris in the 1750s.[11]

Naturally, Paul-François's notions of setting the proper example as an *officier* easily merged into a paternal anxiety for an impressionable son in the "Big City." "I strongly urge you to place the rest of your money beyond the reach of thieves by consigning it to Monsieur Mouchard or to some other reliable person before you spend it all on distractions, especially since you have a new lackey whom you cannot possibly know very well yet" (16 Feb. 1758).[12]

Paul-François's greatest worry about his son's welfare concerned his relation to women. It was not only that Jean-Samuel seemed to spend so much time in their company, but that at the age of forty it was time he found a suitable bride. In this matter, so fundamental both for Jean-Samuel's career and for the respectability and continuity of the Depont family, Paul-François feared that his son was singularly ill equipped to make the right choice. As early as 1758, he had tried to identify the kind of woman who was unsuitable. "It appears to everyone here that Madame de Marcheval and her company were jaded with pleasure [*fades de plaisir*] having nothing better to do than spend the night dancing. Therefore, it seems to me that you have not suffered any great loss here. Madame de Marcheval might be agreeable [*aimable*] in the eyes of a certain society [*monde*], but she does not possess very solid qualities. I believe that she is ill prepared to raise children, which, after all, must be the first function of a woman" (20 July 1758).[13]

But the women Paul-François recommended to his son over the years from 1758 to 1766 were rejected for the "wrong" reasons. Regarding Mademoiselle de Beignon,[14] the father's observations could not have been unexpected in Paris: "She does not seem attractive enough [*pas une certaine présentation*], a fact to which you attach a great deal too much importance. You do not know what true merit in a woman is. The principal thing is that they make good wives and good mothers for their children. Worldly women [*femmes mondaines*] think only about their pleasures and everything that flatters their many different passions" (1 June 1765).

Six months later, when Jean-Samuel had passed over Mademoiselle des Goutes, Paul-François launched a broader attack against *les femmes mondaines,* sources of wasted time as well as "sin," and consequently causes of professional as well as spiritual deficiencies.

It is a very bad sign when women like Mlle des Goutes do not please you. You attach importance only to external qualities, the sure mark of a frivolous turn of mind . . . .

I fear that the frequentation of women is as deleterious to your affairs as it is to your soul, since it must cause a great loss of time. We have an example here in Monsieur Le Pelletier [the intendant], who, despite his many good qualities, makes himself ridiculous by the considerable time he spends with women, apparently only occupied with amusing them and consequently neglecting his affairs. Not satisfied with the ladies here [in La Rochelle], he has brought them from Angoulême [75 miles to the east] and treats them to all the pleasures this city can provide, including banquets [*grands repas réitérés*], concerts, fireworks, and balls. He has had to take them back to Angoulême, then return here on the eve of his departure for Paris where he should be now.

The greatest intendants we have had here, such as Monsieur Bégon and others, were examples to the city by their edifying piety and untiring application to the welfare of the province. They would not have approved of magistrates occupying themselves so much with women and giving balls and the like. I think there is nothing so comical as watching the *Gens de Robbes* mix with all the riffraff of a city, dancing the whole night long. (3 Dec. 1765.)[15]

Serious, dedicated intendants are not distracted by frivolities. Here the practical side of Paul-François's carping moralizing is evident. Perhaps the message was not entirely lost on Jean-Samuel, however much the son rejected its religious garb in these years.

In 1765, when Jean-Samuel was appointed intendant of Moulins, his father began in a businesslike manner to arrange a suitable marriage. He wrote to Madame la Princesse D'Armagnac, a member of the circle of *dévots* at Paris with whom he had regular correspondence, asking her to arrange a marriage for his son. He then informed Jean-Samuel of his action, enclosing a copy of the letter to the princess. "My intention is to find the proper wife for you. I am convinced that with the help of the princess your future wife will have the requisite qualities. I know you to be so incapable of scheming [*si peu intriguant*] that if someone does not find you a wife, you will never get married" (18 June 1765). Paul-François considered his son naive as well as undisciplined, a quite common paternal attitude, even toward a son forty years old. In fact, Jean-Samuel was developing a set of skills more appropriate to Parisian norms of behavior and success. He was neither naive nor undisciplined in the sense of lacking goals and direction.

Although Paul-François said that the princess would place "greater weight on virtue than on wealth and birth," his own comments suggest that his notion of "*honnêteté*" was changing. "I confess, however, that you must still have someone of a respectable family [*honnête famille*] who will give you at least 200,000 livres [dowry] with expectation of an equal sum [inheritance], and who is twenty-eight or thirty years old which would be proper [*sortable*] at your age" (18 June 1765). Apparently, wealth per se was no obstacle to finding those "solid qualities" that make good wives and good mothers. "If you attach importance only to a pretty face and pretty manners, you will later see what a mistake this is, because it is certain that all that will pass very quickly, while a solid piety and a good mind [*Bon Esprit*] are good enduring qualities" (18 June 1765).

Moreover, Depont's friends among the *dévots* at Paris had more than one service to offer. "It will be wise to repeat this to Madame la Duchesse de Villars as well as to M. le Duc de La Vauguyon, thanking him for the favors [*bontés*] he has performed for you *auprès de Monsieur le Dauphin.* You [also] need a lady who knows the Paris convents where one usually places rich heiresses in order to find those who are suitable to you. This is especially important because one can judge the girls by the character of the nuns who care for them" (18 June 1765).

The outlook of Depont *père* perhaps shifted in 1765. He must have been impressed by the congratulatory letters arriving from Paris. Even the Lescure branch of the family at the Luxembourg Palace seemed impressed by the *nouvelle dignité* of Jean-Samuel de Pont de Manderoux, as his name now appeared on the stationery of the intendance.[16] Despite his faults, the man was making something of himself. It provoked Paul-François to reflect again about the relative importance of wealth, patronage, and talent in the choice of a career. How could one be sure to conform to God's Will and to the *état* for which one was "destined"?

The chevalier de Virson was another case in point. He was Paul-François's eldest grandson, son of Paul-Charles, *trésorier de France* at La Rochelle. He was only twelve when Jean-Samuel became intendant in 1765, but already his grandfather was concerned about him. Also named Paul-François, Virson fell considerably short of satisfying his grandfather's expectations of serious application and drive. Whereas Depont *père* criticized his son at Paris for his vivacity and self-indulgence in worldly pleasures, he lamented his grandson's sloth and lightheadedness. He wrote to the boy's mother on more than one occasion: "Virson needs constant supervision so that he does his homework properly. He never stays put [*il se promène toujours*]. On holidays he leaves town, and sometimes travels much farther than I want him to."[17] When Virson was sixteen, his grandfather chastised him for carelessness in his letters. "You do not repeat *Monsieur,* or *Monsieur cher papa* enough. This is not polite."[18] A year later when the boy was in a *collège* at Paris, Paul-François bombarded him with admonitions to go regularly to his confessor, consult his preceptor, and lodge with *un homme de bien.* "You can never fulfill the duties of your *état* if you do not fight laziness and frivolous amusements. . . . Never fail to work incessantly to learn from your teacher."[19]

Depont never spared his grandson's ego. "In order to enter a parlement, one needs more strength [*force*] than you have to fight the evils of this world." As for high administration, "I doubt very much that you will ever be capable of governing a province as an intendant." In short, the Deponts did not have enough wealth and patronage [*la grande protection*] to make up for this much lack of talent. "Nevertheless, you must work hard at your law, as I did."[20] Jean-Samuel had suggested that his nephew pursue a military career, but Paul-François doubted that this would do either. "Virson tells me that he has no attraction to the service. *Entre nous* he appears very cowardly [*fort poltron*] and would crumble at the first shot of a cannon. ... In addition, he is extremely scatterbrained and likely to make the most serious mistakes because of his weakness for distractions."[21]

Incapable of being an intendant like his uncle, too cowardly to be a military officer, lacking the strength of character to be a magistrate in a parlement, much less an ecclesiastic, what was left for the boy? It is worth emphasizing that Paul-François never considered that Virson simply live *noblement*. He must have some *occupation*. At one point in a letter to Jean-Samuel, Depont was ready to "abandon [entirely] to God" the choice of an *état* for Virson, but then thought better of it.

If God does not call him to some *état*, I don't think he will dishonor himself by assuming the office of his fathers without trying to attain the presidency [of the Bureau of Finances]. ... Monsieur de Chassiron's father-in-law, former *Trésorier de France* at Paris, told me that there were a number of men in his corps who could have been *chevaliers de Malte,* but who preferred this *état* in order to have some kind of occupation. I am certain that at Limoges there are many *Trésoriers de France* who have followed father to son for more than two hundred years. I could cite other examples at Poitiers and elsewhere. I would be very surprised if Virson should ever be capable of occupying an office in the *haute Robbe* [*sic*], not because he lacks intelligence, but because of his extreme laziness and his dislike of any serious application [*occupation sérieuse*]. ... Monsieur Dupaty [*président à mortier* at the Parlement of Bordeaux and a law reformer] with fifty to sixty thousand livres revenue preferred giving his children offices of *Trésorier de France* to placing them in the parlement and have them leave their property and their family.

I well understand that vanity and ambition do not easily accommodate to modest [*médiocre*] *états*. But when one has experience and common sense, one knows that it is not the great offices that make us happy, but a perfect conformity with the will of God, in whatever modest *état* we may be (6 July 1765).

At first glance the letter would seem perfectly consistent with the notion of a functional society in which each *corps* had its assigned place, were it not for the last lines addressed to his son which refer to the mundane matter of dividing the family silver and borrowing money at Paris to sustain Jean-Samuel's "new dignity." A closer reading discloses a deep ambivalence toward social mobility and the conflicting virtues of "application" and "conformity to the will of God." Paul-François condemns the sloth of his grandson which excludes him from the "High Robe" and at the same time the vanity and ambition of his son, which have led him to an intendancy. He cites those of his *corps* who advise their sons to follow the careers of their fathers. Yet he seems obliged to defend the "modest *état*" of *Trésorier de France* on the grounds of "common sense" and the "will of God." Moreover, Paul-François obviously endorsed Dupaty's decision to keep his children close to home. In a weak moment, he conceded that young Virson might aspire to an office in the Parlement of Bordeaux "because it was close to his property and his family."[22] Was Depont's reluctance to strive for further social ascent related to his fear of the breakdown of family solidarity and the loss of local roots? Behind the real financial stress of professional advancement was the psychological anxiety of a social ascent which, given French centralization, must lead to Paris. To "move on" was to "move away" and all that this implied. Depont's image of the "whirlpool" was revealing. No wonder he occasionally lost his composure as when he wrote with dubious logic: "Foreigners are right to make fun of the pride that makes the French want their children to be higher (*plus élévés*) than themselves. This is what imperceptibly ruins families and populates the world with idlers" (18 June 1765).

Jean-Samuel and Virson might be taken to represent two extremes to be avoided in the elder Depont's conception of the "golden mean." Jean-Samuel with too much energy and ambition and Virson with too little of both were each in his own way a threat to a static hierarchical society of *corps* and *états*. Paul-François stood at the fulcrum, attempting to balance expenditures of time, energy, and consumption with limited resources of wealth, patronage, and talent, and to adjust personal ambition to prescribed social roles. His world was a delicate mechanism that called for thoughtful management and social controls.

Education was surely fundamental here. Abbé Vazeille, the Jesuit tutor, was greatly missed. Paul-François even asked his niece, Marquise de Lescure, to intercede with the Dauphin himself to obtain a *lettre de cachet* to bring the abbé back from exile in Italy.[23] He asked his son to keep an eye out for a preceptor at Paris. "We need a *bon sujet catholique de bonnes moeurs.* Offer him an honorarium of a hundred *écus*, and if he is a priest we will pay him a supplement for his masses. Try to find such an abbé. Your little nephews have a very great need of one" (17 April 1764). Paul-François bent his own pedagogical inclinations to the task as well. He instructed his two granddaughters in La Rochelle to improve their letter writing by constant exercise.[24]

In writing to their brother, Virson, he turned from admonitions to books. "Henceforth do not buy any book without finding out first if I have it in my library. ... I am enclosing a little book, *Conformity to the Will of God.* I can assure you that if you peruse it faithfully, wanting only what God wills, you will find happiness in this world ... and you will possess life eternal ... and find the means by regular prayer, exactitude in the duties of your *état,* and frequent partaking of the sacraments" (to M. Depont de Virson, 25 Feb. 1769). It would be difficult to find a better example of the joining of religious and secular obligations, in this case reinforcing a prescribed social role. Of course, he was also suggesting that the sixteen-year-old boy choose an *état*.

Unfortunately there is no inventory of the library on the rue de Juiverie among the Depont papers.[25] But there is no doubt about the kind of literature Paul-François Depont preferred. "The abandonment of God," he wrote to Jean-Samuel, "has reduced you to the sad state of all materialists." He pleaded with his son to read "the best authors on such matters, such as Dabadie [Abadie], Pascal, Bossuet, and many others."[26]

Apparently, Paul-François Depont, notable of La Rochelle in 1766, had only a passing acquaintance with the literature of the Enlightenment.[27] His literary world was that of the seventeenth century "Christian apologists," a term he would have found objectionably secular. In one of his never-ending discourses to Jean-Samuel on morality he evinced incomprehension for anyone who could question such authorities. "You believe yourself more qualified in matters of morals than M. Bossuet. All of the best casuists and all the most lucid-minded *gens de bien* can tell you almost nothing. It must be stubbornness and the prejudices of the corrupt world that keep you from listening to such authority" (28 June 1766).

Paul-François consulted the casuists not only about "usury," but also about the morality of putting on plays, especially as staged in Parisian salons. Aside from her dowry, Jean-Samuel's new wife did not possess the qualities held dear by her father-in-law. Among other things, she was a *femme mondaine*. Moreover, since her father was *Intendant des Menus* whose functions included hiring actors and authors, purchasing stage props, and producing royal *spectacles,* play-acting was a normal, even professional activity for her.[28] Depont senior disapproved.

I am a little angry at her for having given way too readily to the tastes of Prince de C. [Conti?] by play-acting. I have abundant proof that it is dangerous to be too close to a prince of his tastes, slavishly adopting everything that pleases him. ... I have even seen lieutenant-colonels censor the officers of their regiments who put on plays among themselves. Furthermore, as we have seen here [at La Rochelle], it often happens that the declarations of love in a play end up as very real so that the poor husbands are often the dupes. ... I am especially angry about the rehearsals. (September 1769.)

Typically, Paul-François linked this argument "from experience" with the prescriptions of the "best casuists." In this instance, he was not sure if the pope and the bishops had decided conclusively on the matter, "but once convinced by their decision, one must submit to it! ... Such a decision would almost be like a revealed truth. We are permitted to use our reason only to find out what God has revealed."[29] Depont had obviously learned his casuists by heart. *La comédie* was as worthy of earnest soul-searching investigation as dancing, gambling, or "usury."

Paul-François was especially partial to the literature of piety. He circulated his books readily, lending the intendant's sister, Comtesse de Tournelle, a number of them. In a letter to Jean-Samuel he said, "Tell her she must have another book of mine, *L'Esprit de Saint-François de Sales*. I shall be obliged to her if she would pass it on to you when she has finished."[30] The persistence of Depont's efforts to convert his son has something almost heroic about it. After ten years of correspondence with Jean-Samuel, he was still quoting Saint-François de Sales. "Self-satisfaction begets the wrath of God" was a favorite passage,[31] but not one that an intendant who had made his way through the social jungle of Paris and Versailles would find very useful.

Depont *père* perhaps gained some satisfaction of his own measured kind from his little country school at Aigrefeuille. He wrote to Sister Bazelle in the winter of 1769: "I am sending you a dozen little books for your schoolgirls. When they have been distributed, I can send you more. I have also enclosed a dozen rosaries. Be sure to give them both as prizes to the most pious and most assiduous [*plus appliquées*] at their lessons" (to Sister Bazelle, Order of Sagesse, Aigrefeuille, 11 Jan. 1769).

It is disappointing that so few of Jean-Samuel's letters have survived. Fortunately, the one short letter written to his father indicates how great the gulf was between father and son, between La Rochelle and Paris. "My dear father, you regard me as the Jesuits used to regard everyone. They readily suspected everyone they encountered of being touched by Jansenism. You, dear father, suspect me of Deism. Why? Because you say I am repelled by the sufferings of Jesus Christ. ... But there is no reason why I should not sample all the tracts that have been written about this subject [Deism]. It has seduced some of the greatest men" (Jean-Samuel to Paul-François, 1 May 1767). The experimental open-mindedness that underlies this approach to ideas was completely foreign to Paul-François. It could only have alarmed him further about what Paris had done to his son.

What would a Paris education do to Virson, already condemned by congenital laziness (*paresse naturelle*)?[32] The views of Carré de Candé and Martin de Chassiron, both colleagues in the Bureau of Finances, who had investigated the *collèges* of Paris, were not reassuring either. "Monsieur Candé has not been happy with the *collèges* of Paris. It is not only the corruption of morals but the manner in which the preceptors behave there. He (and Monsieur Chassiron as well) has decided to put his son and young Chassiron in a *pension* instead" (to Madame des Granges, 15 July 1765).[33] It was indeed a hostile world, and Depont was not alone among the *officiers* in La Rochelle in thinking so.

It was natural that Paul-François would consider those families who shared his general outlook as good influences on his son. Antoine Pascaud was one of the Catholic minority of *armateurs* at La Rochelle who became a *trésorier de France* about the same time (1723) as Paul-François Depont. His son, Joseph, followed him in the office and, like the Deponts, both Pascauds were members of the Chamber of Commerce of the city. Their sons were nominated as mayors of La Rochelle, Joseph Pascaud in the 1740s and Paul-Charles Depont in the 1760s, and, of course, both became nobles, after holding their fathers' office for twenty years.[34] Joseph Pascaud's son, like Jean-Samuel, had left the province to become president of the *Chambre des Comptes* of Brittany, a robe magistrate only slightly less prestigious than a royal intendant. In 1789, along with Paul-Charles Depont, he voted in the Second Estate for delegates to the Estates-General under the appelation of "Alexandre Pascaud, Marquis de Pauléon."[35] Like the Candés and Chassirons, the Pascauds had a family history closely parallel to the Deponts. All four families had much in common—perhaps even the same anxieties.

In 1758 Joseph Pascaud was named delegate to the Council of Commerce and left for Paris.[36] Immediately, Paul-François wrote to Jean-Samuel urging him to call on the Pascauds. "You will be very well received by them. ... They are one of the best houses." A month later, he asked if Jean-Samuel had made his call. "They are the best kind of people, and of very good society."[37] But the young magistrate did not seem anxious to cultivate the company of the Pascaud family. He was apparently more willing to call on some of his father's other friends in Paris.

Depont's religious convictions did not always reinforce his provincialism and his attachment to a functional, hierarchical society. They occasionally broke down barriers between court and country, *grande noblesse* and *anoblis*. Despite his apparent lack of ease with the *haute noblesse*—even when they were members of his own extended family—Depont the elder had established some lasting acquaintances among the circle of *dévots* at Paris with whom he seemed to feel reasonably comfortable. Among these was Duc de La Vauguyon whom he knew many years before he became tutor to the Dauphin, father of the future Louis XVI. That the acquaintance with the duke was more than a matter of convenience is indicated by continued correspondence between the two men even after the duke was replaced as tutor of the "New Dauphin" in 1766.[38] They corresponded at least every six months, usually expressing mutual distress over the "dangers of the *grand monde*" and the "corruption of morals." Occasionally, they talked about more specific matters such as the condition of the clergy at Lyon (1768) or "court politics" in general.[39] From what little evidence exists, the *dévots* constituted a religious society, not to say a party, with correspondents in the provinces.[40]

Paul-François had met the duke when they were both young men, perhaps when Depont was a law student in Paris in the 1720s. Apparently, he admired the duke for his rectitude more than for his rank.[41] He recommended the duke to his son as a "good Christian influence,"[42] with the added virtue, to be sure, of being helpful to his career. "I have spoken to Monseigneur de La Vauguyon about you. ... You will do well to pay your respects to him and let him know about your work on the Council [*Conseil d'Etat*] so that he will mention it to the minister. You should take him as your model especially since he has led a regular life since the age of twenty-five" (1 Apr. 1758).

La Vauguyon was not the only member of the high *noblesse* that Paul-François advised his son "to court from time to time at Versailles."[43] His letters mention Duchesse de Villars, Prince de Talmont, Princesse d'Armagnac, Comtesse de Tournelle (sister of Le Peletier), all of whom seem to have shared Depont's "devotionalism." That these connections at court might be professionally helpful was not lost on Jean-Samuel, but this does not seem to have been his father's main motive for cultivating them. There is no reason to suspect hypocrisy. In a letter thanking Princesse d'Armagnac for her compliments on Jean-Samuel's nomination to Moulins, he wrote: "... in the hope that he will lead a less impious life ... serving as an example to others. ...I place myself on my knees before you, Princess, asking you to pray for him" (to Madame la Princess d'Armagnac at Paris, 4 Jan. 1765).

To point out that Paul-François had a number of acquaintances at court at Versailles is not to say that he treated them as he would the Pascauds or the Chassirons, his colleagues in the Bureau of Finances at La Rochelle. He was always deferential and conscientious about following proper form and protocol. He reprimanded his son for failing to inform him promptly of the death of the mother of Prince de Talmont so he could send his condolences on time.[44] "My Prince, I am much too tenderly (permit me to use this term) and too respectfully attached to you not to express to you how much I share your grief on the death of Madame, your mother" (to M. Le Prince de Talmont, 4 Apr. 1758).

His sensitivity to the social proprieties was even more acute when he dealt with the Lescure branch of his own family. By 1765, his niece had exchanged the bucolic pleasures of Clisson in Lower Poitou for the "high society" of the Luxembourg Palace. Her son's marriage to a Durfort, daughter of the ambassador to Naples and of a lady-in-waiting to the royal sisters at Versailles, presented some awkwardness for a great-uncle in La Rochelle. To Jean-Samuel, he confided: "Madame de Lescure has insinuated that I must begin to pay my compliments to Madame Durfort and her husband, which I shall do, despite a certain discomfort [*ennui*] that this gives me" (1 June 1765). Needless to add, Paul-François performed his duty. He dispatched three letters to the Durforts—father, mother, and bride—replete with the appropriate formulas of *politesse,* including the "pleasure of an alliance with a family as respectable as yours."[45] He also complimented his niece on having obtained a captaincy in the cavalry for her son "since this will lead more quickly to a regiment." But, he quickly added, "God is wiser than we are" in all matters of wordly advancement.[46]

Unfortunately his niece responded to his attentions in a manner that even a person less sensitive than Depont would have interpreted as a slight. First, Comtesse de Lescure turned down her uncle's request that she intercede with the Dauphin to obtain the return of Father Vazeille, claiming that it would be "badly received" by the Dauphin. Second, she kept putting off Depont's invitation to visit La Rochelle with the classic excuse that "she did not want to inconvenience him." Paul-François was obviously hurt; he wrote to his daughter-in-law at La Rochelle: "I will keep quiet about all this. . . . I advise you to do the same."[47]

His new grandniece by the Durfort marriage did nothing to restore his social confidence when she addressed him as "Monsieur." To Jean-Samuel, he commented plaintively: "Apparently, present usage dictates that uncles and granduncles be addressed differently from other members of the family. She addresses me only as 'Monsieur' in her letter to me, as if I had not addressed her as 'niece'" (6 July 1765). Paul-François was never able to accommodate completely and comfortably to the upper nobility and the values and milieu it represented.

The spring of 1765 had been rather upsetting for Paul-François for many reasons. His son's promotion, the Durfort marriage, the doubts over Virson's future, the replacement of La Vauguyon as tutor of the Dauphin—all of these events must have made him uneasy about where the Depont family was headed and where he stood in an uncertain world. Was this the reason he wrote a few months later to his niece, the countess, about those parts of the family fortune that had been "ill gotten"?[48] Yet at the same time he could write to Intendant Le Peletier, who was leaving La Rochelle for another administrative post: "I wish you the very best for the New Year (1766). But this is very little beside Birth, Talent, and Wealth" (to Le Peletier, 24 Dec. 1765). Depont had put his finger on the three cardinal virtues of the secular world of his time. Did he approve of them, after all? He was much too earnest to indulge in irony.

One would give a great deal to know the expression on Paul-François's face when he received a letter improperly addressed to *Monsieur le Marquis des Granges.* "I was obliged to open it," he wrote to his daughter-in-law, "to be sure it was indeed for him [Paul-Charles] because of the word (*qualité*) 'Marquis.'"[49] Was he disturbed by the confusion of ranks or was he pleased that his eldest son had been taken for an authentic *gentilhomme*?

Clearly, he was not pleased by another mistake in a letter sent by Jean-Samuel just after his promotion.

I am justifiably astonished at your affecting to be the only person who does not put my title [*qualité*] of *Trésorier de France* on the address of your letters *as if you blushed at your origins,* which would be almost as reprehensible before the world as it is before God. . . .

You were scandalized at the title of *marchand* given to my father in a contract. In order to reassure you, I will tell you that fifty or sixty years ago both *armateurs* and *négociants en gros* were called *marchands.* I have seen this in the marriage contract of my father and grandfather, who nevertheless were *armateurs.* It has only been in the last sixty years that they have been distinguished from ordinary merchants by the title of *négociant* or *banquier* (3 Dec. 1765, italics mine).

Although Paul-François was describing a more specialized differentiation in the mercantile community, and the increased prestige of the whole-sale merchant and ship-outfitter since 1700, it is very doubtful the new intendant of Moulins would have found this "reassuring." After almost twenty years in Paris, Jean-Samuel surely knew what social "image" was expected of a member of the *Haute Robe.*

Yet Paul-François would make the best of the situation. If Jean-Samuel was to be an intendant, he needed all the help he could get. Congratulating his son on his new post, Depont moved rapidly from one piece of advice to another without separating the essential from the trivial. "Keep your eyes open especially for a good secretary; they are said to be found easily in Paris. Borrow money at 4 percent or below. It will be easier to find in Paris than in the provinces. . . . No doubt you will get all the information necessary for the welfare of your intendancy from your friend, M. de Flesselles. . . . I believe you can use the linen you have here if it is only for the servants" (1 June 1765).[50]

Care and punctuality were the qualities the elder Depont stressed most. He advised Jean-Samuel to re-read all his letters and not let his *"grande vivacité"* cause carelessness. He reiterated that the secretary should be reliable. Depont's views reflect a common suspicion toward agents and stewards.[51] "From my own experience, I have very little confidence in a reputation for reliability that is not sustained by Religion and which fails almost always on those occasions when one can steal with impunity and without being discovered. Can you fire your secretary when you wish or does he come with the position [*intendance*]?" (18 June 1765). In the same letter, he urged that his son be punctual in his tours of the province, which had not always been the case with Le Peletier at La Rochelle.

Depont's advice did not end with imperatives to be prompt and thorough. He had had some experience with local administration himself and his counsel was not devoid of a sense of justice and some concern for these who were defenseless and without influence or wealth. He was afraid Jean-Samuel might be too easily flattered and manipulated by the *grands seigneurs* in his new *généralité*. "I am skeptical about all the compliments [*politesses*] you are receiving from everyone and even from the most important *grands seigneurs* in your *généralité*. ... they do not do anything without some purpose [*ne font rien pour rien*] and most often it is to obtain a reduction in their tailles and other taxes. We have had only too many examples of this here. Under these circumstances only the True Religion can save you because otherwise a careerist [*ambitieux*] can hardly resist a seigneur whom he finds in his path" (3 Dec. 1765).

This observation is an excellent example, not simply of the tax-evasion practices of the high nobility, but also of a major obstacle to common action between the *grands* and the "new nobility" of office, especially fiscal office. *Officiers* like Depont did not defend tax-exemption and in fact were critical of those who escaped taxes. In an earlier letter to Jean-Samuel, father Depont seemed to resent his own son's good fortune in avoiding the tax on his new office of *Maître des Requêtes*. "You are lucky to escape the taxes that fall on almost all offices. Your brother will not be so fortunate. Even I will not be given any special consideration in the taxes on the residents of La Rochelle and it is possible that your brother will have to pay both taxes. Added to the low value of my land due to the frost and worms, this will make things very tight for me" (26 Sept. 1758).

If Depont's comment here is typical of a wider spectrum of *officiers*, which seems reasonable to assume, it is difficult to see how they could join any "aristocratic reaction" in the sense of a movement defending fiscal privileges as part of the "ancient constitution of France." Taking his correspondence as a whole, Depont would appear to view "nobility" as one "dignity" among many. It was not the label for a cohesive order, much less a "class" even as the word was used then. One thing is certain. In Depont's mind *grands seigneurs* constituted a *corps* apart from the *officiers,* and, as indicated by his warning to his son, apart from the intendance as well. Paul-François Depont, for all of his pettiness and lack of wide vision, had some sense of belonging to an administration, even a "service elite."[52]

All of Paul-François's advice was so interlaced with pietist moralizing that it is difficult to separate his Catholic notions of charity from a sense of administrative justice. And in fact they seemed to be inseparable in his own mind. M. Le Peletier, for example, "very far from piety, nonetheless ... gives considerable alms. Every Sunday, he distributes one hundred pounds of bread to the poor [*pauvres honteux*]."[53] As an intendant, Jean-Samuel should do likewise. Despite the obvious importance that Paul-François attached to "application" and hard work and the moral condemnation he reserved for sloth (*paresse*), he did recognize that there were needy people who deserved more than advice to reform their character. Depont's charities had always included local hospices, and he suggested to his son that he pay less attention to his silver service and furnishing for his new residence and more to the poor. "You would be less concerned about your personal expenses if you knew about the pitiful condition of our general hospital which could use a little financial support. We are always living by expedients in order to avoid turning out some of the poor inmates who are there" (28 June 1766). It is worth emphasizing that Depont's austere code of conduct, with its stress on self-denial, did not preclude some sense of compassion or at least Christian duty toward the poor. Jean-Samuel would face this problem in Moulins, which was one of the main way stations for the migratory poor from Auvergne.[54]

Perhaps less disinterested was Depont's advice on public works, new roads in particular.

You are right to work on the roads in your *généralité,* an essential task for an intendant. But be very careful to treat the miserable peasants considerately because they are badly treated here. ... These new roads will cost me dearly because I have been told that they will cross my land for about a league [ca. three miles]. It is a great injustice when the king does not compensate the miserable peasants for the vineyards and fields, while he does pay compensation for many houses. If all of the intendants complained to M. de Trudaine, he might pay more attention to the problem (3 Dec. 1765).

When Paul-François said that the roads would "cost him dearly," he was referring to a forced reduction in the seigneurial dues he collected at Aigrefeuille, his property in the vineyard country east of La

Rochelle. Most of his income in this parish came from the *terrage*, a produce rent on one-eighth to one-tenth of the vine yield.[55] The "miserable peasants" were his *tenanciers,* often called *censitaires* in other parts of France. "The new road," he wrote, "would ruin a large number of my *tenanciers,*" implying that he was not intending to help them himself, beyond forgoing the produce rents on the land removed from cultivation.[56] But the government should help them not only by direct compensation for damages but also by exempting them from the *aides* (wine taxes).[57]

Depont's approach to the problem seems to substantiate Tocqueville's classic indictment of his compatriots for turning to the State to solve problems of this kind. If Depont felt no paternal duty to help his *tenanciers* directly, it was less from personal callousness than from his belief that this was the government's responsibility. He had not proposed a road through this land, however useful it might be for transporting wine and brandy to La Rochelle. In addition, *tenanciers* were not tenants in the English sense, and there were too many for Depont to feel any personal tie to them as he might to his *fermiers.*

But however we may judge him in this matter, he spared no effort writing to the intendant on behalf of winegrowers who had been particularly hard hit in this region between 1755 and 1765. "The hail last Saturday and Sunday has ruined seven-eights of the vineyards in the parish of Aigrefeuille. The revenue of this parish comes almost entirely from wine. ...Ask the intendant to send commissioners to the parish to estimate the damage ... in order to persuade M. Le Peletier to lower the taille in this parish, especially since the vineyards are just recovering from the devastation caused by the worms" (4 May 1765). The government responded and made an inspection, confirming Depont's report.[58] Relief for the small holder was a function that his son should also perform in his own *généralité.* That the royal government lower its fiscal demands in a bad year was a logical assignment of responsibilities.

One gains the impression that Depont felt that "misery" could never be eradicated or even substantially alleviated. The way he used the phrase "miserable peasants" suggests that this was a timeless truth. By his own religious standards, "misery" served to remind the fortunate few not to abuse their wealth by frivolous expenditure and to do their bit for the salvation of their own souls. Indeed this was the traditional attitude toward charity in the Old Regime. While Paul-François did not subscribe to the harsh Calvinist view that "misery" was a sign of damnation, he was wary of indiscriminate giving, not only because of the strain it placed on his own resources, but also because it might sustain the indolent. When the *curés* and even absentee landlords in adjacent parishes asked for Depont's aid for the poor in a bad year, he wrote: "I cannot help. . . . I have so much *misère* on my own land that I feel obliged to help them first. . . . Father Théodore has informed me of the bad condition of his community" (to Mlle. de Messou at Orleans, 6 Dec. 1768).

In a letter to his daughter-in-law living in the family manor house in the difficult spring of 1765, he authorized the distribution of bread to the poor of Aigrefeuille. "The bread is for those who are in the greatest need. Although I am convinced that their misery is great, one must not always believe what they say. There are many loafers [*fainéants*] who should be excluded from the needy" (to Madame des Granges au Château des Granges, 19 June 1765).

Regarding that vast amorphous army of "the poor," Paul-François made at least two distinctions, common to his time. The quotation above reveals one of them, namely, that there were *vrais pauvres* and *mauvais pauvres*. The second was between the mass of the poor and the *pauvre honteux,* the person who had once known respect and better times, who was "newly poor" or at least had not had time to learn the "vices" of the destitute. As Olwen Hufton describes them, these were people whose past lives were verifiable; they did not openly beg, much less "threaten," and they were invariably pious.[59] It was the *pauvres honteux,* no doubt identified by the local clergy, to whom the intendant gave bread every Sunday at La Rochelle. The term also appeared in one of Paul Depont's many codicils. It reads, "to the *pauvres honteux* of their family they are to give six hundred livres in one lump sum."[60] There is no doubt that Paul-François, like almost everyone else above the "poverty line," had his priorities in dealing with this "scourge of society."

Although Jean-Samuel followed more of his father's prescriptions than he might care to admit in his administration and later life, he was less circumspect in his treatment of the *misérables* of his *généralité*. He did not distinguish between the deserving and nondeserving poor, only between those who could work and those who could not. Both were "deserving." Was it, for him, only a matter of law and order?

It is difficult to separate the arbitrariness and harshness of criminal procedures during the Old Regime from the personal inclinations of those obliged to employ them. The *lettre de cachet* was not only used to place wayward sons out of harm's path.[61] Paul-François asked his son to obtain such a "warrant" to put one "Sieur Giraud" in prison, a judicial action he construed to be taken for the "conversion of this *libertin.*"[62] He expressed some regret at the demise of another "criminal," a man, it appears, of some social standing. "Sieur Fouchard, whom I had had put in the Citadel of Ré thirteen years ago, has just died, although the *lettre de petit cachet* was not for life" (17 June 1758).[63]

As for petty crimes on his own properties, Paul-François, like so many seigneurs, found his role as local judge occasionally bothersome and expensive. He urged his son to help him keep criminal proceedings simple and avoid the costs of having a man tried by the royal courts in Paris.

I have been obliged to keep a criminal in my prisons for the last three months. Since I find this report a little weak, I would appreciate it if you would bolster it for me by the appropriate means. The main point will be to prevent the criminal from being taken to Paris which will cost a great deal. Since the object he stole has been restored, it does not seem necessary to pursue the affair further. Banishment will be sufficient punishment. All of the details have been collected by my *sénéchal* who will send them to *M. Le Procureur-Général.*

With characteristic foresight and insistence on detail, Depont added: "But if he must go to Paris, what will be the cheapest way? Will I be obliged to hire a mounted policeman to go with him or will it be sufficient to put him in the coach with his feet in irons?" (23 Jan. 1770). Paul-François Depont was hardly a local Beccaria and he seemed overly preoccupied with the inconvenience the case caused him. He was not unaware of the advantages his "justice" provided when it came to enforcing seigneurial rights on his *tenanciers.* The term "my prisons" probably designates the cellar of his manor house at Les Granges, a damp, unhealthy spot in January 1770.

Yet Paul-François was not a cold person, untouched by the sufferings of others, though he expressed more attachment for those he knew personally—his household servants more than his tenants and *tenanciers.* "Poor Mandrin, my old servant," he wrote, "has lost his job as government tobacco agent because he did not sell enough tobacco."[64] The Depont wills and account books suggest more than a perfunctory concern for the servants. A codicil of Paul Depont and Sara Bernon included a gift of two hundred livres to "Baptiste and his wife ... now in the service of Paul-François" followed by a request that recalls the slave trade: "to Mercure, their black, if he remains in the service of their family, a gift of one hundred livres lifetime pension to help him subsist."[65] Unlike other provincial gentry, the Deponts paid their servants promptly, provided for their clothing, and kept many of them in the family service for twenty and even thirty years.[66] Of course, alternative occupations were not plentiful or very attractive, and it is not surprising that 8 percent of the population of La Rochelle in 1767 were house servants.[67]

Not unexpectedly for the eighteenth century, much of the Depont correspondence deals with sickness and health. Difficult as it is to assess the influence of bad health on one's mentality or what it may reflect about it, it is worth mention that Paul-François's illnesses reinforced his concern with salvation. "I am just recovering from a rather serious illness. An extraordinary depression [*dégout*] still remains. I wish you would think as often about death as I do. ... you will be a thousand times happier in this life and you will infallibly save yourself from the horrible eternity in which you are sure to be engulfed [*englouti*] if you die suddenly. I advise you to make use of these reflections as we approach the Christmas holidays. No doubt you will do just the opposite and dissipate your time in the country" (13 Dec. 1763).

He thought he was near death in 1758, having been through the customary blood-letting and purging. He wrote to one of his financial agents at Paris: "I am anxious to establish a [religious] foundation before my death. It will put me very much at ease to establish this foundation before God ends my career" (to M. Baron, *secrétaire du roi, régisseur des droits réunis à Paris,* 7 Sept. 1758). Paul-François recovered from this illness and lived for another sixteen years.

Most of Paul-François's letters to his daughter-in-law at La Rochelle contained passages about their respective maladies, fluxions, and afflictions.[68] A widower for the last fifty years of his life—his wife having died in 1725 after giving birth to Jean-Samuel—Paul-François had more than one reason to be aware of the transitory nature of this life. Where was the longevity of his own father and mother—eighty-three and eighty-five respectively? No doubt he found some consolation in writing to his favorite daughter-in-law. We have only brief glimpses of his less didactic relations with this branch of the Depont family, but he seems to have felt that "their countryside" was healthier than Jean-Samuel's Paris. In the same somber Christmas letter he addressed to Paris, he added a more cheerful note: "All of the family is in Poitou. The brothers [Virson and his brother, most probably] will be sketched."[69]

Paul-François could not but have felt the contrast between his two daughters-in-law, not only in life style but in a certain zest for life. How often he refers to Madame des Granges as *toujours très languissante.* "The health of Madame des Granges appears bad again. She will not be in a condition to benefit from your stay."[70] Contrast this to his reference to the new Madame de Pont at Paris. "If I spoke of the beauty of your wife, it was because you yourself called her the most beautiful *intendante* in the kingdom" (24 May 1766). And indeed *Madame l'Intendante* was not only very presentable in the company of Prince de Conti, but also a very effective aid to her husband's career in many other ways as well.

Given the fact that so few letters of either of Paul-François's two sons have survived, it would be misleading to suggest that these two brief passages in some sense capture their respective personalities.

Nevertheless, there can be little doubt what their father's reaction must have been.

Paul-Charles: I have no news from my brother. ... I embrace him with all my heart, although his forgetfulness makes me very sad. (M. des Granges to Paul-François, 5 Dec. 1762.)[71]

Jean-Samuel: I am surprised, dear father, that having lived in Paris, you do not see the advantage in having M. de la Touche [his new father-in-law] furnish our apartments. For only 50 louis (1,200 livres) a man alone can have a respectable apartment which he doesn't need to furnish. The apartment of Madame Depont as well as my own will be very well furnished, much better than intendants' apartments usually are. I won't need to bring either an *officier,* cook, or *rotisseur.* I have found a house which will cost neither Madame Depont nor myself anything for a *valet de chambre* or a *femme de chambre.* Next year we will make other arrangements. Doesn't it also count for something to have a pretty little house [*une maison délicieuse*] where I can go in an hour and a quarter and invite all the people I like? (Jean-Samuel to Paul-François, 1 May 1767).

As Paul-François sat in his town house study on the rue de Juiverie or tapped his cane on the flagstone pavement under the bustling arcades of the rue du Palais, he must have shaken his head in dismay. How little impression he had made on Jean-Samuel after a decade of persistent admonition, advice, and pleading! Was the aging Jeremiah also bewildered by the Depont family's social ascent from port merchants to royal intendants? Was his own personal philosophy of the narrow way between ambitious vanity and backsliding sloth violated—even condemned—by his son's blossoming career in the *tourbillon* of Paris? Yet there seemed no turning back. However much he might deplore the ubiquitous threats to his son's salvation, however he might sympathize with his eldest son, Paul-Charles, who had remained in La Rochelle satisfied with a modest *honnête état,* Paul-François would continue to support Jean-Samuel's advancing career by mobilizing the family's resources and employing what influence he had in Paris. For in the end, family solidarity and even pride would be honored, if possible, of course, without losing one's soul. A month before his death in 1774 Paul-François wrote one of his last letters to Jean-Samuel: "We embrace each other possibly for the last time. ... I was touched by your letter and your tender sentiments for me. But ... for the welfare of your soul ..., my satisfaction would be complete, as the dying Saint Monica said to her beloved son, Augustine [if] the Holy Spirit [were] in your heart. I hope you will receive Him at Pentecost" (21 May 1774).[72]

Much of this suggests that the psychological mechanism of over-determination was reflected in Paul-François's letters. He needed more than one argument for every proposition, moving from religious to utilitarian justification without transition. He literally bombarded his son with reasons to avoid this or that activity. Words like "whirlpool" and "engulfed" are signposts to Depont's fear of the unknown as well as of the sinful. The provincial world of La Rochelle permitted one to place other people in a defined social context, by family, *métier* or *état*, residence, age, and personal reputation. It was a world of human dimensions; it could be understood and mastered. The world of the capital was something quite outside his familiar orbit of prediction and control. For what was a person in Paris? To be sure, wealth, birth, and talent counted for something, but they were not so easily identified, weighed, and brought to bear. Appearance and *esprit* counted for much more; an awareness of the latest modes in dress, manners, and ideas might weigh more heavily in that fleeting moment when a career might be made or lost. The virtues of hard work and application were less likely to be valued than *vivacité*, sociability, and *éclat*. Paul-François must have felt completely inadequate in such an exotic and urbane milieu and he would have hated Paris even if it were less "sinful." But of course for him, sin, glitter, flux, and insecurity were inextricably linked in that Babylon on the Seine. They composed the setting for the vain, ambitious careerist, almost a new kind of person for the elder Depont. All this is not surprising. What is more striking is the capacity of the younger Depont to adapt to this new world and make his way upward. Jean-Samuel Depont learned what "social mobility" really meant.

II
Family Fortune

Le vieillard est subjugué par la crainte. Délaissé, isolé, il sent que son existence pèse aux autres, et que ses héritiers en comptent les instans. Sa vie ne peut plus offrir de scènes qui intéressent. C'est alors qu'il s'attriste dans la contemplation de son néant. Effrayé de sa foiblesse, irrité de l'oubli, il cherche un soutien dans l'abandon général, et sa fortune lui offre une ressource assurée. Son bonheur lui paroît dépendre entièrement de sa conservation, de son accroissement. La triste expérience a fait connoître au vieillard le néant de l'amitié, l'a convaincu que l'intérêt seul gouverne les hommes, qu'on ne peut se les attacher que par ce lien indissoluble.

—Sénac de Meilhan
"De l'Avarice"

CHAPTER THREE

Marshaling Assets

The lamentations of Paul-François about pecuniary waste and improvidence were not exclusively attributable to asceticism, religious or provincial. Parisian living was a strain on more than one family's income. For the family of a rising "careerist," the financial burdens were especially heavy. If the office of *Trésorier de France* cost 50,000 livres in 1721, the office of *Conseiller* at the Parlement of Paris cost 48,000 in 1748 and that of *Maître des Requêtes* 100,000 in 1754, not to mention the "reception fee" of 12,000 more in 1755. Nor was this all. Jean-Samuel's pension at Paris, set at 1,250 livres in 1748, had to be adjusted sharply upward—3,000 in 1753, 6,000 in 1754, 8,000 in 1755.[1] Needless to add, Paul-François kept a careful account of these expenditures, just as his own father had kept track of every item purchased in Paris forty years before. He knew to the last *denier* what Jean-Samuel owed the family: "I have already told you why I reduced your pension to 7,000 livres. You press this issue too much. You also owe me 939 livres, 3 *deniers,* which I will carry over on the new account" (24 Jan. 1764).

Paul-François's letters, not only to Jean-Samuel, but to various debtors of the family, suggest that he was hard pressed. In a letter to one Marquis de Champagné, to whom he was more indulgent than to most of his debtors, he wrote: "I beg you, Monsieur, to pay the arrears amounting to 1,369 livres, 11 sous net ... having need of my capital [*fonds*] for the frequent payments I am obliged to make to Paris" (28 Sept. 1758).

In 1758 during the worm blight on his vineyards in Aunis, Paul-François was especially peevish with his son on money matters.

I am astonished. Knowing that my revenue has been considerably diminished by the lack of value of my land, you have the indiscretion to ask me again for an increase in the evaluation of all my property by 10 percent. On the contrary, if the worms continue to plague *my land, which is my principal property,* I shall surely be obliged to reduce your pension in proportion. Moreover, you must remember that I promised to pay you eight thousand livres until you received your reimbursement [from the sale of his first office, no doubt] because otherwise you would have only seven thousand. I am sure that you are in rather tight circumstances. However, you did receive a great deal of help from the inheritance of Madame Bernon [Jean-Samuel's grandmother, Paul-François's mother] and the proceeds from the sale of *la Babotieux.* [2]

This letter points to three ingredients of the family fortune—land, office, and inheritances. Seven years later, when Jean-Samuel was named intendant, his father's tone had changed markedly, and so too, it would seem, had the basis of the Depont fortune. "I would like to be of greater help to you, but *living only from my rentes* which are very badly paid, it is impossible to have much specie [*comptant*]. I will try to help you with some silverware." [3]

One must not take Paul-François too literally. It was not that he consciously misled his son about the resources of the family; he believed that the "appetite" of Paris was insatiable; the "bottomless pit" of Mirabeau *père* could drag down even the best-ordered house. With three separate households to maintain in the 1750s Paul-François had to be careful.

The solidity and continuity of the family fortune was much more than a matter of meticulous bookkeeping and a firm hand on expenditure. Even a regular excess of income over expenditure only guaranteed a certain standard of living for a generation at best. But a family of the status and pretension of the Deponts of La Rochelle had to consider its financial position over several generations. What would its "marriage strategy" be? What dowries and marriage portions could it assign to its children and what kinds of marriage alliances—of what wealth, status, and influence—could it hope to attract? [4] Although the customary law stipulated certain rules for the division of the family fortune in each generation, there was considerable room for testamentary freedom even in those provinces like Aunis and Saintonge which were not governed by Roman Law (*Droit écrit*). How would the head of the family use this testamentary power? Should he "advantage" one of the children in order to concentrate the family fortune and accentuate, or even maintain, family *éclat,* or should he treat all the children alike? And in the calculated *partage* of paternal and maternal property, should certain categories of property be kept together, even if the total family fortune was divided equally in terms of value? The land, for example, might go to the eldest son, the office to the younger son, the *rentes* divided among the other children, and so on. If sufficient capital could not be raised from current income, should one borrow? If so, on what terms? Under what circumstances should one sell part of the patrimony? And how should an influx of capital—a wife's dowry, a spinster aunt's inheritance—be invested, provided it could be converted into other forms of wealth without too great a loss of value? Finally, how much should one save from current income in order to invest in income-producing capital for the future and how much should one spend on current consumption, an elastic term that embraced such items as equipage, furnishings, servants, trousseaux, and even gambling—costs Paul-François tried so doggedly to limit, but which Jean-Samuel surely considered a kind of investment in his own future at Paris. Thus, the *livre des comptes* joined the marriage contract, will, and *partage* as instruments of control of the family fortune.

The occasions that marked the signing and notarizing of the latter three documents were appropriately solemn and ritualized. At these moments, the accumulated family wealth of a lifetime—indeed many lifetimes—and the saving, planning, and negotiating it represented, was parceled out and redistributed. If there was a time when a family had to weigh—in livres at least—present status, future prospects, and even emotions toward offspring, it was when the extended family gathered before witnesses and notaries and listened carefully to those well-known legal formulas in which the round sums were couched before passing the quill to scratch a signature. In this respect the gathering on the *Grande Rue* at La Rochelle in 1710 that witnessed the marriage of Françoise Depont to the banker Pierre Moreau in the company of Bernons, Carayons, Seignettes, and Viviers—local *armateurs* and *banquiers* all—was not so different from that more elegant assemblage at the Palais de Luxembourg in 1788 when Marie-Madeleine-Pauline Depont married Justin de Fontanges, Marquis de Fontanges, in the company of an array of bishops, Parisian financiers, and members of the High Robe.[5] For a brief moment the two worlds drew closer as one generation bequeathed its legacy—a legacy of values as well as of hard capital—to the next.

What effect did the local customary law of inheritance have on the transmission of the Depont family property in the eighteenth century? A succinct answer is difficult because the Deponts were changing their legal status. Paul-François had attained *noblesse personelle* in 1721 and his eldest son, *noblesse d'ancienne extraction* in 1773. Jean-Samuel became a hereditary noble with his acquisition of the office of *Conseiller au Parlement* in 1748, thus placing the cadet branch in the Second Order of hereditary nobility as well. There is no doubt that both of Paul-François's sons could avail themselves of those articles in the customary law of La Rochelle or of Paris entitled *"succession noble."* Presumably, Paul-François could also do so. But before deciding whether the Deponts practiced "noble succession," we should examine the provisions of the law.

Recall the basic distinction in French customary law, "noble" or "common," between those immovables acquired by the fruits of one's own labors (*acquêts*) and those received from one's parents (*propres*). The former could be freely disposed of by lifetime gifts or by testament upon death. *Propres,* on the other hand, were considered lineage property and the right to dispose of these properties was limited by the customary law.[6] Restrictions under the succession law therefore affected the *propres*, not the *acquêts.* Moreover, the customary law of noble succession for Aunis and Saintonge where the Deponts had their property was exceptionally generous to the younger children. An authoritative legal commentator wrote in 1701: "Our Customary Law, article 61, permits one to dispose freely of the movables, the *acquêts,* and one-third of the *propres,* so that the two-thirds remaining are reserved for the portions of the children."[7] In other words, the eldest son could have no more than one-third of the lineage property. The commentator rightly went on to contrast this provision with the two-thirds permitted to the eldest son in Poitou, Touraine, Brittany, and Bourbonnais.[8] In short, the law of noble succession in the region of La Rochelle did not greatly advantage the eldest son and the concentration of family wealth unless there were only two children.[9]

On the other hand, the head of the family had free disposition over the *acquêts* and movables, including commercial assets, specie, and personal possessions. Another commentator on the customary law of Aunis noted that in the city of La Rochelle "fortunes are most often in movable goods," that "all immovables are presumed to be *acquêts* rather than *propres*," and that "when there is [some] lineage property [*propres*], the free disposition of all movables and *acquêts* is permitted."[10] Thus the father could advantage the eldest son by testament and, if most of the family fortune was in movables and *acquêts,* as were most commercial fortunes, this son's portion could represent almost the entire family fortune. Younger sons and daughters had a legal claim to their share of the lineage property; they had no legal claim to acquired property. This "acquired wealth," commercial or landed, could be freely assigned to one child under the provisions of the law.[11]

These, in brief, were the provisions of the inheritance law. How were they employed by the Depont family? First, it does not appear that either Paul-François or his two sons employed the *succession noble* to advantage any of their children. Did they, like the gentry of Toulouse, use their freedom *inter vivos* or by will to favor one child in the interest of preserving the family wealth?[12] Three generations of Depont patriarchs—Paul, Paul-François, and Jean-Samuel—stated in their wills and the marriage contracts of their children that they would divide their inheritance *"par égales portions."* The prominent place they reserved for this phrase in these precious documents of property transmission suggests that equality of treatment of children was an operative principle for all three of them. But it may not have been the only one. In fact, there were some contractual clauses that seemed to work against equality. A certain ambivalence appeared with Paul Depont at the beginning of the century, and with Jean-Samuel Depont at the end. Paul-François in the second generation, so anxious, undecided, and downright illogical on so many issues, was singularly consistent on this one; his two sons would be treated with scrupulous equality when it came to division of the Depont fortune.

Was there a relation between ambition or "upward mobility" and an attempt to preserve the fortune intact by legal instruments into the third generation?[13] Both Paul Depont, the ship-outfitter, and Jean-Samuel, the intendant, must have been aware of how far the family had come in their own lifetimes. Does this help account for Paul's entail of land to the children of his only son? Why did Jean-Samuel by his will legally bind his son and daughter, their spouses, and future offspring not to demand an accounting of his inheritance? These two fathers hesitated to give the succeeding generation complete freedom to dispose of the family property. On the other hand, Paul-François hesitated about "ambition" and defended the *honnête milieu* all his life. Did this make it easier for him to treat his two sons equally and transfer the family fortune to them without any legal obligation toward future generations? Was his avoidance of entails and preference legacies consciously anti-aristocratic? It may be that equal treatment of children is less compatible with "rising families" than with stationary ones, especially when the families at the apex of the social pyramid proffer entails and the "right of the eldest" as well as fine manners and fine carriages as the badges of status and success.[14]

Paul Depont, the *armateur,* died in 1744 at the age of eighty-three. In 1715 at fifty-four he made his first will; in the following thirty years he drew up nine codicils and two entails. Not as intimate and personal as a diary, to be sure, nine successive codicils still tell us something about the views of an aging father toward his family that go beyond a statistic. The codicils reveal hesitancies and changes of mind as the family fortune continued to grow and change its composition in these years. Like so many fathers, Paul Depont was torn between the customary *roturier* law, which affirmed the human inclination to treat all children equally, and an apparently newer concern for Paul Depont to keep his wealth intact for his grandchildren. No doubt he shared these hesitancies with his wife Sara Bernon, who would live until 1759 and die at eighty-five. How many times do these codicils begin with the words "*ayant encore reflechy*," or "*ayant pesé la chose et voulant ôter tout sujet de mécontentement que leurs autres enfants en pourraient avoir*," or "*comme lesdits Sieur Depont et son épouse ont des raisons pour soulager laditte Dame de Clisson, leur fille*"! Paul's case was further complicated by the fact that one of his three children had married into the Poitou nobility, an "alliance" in which the promise of a respectable portion and future inheritance played no small role. At the same time he wanted to establish an entail to convey his landed property to the children of his only son, Paul-François. Thus one codicil supplemented the entail as new lands were acquired, to be followed by another codicil a year or two later increasing the portions of the daughters, compensating them either for the enlargement of the entail or for an increase in the overall value of the fortune. Over the years, *métairies* and mills were shifted from one portion to another, money gifts revoked, pensions increased, domains reevaluated after "major repairs," and mortgage obligations reduced or canceled as a form of gift to an indebted son-in-law.

Nor was the landed property the only part of the fortune subject to constant reassignment among the future heirs. The commercial elements in the fortune—still considerable in the 1720s and 1730s—also had to be divided. The seventh codicil would seem to have clearly separated the commercial fortune from the entailed land and *rentes*. "It is their will [of Paul Depont and Sara Bernon] that the ships and cargoes which they own or in which they have an interest will *not* be included in the said entail. Their children will have free disposition of their property." [15]

But this did not include the *pacotilles*, the smaller shares in ship cargoes, which the Deponts assigned to their grandchildren, and not in equal lots. "With regard to the proceeds of their *pacotilles* assigned to their grandchildren, they want them to be divided as follows: for their grandson, Clisson, one-fourth, for his sister, another fourth, his sister, Pauline, a sixth, and the rest to the eldest son and daughter of our son, Paul-François Depont, if he has any in his marriage." [16] In all of these complicated arrangements, land and *rentes* were apparently considered more permanent, more worthy of entail, but divisibility counted for something too; a *pacotille* could be readily converted into coin. It was almost like buying a share of stock for a grandchild.

Despite all apparent efforts to adhere to the spirit of the lines in the first will of 1712, "to divide *acquêts et propres* . . . in three parts and equal portions," the daughters, especially Comtesse de Clisson, were not altogether happy with the entail to their brother's children. This is what the entail provided:

Paul Depont and Sara Bernon ... have three children whom they have married and to whom they have already given a considerable part of their fortune, sufficient for them to live honorably according to their *état* and *qualité*. It has pleased God to give them this property by the blessing He has shed on their commerce and labor [*travail*] since their marriage. He has also given them the means to make acquisitions of land and seigneuries, manors, domains, *rentes* of different kinds, ... and salt marshes. It is their intention, by foresight and by paternal and maternal affection to assure the possession and use of this property for their children and for the children of their children born or to be born, ... male and female in succession until the third generation, without the power ... to sell, alienate, mortgage, exchange, or dispose of it in any way whatsoever. This real property [*biens immeubles*] was acquired in their lifetime and they have the freedom to dispose of it according to the customary law of this province where the major part of this property is situated. For this purpose and by this act they do entail this property. [17]

By itself the entail did not give all of this property to the eldest son; it simply provided that the "immovables" (*terres, domaines, et rentes sans exception*) could not be sold or even mortgaged "in order to prevent [the second generation] from consuming their wealth and to conserve it for their grandchildren in the third generation." [18] But linked to an *inter vivos* gift of all the landed property to the only son, Paul-François, in 1712, the entail in fact transmitted the landed portion of the patrimony to the children of Paul-François alone and not to the other grandchildren unless, of course, the male branch died out before the third generation. Both daughters had been dowered for fifty-five thousand livres by their marriage contracts: Françoise to receive most of hers in coin and Marie-Anne-Sara most of hers in the form of canceled mortgage loans to her husband, Comte de Clisson. In 1712, it seemed possible to keep all the land for one son.

By the gift of 1712, Paul-François received the family domain at Les Granges, situated some twenty kilometers east of La Rochelle in the vineyard country of Aunis. It had been purchased in 1687, a half century before there was any thought of leaving trade. Together with the dependencies, Chaumeau and Manderoux, which were more recent acquisitions, the Terre des Granges was evaluated at 100,000 livres. A few years later, in 1723, after Paul-François had become *Trésorier de France,* his father and mother added the following items to his share:

1. Linens, wine containers, and boiling apparatus for making brandy at Les Granges.
2. The mill at La Brande [a neighboring seigneury].
3. Certain fiefs, *cens,* and a wood also detached from La Brande.
4. The family town house on the rue de Juiverie.

These supplements increased the evaluation of Les Granges to 104,000 livres; the town house added another 25,000. In the same codicil, Paul and his wife compensated the daughters *"pour venir à égalite"* with the income of *rentes* or specified farms. [19] The dependent economic position of Comte de Clisson is suggested by the provision giving "grandson Clisson" the revenue of a *métairie* in Poitou sold earlier to the Deponts by the count, his father, while the Deponts retained *pleine propriété.*

Paul Depont continued to buy land in Aunis. The seigneury of La Brande had been purchased in 1716 for 38,000 livres; it underwent "major repairs" between 1723 and 1726 and was reevaluated at 60,000. In 1726 Paul bought Aigrefeuille for another 60,000 livres. [20] Both were included in the entail. Smaller pieces were also added. In 1729 Paul acquired a farm at Virson by using the seigneurial right of *retrait féodal* and "incorporated it into the seigneury of Les Granges" in addition to a tract of forest, another *métairie* at Forges, and five acres of drained meadow at Voutron in the direction of Rochefort. [21] The acceleration of land purchases, large and small, after 1715, the interest in consolidating domains and rights, both pecuniary and honorific, in a cluster about the manor house at Les Granges, and the substantial repairs with special attention to the fabrication of brandy suggest that Paul Depont was interested in more than securing his commercial loans. He was concerned with making the land pay, especially through producing and marketing brandy. [22] The entail suggests that the land was now considered the most prestigious part of the family fortune and the only son was to convey it to his children intact and unmortgaged. [23]

By 1733 Paul-François had the usufruct, if not full possession, of most of his father's real estate, valued at over 250,000 livres. At the same time, both of his sisters had received increments on their 55,000-livre dowries, but it was becoming increasingly difficult to pay them all in coin, *rentes,* commercial paper, or cancellation of previous loans. Fortunately, Paul and Sara Depont had also accumulated a number of residences and warehouses in La Rochelle which they began to distribute to the Moreaus and Clissons. They no doubt found it harder to part with the salt marshes on the island of Ré and the drained marshland in lower Poitou, but at least these lands were far from the principal family domain at Les Granges. [24]

Nature or accident would also come to the aid of Paul-François. By 1734 it was clear that Françoise Moreau would bear no children; she accepted a life annuity of 500 livres to satisfy her last claims on the estate. In the same year Paul remitted 50,000 of the 70,000-livre mortgage he held on the Clisson property in Poitou "for the benefit of their grandson, Clisson, and his three sisters," but not to go to collaterals on the Clisson side of the family.[25] The sturdy elder Deponts had by now outlived their son-in-law the count, giving them at least temporary bargaining advantages with this branch of the family. Madame Depont even outlived their other daughter, Françoise Moreau and her husband, and her dower rights returned to the Deponts in 1746.[26]

By 1735 it appears that Paul and Sara Depont had successfully executed their wishes in the assignment of their fortune. The landed core of the fortune had been kept intact by entail and lifetime gifts, and by paying the daughters and sons-in-law largely in non-landed assets. They also outlived most of them. Then, in 1743, the last year of his life, Paul summoned the notaries again to his town house on the rue de Juiverie and in the lower salon looking out on the court, he and his wife "for reasons of their own" revoked the legacies assigned to their grandchildren in the Clisson branch and reassigned them to their daughter, the widow Clisson. The very next day they summoned their three children to the presidial court next door on the rue du Palais and revoked the entail of 1727 on the landed property.[27]

At first blush this would seem to reverse the policy of the previous thirty years. In fact, it affected the distribution of the fortune very little. Paul-François would not only retain the lion's share of the property; he would gain free disposition over it. This seems to have been his parents' intention. The wording of the revocation is revealing. The land was "not to be burdened and charged with any act of entail or other *obstacle* which could prevent the entire and free disposition" of the property.[28] The older generation had decided not to tie the property to an entail. Why? Had they decided that Paul-François, now in his forties, was fully capable of managing the family fortune? Had the entail already served part of its purpose by keeping the land free of mortgage for sixteen years in the face of the dower claims of two sons-in-law? Had they decided that entails were on the wane as Chancellor D'Aguesseau began to limit their use by new ordinances from Paris?[29] Or did they draw closer to all their children as they entered old age? The old couple must have been venerated indeed as Paul passed eighty and Sara seventy-five, both in good health to the very end.[30] Had they finally decided that their children were worthy and deserving of managing their shares of the family fortune?

Even from this close perch of investigation it is impossible to isolate the role of affection from more "practical" considerations. Only one shred of evidence suggests unadulterated sentiment: the gift of a house by Sara Bernon-Depont in her widowhood to the nephew of her deceased son-in-law, Pierre Moreau. There was no family obligation to make this gift, and therefore no reason to doubt the sincerity of her words, "out of affection for him and his family."[31] The Bernon and Moreau families had been linked by marriage and trade since the seventeenth century.

When he became head of the family, Paul-François did not feel the need to write nine codicils to his will. Much as he might appear the irascible patriarch at certain moments in his correspondence, he never questioned the principle of equality of treatment of his two sons in the matter of transmission of the Depont fortune. He might not like Jean-Samuel's prodding him on such questions as reevaluation of the properties,[32] but there is no doubt what his underlying assumptions were. Equality, of course, had long been the practice in the account books. The credits (*Avoir*) and debits (*Doit*) of Jean-Samuel and Paul-Charles on their father's accounts are clearly itemized in his journal. One item reads:

Debit: M. de Manderoux, 311 livres for half of the 622 livres which I have paid for him and his brother [Jean-Samuel and Paul-Charles Depont] for merchandise sent to them from Venice according to a bill of exchange dated 7 December, 1753.[33]

Twelve years later, when Paul-François was making an inventory of the family silver, he wrote that Jean-Samuel must furnish receipts for his share "to be recorded at my death so that this silverware can be divided *equally* between you and your brother."[34] Paul-François kept account of all Jean-Samuel's expenses at Paris, especially the capital cost of his offices, to be included in the total evaluation of the inheritance before final division. But the father's belief in equality of treatment is best indicated in this passage written two weeks after Jean-Samuel's marriage in Paris.

With regard to the wedding gift for your wife, I shall limit myself to the necklace and the candelabra, having done a great deal less for Madame des Granges. Moreover, when I am about to give you a gift, I do not need your suggestions . . . .

You are always lamenting, though *I have surely done more for you than I ought to, and a great deal more than I have for your brother.* Therefore, I shall limit myself to what I have already told you regarding your marriage portion [*dote*]. You will receive the interest [*produit*] as it comes in, which is common practice at the time of a child's marriage. I have even done more than this by guaranteeing your solvency. My own father acted quite differently when he gave me some shipping interests for my portion [*dote*] that I lost three or four years later when the vessels were judged unseaworthy.[35]

Throughout his life, Paul-François was scrupulously equitable toward his two sons and two daughters-in-law. Part of his objection to Jean-Samuel's style of life in the capital was due to the difficulties it created for treating the two branches equally. It was not simply petty-mindedness when Paul-François asked his favorite daughter-in-law to give back some of the family silver for division with her new sister-in-law in Paris.[36] Every item, large and small, was counted. When he died, his fortune was divided in two equal lots after all previous gifts and loans to each son were itemized and collated to the total fortune before final division. When the value of the individual share was determined, earlier donations were then deducted from it. While it is true that Paul-Charles received a larger share of the land, Jean-Samuel's administrative functions far from La Rochelle made this a practical arrangement. Jean-Samuel received the lion's share of the *rentes* and other non-landed assets. And Paul-François never alluded to an entail.

From his letters to his son, one would think that Paul-François's resources were limited. By provincial standards, he was a wealthy man. Consider first the inheritance of his father, Paul Depont (table 3.1).

Even after the family advances and the bad debts in the West Indies were deducted, this still left a fortune of over 800,000 livres. Since one can estimate the average return on Depont's real estate and *rentes* at 4 percent in 1746, this would represent an annual revenue of 32,000 livres.[37] In provincial France, this was an income four or five times the revenue of a *gentilhomme-campagnard* at Toulouse, two or three times that of a robe noble at Bordeaux, and equal to the richest parlementary noble at Rennes or Dijon. Even by Parisian standards this fortune was "*sortable*", but of course it could not compare with those of court finance and *les grands*.[38]

How did the Depont fortune compare to those of other La Rochelle merchants who remained in overseas trade? Here too the Depont wealth ranked high. More important, it was more securely based, an advantage that would become much more pronounced after the commercial disasters of the Seven Years' War. The *armateurs* Rasteau, Belin, Bonfils, and Vivier, partners of Paul Depont in the 1730s, had fortunes at mid-century of approximately the same size, but their capital was much less secure. True, Jacques Rasteau, despite heavy losses at sea in the 1740s, managed to amass 208,286 livres in real estate and *rentes* by 1756, but still less than one-third of the value of Depont's capital assets a decade earlier. Allard Belin had 510,700 livres, of which 300,000 was in real estate and *rentes* by 1748, half of Depont's total. Tresahar Bonfils had a capital of 572,000 livres in 1768, but after deducting his debts of 190,000 and his claims on the planters at Saint-Domingue of another 125,000, his net fortune was much closer to 250,000. The three sons of Jacques Vivier inherited a substantial fortune of 800,000 livres in 1737, but when Jean Vivier died in 1761 there remained only debts in his share. He had been ruined by the Seven Years' War, having

Table 3.1. *The Family Fortune in 1746 (after the death of Paul Depont,* **armateur** *and banker)*

	Capital	Percent of Fortune
I. Real Estate		
1. Land in Aunis (Les Granges, Virson, Manderoux, Aigrefeuille, La Brande, etc.)	248,000	
2. Salt marshes in Lower Poitou and Island of Ré	92,000	
3. Drained marshland near Rochefort (3 *cabanes* purchased by Paul-François)	25,000	
4. Three houses and one warehouse at La Rochelle and one house at La Jarrie	38,500	
5. Town house, rue de Juiverie	25,000	
Total real estate	428,500	(32.5)
II. *Rentes*		
A. *Rentes* of Paul Depont in 1744:		
1. 16 mortgage loans (*rentes foncières*) at 2% (5) and 5% (11) 30,260		
2. 35 constituted rents at 2% (9) and 5% (26) 154,673		
3. 1 *rente* on the *Aides et Gabelles* at 2.5% 12,500		
Total 53 *rentes* (1744) 197,433		
B. *Rentes* purchased by Paul-François, 1744–46:		
1. Constituted rents on individuals 70,500		
2. *Rentes* on the Clergy of France 60,000		
Total new *rentes* 130,500		
Grand total of *rentes* (1746)	327,933	(25.0)
III. Notes and Drafts (*Billets sur Place*) (1746):		
1. Payable (*bons et exigibles*) 16,460		
2. Bankruptcy claims (*biens douteux*) 37,582		
3. Notes due (mostly claims on West Indies planters) 218,315*		
Total notes	272,357	(20.5)
IV. Specie Gold and Silver (*en caisse*) (1746):	59,068**	(4.5)
V. Advances to Children:		
1. To Paul-François 47,462		
2. To Marie-Anne-Sara, Comtesse de Clisson 161,224		
3. To Françoise, Madame Moreau 15,481		
Total Advances	224,167	(17.0)
Total Fortune	1,311,883	(99.5)

Source: Archives Départementales, E–483, *"Succession,"* 22 June 1744; *"Partage,"* 2 Nov. 1746.

*Also, *biens douteux.* See chapter 1 above.

**Sara Bernon, Paul Depont's widow, had 87,500 livres in specie in 1754. E–483, *"Etat de la Succession de ma mère,"* 15 May 1754 and 4 June 1754.

failed to place enough of his commercial profits of the "good years" before 1744 in land and *rentes*. Other *armateurs*, such as Harouard and Rodrigue who had left trade, their sons, like the Deponts, having entered offices, fared much better. And a few, like the Garesché, weathered all the vicissitudes of war and uncertainty to be counted among the richest ship-outfitters in 1789.[39] But there can be little doubt that the Deponts had secured the bulk of their capital at the right moment.

If economic historians point to this kind of decision as contributing to the "decapitation" of French capitalism,[40] who can deny that subsequent events confirmed the wisdom of this shift to security? Continuous commercial reinvestment may suggest a Schumpeterian dynamism in late nineteenth-century Europe; such a course of action had very definite limits in mid-eighteenth century La Rochelle. Were Jean Vivier or even Jacques Rasteau rewarded for their persistent commercial enterprise? In retrospect at least, who had been most "rational" in their economic choices: the Viviers or the Deponts?

In 1746, the Depont fortune contrasted with those of other prominent merchants in more ways than one. Not only did the Deponts have 58 percent of their wealth in real estate and *rentes*—a larger proportion than the *armateurs* described above—they had almost half of their income-producing wealth in land; they would soon sell or alienate most of their urban property except the town house. The amount of specie *en caisse* was also exceptional. Most ship-outfitters could not afford to keep this much capital idle.[41] Some of the silver and gold stayed locked in the strongbox for years. In 1753, Comtesse de Clisson bequeathed 100 *pistoles* (1,000 livres) to her brother, Paul-François, in recompense for executing her will. Twelve years later, Paul-François asked his son to buy the wedding gift for his great-nephew (in the Clisson branch) with the same 100 *pistoles*.[42] Of course, we are examining the fortune at the moment of transition. Between 1744 and 1746 Paul-François liquidated most of his father's investments in overseas trade and reinvested the capital in land and *rentes* wherever he could find a good *placement*. The large sums in gold and silver—over 140,000 livres if his mother's *deniers* are added—probably reflected the absence of immediate investment opportunities other than overseas trade, and even here the effects of the war starting in the 1740s were beginning to tell. The notes (*billets*) would almost disappear from the family portfolio over the next thirty years. A letter in 1769 refers to claims of only 1,384 livres at Saint-Domingue of which "we can take possession (*saisie*)," and this twenty-five years after Paul-François had left the trade.[43]

The land market in the region around La Rochelle was not large or fluid enough to absorb several hundred thousand livres of Depont capital in a short time. The *armateurs*, as well as the old resident nobility, were naturally reluctant to sell. This was one reason why the family holdings of *rentes* substantially increased. The capital in *rentes*, both private and public, rose from 200,000 to almost 400,000 between 1744 and 1776.[44] When Paul-François wrote in 1765 that he lived from his *rentes*, he was not greatly exaggerating. They represented close to 40 percent of the income-producing capital of the family and about 50 percent of its revenue by 1770.[45]

Paul Depont's *rentes* consisted largely of loans to individuals ranging from 800 to 20,000 livres, thirty-seven at 5 percent and fourteen at 2 and 2.5 percent. His son, Paul-François, had increased the number of *rentes* on public institutions from 12,000 to 75,754 livres over the following thirty years. He also increased the number of constituted *rentes* (perpetual annuities from individuals) from fifty-one to eighty-one and converted almost all of them to *rentes* at 5 percent by 1774. If his father had dispersed his commercial investments in an assortment of ventures large and small, Paul-François did the same with his *rentes*. His public *rentes* included loans to the Clergy of France, the *Aides et Gabelles*, the *Tailles* of Poitiers and La Rochelle; his *rentes* on individuals were distributed among four-score local notables, financiers, merchants, artisans, and *laboureurs*.[46]

Table 3.2. *The Income from* Rentes *of Paul-François and Paul-Charles Depont* (*at 5 percent unless otherwise specified*) (*in livres*)

Capital	Property or Occupation of "Borrower"	1730	1740	1750	1760	1770	1780	1790	1800
			1744 Death of Paul Depont			1774 Death of Paul-François			1800 Death of Paul-Charles
1000 liv.	2 houses					40 (4%)		40 liv.	
1000	2 houses					40 (4%)			
2400	1/2 mill					120			
1222	small farm					61		61	
1000						50		50	
200						10		10	
4000						200		200	
2000	small farm					100			
3000	(of Intendant Depont)					150		150	
4000						200		200	
3000						150		150	
2000	Morin, *avocat* of this city							100	
1500						75		75	
4000						200			
300	locksmith					15		15	
4000						200		200	

Table 3.2. (*Continued*)

Capital	Property or Occupation of "Borrower"	1744 Death of Paul Depont	1774 Death of Paul-Françoise	1800 Death of Paul-Charles
1200			48 (4%)	
8710			435	
4000			200	
3240			162	
2000			100	
3000			150	
1600			80	
1400			42 (3%)	
1000			50	
8000	merchant			400
1500			60 (4%)	
2000			100	100
1200	(of Indendant Depont)		50 (4.2%)	50
1450			72	72
900	1 house		18 (2%)	18
1971			98	
3000			150	150
2000			100	100
2000	1 house		100	100
500			25	25
2700			135	135
600	1 house (in village)		30	
2000			100	100
800			40	40
2000			100	100
6000	chief clerk		300	300
3200			160	160
8000	royal councilor, judge		400	400
3000			150	150
6000			300	
425			21	21
1000			50	50
1530			76	76
2000			100	
2000			100	?
100	1 house		5	5
1280	1 house		64	
3000			150	?
1000			50	
1200	1 house		60	?
4000		200		

Table 3.2. (Continued)

Capital	Property or Occupation of "Borrower"	1744 Death of Paul Depont	1760	1774 Death of Paul-Françoise (1770)	1780	1800 Death of Paul-Charles (1790)
1000				50		50
5000				250		250
1320	1 house			66		
4000	(of my father)			200		
4000	1 house			200		
4000				200		
700	widow Gresseau			35		35
4000	1 house			200		200
4833	wood merchant			241		241
4123	merchant in Angoumois					206
4000	Clergy of France		200			
8000	France				400	
8234	Tailles of Poitiers			192 (2.3%)		192
2200				110		110
300				15		
420	1 house			21		21
1200				60		60
4356	Tailles of La Rochelle			217		
32,500	life annuity on the *Aydes* at *Gabelles*			2600 (8%)		2340 (7.2%)
196,191 Total capital (1770)	Total revenus from *rentes*			10,464 (1770)		7,019 (1790)

Source: Archives Départementales, E–484, "Livre conçernant mes rentes et prix des fermes" (1757–1804). "Mes" refers to Paul-Charles Depont after 1774. There is a small discrepancy between this account and the *rentes* listed in the *partage* of 27 June 1776. Presumably, the *rentes* given to Jean-Samuel in 1765 at the time of his marriage are not included in this account book.

Paul Depont had lent considerable sums to Comte de Clisson, and the subsequent marriage of his daughter to the count was not unrelated to these loans. Sara Bernon, Paul's widow, had lent another noble landlord, François Gasseau, Baron de Champagné, 40,000 livres in 1748 from her half-share in the marital "community of property." The baron, like the count, needed the money to pay off earlier debts. The contract noted succinctly that the baron had "lost his lawsuit." It also pledged all of his property to secure the loan, specifying one farm and its tenant to pay the *rente*.[47] Ten years later when Gasseau fell two years behind in his *rente*, Paul-François reminded him of the delay "due no doubt to the negligence of your agent, Sieur Ferrachim."[48] Twelve years later in 1770, Paul-François "purchased a *rente*," that is, lent the Gasseau family another 7,000 livres at 5 percent.[49] Paul-François was not the sort to transfer capital to negligent *rente*-payers. The baron's land consisted of drained meadowland (*cabanes*) near Luçon, some fifteen miles north of La Rochelle; the Deponts had owned land in this region before. Perhaps Paul-François had an eye on the baron's farms.

Descending the social scale, one notes a family of tenant farmers (*fermiers*). The account book reads:

Debit: François Roblet and Elizabeth Giraud, his wife, living at the farm of Chaumeau, owe 121 livres, 6 sous interest on the principal of 2,426 livres that M. Des Granges has lent to them.[50]

Still further down the scale we find:

Debit: Jacques Refin, *laboureur* of the parish of St-Vincent des Chaumes, and his wife:
1. One *boisseau* of wheat and one capon.
2. Two days labor-service per year.
3. *Rente foncière* of 300 livres to be amortized in four equal payments . . . *rente*: 15 livres.
4. *Rente hypothéquaire* to be amortized at their discretion (*leurs bons points*) . . . 3 livres, 15 sous.[51]

Here the *rente foncière* is almost indistinguishable from a *cens*, since a particular piece of land was pledged; however, unlike the *cens*, it could be amortized or repaid. Sometimes even Depont was not sure where seigneurial terminology ended and the nomenclature of *rentes* began.

Debit: Jean Thibaud, *laboureur* and his wife, 8 livres 14 sous *rente hypothéquaire* on a capital of 174 livres, payable 11 December (of each year) by an act of *retrait lignager* passed 11 December, 1750.[52]

It appears that Depont had exercised the right of *retrait lignager*, attaching Thibaud's holding to his domainal property, but retained an annual payment.[53] Depont finally decided that the annual charge was a *cens*, not a *rente*. Consequently, Thibaud could not liquidate this annual charge by "repurchasing the *rente*," that is, by paying back the capital.[54] It had become a perpetual ground-rent.

Rente contracts, as the jurist Pothier said in 1763, were very popular, "composing the largest part of the patrimony, often all the patrimony, of a great number of families."[55] Legal refinement proceeded apace. Credi-renters, (technically, those who "bought a *rente*") in order to protect themselves against withholding taxes of the crown, inserted clauses in the contracts limiting the sums the debi-renters could deduct from their *rente* payments for taxes. This was impossible to do on public *rente* contracts, of course. Although mortgage liens were usually assigned on all the property of the debtor, occasionally a specific piece of property (a house, a farm, an office) was identified as collateral or "guarantor" of the loan. The *rente* never departed from the legal notion that it represented a transfer or alienation of property.[56] One "purchased" a *rente* as if it were a piece of land with an annual revenue. Otherwise, it would be a loan and therefore usurious and contrary to the law.

More significant as examples of the popularity of *rentes* were the provisions for amortization or "repurchase" of the *rente*. The debtor could not repay the capital without warning the creditor "in writing" at least three months in advance, and usually six. Nor was the capital always payable in a single lump sum; payments were spaced over many months. In the Depont case, these clauses did not seem to bear any relation to the amount of capital on loan. Jean Thibaud, the *laboureur* discussed above, could liquidate his 300 livres in four equal payments, while M. Cantier, wood merchant, could amortize his capital of 4,833 livres "in one single payment."[57] Both provisions demonstrate that the creditor was not anxious to have his capital refunded, and clearly not without being given sufficient time to find a new *placement*. The stories Montesquieu once told about debtors laden with Law scrip rushing about Paris after their creditors, armed with quills and ink, and with notaries at their heels, can be applied—with less force, to be sure—to those who would repay their *rentes* too soon, even with sacks of solid silver and gold.[58] The law in this instance is testimony to the relative shortage of good investment opportunities and to the preference for long-term loans at a fixed return of 5 percent. In fact, credi-renters were willing to accept even lower rates rather than recover their capital. The legal provision whereby the creditor could not demand repayment of the capital without the consent of the debtor was not considered a great disadvantage to a potential investor as long as the interest (*rente*) was paid. *Rentes* were not intended for short-term investment and in fact precluded any notion of rapid turnover of capital.[59]

Although the accounts do not describe the occupations of most of the debtors, there are indications of the range of people to whom the Deponts lent money between 1750 and 1790.[60] Many, indeed most, seem to have been local notables who often pledged a house for a loan of 2,000 livres—the widow Gresseau, the chief clerk (*greffier-en-chef*) of the city, a councilor at the *Eaux et Forêts*, a local nobleman draining marshland near Rochefort, and scores of anonymous "Messieurs." Occasionally, one detects a wood merchant borrowing several thousand livres or a butcher and a locksmith a few hundred, but these are rare cases. Nor does one find a large number of small mortgage loans to

Table 3.3. Distribution of Loans in 1772

Capital on Loan	Number of Debi-renters*
4,000 and over	15 (largest: 8,710)
3,000 to 3,999	8
2,000 to 2,999	12
1,000 to 1,999	20
500 to 999	5
100 to 499	6 (smallest: 100)
	66 (total)

Source: Archives Départementales, E–484, "Livre concernant mes rentes."
*"Debi-renters" used by Ralph Giesey ("Rules of Inheritance," p. 279) in order to make a legal distinction from the modern term "debtor." Contemporaries used *"débiteurs de rentes."*

laboureurs and winegrowers comparable in quantity to those found around Beauvais, Toulouse, or Dijon.[61] Consider the distribution of loans to individuals in 1772 just before Paul-François's death (table 3.3).

Hence, four out of five of the Depont loans represented capital sums of 1,000 livres or more. These are not the small loans (the median falls between 2,000 and 3,000 livres) that one usually associates with petty moneylending in the countryside. But they are not large enough to launch substantial commercial or financial ventures either. The impression—and it is no more than that—is one of loans to middling town notables, most of whom owned a house and some land in the hinterland, and who needed ready coin for marriage portions or the promotion of their children in a local office or profession—law, army, or church. Unknowingly, Paul-François Depont was probably helping other "mobile", if more modest, families along the incremental path to higher social status.

Whether collected from a widow at La Rochelle, a *laboureur* in Aunis, a tax farm at Poitiers, or the Clergy of France in Paris, Paul-François was able to assure himself a return of 5 percent from his *rentes*. In the years after his father's death in 1744, he liquidated by sale or gift almost all of the family *rentes* that had been established earlier at lower rates. The new public *rentes* issued by the government at 5 percent and even above no doubt raised the rate on private *rentes* as well. The long-term decline in annuity rates was halted and even reversed. Near the end of the Seven Years' War, the government began to float large issues of lifetime annuities (*rentes viagères*) on very attractive terms, a policy that would have disastrous budgetary consequences twenty-five years later. In 1762 Paul-François bought a *rente viagère "sur les têtes"* of his grandchildren, Virson and Pauline, both of whom were not yet ten years old, and would live another fifty years.[62] He invested 32,500 livres at 8 percent (2,600) "tax exempt," to be paid by the *Aides et Gabelles*, a very reputable tax agency. The *rente* was still being paid in 1780, representing an accumulated income at this date of 46,280 livres. Even after partial repudiation of the national debt during the Revolution, the Deponts could hardly complain about this investment.[63] The Depont case seems to substantiate Marcel Marion's comment that the average life-expectancy of French *rentiers viagers* was substantially above the national average; the government's actuary tables had not yet drawn upon the expertise of modern statisticians and demographers.[64]

Paul-François could not always avoid the uncertainties of public finance. The *rentes* on the *Tailles*, though backed by royal tax collections, were particularly susceptible to arbitrary reduction. Depont's *rentes* on the *Tailles* of Poitiers, inherited in 1724 from his maternal grandfather, *Trésorier de France* at Poitiers, were reduced in 1761 from 20,945 livres to 8,234 and returned 192 livres per annum in 1767, only 2.3 percent.[65] Moreover, the government was often tardy in its disbursements to *rente*-holders. Paul-François frequently called upon Jean-Samuel in Paris to track down arrears as well as to obtain the latest information about public *rentes*. "The arrears on the *rentes* on the *Tailles* amount to 1,300 livres per year. Go to the office of M. d'Ormesson and find out why the delay for 1764. I also acquired 300 recently from M. de Séline, Receiver of Tailles. I am "Paul-François," though the records have me down as "François-Paul." Correct the register at d'Ormesson's office for the 1765 *rentes*. Is it true that the *rentes* will be reduced to 4 percent?" (24 May 1766).

Paul-François had been self-righteous about transferring some 60,000 livres from the *"intérêts mal acquis"* of his father to *rentes* on the Clergy back in 1746. By 1765, however, he was less sanguine about the financial wisdom of the decision. "My loan to the Jesuits, twenty years ago, appears lost," he wrote with some alarm at the time of the suppression of the Society.[66] Six months later, he was more optimistic. "Don't forget my credit on the Jesuits. There are no new laws on this subject here."[67] The uncertain state of this loan did not affect Depont's other loans to the Clergy of France, though he was concerned that the Assembly of the Clergy might reduce the interest to 4 percent.[68] In 1766 Paul-François was still able to deliver 33,000 livres in Clergy loans returning 5 percent as part of his son's marriage portion.[69]

From his accounts and letters it seems clear that Paul-François went to great pains to find *placements* at 5 percent. When he had to *borrow* for immediate needs of liquidity, he went to equal pains to find an interest *below* 5 percent. Again, he used his son's presence at Paris to the fullest. "I am surprised you cannot borrow at 4 percent. Perhaps you can borrow at 5 percent but with all taxes deducted."[70] Paul-François had many contacts among financiers in Paris and the provinces. He often referred Jean-Samuel to Monsieur Mouchard, receiver-general of finances, for advice in financial matters.[71] Here is an example of Paul-François's meticulous efforts to negociate a loan for his son. "Money is extremely rare here. With the help of M. de la Neuville or other financiers can't you find someone who can lend you money by private signature [*sous signature privée*] without a notarized contract? You can then calculate which will cost the least, the fee of the notary or the cost of a 'private signature.' Your brother could easily borrow at 6 percent by draft [*billet*] but without deducting the *vingtième* tax."[72]

The heaviest single demand on Paul-François for ready capital was for his son's office of *Maître des Requêtes* in 1755—100,000 livres. He had managed to pay for the office of *Conseiller* with contracts on the Clergy (20,000), bills of exchange (10,425), and louis d'or (13,200).[73] But he had to find 60,000 more to pay for the second office. He borrowed 48,000 from Jean-Antoine Carré de Candé and 12,000 from Jean-Baptiste Veyssière, both colleagues in the Bureau of Finances at La Rochelle. The debt was liquidated from the dowry of Jean-Samuel's bride in 1767, twelve years later.[74] Paul-François had always been on good terms with his colleagues.

Although Depont relied heavily on the Parisian money market, he was also able to find money at La Rochelle, sometimes from old acquaintances among the *armateurs*, like Rasteau, though more often, especially for long-term loans, from tax officials of the crown. John F. Bosher has informed us about the financial opportunities open to tax farmers and an army of lesser receivers who had many months' use of tax funds before they had to transfer them to a central collecting agency.[75] Was Paul-François one of these? There is no evidence from any of his carefully preserved accounts or his correspondence that he lent money on short-term at commercial rates or that he speculated in any way with public funds. His recorded loans are all *rentes* at 5 percent (never more) and there is no sign of any hidden interest such as one would expect to appear later in his eldest son's accounts of the 1780s. Paul-François, it seems, was not that kind of a "banker." But of course he was close to the milieu of provincial and even Parisian financiers, and he occasionally "purchased *rentes*" from them on long-term, ten, twenty, even thirty years. It was also natural that he would borrow from them when necessary.[76]

There can be little doubt that Paul-François's "mentality" precluded any notion of speculation, especially where the danger of incurring "usury" was present. On the other hand, everything conspired to make him a superb accountant, a *rentier né*. A man of few passions, Depont surely took some satisfaction from his account books—a smile for every payment received, a scowl perhaps for every *arrérage*. Unfortunately, there were arrears. In 1769, he wrote to Jean-Samuel: "There is no doubt that times are very hard here on debtors because of the low return on the land. Since they owe me more than you, I will give you half of what comes in. I am more poorly paid by my *rentes* than you are" (April 1769).

Paul-François collected some of the *rentes* of his son, having retained for himself the usufruct of some *rentes* whose proprietorship had been alienated by the marriage contract in 1766.[77] He felt more secure administering Jean-Samuel's property—land and *rentes*—in Aunis. He was also capable of hiding behind his son's name if it served to enforce payments. "M. Depont [Jean-Samuel] has been willing to wait, Monsieur, until 15 October (last). M. Depont is very surprised, Monsieur, that you have not kept the promise you made in your letter of 4 August in which you said you would pay by 15 October at the latest. Consequently, he has instructed me to warn you for the last time that if you do not pay in the next eight days, he will send a process-server [*huissier*] to force you to pay. Don't bother to write to him because he is decided not to wait any longer".[78]

To Madame de La Coudraye and to Baron de La Rochebaron he gave extensions of a fortnight, warning them to avoid the legal costs of *les facheuses suites*. Characteristically, he estimated the fees of the process-server at 24 livres on a *rente* of 150.[79] Nor were Depont's warnings empty threats. In a letter to Monsieur Chevalier, *conseiller* at the Parlement of Paris, he referred to the necessity of a number of foreclosures (*saisies*) on the debi-renters (*débiteurs de rentes*). In 1764 he had obtained a favorable judgment at the local presidial court promising 2,320 livres, but he had collected only 936 livres in the following five years. He was considering further legal action in the highest court of the kingdom.[80]

Rentes were an honorable form of investment. They were not considered "usurious" by the Church; under the law, they were "immovables by fiction" and could become lineage property (*propres*) in the second generation just like acquired land.[81] Despite delays in payment by either public agencies or private parties, *rentes* were a sound economic investment. The main risk was not that the capital *would not* be repaid, but that it *would* be repaid. It was the notion of perpetuity that gave the *rente* its special status as an immovable and made it attractive as a long-term familial investment. Paul-François rarely had his *rentes* reimbursed before ten years had expired, and the great majority were in force over twenty years, some for over forty, repaying the capital twice over.[82] Nor did he have to renegotiate his *rentes* at lower rates to prevent reimbursement, a practice that was common a century earlier.[83] Moreover, when one recognizes the effects of compounding, that is, reinvesting the interest in new *rentes*, it becomes clear that *rentes* were not only steadier and safer than returns on commercial ventures, but over the long run equally profitable, excepting the lucrative operations of the tax farmers, of course.[84]

In 1746 Paul-François received as his share of his father's inheritance about 100,000 livres (capital) in *rentes* at 5 percent. If one assumes for a moment that he invested the entire interest on this 100,000 livres every five years in new *rentes* and reinvested the revenue from the old and

Table 3.4. *The Inheritance of Paul-François Depont,* Trésorier de France, *in 1776*

"Mass of Property of the Inheritance of M. Depont *père*. This mass is composed of the collations [*rapports*] to be made by MM. Des Granges and Depont, his sons, for the "objects" that said Sr. Depont *père* has given to his sons before or since their marriages as well as the property existing at the time of the death of the said Sr. Depont *père*."

Property already given to M. Paul-Charles Des Granges:
1. Domains of Les Granges and Chaumeau, and the office of *Trésorier de*		
France by his marriage contract, 11 May 1751		109,700
2. *Rentes* on individuals at 5 percent (1,485), also by his marriage contract		29,700
3. Domain of La Brande with a revenue of 3,150 given to Sr. Des Granges at		
his brother's marriage, 11 May 1766		
Domain worth 63,000, but burdened with a mortgage of 6,300. Net value		56,700
Total given to M. Des Granges		196,100

Property already given to M. Jean-Samuel Depont, Intendant:
1. Advance in 1748 for his office of *Conseiller au Parlement*		48,000
2. Advance in 1755 for his "reception fee" for the office of *Maître des*		
Requêtes		12,000
3. Domain of Manderoux given by his marriage contract, 11 May 1766		55,000
4. *Rentes*:		
on the *Tailles*	28,004	
on the Clergy	33,000	
on Municipality of La Rochelle	8,000	
on *Hôtel de Ville* of Paris	6,750	
on 5 individuals	49,013	
on inheritance (to be adjusted)	233	
Total *rentes*		125,000
Total given to M. Depont, Intendant		240,000

Immovables Remaining on the Death of Sr. Depont, *père*:
1. Domains of Aigrefeuille, Chagnées, 2 farms, 1 mill, and 1 town house at	
La Rochelle	210,200
2. *Rentes* on individuals at 5 percent	240,777
3. Specie on hand (*deniers comptants*)	65,245
The movables in town house, La Rochelle	6,000
Total fortune	958,322

"From which sum 10,000 livres must be deducted in favor of M. De Virson, Grandson of Sr. Depont, conforming to his verbal intention."
Net fortune	948,322
To be divided in equal portions, each son entitled to:	474,161

Source: Archives Nationales, Minutier Central, *Etude* 66:628, "Partage Depont," 27 June 1776.

new *rentes* every suceeding five years, the original capital would grow in the following manner:

After	Date	Capital Compounded	After	Date	Capital Compounded
10 years	1756	156,250 livres	40	1786	596,050 livres
20	1766	244,140	50	1796	931,320
30	1776	381,470	100	1846	8,673,570

This is only a theoretical calculation,[85] but it is a recorded fact that during the thirty years 1746–76 Paul-François accumulated *rentes* very close to the theoretical model, that is, 395,477 livres, including those he had given to his sons as marriage portions in 1751 and 1766. He had invested most of the remains of his father's commercial assets in *rentes*, so he would not be required to follow the discipline of the model rigidly in order to increase his *rentes* fourfold in this period. In any case, there is no need to look for some hidden source of income—lending public funds on short term, for example—to account for this growth of capital. Recall again that Paul-François's entire outlook and style of life at La Rochelle were admirably adapted to this kind of wealth accumulation. Here indeed the Weberian notion of "worldly asceticism" makes sense. The fruits of thirty years of management of the family income could be regarded by the two surviving sons with no small satisfaction, whatever their own intentions as to its future employ (table 3.4).

Recall that at the death of Paul Depont in 1746 the total family fortune before division totaled 1,300,000 livres, but that only about 800,000 of this could be considered safe and income-productive. In 1776 the fortune of one son (his two sisters having been paid their shares from the father's patrimony) was again close to one million livres and much more securely anchored. In absolute numbers, compare the fortune of father and son at the two dates:

Table 3.5. *The Family Fortune in 1746 and 1776*

	The Inheritance of Paul Depont, 1746 (livres)	The Inheritance of Paul-François Depont, 1776 (livres)
Land	428,500	381,600
Rentes	327,933	395,477
Notes	272,357	–
Advances	224,167 (50,000 for office)	110,000 (all for office)
Specie	59,068	65,245
Total	1,312,025	952,322

Source: See Table 3.1 and Table 3.4.

In the division of the fortune following Paul Depont's death, Paul-François had received the bulk of the land, but only a fraction of the *rentes*. The claims of Comtesse de Clisson were a substantial drain, despite the accumulated mortgages held by Paul Depont on the count's estate in Poitou. When we remember that Paul Depont's fortune was to be divided in three almost equal shares after the entail was revoked, Paul-François's accomplishment in rebuilding his share almost to the total family wealth of 1746—and supporting a son in Paris besides—must elicit some respect. It had taken some restraint on all sides and a good bit of cajoling and even threatening of a younger son. Perhaps his greatest success was providing that Jean-Samuel's marriage contract "assign" part of his wife's dowry in 1766 to liquidate 60,000 livres borrowed ten years earlier for his office of *Maître des Requêtes*. [86] Aside from a small mortgage (6,300) on the domain of La Brande, Paul-François had no obligations in 1774; the estate was debt-free. Many a great nobleman at Paris with five times his fortune—but *criblé de dettes*—might envy Depont's resources. Moreover, with the *rentes* now invested almost entirely at 5 percent and with land values beginning to rise dramatically after 1770, the income in 1774 must have been close to 35,000 livres. Paul-François died a millionaire on the threshold of a "noble-worthy fortune." [87]

One aspect of Paul-François's fortune deserves special attention, the large amount of specie. Despite the major shift of family investment from shipping to *rentes*, the amount of gold and silver kept in strong boxes remained at about 5.0 percent of the total fortune. In fact, assuming that Paul Depont's specie had been divided equally among the three children in 1746, Paul-François had increased his share more than threefold in the following thirty years, from 20,000 to 65,000 livres. A large hoard in Paul Depont's hands might suggest the banking operations of an active Protestant shipowner. But what was Paul-François, a rentier and outspoken opponent of usury, doing with 65,000 livres of silver *en caisse*? One can only conclude that, despite his prodigious efforts to find investment outlets via land and *rentes*, Paul-François still had a surplus, a nest egg he preferred to keep locked up in his townhouse in La Rochelle rather than see it squandered on conspicuous consumption in the *tourbillon* of Paris. Something might also be attributed to the anxieties of a provincial *anobli* who looked to solid silver as ballast against the stormy seas of upward mobility.

Paul-François had spent most of his life managing, indeed nurturing, the family fortune. His constant entreaties to his son were as much a part of this "management" as his methodical reinvestment in *rentes*. No wasteful consumption would be allowed to undermine his resolve to muster a surplus each year to "build" the family capital. This is not to say that the righteous moralizing of his letters to his son was hypocritical and insincere. More than one imperative was at play and they were mutually compatible. In the end, Paul-François was less interested in his own material self-gratification and even his own social *éclat* (beyond his *honnête milieu*) than in passing on a solid fortune to the next generation, unburdened by family charges and untainted by obligations to "outsiders." If his attitude toward pretensions to the High Robe remained ambivalent, he assumed his financial obligations toward the future of the Depont family without equivocation.

Paul-François took understandable pride in his own expertise in the administration of the patrimony. If he suffered occasional social slights at the hands of his niece, Comtesse de Lescure, he seemed to have the upper hand when it came to family finances. He could even be peremptory in these matters. "Having assured you, my dear niece, of the continuation of my friendship, I give you notice of an informal arrangement [*petit arrangement*] that I find advantageous for both of us in my father's inheritance ... [1,337 livres, half for you] Please give me your approval on the form I have enclosed [*forme de petit modelle*]."[88]

On the occasion of the marriage of his niece's son, he might have to be prompted to write his congratulatory letter, but he knew the exact value of the king's gift. "If it is not eight thousand livres *rente* on a domain, it is not worth very much," he wrote almost with disdain toward a branch of the family whose social pretensions were not always matched by their financial acumen.[89] Family continuity was worth more than immediate social gratification. To that end, Paul-François Depont would see that the economic underpinnings were secure.

CHAPTER FOUR

The Land: The Depont Domains Over Three Generations (1700-1789)

The Atlantic coast immediately north and south of La Rochelle is drained marshland. To this day, these flat, treeless stretches give a distinctive, almost eerie aspect to the region. Looking north from the parish church of Esnandes, for example, when the village is shrouded in evening fog, one can barely make out the slow-moving outlines of livestock grazing on table-top meadowland, stretching some twenty miles to the north and east along the estuary of the Sèvre-Niortaise. In the sixteenth century La Rochelle was an isolated port at the tip of a peninsula jutting into the Atlantic and almost surrounded by seawater, which reached Niort to the northeast and Tonnay-Boutonne to the southeast of the port. It is not too far from the truth to say that Aunis did not exist before the reign of Henry IV. Draining this land was not new to the eighteenth century. The Dutch had already put their expert hand to it at the turn of the seventeenth century.[1] But as the "science" of land reclamation and financial organization improved, and as government promotion became more persistent, the water was channeled more rapidly into a thousand canals and ditches that fed into the Sèvre and Charente rivers.

Jurisdictional problems and local opposition remained formidable, however. Agricultural improvers like Abbé Arcère and Martin de Chassiron complained that, without a uniform plan for draining the entire region, progress would be slow.[2] The forces of resistance formed an unlikely but effective alliance. Absentee *grands seigneurs* who owned mills and salt beds on marshlands or drew seigneurial rights from them joined with that peculiar world of marsh people—salt-makers, boatmen, fishermen, scavengers for oysters and seaweed—to fight the "new companies" of local proprietors, large and small, who wished to drain and convert the marsh into compact farms of rich grainland and pasture. The Minister Bertin, champion of land-draining, had to face local realities when he attempted to drain 2,500 acres of marsh on his own newly acquired estate north of Mauzé. The villagers fought tenaciously for their communal rights to the marsh, and the law case cost Bertin more than 150,000 livres and a decade of delay before he won, only to face a revived communal protest in 1789.[3] In 1750 an assembly of seventy-two individuals with "interests in coastal marshland" met at Marennes to protest a drainage project which, they claimed, threatened to divest them of their patrimony of valuable salt marshes. The list was headed by such illustrious names as Marshal de Richelieu, Dame Durfort de Duras, and Prince de Soubise, followed by constituencies of robe magistrates from Bordeaux, local military nobility, and an array of smaller proprietors of salt marshes on the islands and the mainland south of La Rochelle. Well sustained by a battery of attorneys, the assembly at Marennes described the reclamation project as "the odious fruit of the sinister machinations of an avaricious company concerned only with the selfish interest of its members."[4] Intra-regional disputes complicated matters further. The notables of the city of La Rochelle wanted to combine a large-scale effort to drain the Sèvre estuary with a canal that would link the Atlantic port with Niort, the major *entrepôt* of grain from Poitou. But the grain port of Marans to the north objected to a canal which would weaken its monopoly on grain shipments from the interior. One had to be careful not to threaten *situations acquises*; even President d'Aligre, a large proprietor of marshland near Marans who favored drainage "companies," fought all projects that included a canal from Niort to La Rochelle.[5]

Nevertheless, despite these many obstacles, draining continued. Energetic local notables like Martin de Chassiron, Pascaud, and Seignette, all *officiers* like Depont, at La Rochelle, country residents like Marquis de Saint-Georges at Thairé, and Dr. Pivet at Marans directed "companies" of one hundred proprietors who contributed to a common fund to drain the land and maintain the canals and levies thereafter.[6] Individual entrepreneurs occasionally exhibited exceptional drive and skill. Marquis de Saint-George drained 400 *journaux* (320 acres) at Voutron south of La Rochelle. His enthusiasm testified to the fact that not all rural seigneurs were content to sit back and draw rents from the land. Returning from Paris where he had to establish his titles to the land, the marquis wrote a letter marked 4 A.M. in the morning: "I am arriving tomorrow in Saintonge. I wish the day were sixty hours long. ... My sluice gates are finished. We shall dispatch the sweet water into the ocean. ... We begin plowing Monday. My tenants [*colons*] are moving today."[7] Paul-François and his father profited from this project without doubt. They acquired three *cabanes* in the same area in the 1730s.[8]

The marquis's project was small compared to those attempted by the "companies" later in the century. The association of landowners that proposed to drain over 4,000 acres of marshland north of La Rochelle was composed of 150 members ranging from large proprietors (200 to 1,000 acres of marshland), such as President d'Aligre, Cadoret de Beaupréau, and a number of religious houses, to numerous middling holders of 10 to 40 acres. Each member contributed 12 livres per *journal* (0.8 acres) for a total of 63,000 livres working capital.[9] Maintenance was as important as the initial draining. In 1780, one member of the Society of Agriculture at La Rochelle claimed that the major drainings in the region were completed; henceforth, it was only a matter of upkeep. Unfortunately, it was not always possible to maintain the initial spirit of cooperation; contributions fell off, and proprietors refused to let water from higher levels cross their own farms. There were innumerable disputes among landlords attempting to fix responsibility for the collapse of a levy, the stoppage of a canal, or some other damage.[10] Yet somehow the work was done and new farms or *cabanes* were created.

Paul-Charles Depont was one of the contributors to the upkeep of drained marshland in the region between the *cabanes* of Marquis de Saint-Georges at Voutron and the mouth of the Charente.[11] Like those of the marquis, Depont's three *cabanes* measured about two hundred acres each, which was much larger than the usual *métairie* in the interior. More important, they were compact, broken only by the drainage canals and levies, and of course free of trees, scrub, and heath. Located near the coast, meaning cheap water transportation, the new farms could be readily commercialized, and the grain shipped as far as Bordeaux. The rich tidal soil was equally suitable for grain and pasture, the best in Aunis. A report of the Society of Agriculture in 1764 alluded to the "abundance of grain, vegetables, beans, hay" produced by the *marais desséchés*,[12] and another in 1780 was equally enthusiastic: "One only has to look at the drained marshlands about Rochefort and Marans, so rich in grain and livestock, to realize the promise of those not yet drained." In fact, livestock raising for commercial purposes was restricted to the coastal flat-lands, especially near Marans, and much of it was sold at the fairs of Fontenay-le-Comte for export out of the province.[13] As all readers of Arthur Young know, abundant livestock suggests modern farming, and the *cabanes* of Aunis came closer to the English model than almost any other farms (*métairies*) west of the Paris basin. If the simple cabins that lined the countless estuaries of the Sèvre looked even more primitive than the "hangars" in the southwest near Toulouse, they nonetheless housed the families of commercialized tenant farmers. None of Depont's rents rose as abruptly after 1780 as those from his *cabanes*.

In the decade of the 1760s the royal government, led by Henri Bertin, a veritable secretary of agriculture for seventeen years, made a major effort to encourage agricultural production.[14] Land reclamation was one aspect of this policy; the establishment of societies of agriculture was another. In 1761 a group of notables at La Rochelle, organized by a local seigneurial judge, de Bussac, responded to Bertin's urging and formed such a society. But despite Bussac's laudable desire to enlist a wide spectrum of local leaders, the new society appeared to have little impact on agricultural practice. Bussac even intended to consult the local *laboureurs*, "without, of course, having them join the academy."[15] An obvious concession to local attitudes, the reluctance to include real farmers as regular members is an indication of the social gulf that separated landlord from small holder and tenant farmer. It was an impediment to communicating new techniques that Arthur Young decried again and again.

Arcère, the local Oratorian historian, also blamed habit and routine. The Society had tried to propogate Jethro Tull's methods of soil preparation and seed planting, but without success. "Of 10,000 of our small *laboureurs*, there are not a hundred who understand anything about Tull's principles of farming, publicized by M. Duhamel. Our peasants do not understand French, at least written French. ... Why not teach them orally? One does not need much intelligence to use one's eyes. But they are stubbornly attached to their old routine. This is the major obstacle to all new farming."[16] Nor did Arcère exempt the large landlords from blame. "How many people in an *état* superior to the *laboureur* are any wiser about farming?" As for the English, whatever the local notables thought about their political machinations—and the many Rochelais ships they had captured on the high seas—French landlords should not be ashamed to adopt "the wise maxims of her rural economy."[17]

Bussac proposed a score of Rochelais notables for membership in the Society divided by *états*:

Noblesse: Châtelaillon, Pauléon, Voutron, Bussière
Gens de Robe: Griffon, Beaupréau, Martin de Chassiron
Jurists: Reynier, Bussac, Bougie, Valin
Négociants: De La Croix, Rasteau, Goguet, Lefebvre
Bureau des Finances: Busseau, Lambert, Meanne, Depont des Granges.

The structure was formal enough, but results were meager. Of these notables, only Martin de Chassiron attained a local reputation as a farm improver, and this came about largely because he retired to his domain at Beauregard during the Revolution. Depont, like most of the others,

Map 3
The Landed
Property of the
Depont Family in
the Eighteenth
Century

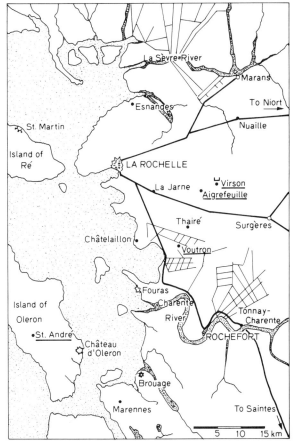

Note: Underlined parishes indicate vicinity of property of the
Depont family.

was honored as a town notable and important landlord, but he may well
have been among the "half of academicians" who, as Bussac said, were
"always absent."[18] Neither Paul-François nor Paul-Charles Depont were
local Jethro Tulls or "Turnip" Townshends, and their activity in the
Society of Agriculture was limited.

Contemporary observers were convinced that Aunis was being depopu-
lated. A survey of the province by the Society of Agriculture in 1764
painted a sad picture of the back country. "In our hamlets and villages
too far from the capital, what does one see? Habitable dwellings un-
occupied, houses threatened with ruin, crumbling to pieces ... left to
solitude. ... The *curés* all tell us that the number of marriages has considerably diminished. Depopulation is certain."[19] But efforts at systematic

counting left much to be desired; no modern demographer would accept the government's method of multiplying the number of recorded births by a factor of twenty-seven for the towns and twenty-five for the parishes.[20] In fact, other evidence points to a large floating population of migrant labor who deserted their native villages for part of the year and may account for the reports of abandoned cottages. The syndics of Marennes south of Rochefort ascribed the slight increase in the town's population to migration. "The small increase ... comes from families who have been chased by misery from the island of Oleron in order to work at Marennes, where they are paid in coin for their labor rather than in produce and cloth as on the island. There is also a large number from upper Saintonge, Angôumois, Périgord, and Limousin who have come as refugees, most of them finding work as salt-makers. ... Mortality in this region has been high in recent years because of the bad air, the marshland ... and the English prisons."[21]

In any event, the majority of the population of the region was far from affluent. Once the pockets of prosperity have been identified—the larger landlords, the *officiers* and merchant elite of La Rochelle, the grain merchants at Marans, the brandy speculators along the Charente, a few cattle dealers, the larger tenant farmers and naval procurement officers in the Marenne-Rochefort area—the bulk of the thirty-five thousand inhabitants in the province were micro-owners, *bordiers,* sharecroppers, vinedressers, day laborers, and salt-makers, trailing off into a world of petty hucksters, oyster-gatherers, fishermen, and handymen, a euphemism for bare subsistence. As one left the coast for the interior of Aunis, Saintonge, and Lower Poitou, the intermediary groups between landlord and subsistence farmer tended to disappear altogether. In these remote parishes the word *paysan* appears more frequently in local records, testimony to an undifferentiated mass of human beings who ate black bread, drank the *arrière vin* or none at all, and frequently migrated toward the coast to find work in the dead season.[22]

Contemporaries who advanced explanations of alleged depopulation pointed to the lassitude and bad health of the rural population, usually related in the final analysis to *misère*. One observer confused aspects of the problem with its causes, mixing premature death, low fertility of females, the indifference of the husband to his marital rights, malformed children, and desertion of the countryside. But he was surely close to the mark when he asserted that the food was of such bad quality that the human body was often not strong enough to sustain heavy farm work. "Thus the human species perishes in our countryside and is silently engulfed in an abyss." The same observer also presented a clear picture of the day laborer.

The rural day laborer in our province earns only 183 livres, 15 sous annually and must spend a minimum of 189 livres 13 sous for his own needs. Therefore, nothing remains for the support of his family or for the payment of his taxes. Thus he must deprive himself of necessities, *ne vivre qu'à demi,* and his miserable clothing is scarcely better than that of a beggar. To protect himself against the misfortune that plagues him on all sides, he is often obliged to rely on rapacious moneylenders and he becomes insolvent. If the tax collector comes, he is struck down again. He does not even have the consolation of inspiring pity.[23]

This was a "normal" situation. What was it like in a "bad year"? In 1754 and 1765, not to mention 1788 and 1789, the province was beset with a series of calamities, which broke the composure of the most stolid bureaucrats. The year 1754 was horrendous. A harsh winter, heavy snow, late spring frost, followed by intense heat and dryness, a worm disease in the vineyards, a cattle plague in the coastal meadows, and insufficient seeding of spring grains produced a severe shortage of all farm produce at once—wheat, barley, oats, forage, wine, maize, millet, fruits, vegetables, even nuts, flax, and hemp. The worms had already destroyed two-thirds of the vineyards from Aigrefeuille to Surgères when the August drought destroyed the rest. Without forage, the proprietors sold the livestock—"at a vile price." The spring grains were also burned by the intense heat, and the local inhabitants were too poor to plant new seed. The subdelegate of La Rochelle said that if taxes were not reduced and other aid not forthcoming, the people would have to beg for bread. "The *taillables* are reduced to the greatest misery."[24]

The year 1765 was only slightly less disastrous. The subdelegate's report was more systematic; each village was now listed with an estimate of the crop loss—Aigrefeuille, three-fourths of the wine lost; Virson, one-half of the wine lost and "the worms multiplying"; La Jarne, one-half the wine lost and "in the marshes, the inhabitants have nothing," and so on for the entire election of La Rochelle.[25] Stable grain prices at La Rochelle in the 1770s appear to have been a respite before the new price rise in the 1780s.[26] Still, at Saint-Jean-d'Angély, 1775—a good year—seemed grim enough. A local attorney and grain administrator, Pelluchon du Breuil, wrote to Turgot who had inaugurated a policy of "free trade" in grain the year before: " . . . with piercing cries the mass of artisans and country people, vinedressers with sacks on their backs, somber faces and tears in their eyes, tramp through our streets."[27]

La Rochelle lacked sufficient grain storage and was heavily dependent on Marans, the grain port to the north. Marans was not only less accessible to inspection for fraud, but was set in the center of the northern marshes where the humidity often spoiled the grain. At these moments of grain shortage one paid the price for having converted almost all of

Aunis into vineyard. In the 1780s La Rochelle experienced at least three major bread riots involving several hundred *garçons ouvriers*—construction workers, dockhands, and sardine hucksters—who broke into the bakery shops, lifted the bread, hauling away clothes and furnishings, and smashing the windows. The city government, showing some restraint, arrested forty-eight of the rioters, but detained only five after the riot of 1788. The municipal government of Rochefort was less lenient after a riot in April 1789; of twenty arrested, three youths were sentenced to death, two were branded and imprisoned for life, and one was sent to the galleys. Wheat reached the highest price of the century in the spring of 1789—400 livres per *tonneau*! The departmental office of provisioning in 1790, not the historian C.-E. Labrousse, stated: "We can regard the price of our bread as the thermometer of public tranquillity."[28]

Yet apart from government efforts to control fraud, limit speculation, buy grain abroad and provision the port, what could be done? There was resignation in the last phrase in one official's report—"*fascheuses évenements impossibles à prévoir*"—and impossible to solve. In the face of such staggering problems charitable efforts by individuals or by the few welfare institutions at La Rochelle were doomed to failure. The General Hospital, for example, a receptacle for the poor, for beggars, foundlings, and the sick, had no more than a hundred beds for a city population of seventeen thousand, not to count the refugees from the countryside.[29]

Paul-François Depont's contact with the mass of country people was intermittent, though he must have seen them on his trips by coach to and from his manor house at Les Granges in the spring and fall. His charity school at Aigrefeuille, his contribution of a thousand livres to the General Hospital, and his distribution of bread to the villagers during a bad year point to a charitable Catholic, within the limits prescribed by a newer view toward the poor, including the importance of self-help and moral worthiness.[30] Knowing the vinedressers, *bordiers,* and day laborers through the intermediary of his tenants and agents, Depont had the advantage of a regular money income without the *souci* of direct management, to quote Pierre d'Harouard's agricultural manual. Part of that *souci* was dealing with the *malheureux.*

The center of the Depont family's domains was Aigrefeuille, one of the larger villages in Aunis with a population of about eight hundred inhabitants. Between 1773 and 1786 the number of burials exceeded the number of births by forty, indicating an absolute decline in population of at least 5 percent in sixteen years. The death rate was especially high among children under five, partly attributable to the wet-nursing of children from La Rochelle.[31] Nor was the high infant mortality rate limited to the children of city-dwellers and the rural poor. For nine years ending in 1789, Pierre-Gabriel Faurie, the local notary, lost four children, ages twelve, three, two, and nine months, and baptized three others. The Fauries had a child every fifteen months in a frightful battle against death.

If infant mortality recognized no hierarchies, marriages followed a decided social pattern. Intermarriage was within the same occupation or *métier*. This was as true for coopers and winegrowers as for *marchands-fermiers* and notaries. The Mainguets, Bernards, and Boutards, Depont's tenants at one time or another, were all related by marriage. So were the local notaries, Faurie, Moreau, and Chauvet. Faurie's connections extended beyond marriage and blood ties, however. After 1770 the name "Faurie," appears on almost every page of the parish register either as parent, godparent, friend, or witness. It was a clear sign of his status as local notable in this little world in the vineyard country of Aunis.[32]

In fact, the Faurie family had been attorneys (*procureurs-fiscaux*) of the seigneury of Aigrefeuille from 1738 until the Revolution. Three generations of Fauries had served the Depont family: Sieur Pierre Faurie for twenty-four years until he died at the age of seventy-one; his son, Maître Pierre Faurie, for the next thirteen years (1762–75), until he died at fifty-three; and *his* son, Maître Pierre-Gabriel Faurie, seigneurial agent and royal notary from 1775 to 1789 and perhaps after. The Faurie family had pretensions even outside the immediate circle of parishes. Pierre-Gabriel's wife was the daughter of a "royal printer" at La Rochelle. His sister, Françoise-Esther, married the son of a notary from Niort, an important market town on the royal road to Poitiers. In 1789 this Sieur Jacques-Louis Recapé was named in the parish register as "bourgeois" of the parish of Thairé," an authentic "rural bourgeois."

Remote and tiny as Aigrefeuille was compared with La Rochelle, it spawned its own hierarchy, its own notability.[33] The Faurie family owed its status as much to long years as resident notaries with a network of friends and relations as to its "borrowed" prestige as Depont's attorneys and agents for the seigneury. Three generations of Fauries paralleled three generations of Deponts over the century. They were an important link between the town house in La Rochelle and a cluster of seigneuries in Aunis, a hybrid relation, half clientage and half professional service.[34]

In 1787 more than three-quarters of the Depont income came from the land. The properties had been assembled over three generations, beginning in 1707 with Paul Depont's first major purchase at Les Granges. The following table traces this accumulation, indicating the price and dates of the major acquisitions, the capital values at various times and the revenues in 1751 and 1787. In 1751 Paul-Charles married, and Les Granges was entailed to the third generation in the marriage contract. However, Paul François did not divide his estate between his two sons until 1766. The year 1787 represents the estate at its apex on the eve of the Revolution, and 1797 gives the landed income and areas remaining after the abolition of the seigneurial rights. Despite the division of the family fortune in equal portions between Paul-Charles and Jean-Samuel in 1766, Paul-François had been most successful in keeping most of the land in the hands of one son.[35]

The core of the estate was acquired in the first quarter of the century when Paul Depont's slave ships were at the peak of activity. Like other merchant families of La Rochelle—the Pascaud, Carré, Fleuriau, Chassiron, Goguet—Depont looked toward Aunis for a good investment in land.[36] Would it be drained marshland in the direction of Marans or Rochefort along the coast, or a domain in the older vineyard country on the route eastward to Surgères and Niort? Paul Depont decided on the

Table 4.1. The Landed Property of the Depont Family

Name of Property	Price and Date of Purchase (in livres)	Evaluation and Date (in livres)	Revenue (in livres) 1751	1787	1797	Domain Area in 1797 (in acres)
Seigneuries in Aunis:						
1. Les Granges	1707		2,200	5,000	3,200	501
2. Chaumeau	1711	(68,000) 1744	1,200	1,400	450	75
3. La Brande	(38,000) 1716		2,200	4,500	750	112
4. Chagnées	(33,250)[a] 1718	(60,000) 1744	820	1,600	–	–
5. Aigrefeuille	(60,000) 1726	(80,000) 1744	4,280	8,000	500[b]	17[b]
Cabanes near Rochefort:						
1. Grand Moindreau	1735	(60,800)[b]	800	2,400	2,000	240
2. Sousliron	(25,000) 1735	(38,000) 1754	500	1,600	1,200	160
3. Galais[c]	1735	(45,600)[b]	600	–	–	–
Métairie in Bas-Poitou:						
Pezotière	(5,643) 1764	(4,470) 1797	–	650	450	80[b]
Salt Beds on Oleron:						
(five parishes)	ca. 1780, 1792, 1796	(84,530) 1797	–	3,870	2,926 (1796)	211 acres 96 *livres*[b]
Total			12,600 (1751)	29,020 (1787)	11,476 (1797)	1,396 acres (1797) (581 hectares)

Source: Archives Départementales, E–483, E–484, Depont's account books; E–490, E–491, E–492, E–493, Seigneuries of Les Granges, La Brande, Aigrefeuille, and Chaumeau; E–499, Purchase of Marshlands, Inventory of Contracts; E–501, Salt Marshes; Q–250, "Biens des Emigrés"—Depont des Granges.
a. Paid in Law paper
b. Approximate. The *livre* of salt-bed varied between 1.2 and 2.2 acres.
c. The *cabane* of Galais was sold before 1787.

vineyards and purchased five properties in the neighborhood of Aigre-feuille, twenty kilometers east of La Rochelle. Paul Depont usually paid in silver *"manuellement et comptant"* within six to fifteen months after the act of sale. There was one exception to this, which resulted in a *très bonne affaire* for the shipowner. He managed to complete payment for the domains of La Brande and Chagnées in Law paper before the collapse of the famous *Système*. The acquisition of La Brande and Aigrefeuille involved Depont in a series of lawsuits before the land was finally cleared of competing seigneurial claims.[37] Both of these *châtellenies* consisted largely of seigneurial rights with little domain land.[38] However, the right of *terrage* was collected in kind and amounted to one-eighth and one-tenth of the wine harvest of four thousand acres.

Gradually Paul Depont began to consolidate his principal domain of Les Granges. A modest but dignified manor house was built, and four substantial farms (*métairies*) of over eighty acres each were formed into compact fields of wheat, barley, and oats. About 1714, he began detaching blocks of vineyard, wood, and meadow, as well as a mill and some seigneurial rights from his neighboring domains and added them to his favorite seigneury of Les Granges.[39] By 1739, the new seigneur was reserving "fountains, canals, fruit trees, and the *grand allée*" for his sojourns in the country.[40] No doubt the former director of the Chamber of Commerce was proud to render formal homage to such illustrious overlords as Marquis de la Rochefoucauld, seigneur of nearby Surgères, and Duc de la Trémouille, Prince de Talmont.[41] Indeed, Paul Depont staffed his own *châtellenie* with a seneschal judge and a resident attorney (*procureur fiscal*) who were to become more than mere symbols of seigneurial prestige.[42] They were to be the active instruments of a domain-building landlord.

The major features of the growth of the Depont estate over three generations are clear enough. After Paul Depont's initial acquisitions around Aigrefeuille, three other additions were made before the Revolution. In 1735 Paul-François purchased three large farms of grain and meadow-land reclaimed from the marshes north of Rochefort. Two of these *cabanes* were bequeathed to Paul-Charles in the third generation. In 1764 Paul-Charles bought a *métairie* that his father-in-law had sold shortly before, employing the seigneurial right of *retrocession*. The last large purchase, or series of purchases, consisted of salt beds. Salt beds were not new to the Deponts. Paul Depont had bought some on the island of Ré and given them to his daughter as part of her inheritance in 1744. But his grandson, Paul-Charles, became one of the largest holders on the island of Oleron and made substantial speculative profits in the 1780s.[43]

Less spectacular, but no less important to the process of domain-building, were small acquisitions. All three generations of eldest sons participated in the piece-by-piece accretion of the estate in Aunis. In this regard, the landlord with seigneurial claims had certain legal advantages over the local peasant holder. Several methods of acquisition were employed, including outright purchase, foreclosure, and manipulation of seigneurial rights.

Purchases of plots as small as one-fifth of an acre were numerous, and not a few of the contracts specified that Paul-Charles Depont had been paid *auparavant*, suggesting that the sales may have been foreclosures for debt.[44] In a few cases, foreclosure was explicit in the contract of sale. For example, on March 28, 1781, Jean Bevin, *laboureur à bras* "sold" Paul-Charles one *journal* (0.8 acre) of land near Les Granges for 24 livres. The sum was applied toward payment of fifteen years' *rente* arrears at 10 livres per year, "without prejudice to the balance owed."[45] In another case, Jean-Baptiste Rousseau, *laboureur à charrue*, sold over ten thousand vine plants (*ceps*) near Les Granges to Paul-Charles Depont for 310 livres. The entire sum was deducted from rent arrears Rousseau owed Depont as his *fermier* eleven years before.[46]

The Deponts enforced their seigneurial claims with the requisite manorial judges, appealing to the presidial court at La Rochelle when necessary.[47] Among these claims was the right of retrocession or *retrait féodal*. The *retrait* gave the seigneur the option of purchasing any piece of property recently exchanged or alienated within his jurisdiction. The Depont papers contain five examples (in 1730, 1735, 1751, 1764, and 1778) of the use of the *retrait* to force sales. Three farms, totaling almost two hundred acres, were purchased from two local merchants and from a *laboureur à boeufs*. The other two plots, less than an acre each, were acquired from a carpenter and a day laborer. The merchants contested Depont's claims but finally surrendered to the decisions of the seigneurial judge.[48]

On 2 June 1758, the seneschal judge of the *châtellenie* of Aigrefeuille ordered Pierre Ligneron, *laboureur*, to pay his *cens* arrears since 23 August 1730, that is, for the past twenty-eight years, and to furnish a declaration (*reconnaissance*) of his obligations to his seigneur, Paul-François Depont. Twenty-nine years was the longest period a seigneur could wait to collect arrears before forfeiting the right altogether.[49] The total was only forty-eight livres, but Ligneron could not pay it. The seneschal then ordered that Ligneron's scattered pieces of vineyard and arable land be "reunited to the former domain of the *châtellenie*." Plaintively, Ligneron declared "that he had no means to prevent this." Included in this seizure (*prise de possession*) was an inventory of the peasant's one-room habitation with a "detachable" door, part of one wall on the ground, and the roof about to fall in. On the back of the document is the name of M. Jean Provaud, Depont's steward (*régisseur*) followed by the name Ligneron and the common formula *ne savoir signer.*[50]

Here the seizure was employed as a foreclosure on *cens* arrears. More often this procedure was used to claim land uncultivated by peasant holders and judged "abandoned domain." Valin, the eighteenth-century authority on the Customs of Aunis, stated that, if the land was abandoned "for a long time" and could be considered *terres vagues* or wasteland, the seigneur could legally incorporate the plot into his domain. Moreover, he had the right to hold his *tenancier* to the lease terms requiring specific farm tasks. If the *tenancier* neglected to satisfy the seigneur in this matter, the seigneur could evict him after sufficient warning.[51] Paul-Charles Depont employed both provisions of the customary law. In 1775 he condemned eight *laboureurs* and one of his own *fermiers* for having abandoned seventeen acres of land in his jurisdiction. He took possession. For eight years he pursued Thomas Lapitaux, *laboureur à bras,* for failing to cultivate eleven pieces of land "*bien et convenablement.*" In 1782 Paul-Charles obtained a judgment from the presidial court which awarded him twenty acres of Lapitaux's land. In 1784 he condemned six peasants for neglecting certain vineyards for three years and added nine acres of vines to his domain.[52] That these lands were not always "voluntarily abandoned" under the provisions of Valin's Customs of Aunis is suggested by the law case of two peasants who attempted to regain their land during the Revolution twenty years later. Gabriot and Fourestier claimed that they had been "forced to abandon their land by the *puissance féodalle.*"[53]

According to the family papers, the Deponts added over 175 acres of land and no less than 14,700 vine plants to the estate in Aunis in addition to about 80 acres in Bas-Poitou in twenty-three transactions of this kind between 1730 and 1790. Although complete figures are not available, the principal domain at Les Granges increased from 222 acres of arable land in 1730 to 342 acres in 1797, not including meadow, wood, and vineyard.[54] Small acquisitions played an important part in forming this domain. By 1789 the entire landed estate in Aunis, near Rochefort, and on Oleron counted 1,400 acres of domain with seigneurial rights over about 4,000 acres more.[55] (See map 3, p. 81.)

Paul Depont had not neglected his seigneurial claims, but it was Paul-François who conducted the first general survey (*arpentage*) of the seigneuries after his father's death in 1746. The survey was intended to determine the exact amount of seigneurial dues owed by each peasant.

Depont entrusted the work to Pierre Faurie, his agent (*procureur fiscal*) at Aigrefeuille since 1738. Faurie received 3,000 livres in advance from Depont and agreed to collect the balance of the surveying costs from the quit-rent payers (*redevables*). Apparently collection moved slowly. Four years later Faurie had not yet been paid for the operation. He explained the situation to the *trésorier de France* as diplomatically as possible: "Your inhabitants of Aigrefeuille have no doubt forgotten the notice you have given them to make their declarations [of land for the survey], since no one has presented himself to make them."[56]

Faurie kept an alphabetical list of the peasant *tenanciers* at Aigrefeuille who owed from 2 to 12 livres each and a total of 1,119 livres for their share of the survey costs. By 1756, ten years after the surveying had begun, Faurie had collected only 170 livres of this sum. Nevertheless, all of the seigneuries in Aunis were finally surveyed at a total cost of 6,608 livres. This was a substantial sum and indicated the importance Paul-François attached to the operation.[57]

The next major land survey for the purpose of enforcing seigneurial obligations took place in 1787. Pierre-Gabriel Faurie, the third generation of resident attorneys for the Deponts at Aigrefeuille, assumed general supervision. But this time Paul-Charles Depont decided to employ a professional expert on seigneurial rights as well.[58] Since the new *feudiste* came from Metz, it is possible that he had been recommended by Paul-Charles's brother, Jean-Samuel, the intendant of Metz. Both Deponts were seigneurs at Aigrefeuille after the division of their father's estate in 1766. In any event, Jacques d'Otrenge Sarralbe had excellent credentials. He was *ingénieur-géographe du roi* and offered his services to seigneurs throughout the kingdom. Just before coming to Aunis he had surveyed the seigneuries of the chevaliers of Malta in Lower Poitou. He arrived in the province with his two assistants, under contract to draw up a new *terrier* or quit-rent roll for Depont's seigneurial jurisdictions around Aigrefeuille. Sarralbe charged 450 livres per year and 12 sous for each *journal* of land surveyed.

It was no easy task. Depont's seigneurial claims extended over a large area. His seigneuries of Aigrefeuille, La Brande, and Chagnées measured 4,829 *journaux* (3,863 acres) "outside the domain" which totaled only 130 acres for all three jurisdictions. Half of this or 2,316 *journaux* (1,853 acres) was in vineyard, the main source of Depont's income in this area. The vineyards were divided into 4,093 parcels and were held by over 600 small proprietors! At Aigrefeuille alone 1,722 *journaux* (1,422 acres) of vineyard were held by 306 *tenanciers* or quasi-owners, distributed as follows:[59]

Size of Plot	Number of Owners	Percent of Owners
Under 3 *journaux* (1 hectare)	176	(57)
3 to 6	51	(17)
6 to 15	50	(17)
15 to 30	16 ⎫	
30 to 60	10 ⎬	(9)
Over 60 (20 hectares)	3 ⎭	
Total	306	(100)

It is a classic picture of a swarm of micro-owners, especially marked in vineyard country. Claude Laveau calculates that one would need 8 *journaux* (6.4 acres) of vineyard to support a family. Hence, no less than 227 winegrowers, about three-quarters of the total, did not have enough vineyard to live on the product, even before they paid dues, tithes, and taxes. Laveau's occupational analysis indicates that over one-quarter of the smallest owners (below one hectare) were also artisans, mostly coopers, while another half were simply day laborers (*laboureurs à bras*).[60] Although we do not know the precise population of Aigrefeuille in 1787, it appears that most of the households owned some vineyard, though only about 10 to 15 percent could attain self-sufficiency from their sales of wine. Small holders like these are not likely to appreciate *feudistes* equipped with boundary stones, measuring lines, and legal titles.

Indeed, Maître Sarralbe's first visit to Aigrefeuille was far from uneventful. If Paul-François's efforts to "reform" his rolls forty years before had met with passive resistance from the *redevables,* Paul-Charles's new *feudiste* was greeted by "a howling mob of peasants armed with pitchforks" and was forced to flee. Nevertheless, after eight months of persistent labor, Sarralbe completed the surveying and produced a terrier at the cost of 9,323 livres. The terrier combines meticulous detail with artistic beauty. It is a sturdy, cloth-bound volume, a full yard in length, and contains almost eighty pages of carefully colored maps, indicating each scrap of vineyard, each meadow, each farmhouse, each mill. The terrier is accompanied by a register of *tenanciers*, listing every obligation, in money and produce, fixed or in proportion to the harvest, owed the seigneur.[61]

The fact that the *feudiste* completed his work quickly, given the dimensions of the task, is surprising enough. But one chapter of the terrier even contains a testimonial of appreciation by the local inhabitants! Part of the passage reads: ". . . far from considering ways of opposition, [the inhabitants] declare by their attorney that, on the contrary, they . . .

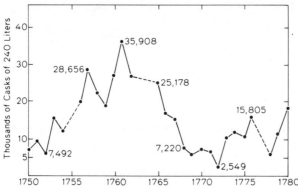

Figure 4.1
Exports of Brandy
from La Rochelle
by Volume

Source: Claude Laveau, "Le Monde rochelais de l'Ancien Régime au Consulat" (*thèse de doctorat,* 1972), p. 758.
Note: Laveau presents the quantity of annual exports that I have graphed. Unfortunately, Laveau's figures do not include the decade of the 1780s.

wish to express public recognition to their seigneur for a deed well done, assuming that in this instance he has had only paternal intentions to reestablish the natural order [*l'ordre naturel*] in the collection of his seigneurial rights, thus ending a long sequel of lawsuits which have lasted more than a century under the name of verifications."[62]

This apparent volte-face deserves some comment. First, Depont did not repeat the mistake of his father and refrained from asking the *justiciables* to share the expenses of the survey. He paid the entire 9,323 livres himself. Moreover, it is true that Sarralbe's terrier did make the obligations clear. He himself commented in the terrier that he intended to protect the *tenanciers* from the *fermiers*, who leased the seigneurial rights from Depont, and who had not always honored the *baillettes*, the subleases of seigneurial obligations, in the past. Sarralbe also claimed that his definitive terrier would prevent the seigneurial officials from adding any new charges "captiously," as they had often done since the earlier terriers of 1606 and 1684. He even insisted that, far from increasing seigneurial burdens, he had in many cases eased them, reducing the seigneur's produce rents from one-eighth to one-tenth, for example. Sarralbe's comments throughout the terrier give the impression of a humane person who had combined administrative order with paternalism and, by eliminating the "confusions" of the past, had removed the causes of countless lawsuits so burdensome for the small *cultivateur.*[63]

However, one should not lend too much credence to Sarralbe's view of the matter. Three years later in 1792, many parishes in Aunis and Saintonge, though not Aigrefeuille, demanded the elimination of the seigneurial produce rents.[64] It is not clear that on balance Sarralbe was

Figure 4.2
Ad Valorem
Exports of Brandy
from La Rochelle

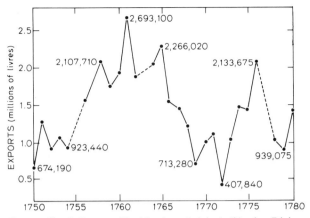

Source: Claude Laveau, "Le Monde rochelais de l'Ancien Régime au Consulat" (*thèse de doctorat,* 1972), p. 758.

lessening the burden of obligations. A directive from Paul-Charles in 1786 specified that the terriers were to indicate the nature of the land and "to add the amount of seigneurial *cens, champart,* and *terrage,* and, in cases where the obligations are unknown, *establish them in proportion to the dues in neighboring plots."*[65] This approach was also "natural and reasonable," but its effect was to increase obligations by "finding" new ones. No doubt in a few cases Sarralbe did reduce the *terrage* from one-eighth to one-tenth, as he claimed, but when he had finished his surveying and calculating, the areas subjected to one-eighth remained extensive.

Sarralbe may have written that *"le dixain paraît naturel."* In practice, 683 of 1,832 acres of vineyard were subject to one-eighth or more, and 911 to one-tenth the wine harvest. Only 130 acres were exempt, which is curious, given Depont's directive. Altogether then, these were heavy produce rents, especially for the majority of the winegrowers with less than one hectare. Sarralbe presented an image of paternalism, but his "natural order" legally secured Depont's *droits,* and by obtaining the explicit

Table 4.2. *The* **Terrage** *on Wine on Three Seigneuries* (*1788*) (*in* **journaux** *or 0.8 acres*)

Aigrefeuille	La Brande	Chagnées
9 at 1/6th	9 at 1/7th	180 at 1/8th in 95 tenures
636 at 1/8th	20 at 1/8th	
861 at 1/10th	278 at 1/10th	
135 at 1/16th	25 no *terrage*	
137 at no *terrage*		
1778 *jx.* in 306 tenures	332 *jx.* in 430 tenures	

Source: "Terrier d'Aigrefeuille," 1788, analyzed by Laveau, "Monde rochelais," p. 323.

consent of the communities, he undercut all legal justification for resistance to payments in the future.

The presence of a professional *feudiste* like Sarralbe on the Depont properties in 1787 marks an important difference from the survey of seigneurial rights conducted by Paul-François in 1746. The terrier of Aigrefeuille is testimony to a considerable advance in the science of measurement, representation, classification, and the general *police* of a seigneury in forty years. This is the sense in which one must regard the so-called seigneurial reaction here and I suspect elsewhere in the kingdom. The evidence does not suggest that any one of the three Depont seigneurs—Paul, Paul-François, or Paul-Charles—was more strict or hard-nosed in the enforcement of seigneurial rights than the two others. Nor does it appear that the first generation of domain-builders, fresh from overseas trade, was any more "businesslike" or attentive to seigneurial income than the second and third generations of more settled landlords and *rentiers*. However, the techniques of estate administration were improving, techniques which mobilized "feudal law" as well as more modern legal instruments and contracts in order to assure any seigneur, regardless of his personal temperament, a maximum return. Paul-Charles Depont, like any other alert seigneur of the 1780s, must have considered it entirely normal to employ a *feudiste*. One must move with the times.[66]

Before 1740 the farms at Les Granges were administered by shares (*métayage*). The leases of Paul Depont for a seventy-three-acre *métairie* at Les Granges indicate rapid changes in lease terms between 1719 and 1730. In 1719 the landlord and sharecropper furnished the seed and divided the harvest in equal shares. In 1725 the sharecropper furnished the seed entirely, and two-thirds of the harvest went to Seigneur Depont. In 1730 all of the grain was earmarked for Depont, and thirteen acres were converted into vineyard, presumably for brandy-making.[67] However, management by sharecropping was not to last.

Even before he died in 1744, Paul Depont, the *armateur*, had abandoned direct management and eliminated the necessity of marketing his own grain and brandy. After 1750 all of the Depont properties (except the salt marshes) were administered by leases at money rents (*fermage*). Fortunately, the Depont journals and accounts furnish a complete series of rents for all of the seigneuries and farms from about 1750 to the Revolution.[68] The table clearly demonstrates a sharp rise in rents, especially after 1779, and the frequent change of *fermiers*, most of whom were local grain or wine merchants. None of the Deponts placed much value on continuity of tenants. They preferred *fermiers* who bid highest for the lease and then paid promptly. Since the value of the land was rapidly

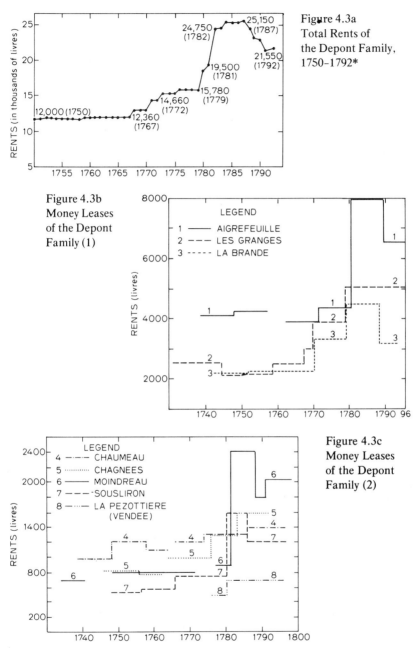

Figure 4.3a
Total Rents of
the Depont Family,
1750-1792*

Figure 4.3b
Money Leases
of the Depont
Family (1)

Figure 4.3c
Money Leases
of the Depont
Family (2)

Source: Claude Laveau, "Le Monde rochelais de l'Ancien Régime au Consulat" (*thèse de
doctorat*, 1972), p. 758.
*This is a total of the money leases; it does not include the revenues from the salt-beds which
were administered directly.

Table 4.3. Seigneuries and Farm Leases of the Depont Family

1. Seigneury of Les Granges

Lease	Years	Annual Rent	Fermier
1707-15	8	–	Chieze
1715-24	9	1800	Rebecon
1724-31	7	–	Dames
1731-39	8	2500	Trocquet
1739-45	6	2500	Trocquet
1745-50	5	2150	Lapitaux
1750-59	9	2200	Audry
1759-68	9	2500	Jacques
1768-70	2	3000	Jacques
1770-79	9	3800	Giraud
1779-88	9	5000	Rondeau
1788-97	9	5000	M. Chevelleau

2. Seigneury of La Brande

Lease	Years	Annual Rent	Fermier
1743-52	9	2200	Fenion
1752-61	9	2300	Bernard
(Mill added in 1752)			
1761-70	9	2300	Bernard
1770-79	9	3300	Bernard
1779-88	9	4500	Chaignard
1788-93	5	3200	Mainguet

3. Seigneury of Aigrefeuille

Lease	Years	Annual Rent	Fermier
-48	–	4100	Boutard
1748-57	9	4280	Boutard
1757-63	6	-	–
1763-72	9	3800	Bernard
1772-81	9	4300	Mainguet
1781-90	9	8000	M. Challou
1790-99	9	6500	M. Challou

4. Seigneury of Chaumeau

Lease	Years	Annual Rent	Fermier
1739-48	9	1000	Rousseau
1748-57	9	1200	Jacquet
1757-64	7	1100	Giraud
(Mill detached in 1752)			
1766-75	9	1200	Rousseau
1775-86	9	1300	M. Challou
1786-95	9	1400	Widow Bernard

5. Seigneury of Chagnées

Lease	Years	Annual Rent	Fermier
1746-55	9	820	Bernard
1755-62	7	750	Bernard
1762-67	5	–	–
1767-76	9	1000	Widow Bernard
1776-83	7	1300	Tétaud
1783-92	9	1600	Mainguet

6. Métairie of La Pezottière

Lease	Years	Annual Rent	Fermier
1775-80	5	470	Fouchard
1780-87	7	650	Fouchard
1787-96	9	650	Frappin

(at Saint-Fulgent, Lower Poitou)

7. Cabane of Moindreau

Lease	Years	Annual Rent	Fermier
1734-41	7	675	–
1741-49	8	–	–
1749-56	7	800	Bourday
1756-61	5	800	Bourday
1761-66	5	800	Chay
1766-71	5	800	Chay
1771-76	5	–	–
1776-81	5	850	Moquet
1781-88	7	2400	Moquet
1788-91	3	1800	Moquet
1791-98	7	2000	M. Challou

8. Cabane of Sousliron

Lease	Years	Annual Rent	Fermier
1748-57	9	500	Solleau
1757-66	9	560	Solleau
1766-73	7	760	Questron
(meadow added)			
1773-80	7	760	Moquet
1780-87	7	1600	Combau
1787-94	7	1200	Routhe
1794-99	5	1200	Moquet

Source: Archives Départementales, E-483, E-484, E-490.
Note: The most dramatic increases in rent came after 1779-80. In addition to the money rents, each tenant owed rents in kind and other services known as *suffrages*. For example, at Les Granges the *suffrages* in 1759 included two casks of white wine, one cask of red wine, two carts of hay, two carts of straw, twenty *boisseaux* of oats, six capons, six cheeses, and six cart trips to La Rochelle. In 1779 these *suffrages* were increased by five *boisseaux* of oats, six capons, six cheeses, one lamb, two days' plowing, and ten pounds of wool. The *suffrages* on other seigneuries and farms were less heavy. In 1779 they included three casks of

Figure 4.4
Wheat Prices
at La Rochelle

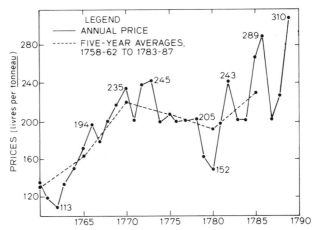

Source: Claude Laveau, "Le Monde rochelais de l'Ancien Régime au Consulat" (*thèse de doctorat,* 1972), p. 764.
Note: Figures are in *Tonneaux de Marans* of 42 *boisseau;* 1 boisseau = 34 liters.

increasing, it was tempting to adjust the lease frequently. The longest leases were for nine years, but Depont could alter lease terms or find a new *fermier* any time the old one defaulted on his rent payments.

In 1731 Paul Depont noted that, "although there are still a few years before the expiration of the lease for Les Granges, the *fermiers* (two local merchants) are not in a position to manage the property." Hence, Depont offered a new eight-year lease to the highest bidder. On 8 July 1731, in the village of Virson "at the ring of the church bell after mass, posted and proclaimed in a high and clear voice," the auction began. Sieur Trocquet, a merchant from Marans, offered 2,000 livres; Dames, one of the former *fermiers*, bid 2,200; and Tocquet outbid him at 2,500.[69] Trocquet lasted through two lease terms to be replaced by Louis Lapitaux who quickly fell behind in his rent and was in turn replaced in 1750.[70] As Table 4. 3 indicates, Les Granges had ten different *fermiers* between 1707 and 1797, an average of one every nine years. Whatever the disadvantages in terms of a lack of incentive on the part of the *fermier* to make farm improvements, such a rapid turnover brought immediate returns to the landowner. The total revenue of the entire landed estate rose from 12,600 livres in 1751 to 29,020 livres in 1787, an increase of 130 percent in thirty-six years. The revenue from the *money* rents alone

---

Note to Table 4.3. (continued)
white wine, twelve capons, and one-half cart of hay at La Brande, twelve capons and six chickens at Aigrefeuille, and two carts of hay and twenty pounds of butter at Moindreau. No doubt most of these products were consumed by the Depont family either at La Rochelle or at Les Granges during the summer. I suspect the wool was used for servants' clothing.

(excluding the salt beds) rose from 12,000 livres to 25,150 livres, an increase of just over 100 percent in thirty-six years.[71] Notice too that most of this increase took place after 1780. (See table 4.1, p. 86.)

Were Depont's *fermiers* still able to make a profit despite these rising rents? The return from the *terrage* of wine at Aigrefeuille in an average year was about 700 casks. Sold on the local market this wine might have brought 9,000 livres. But considerably more could be made by converting the wine to brandy. In fact, Depont's tenants—Mainguet, Tétaud, Challou, Widow Bernard—who leased the privilege of collecting the *terrage* along with the domain farms and other properties could not have paid their rent unless they entered the brandy trade. At a ratio of one cask of brandy for every five of wine, the *terrage* would yield about 140 casks of export brandy annually.[72] Taking 100 livres as an average price per cask in the 1780s, this would mean a gross income of 14,000 livres from the sales of brandy. Deducting the rent at Aigrefeuille of 8,000 would leave a net income of 6,000 livres for the *fermiers,* plus whatever income they could extract from the small domain, mill, winepress, and other "utilities." Compared to an ordinary vinedresser or *laboureur*, this appears to be a substantial income. But the rent represented a very high fixed cost all the same.

Three factors might be considered in appraising the economic situation of Depont's tenants engaged in brandy manufacture and sale: (1) the export market, (2) fixed costs, (3) alternate investment opportunities. The volume of brandy exports from La Rochelle had fallen steadily since the end of the Seven Years' War, reaching a low point in 1772.[73] Unit prices, however, rose abruptly after 1767, and because of a partial recovery in the volume of exports after 1772, the years from 1773 to 1776 were good years, until overproduction in 1778 and 1779 drove prices down again. This was the year Paul-Charles raised rents sharply on his vineyard properties in Aunis.[74] After 1779–80, all tenants were subjected to the higher fixed costs the rents represented, and that in a less favorable market. The 1770s had been years of steady, even declining grain prices at La Rochelle. In the 1780s, however, a continuous rise in the price of all the grains—wheat, barley, oats—placed an added squeeze on the tenants as consumers, whose labor costs increased, since even day laborers have to be fed.[75] In short, the 1780s must have been very difficult years for the large distillers, Depont's *fermiers*. It is not surprising therefore to find that Challou at Aigrefeuille was in arrears in his rent payments in 1786 along with most of the other *fermiers* by the mid-1780s.[76] (See figures 4.1, 4.2, 4.3, and 4.4.)

True, larger operators had some room to maneuver. They had contacts in the port, knew when the Dutch ships arrived, and were able to choose the best moments to sell. They might even circumvent the export merchants and brandy brokers, though the royal government attempted to restrict all decanting to the city in order to eliminate fraud—short measurement, poor quality of casks, dilution, and so on. The larger distillers also bought the wine of the mini-growers at low prices immediately after the September harvest or at a prearranged price before the harvest. They then stocked the brandy and waited for the best price of the year to sell. Clearly the government acted as if these were widespread practices,[77] and popular dislike of the speculator was legend. The large *fermier*—hoarder, speculator, usurer, fraud—has never received very flattering treatment from French historians and he was generally hated by contemporaries, especially by the *vignerons* and small distillers in the countryside.

Perhaps the *fermier* deserves some sympathy.[78] His resort to speculation, even to fraud on occasion, was at least in part imposed by the pressure of high and increasing rents. Nor is it clear that with such high fixed costs speculation was a solution. One miscalculation, and several years' supply was sold at a loss. Risks were greatly increased. The purchases of wine from the mini-growers may not have been speculation at all, but rather an effort by the hard-pressed distillers to increase the volume of sales and to cover the high fixed costs. Could Depont's tenants have shifted to wheat in the 1780s? There is evidence that some of the smaller distillers were doing so.[79] Here too, several local conditions must be remembered. First, at Aigrefeuille and the adjoining properties, the wine was supplied by the *terrages*, an eighth or a tenth of the harvest on about four thousand acres of semi-independent holders (*tenanciers*). Depont's tenants did not have direct control over this land and could not shift production from vine to grain at will. Nor could the *tenanciers* themselves change crops easily. Even apart from costs and delays, the seigneurial obligations, fixed by the new terrier of 1788 *in wine,* could not be altered by a small bookkeeping change; Paul-Charles had spent almost ten thousand livres surveying the region and estimating the size and production of the vineyards. The terrier, beautiful as it was, became an obstacle to changes in crop courses and farm methods. It would also be a sticky legal problem to determine if Depont had a "right" to a *terrage in grain*. What *feudiste* would be able to calculate the equivalent in wheat or barley or buckwheat? Finally, one must return to the quality of the soil. Harouard, a practical landlord, replied to a member of the Society of Agriculture who proposed a general conversion from vineyard to cattle raising in Aunis: "Our land is good only for vineyard. ... One plants wheat on a few *métairies* and I can see for myself how unprofitable these exploitations are, although we must not discourage them entirely or the land will be left idle."[80]

"Alternate investment opportunity" has a very modern ring about it, suggesting that such decisions can be reduced to comparative cost analysis. Depont's tenants had neither the information, the capital, nor indeed the opportunity to circumvent the obstacles presented here. What is surprising perhaps was the continued willingness of new tenants to try their luck on Depont's properties. It is possible that landlords were right when they claimed that the land was not returning its "true value," and that by raising rents they were only catching up. It is also curious at first glance to see that the turnover rate of tenants did not change very much and indeed that many of Depont's *fermiers* in the 1780s simply changed leases—Bernard, Mainguet, Challou, for example. It may be that the tenants had to hang on longer to make enough money to invest in land of their own. Moreover, there was a high density of population in Aunis,[81] and the opportunity to make even one thousand livres as a *fermier* was still attractive in a rural world where ten thousand or more *bordiers* and day laborers made two hundred livres a year at best. One may become "hardened" to rural poverty; it still represented an abyss into which one could fall if a leasehold was lost.[82] The *fermier* had little bargaining power and his skills were not "transferable." Brandy-making also carried a certain status as a traditional art and like so many "arts" was not susceptible to much technological amelioration.[83] In any case, with Depont extracting at least 50 percent of the gross income in rent, there was little margin for tenant improvements of any kind. It was the same with leaseholds of grainland.

Throughout the century, the lease terms obliged the *fermier* to follow the agricultural methods and routines of his predecessor, though he might be required to build a storage loft or make other designated repairs on the property. But there was little if any leeway for his own initiative. *Fermiers* who neglected specified work, such as two vine cuttings or two plowings on the fallow, or who seeded land not included in the lease were fined. Exact assessments were made of the livestock and farm tools, including the equipment and fuel for making brandy.[84] In a letter to his agent at Aigrefeuille in 1757, Paul-François itemized the materials for brandy-making and added: "Note that I am not obliged to repurchase in coin any boiler or wood included in this list. Boutard and Challou were required in the private act of 3 July 1739 to pay the full amount by my father [twenty years before]."[85]

The leases also obliged the *fermiers* to collect the seigneurial dues, forming, as we have seen, the largest part of the income at La Brande and Aigrefeuille. This greatly simplified administration for the Deponts, but placed the *fermiers* in the unenviable position of enforcing the seigneurial titles on hundreds of winegrowers and other small peasant owners. Finally, the *fermiers* were responsible for the taille to a maximum of eight sous per *journal* (ten sous per acre) on the domain lands and usually for *half* of Depont's *vingtième* tax. Paul-Charles paid only the remainder of the *vingtième* and his capitation tax at La Rochelle of seventy-two livres in 1789.[86]

The mark of a good *fermier* was not improvement of the property, but prompt payments of the rent in silver. One of the reasons for Michel Bernard's longevity as *fermier* at Chagnées, La Brande, and Aigrefeuille was his reliability in financial matters. In March 1762, he bought the future harvest at Aigrefeuille and the concession of *cens* arrears. On 27 August 1763, seventeen months later, he paid Depont in full.[87] Subsequently, he received the lease on this property for the next nine years. On the other hand, *fermiers* such as Boutard, Lapitaux, Jacques, Rousseau, and Giraud frequently did not pay on time and were usually replaced. Paul-François pursued Lapitaux for twenty-seven years after he ceased to be the *fermier* at Les Granges, collecting rent arrears in produce from the man's descendants until the debt was reduced to 100 livres in 1771.[88] Pierre Giraud left his tenure at Les Granges in 1779, signing an obligation of 5,293 livres plus interest, presumably for rent arrears. Paul-Charles did not follow the long procedure used by his father in Lapitaux's case. By 1782 he was prosecuting Giraud in his seigneurial court, and by 1788 he had collected 1,230 livres.[89] It is worth noting that Paul-Charles was employing his seigneurial court to collect regular rent arrears, not simply seigneurial dues.

Relations between landlord and *fermier* appear to have been strictly "business" with little place for personal interchanges, much less something deeper. If Paul-François Depont was not given to an easy generosity toward his family, one would hardly expect him to be more favorably disposed toward his *fermiers*. In March 1769, he seemed particularly irritable. In a letter to his eldest son he said that Faurie, his agent, was negligent and had not had a new lease signed. As a result, Mainguet, the *fermier*, was not performing his carting obligations.[90] A few weeks later Paul-François wrote this crisp note to Faurie: "If Mainguet does not sign the lease for Aigrefeuille as soon as this note is received, tell him that there will no longer be any question of making a sacrifice of two hundred [livres] per year for him. Tell me immediately if the lease is signed and do not fail to find another tenant to take his place."[91]

In the same spring Paul-François wrote his younger son at Paris that times were hard in the province for debtors because of a poor return on the land that year.[92] This observation, however, did not deter him from writing a terse note to his *fermier* at Sousliron, the *cabane* near Rochefort, asking him to pay his rent like the other *fermiers* or "I shall be forced to get a court order."[93] Later in the year Depont wrote to another *fermier* renewing his lease and stating that he was adding "*only* fifty livres" to the annual rent, even though he could justify "a greater in-

crease."[94] Paul-François did not subscribe to Tocqueville's moral imperative that "in aristocracies the hire of a farm is paid to the landlord, not
only in rent but in respect, regard, and duty."[95] Since he had given his
younger son his full share of the family fortune only three years before,
this was hardly the moment for *largesse*—or "sacrifices"—to the *fermiers.*
After all, with most of family *rentes* in Jean-Samuel's easy hands, the
Depont domain had to be more carefully husbanded than ever. Family
obligations surely came before coddling tenants.

In 1757 a worm disease ravaged two-thirds of the vineyards at Aigrefeuille. Paul-François's first reaction was to write to the parish priest
and the bishop of La Rochelle urging public prayers "and even a pro-
cession in order to beseech the Lord to end the vine disease caused by
the worms."[96] Seigneur Depont also provided bread. His account book
for this year contains a list of individual debts for bread distributed between June 20 and August 29, the lean time before the harvest, and
subsequent repayments. Among others, Paul Reinjomeau repaid his
debt in piece work. The account reads: "For six days I have had Reinjomeau cut down dead trees for 3 sous each. He has cut down 102 of all
sizes which makes 15 livres, 6 sous."[97] This sum was deducted from his
debt of exactly 75 livres, 19 sous, 11 deniers. Jean Meschad amortized
his debt of 27 livres, 14 sous by having his children collect firewood
in the forest of La Touche at 12 sous per day.[98] This is not to suggest
anything sinister or even inconsistent about Paul-François's treatment
of his *tenanciers.* But it would be difficult to classify him as a paternalistic seigneur.

Paul-Charles Depont did not assume complete control of the family
properties until after his father's death in 1774. Shortly after this, he
employed a professional *homme d'affaires* to administer the property of
the entire family, even including that of his younger brother and his
brother-in-law. Although Jean-Samuel already had title to one-half of
his father's estate, the new general manager, now installed in the town
house at La Rochelle, was given "full power" to buy and sell the younger
brother's property.[99] It seems, therefore, that Paul-Charles retained
virtual control over the administration of all his father's land, sending
his younger brother the revenues of certain specified farms.

M. Arnault Bonnet was a cut above Depont's other agents and *fermiers.* He was referred to as a *négociant* as well as an attorney (*procureur*) of parlement. Bonnet's voluminous correspondence reveals a
man of affairs who had a certain education as well as commercial and
legal experience.[100] He was not, however, a *fermier-général* who sublet
the farms and seigneuries; he remained a salaried employee of the
family, and was not always promptly paid.[101] Like Sarralbe, the *feudiste,*
Bonnet, *homme d'affaires,* was a mark of proper estate management in

the 1780s. Was it Bonnet who urged a major increase in rents after 1775? A glance at the table of leases above indicates that at the renewal of each lease after Bonnet assumed management of the properties, all rents rose steeply, an increase of about 50 percent for the seigneuries around Aigrefeuille and of over 100 percent for the *cabanes* near the coast. Of course it might have been at the initiative of Paul-Charles himself and Bonnet served as his advisor and instrument (figure 4.3, p. 96).

Placing the administration of the estate in the hands of a *chargé d'affaires* apparently did not signify any relaxing of the eldest son's interest in his *fermes*. In a letter to Bonnet, Paul-Charles insisted that Mainguet and the other *fermiers* pay for a *bon garde* to keep the woods clear of poachers and peasant livestock. He cautioned: "... it would be a mistake not to put this [provision] in the lease because you know that for those people [the *fermiers*] anything that is not written down never happened because they deny it without the slightest hesitation."[102]

Not that all relations between landlord and *fermier* were so diffident, not to say distrustful. Antagonism to the royal administration sometimes united Depont, *fermiers*, and local peasants in a common cause. In 1783 Paul-Charles was asked by his tenant, Mainguet, to falsify the amount of his rent to the royal tax collector in order to avoid an increase in the taille. Mainguet pleaded that his two *fermes* already paid a taille of 984 livres (one-fifth of the rent). To his landlord, he wrote, *"Monsir vous save que nous ganons point sur vos ferme."*[103]

On this occasion Paul-Charles made a "sacrifice": "If you were to give me a million, my dear Mainguet, it would still be beneath my dignity to lie either in word or writing. Therefore, I am sending you under private seal a lease similar to Tétaud's [the previous tenant] and I will not oblige you to pay the extra three hundred livres that you were supposed to pay."[104]

Even Paul-Charles's stern and frugal father had appealed for tax relief on behalf of the local peasantry. In 1765 a late spring frost had ruined seven-eighths of the vineyards at Aigrefeuille, the principal source of revenue. Paul-François asked his younger son to contact the intendant of La Rochelle who was visiting Paris and persuade him to reduce the taille that year.[105] Regarding Jean-Samuel's own intendancy, Paul-François advised him to take care of "the miserable peasants" who had not even been indemnified for the property damage inflicted by the new royal roads. He added that such public works had cost him dearly as well, presumably by reducing the revenue from the *terrage* on the wine harvest.[106] He suggested that compensation take the form of an exemption from the *aides* (wine tax).[107]

Of course, reducing royal taxes on tenants and winegrowers was in Depont's interest. The more taxes they paid, the less remained for rents and dues, and collection became difficult. And well might the Deponts lend a helping hand since as "Bourgeois de La Rochelle," they were exempt from the taille. In this respect the hereditary nobility that Paul-Charles attained after twenty years in his father's office gave him no additional fiscal privileges.

In 1808 Harouard de Beignon, seigneur of La Jarne, recalled the modest estate expenses under the Old Regime. "How light taxes were in our fathers' time, sixty years ago," he wrote. "We paid only a tenth of our revenue, a sum which in practice did not reach a fifteenth."[108] When historians have ransacked the tax and rent rolls, they will probably come no closer to the actual tax burden on landlords than this. In theory, the two *vingtièmes* and the *capitation* should have claimed 11 or 12 percent of landed revenues. In practice, they could not be enforced. Tocqueville and Taine, Mathiez and Lefebvre have always said this, but listen to the subdelegate of Saintes telling about his father's effort to collect the *vingtième noble* from the Prince de Chalais: "I remember the time the family of Prince de Chalais lodged a complaint with M. Orry [Controller-General] against my father, the most gentle and respectful of men, because of a simple notification—containing all due respect for the rank of the prince—to pay his *vingtième*."[109] He went on to say that not half of the 175 parishes in his district had paid the *vingtième noble*. The seigneurs who held land in many parishes paid only for one, usually the least valuable. It did no good to assure them that their rolls were kept separate from those of the *taillables*. In 1779 one-third of the taxes of the previous year remained unpaid, "most of them owed by the most important people in the province who are several years in arrears."[110]

Paul-François, as *trésorier de France*, did not condone such behavior on the part of the *grands seigneurs*, but he said less about the tax exemptions of the Bourgeois de La Rochelle. By agreeing to pay a lump sum in advance, the residents of the city reduced their taille appreciably. In fact, they avoided paying the taille on their properties in the countryside altogether. Under the letter of the law, taxes on leased land were to be paid by the tenant, not by the owner. What an incentive not to work the land by direct administration! In fact, many Rochelais landlords went one step further and maintained that the vinedressers who worked by "task" were in fact tenants or *bordiers* and must pay the taille. The intendant at least saw the injustice of this argument and wrote with obvious exasperation to Necker, controller-general.

I have had a terrible time persuading them of the absurdity of this reasoning and making them understand that their *bordiers* are only day laborers paid by the task instead of by the day. The proof is that the *bordier*, hard as he may work, scarcely earns more than two hundred livres per year, about the same as a day laborer. A *fermier* [a true tenant] has a share of the income either in money or a half or third of the harvest, while the *bordier* has no share of the harvest [or income in any form].

... But since this is contrary to their personal interest, they [the landlords] are not convinced. The resulting abuse is that gradually all the inhabitants of La Rochelle buy domains in the neighboring countryside with real advantage since they do not pay the *taille*, while the unfortunate day laborers and small peasant farmers (*cultivateurs*) see their taille increased every year because of the acquisitions made by the "Bourgeois of La Rochelle." Unfortunately, this evil is slowly growing and spreading to many towns in the *généralité*. [111]

Since the Deponts employed money leases (*fermages*) to substantial *fermiers*, they were not guilty of shifting the taille to their vinedressers and *laboureurs à bras*. True, they made no efforts, unless circumstances were exceptional, to share this tax burden with their tenants. But they were following the Declaration of 1728 to the letter, and they saw no inconsistency between this distribution of the burden of the taille on their own land and the requirement that the *grands seigneurs* pay their *vingtièmes*. After all, the taille carried a social stigma; it was a commoners', even a peasants' tax; the *vingtième noble* was quite different. Both the Deponts and Prince de Chalais should pay the *vingtième* or at least share it with their tenants. Each *état* had its fiscal obligations.

Paul-François tried his hand at direct administration only once in his twenty years as head of the family estate. This was between 1757 and 1763 when he installed new boilers for making brandy at Aigrefeuille. Despite the worm disease, he was able to sell fifty-three casks (less than half a normal yield) of brandy for 8,553 livres in 1762, or 161 livres per cask, a very good unit price. The early 1760s were exceptional years when brisk foreign demand placed Rochelais brandy exports at record highs. [112] But in 1763 Paul-François reverted to money leases, presumably because he was unwilling to take the risks of a very unpredictable harvest and market. [113] As with his shipping ventures, he seemed to sense the best moment in which to leave the "trade."

Twenty years later, his son, Paul-Charles, acquired an interest in salt beds on the island of Oleron, a center of European salt trade since the sixteenth century. [114] In 1789 Paul-Charles owned about sixty *livres* of good white salt marsh. The *livre* contained twenty rectangular basins about 12 by 15 feet each and produced about 4.5 metric tons of salt annually. The largest holding on Oleron belonged to seven *parlementaires* of Bordeaux who averaged sixty-eight livres each, followed by over forty members of the local notability who held between three and sixty livres each. [115] Hence, Depont's holding was quite respectable in terms of production and in relation to other proprietors on the island.

Relegated to the picturesque in our own century, salt-making on Oleron was a serious enterprise in the eighteenth century. Officials on

the island in 1780 said it produced "the best salt in the kingdom," especially for the preservation of cod fish. Paul-Charles employed twenty-two
salt-makers on his salt basins scattered over five parishes. Like other
landlords, Depont worked his salt beds by shares. Two-thirds of the production was sold on Depont's account, one-third on the salt-makers',
after deduction of the seigneurial dîme of one-tenth. In effect, Depont
received 70 percent of the product. He alone was responsible, however,
for all repairs to the basins. These costs were not inconsiderable, averaging 1,000 livres per year from 1783 to 1789 and reaching 5,483 livres in
1791.[116] The salt basins were extremely vulnerable to flooding.

Production varied considerably from year to year—sometimes by more
than 100 percent. Since the royal tax farm for the gabelle bought only a
portion of the production and did not fix prices, the market price also
varied a great deal.[117] Therefore, in order to make profits it was necessary to stock and wait for a favorable moment to sell. Often this meant
waiting for a number of seasons. In the meantime the salt-makers had
to be fed and a reliable agent employed to see that no salt was sold and
the bread from the mainland carefully husbanded. Such an agent Depont found in one Chauvet, described by a contemporary report as a
man who could measure the salt basins accurately, keep good accounts,
and "terrorize his men."[118]

Paul-Charles held his salt for seven years before selling 1,625 metric
tons (muids ras) in 1789 at 24 livres the ton. This was a good price. Depont's share (two-thirds and his dîme) totaled 27,023 livres or 3,860
livres per year. The twenty-two salt-makers received 11,991 livres from
the sale, but their debts to Depont for seven years' supply of bread absorbed almost the entire sum. In fact, eight of the men were still in debt
while fourteen others were ahead by sums ranging from 40 to 180 livres
each. Obviously, the salt-makers were "partners" only in the most eu-
phemistic sense. Their small scraps of vineyard, some seafood, and
Depont's provisions kept them at bare subsistence. It is true, of course,
that had the individual salt-makers not been sustained for seven years
by Depont, they would have been obliged to sell their product at a much
lower price.[119]

Pierre d'Harouard began his agricultural manual with this passage:

In the greater part of Aunis the land is poor, dry, and stony with scarcely four or
five inches of top soil. In general, it is good only for vineyard. Some areas have
drained marshland; there are even large areas flooded part of the year; there are a
few salt beds in the communes of Aitré, Angoulin, Saint-Maurice, and Laleu. The
cultivated land is either in métairies or fermes, but the greater part is in petite
culture. ... The inhabitants are very hard-working and labor almost all the land
by hand [à bras]. About 40,000 journaux (32,000 acres) of vineyard produce 37,000

tonneaux of wine. Of this total, 5,000 are shipped to La Rochelle for local consumption or for ship cargoes, 6,000 are consumed in the countryside or transported to the Vendée via Marans, and 26,000 are converted into brandy. ... Lacking manure, wheat returns barely four to one on the seed. There are 22,000 *journaux* [17,600 acres] of grainland producing 90,000 *quintaux* of all grains. Local consumption is 182,500 *quintaux* or 550 pounds per capita [35,000 people]. There is no livestock raising because of the lack of pasture.[120]

This concise description of land use in Aunis was written in 1802. It might have been written a half-century earlier. True, the abolition of the seigneurial system lightened "rents" on a mass of vinedressers, and the sale of church and émigré lands increased the number of small holders, though we do not yet know by how many.[121] But clearly, the basic agrarian structure remained unchanged as did the ways of managing and leasing the land.

The Deponts were unexceptional landlords. They were neither agricultural entrepreneurs nor paternalistic guardians of their agents, tenants, salt-makers, or *tenanciers.* Nor do they seem to have been markedly sentimental about the land like Harouard at La Jarne who evoked the *douces jouissances* of a domain in the country. Yet the Deponts were not indifferent to the land. They were not absentee landlords, like the *grands seigneurs* at Paris, interested only in aggregate returns as reported by their estate intendants.[122] Each domain and the tenants on it, each seigneury and the *tenanciers* belonging to it, received their regular close attention. To the charge that they were "acquisitive," the Deponts could reply that their land had to support more than one branch of the family. For more than twenty years, from 1740 to 1766, Jean-Samuel in Paris needed money. Even after the death of Paul-François in 1774, Paul-Charles continued to manage his brother's properties as well as his own, an indication that Jean-Samuel knew the pecuniary advantages of close supervision. Moreover, I suspect that the Depont style of management was much more characteristic of local landlords than that of Harouard. After all, when Harouard urged landlords not to ask too much from their domains, that the land would not respond to their "cupidity," was he not revealing common practice?

The Deponts of La Rochelle—especially Paul-François and Paul-Charles—were tenacious landlords, and if their sternness hardly strengthened Tocquevillean "ties" with the country people, this same tenacity helped them survive—even a revolution.

III

Royal Administrator

Il ne faut qu'une dose très médiocre d'esprit pour avoir des succès dans les affaires. On est borné à décider dans la plupart des places des questions mille fois décidées. On n'a besoin que d'une certaine activité nécessaire pour une prompte expédition, que d'embrasser des détails familiers par l'habitude, d'avoir présent à l'esprit le texte de quelques réglements, des formes prescrites, des usages qui ont force de loi. Les lumières, les secours, arrivent de toutes parts à l'homme en place, en raison surtout de son élévation. Les affaires sont à l'avance examinées, discutées. On ne les lui présente que tamisées en quelque sorte, éclaircies, mises dans un tel jour, qu'à moins d'être stupide, la décision saute aux yeux. Un homme doué d'une médiocre intelligence, qui a quelque mémoire et de l'application, peut acquérir une grande réputation, surtout s'il a une physionomie imposante ou spirituelle. L'expérience nous apprend d'ailleurs que la plupart des succès sont dûs au caractère de l'homme en place, bien plus qu'à son génie.

—Sénac de Meilhan
"De l'Esprit d'Affaires"

CHAPTER FIVE

Apprenticeship and Marriage

In May 1766, Jean-Samuel De Pont, Intendant of the Generality of Bour-bonnais, married Marie-Madeleine-Françoise l'Escureul de la Touche. Depont *père* was informed that his new daughter-in-law was "the most beautiful *intendante* in the kingdom."[1] Her other more solid assets not-withstanding, Paul-François found it necessary to temper his son's "natural vivacity." "It is only fair that you pay for the luxury of satisfying your vanity. For example, I understand that it will cost 50 louis [1,150 livres] to have the marriage contract signed by the King. If this is so, you might avoid this expense. After all, you seem indifferent to this honor, which really does not amount to much since it is so common nowadays."[2]

It was already too late. The contract had been signed ten days earlier before an assembly of the most distinguished representatives of Parisian *haute société*. Perhaps that is why Depont *père* did not attend in person. The month before he had drawn up a contract making Jacques Flesselles, new intendant of Lyon and colleague of Jean-Samuel, his legal represen-tative at the official signing of the marriage contract.[3] For Jean-Samuel, surely 50 louis d'or was a small sacrifice indeed for the *éclat* of this mo-ment.

Although a systematic listing of forty-three witnesses does not do justice to the pomp of the occasion, it tells us something about the social milieu Jean-Samuel frequented, or at least approached. Thirteen members of the royal family signed the contract, although they did not gather in person at the Châtelet Court to witness the transaction or attend the church ceremony on the following day. But they added no small luster to the con-tract. Immediately after the signatures of the King and the Queen are the names of Louis, Dauphin of France, the Comte de Provence, the Comte d'Artois, followed by five Princesses of the Blood and the four Princes—Condé, Bourbon-Condé, Conti, and Bourbon-Conti. These were followed by high functionaries of the crown in actual attendance; the vice-chancellor and *garde des sceaux*, Le Vue, the ministers of state, Saint-

Florentin, Choiseul, Praslin, Bertin, the new controller-general, L'Averdy, and three members of the royal household, the dukes de La Vauguyon, d'Aumont, and de Villeguier. Jean-Samuel and his friend, Jacques Flesselles, could not have wished for a more elite audience, one that blended the highest royalty with the most distinguished civil servants, and included their own immediate superiors and potential patrons in an increasingly complex royal administration.

The remaining twenty-one "guests" at the signing tell us more about the "mixed society" through which Jean-Samuel had made his way since law school some twenty years before. They included three bankers or sons of bankers, a *sécretaire du roi*, a *conseiller au parlement*, a *conseiller du roi*, a dean of a cathedral chapter, the chamberlain of the Elector of Bavaria, the Princess d'Armagnac, the Marquise de Montesson, Intendant Flesselles's brother, and two Durforts, relatives by marriage into the Lescure branch of the Depont family, on this occasion demonstrating none of the social diffidence they exhibited toward Paul-François in La Rochelle. But perhaps more important to the advancement of Jean-Samuel's career even before the marriage was the father of the bride, Charles-Francois-Joseph L'Escureul de la Touche. Immediately below the distinguished ranks of ministers and courtiers one senses a level of society where office, finance, and salon easily mingled. [4]

Who was M. L'Escureul de la Touche? He was the son of a receiver-general of the royal domain and wood in Normandy. François de la Touche the elder had lived in the provincial town of Alençon most of his life. His modest inheritance consisted of diversified investments in land, wood, forges, rural textiles, and a score of loans to local residents ranging from the widow Garnier (75 livres) to the intendant of the province (1,146 livres). The elder La Touche does not fit the stereotype of the parvenu financier growing fat on the windfall profits of public finance. [5] One must not overestimate the wealth of a rural "receiver," whose accounts were subject to periodic inspection. After his death in 1748, François's fortune of 76,690 livres was further pared down, by a series of audits that found his books "wanting," to 42,429 livres. But perhaps the real balance sheet was not quite so modest as the death inventory suggested. La Touche *père* had furnishings and silverware worth 11,310 livres and 15,000 more in specie, sums inordinately large compared to his modest assets in land and *rentes*. And where had he found 80,000 livres to pay his son's marriage portion in 1745, three years before? Presumably, he had chosen his son's marriage as the moment to transfer the bulk of his liquid assets to the next generation. The effort was reciprocated by the bride's family. The Cromots, also *officiers de finance,* had mobilized another 40,000 livres for the dowry *en espèces.* Beginning with this capital—probably raised at some sacrifice for both families—the next generation transformed a modest provincial fortune into a substantial Parisian one.[6]

Charles-Francois-Joseph L'Escureul de la Touche—his name somewhat lengthened—increased the family capital by a wide variety of enterprises, most of them originating in government contracts. In 1755 he bought the office of *Intendant et controlleur général de l'argenterie, menus plaisirs et affaires de la chambre du Roi*. In this post, he was in charge of the royal theaters, their construction and maintenance, the purchase and leasing of stage properties, and the preparation of state pageants. The accounts of his "department" refer to sums owed for "various constructions," to roofers, painters, ironworkers, and other artisans in the building trades, suggesting extensive subcontracting. La Touche dealt regularly with a host of royal suppliers (*fournisseurs*) of clothing, draperies, horses, hunting gear, and other luxury goods, stocked in the royal warehouses and placed at the disposition of the First Chamberlain of the Royal Household. Louis XV's well-known passion for the hunt—and other needs for distraction from routine—often led him to leave Paris suddenly for Marly or Fontainebleau. His *garde robe*, a convoy of wagons and equipage, had to be ready at a moment's notice.[7]

The office drew a salary of 10,000 livres in 1756, 12,000 after 1771. But the cost of the office—236,000 livres—was an indication that it was an entree to much greater rewards. First, there were royal gifts. La Touche's colleague, Papillon de la Ferté, refers to the *très belle tabatière du Roi* received by both men in 1768 "because the king loved the theater" and to the jewel boxes from the young princess, Marie Antoinette.[8] More important were the opportunities for profits from subcontracting. Papillon noted that all of the building expenses could not be accounted for on the *états* and warned La Touche of potential "difficulties" if there was a change of ministers.[9] It is well known that royal procurement was an open door to supplementing one's income. It also provided valuable contacts in high court circles. La Touche and his two colleagues were in a position to lend or "circulate" the stocks in their warehouses. In January 1769, for example, La Touche lent the foreign minister, Marquis de Choiseul, curtains, cords, and tassels, no doubt for a stage production at court.[10] But the impression should not be only that of royal haberdasher or theater manager. Jean-Samuel's father-in-law had invested in countless enterprises in the twenty years since his marriage in 1745.

In contrast to the clear balance sheets of Paul-François Depont, made "cleaner" by the uniform mass of five percent *rentes*, the inventory of L'Escureul de la Touche appears, at first glance, fragmentary and obscure. True, there is an aggregate total at the end of the twenty-nine articles of his *partage* of 1766 when he transferred half of his assets to his only child, but the precise composition of his fortune and the returns of individual investments are not quickly grasped. The reasons for this go beyond the vagaries of recording; French notaries were not careless. Uncertainty and complexity characterized the world of finance in which La Touche lived, and secrecy was one condition of its successful operation.[11] Not only were the rates of return on these investments variable, but there also was a continuous reinvestment of capital which the

Table 5.1. The Fortune of L'Escureul de la Touche, 1766

	Capital	Percent of Fortune
I. Office, *Intendant des menus* (1755)	236,000	36.1
II. Land, Fief of Rancy, purchased from Brunet d'Ivry (1757)	68,200	10.4
III. Investments in Tax Farms:		
1. Lease, Richard (1757)	40,000	
2. Lease, Lashy (1757) and Augeard (1759)	50,000	
3. Lease Mezières (1760), 5 *billets*	22,000	
4. Lease Augeard (1760), 6 *billets*	27,500	
5. Thirty shares on the General Farms	30,000	
6. Six *billets* on the General Farms of Brittany	30,000	
7. Two *billets* on the General Farms	8,000	
8. Loan to receiver-general of finance	2,494	
Total	209,994	32.2
IV. Investments in Enterprises:		
1. Army supply (*fourniture des étapes*) Partnership, Robin (1756–59), 6 "*deniers d'intérêts*"	45,000	
2. Bill (*rescription*) on army-supply contract	2,480	
3. Share in three shipping ventures at Boulogne-sur-Mer, *armateur* Merlin (1757)	2,000	
Total	49,480	7.6
V. Lifetime annuities (*Rentes viagères*):		
1. "On the Head of Daughter" (1758), (1,000 *rente*)	13,000	
2. "Received from an unknown person" (1761), (1,500 *rente*)	15,000	
Total	28,000	4.3
VI. Specie on hand (*en caisse*):	1,436	0.2
VII. Personal Possessions:		
1. Silverware	5,677	
2. Diamonds, jewelry, wardrobe	9,692	
3. Personal Property of Madame de la Touche	44,570	
Total	59,939	9.2
Total fortune	653,049	100.0

Source: Archives Nationales, Minutier Central, *Etude* 95:302, "Partage," 3 June 1766.

inventory does not always clearly indicate and which is further obscured by a certain number of financial failures or partial failures; nor does the final *bilan* ever appear. But however unsure one is of the long-run profitability of certain *placements*, one thing becomes immediately clear: La Touche was no *rentier*. He was an active participant in the risky ventures of French "court capitalism." [12] His inventory reveals a series of temporary partnerships involving substantial capital sums, a network, not of *rentes*, but of notes (*billets*), shares (*actions*) and treasury claims (*rescriptions*). Consider the summary of the La Touche fortune in 1766 presented in table 5.1.

Inferring economic behavior from a single balance sheet has obvious risks, but the La Touche fortune undeniably reveals economic activities and investments strikingly different from those of the Depont family of La Rochelle. Only 10 percent of the La Touche fortune was in land, and it was not highly prized as an economic asset. In fact, an "observation" attached to the inventory said that the "fief of Rancy is more *agréable* than useful." [13] Having bought it from the Brunet family, tax farmers, and "other co-proprietors" in 1757, [14] La Touche had no interest in living in the country, at least not after his wife's death in 1761. The lease on the land returned only 1,750 livres, less than 3 percent on the purchase price, and 1,577 of this was absorbed in taxes, maintenance costs, and an annual mortgage payment of 1,000 livres. Rancy with its château, park, fountains, and "dependencies" had been on the market for four years (since 1762), but "no one had offered a price that Sieur de la Touche considered large enough." The family's lack of attachment to real estate of any kind is also indicated by the habit of renting a town house in Paris—at 1,500 per annum—in the parish of Saint-Germain de l'Auxerois. [15] La Touche's investments were clearly elsewhere.

The office, to be sure, represented a very large investment, almost 40 percent of the total fortune, though it bore a mortgage of 71,000 ten years after its purchase in 1755. But it was worth a good deal more than the *gage* (4 percent of the purchase price) in opportunities for subcontracting and other "arrangements" emerging from the custodianship of government warehouses of luxury goods. Indeed, regarded closely, the office was as much an enterprise as a bureaucratic function and reflected the skills La Touche employed in his other business ventures.

L'Escureul de la Touche was a financier, not of the wealth and importance of a Pâris-Duverney or an Antoine Crozat, but one of those lesser creditors of the state without whom the entire system of public finance would have broken down. The Company of Farmers-General had to keep about 20 to 30 million livres in notes constantly in circulation in order to bridge the chronic deficit in royal revenues after 1750. The great financiers and bankers of the crown had to depend on a much larger network of creditors who were willing to lend substantial sums on relatively short term (two or three years) to fill out the huge advances promised to the Royal Treasury. Their credit, of course, depended in large measure on the secrecy surrounding the anticipated receipts from royal taxes.[16] La Touche's account indicates his loans to well-known farmers-general such as Richard, Mezières, and Augeard with whom he shared the risks of deficient tax receipts and also the potential profits of a surplus, and a return above the usual 5 percent on regular public and private *rentes*.

Consider an operation in 1756. La Touche and his partner Boisneuf advanced 70,000 livres to Richard, farmer-general, "who was obliged to pay interest at the same rate (*sur le même pied*) that is agreed in the contract between (all) the investors and the General Farm."[17] Richard agreed to pay the interest quarterly to La Touche and Boisneuf. Apparently the returns were above the legal rate for a time since we read "the interest has been reduced to 5 percent." Another investment in the tax farms during the Seven Year's War was less fortunate. In 1757, La Touche lent 50,000 to the "Lachy Lease," representing one-fiftieth of the total capital raised and was reimbursed two years later with an added "dividend" of 5,044 livres. He immediately reinvested the same capital in the "Augeard Lease." But 1759 was a year of military defeat and excessive strains on public finance.[18] The account reads: "The capital has not been refunded. There is even reason to fear that there has been a loss on this capital." La Touche lost 12,600 livres of the 50,000 "without hope of being reimbursed," along with the interest on the total capital during the two-year lease. Nevertheless, he did receive a partial indemnification from the crown so that his overall losses in the four years were reduced to about 3,000.[19]

Not all of the investments were so risky. Each of La Touche's thirty shares of the *Fermes Générales* of 1,000 livres had coupons attached with fixed dividends payable at stipulated dates, like modern U.S. treasury notes; on these he received assured returns, though less than 4 percent on a 30,000 investment in 1760. If the war played havoc with public finance, it had some benefits for investors in army supplies. In 1756 La Touche joined a "*société* of investors" along with his brother-in-law, Cromot, for 45,000, and received dividends of 6,400 livres over three years, about 5 percent per annum. The war was of course disastrous for overseas trade. La Touche's foray into shipping ventures at Boulogne in 1757 was a "pure loss"; fortunately, the investment was small.[20]

Altogether, La Touche's commercial ventures were limited, but his range of investments still substantiate a close relationship between office, public finance, and large-scale enterprise.[21] La Touche was willing to take risks with his capital, move in and out of short-term leases on the tax farms, enter temporary partnerships in army supply, and dabble in shipping ventures. He kept almost no specie in the strongbox, despite the large capital sums at his disposal; he was uninterested in real estate as an investment and even as a source of status or pleasure; he did not invest in perpetual *rentes*, preferring more speculative lifetime annuities, and very few of these.

Reading this article in La Touche's inventory, one might share some of the popular prejudices against financiers: "The said M. Duttion de Boissy [notary] declares that he was given 15,000 livres by an unknown person who did not wish to give his name, to be employed for the acquisition of a lifetime annuity of 1,500 livres [10 percent] in favor of Sr. de la Touche, transferable in case of his death to Madame de la Touche, in case of her death, to his daughter, and thereafter to her children."[22] That the notary was able to buy such an advantageous *rente* in 1761 is a reminder of the crown's increasingly desperate need for money. It also makes one wonder how long L'Escureul de la Touche would continue to prefer risky short-term loans to the tax farms to high yield government annuities even if the capital was permanently alienated. The year 1760 was a kind of turning point for financiers and *gens de finance.*[23]

In any case, La Touche decided to divest himself of his entire estate only one year after his daughter's marriage to Jean-Samuel Depont. Most likely, La Touche had accumulated enough money in the twenty years since his marriage in 1745 that he could now think of social promotion. His father had died in 1748, his mother in 1756; his wife in 1761; his only daughter was a young and beautiful heiress. An "alliance" between "finance" and "high administration" was common enough in the second half of the eighteenth century.[24]

Charles-François L'Escureul de la Touche and his son-in-law Jean-Samuel Depont must have been about the same age. In some ways their careers had been parallel. Both born in the provinces in the 1720s, they had made their way in Paris with little parental help or patronage. La Touche's father had died in 1748 and Paul-François Depont, though never short of advice to his son, was far away in space and *mentalité*. Both men bought their key offices in 1755 at considerable cost and had borrowed heavily to acquire them. But while La Touche was pyramiding his fortune in the tax farms and in royal procurement services, Jean-Samuel had entered those long, lean years as a *maître des requêtes*. Living on modest *gages* and his father's tight pension, deprived of the dowry and influence of a "good alliance," he must have despaired at times of ever attaining the coveted post of Intendant and the security and status it would provide. He could not know in 1760 that two fortunes-in-the-making—one by the patient discipline of a *rentier* and the other by the risky ventures of a *"capitaliste"*—would one day be his. Still, in statistical terms, his years of "internship" were not exceptional; his labors at the royal council and in the demanding salons of Paris were the lot of most men of his *état* or profession.

In fact, regarded from the perspective of the collective careers of a generation of intendants, Jean-Samuel did well. [25] He became a *conseiller* at the Parlement of Paris at the age of twenty-three, two years below the required age. Like so many of his colleagues, he obtained a dispensation for his age with the proviso that he would not have a "deliberative voice," the right to speak and vote, until he reached twenty-five. [26] Successively, he had attended a Parisian *collège* and law school to become an advocate attached to the Parlement—all before twenty-three. Etienne Pasquier, who later became chancellor of France under Louis XVIII, commented about the youth of the magistrates in the eighteenth century: "One entered the magistracy at twenty; at twenty-five one had a voice in its deliberations. There was (in practice) no rule governing the age of admission in the parlements." Contrasting these young men to magistrates of his own time, he said they knew they had to learn from experience and from the great city in which they lived. They could have no illusions that their formal education before the age of twenty was sufficient. [27] It seems they had none of the intellectual smugness associated with the graduates of the *Grandes Ecoles* of more recent times.

The "long years" extended from the moment one entered the Parlement to the day one obtained an intendancy. Jean-Samuel spent seven years as a *conseiller* and ten years as a *maître des requêtes* before obtaining his commission as intendant at the age of forty. But this long apprenticeship was not exceptional. Even Turgot, Jean-Samuel's brilliant contemporary, spent eight years as a *maître des requêtes* before becoming intendant at thirty-four. Depont's "professional minority" was only slightly longer than the average for his generation of future intendants. [28]

All sixty-seven *maîtres des requêtes* served three months of the year (*par quartier*) as judges at the *Requêtes de L'Hôtel du Roi*, a court that processed petitions from individuals or from *corporations* requesting royal letters patent. The *maîtres* studied these petitions, attempted to determine to which courts or jurisdictions they pertained, and then submitted them, properly annotated, to the chancellor, the chief judicial officer of the crown. The chancellor also named one *maître des requêtes* to serve as *rapporteur* (committee chairman and spokesman) for each case brought before the *Conseil d'Etat Privé*, which acted as a high court judging the legal competence of the lower courts, settling conflicts of jurisdiction, and annulling judgments that had been improperly made. Here again, the *maître* studied the entire dossier (those bundles of *factums* and *mémoires*, so much a part of this litigious century) and submitted it to the *Conseil* with his recommendations. Finally, the *maîtres* served in the *Direction des Finances*, a division attached to the *Conseil du Roi*. This department had jurisdiction over litigation arising from royal finances. The *maîtres* were called upon either to participate directly in the deliberations of the *Direction* or to serve on one of its commissions or *bureaux*. The *bureaux* prepared the work of the councils. There were six "ordinary" *bureaux des finances* and sixteen "extraordinary" ones, each composed of about two councilors of state and eight *maîtres des requêtes*. [29]

There is no doubt that this training provided an exposure to a wide variety of litigation and not only instructed the *maître* in the fine points of the law, but also familiarized him with the various problems involved in local administration. For these petitions and *procès* were not limited to tax cases. The cases reported by Depont to the *Conseil Privé* dealt with a whole range of issues, including contested inheritances, wardships, ennoblements, privileges and communal rights; they touched all levels of society, from cathedral chapters and municipalities to artisans and villagers. [30]

In addition, this training taught a young magistrate to synthesize disparate factual material and to present reports with clarity and precision. Even so promising a young man as Turgot was treated as an apprentice by the councilors of state when he reported to the *Conseil Privé*: "You have spoken very well, but a little too long. Next time, please be more brief." In his subsequent reports to the *Conseil,* Turgot was careful to summarize each section of his *discours* and to present a general résumé at the end. "You have greatly improved. You have said a great deal, and you have been brief." [31] The incident indicates that the work of the commissions was intended as an authentic apprenticeship. However valid may be the criticism of favoritism and privilege in government, it would be difficult to accuse the *Conseil d'Etat Privé* of a lack of professionalism. It conscientiously inculcated an administrative expertise and a sense of service in its future intendants.

Depont was named *rapporteur* before the *Conseil Privé* thirty-seven times in nine years, somewhat below the average but not markedly so. [32] Work for the *Conseil* gave the *maîtres des requêtes* an excellent opportunity to display their legal and administrative acumen to the councilors of state, professional undersecretaries such as Ormesson, Trudaine, and Bertin, and to compete for posts in the high administration. It was a demanding forcing ground, not unlike the *Grandes Ecoles* in France today. The pressure was not relieved by a very modest stipend of 1,000 livres. [33] Given the style of life prescribed for a royal administrator in Paris and the reluctance of his father to sustain it, Jean-Samuel must have been eager to apply for service on the committees in the finance department which offered supplementary emoluments. Depont had to wait five years before being named to one of the sixteen "extraordinary bureaux." By 1765 he was serving on five of them in the company of such councilors of state as Moreau de Beaumont and Feydeau de Marville as well as such distinguished prelates as Cardinal de Luynes and the Archbishop of Albi.[34] The subjects treated by these committees ranged from the administration of the property of "religious fugitives" and religious communities to the liquidation of the debts of the craft guilds and the reimbursement of certain venal offices abolished by the crown. *Bureau* VIII was concerned with "litigation involving shares of the *Compagnie des Indes* and concessions of lands in Louisiana," a reminder to Jean-Samuel that his grandfather had been director of the royal company at La Rochelle forty years before.[35]

In the performance of his duties as *maître des requêtes* Jean-Samuel appears competent without being exceptional. Like his colleagues and contemporaries—Flesselles, Le Peletier de Morfontaine, Taboureau des Réaux, and Perrin de Cypierre—names that do not evoke the prestige of a Calonne, Turgot, Joly de Fleury, or Bertier de Sauvigny—Depont served his internship to be rewarded finally with an intendancy by the controller-general, L'Averdy. What *is* exceptional was Depont's move as a youth directly from the provinces into the Paris Parlement to become an intendant all in one generation. Of the ninety intendants studied by Vivian Gruder, "only four and possibly five 'new Parisians' succeeded in transplanting themselves from their province and becoming Paris magistrates and then royal intendants."[36] Jean-Samuel was one of these five.

This statistic tells us something about the man's speed and agility of adaptation to the imperatives of Parisian society, one for which his background at La Rochelle had not prepared him. Lacking outstanding administrative talent, with limited financial means and local patronage—at least at the outset of his career—how did he do it? "To become an intendant," writes Roland Mousnier, "it was necessary not only to be a good *maître des requêtes*, but also to have a protector in the *Conseil d'Etat*."[37] To reach the ear of the minister, as even Paul-François in La Rochelle knew, one needed connections, contacts, and influence. The evidence available suggests that Jean-Samuel's chief skill was knowing how to cultivate patrons. To "Birth, Talent, and Wealth," his father had once ascribed the success of the intendant of La Rochelle.[38] Perhaps he had underestimated "*Protection*"; it might compensate for modest endowments of the other three virtues.

Anne-Robert-Jacques Turgot, descendant of an old robe family, spent much of his "term" as *maître des requêtes* in the 1750s frequenting some of the most distinguished salons of Paris. Here he met d'Alembert, Condorcet, Grimm, Holbach among *philosophes,* Quesnay, Dupont, Baudeau, and Gournay among physiocrats and *économistes.*[39] Jean-

Samuel's Parisian connections were quite different. Intellectually less distinguished, they represented another part of the complex social world of the capital, one where affability and wit played a larger role than sustained intellectual discourse. For evidence of what Depont's "society" was, let us consider again the guests at the wedding of Jean-Samuel to Marie-Madeleine-Françoise l' Escureul de la Touche in 1766.

Among the ministers of state was Monseigneur le Duc de la Vauguyon, tutor to the Dauphin, and correspondent of Paul-François in La Rochelle. One also finds "on the side of the groom" Princesse d'Armagnac, another *dévote* and correspondent of the *trésorier de France*. Jean-Samuel had not ignored his father's advice entirely; he had "paid his respects" to the duke and the princess. Yet one wonders what influence they had with the controller-general or other members of the *Conseil d'Etat Privé*. The Dauphin was notoriously lethargic and little help could be expected from that quarter. [40] Perhaps La Vauguyon did "speak to the minister," but his influence was clearly declining as indicated by his loss of the post of tutor to the future Louis XVI. Directly after the name of Princesse d'Armagnac comes that of Marquise de Montesson. This "friend" was surely much more important to Jean-Samuel's career advancement.

Madame de Montesson was a member of the inner circle of the Duc d'Orleans, a much more politically active branch of the royal family. [41] She later became the morganatic spouse of the duke. Fortunately, her niece, Comtesse de Genlis, the well-known novelist and educator, gives us a glimpse of the "intimate circle" of the Palais Royal in the early 1760s. Among the many roles created by this society was that of "confidant." "At that time," wrote the countess, "many men who were not attractive enough to have many conquests among the women assumed the more modest role of "confidant," which in this society was not negligible in helping many of them make their way." Among the names on her list was Jean-Samuel's. "M. de Pont, the intendant of Moulins, also a very amiable man who a few years later married a charming person, the mother of the present Madame de Fontanges." [42] Madame de Genlis was not a superficial person; she did not use adjectives like *aimable* and *charmant* indiscriminately; they were virtues.

That Jean-Samuel cultivated his role of "confidant"—and even overstepped its bounds on occasion—is indicated by the following story. It is worth quoting at length because it reveals a great deal about the norms and *milieu* of Parisian high society.

M. de Pont, the intendant of Moulins, was in love with my aunt, Madame de Montesson, who was unaware of this; he had been her friend for several years and he had never given her any hint of his feelings. One evening, finding himself alone with her, he was no longer able to constrain himself and, without any warning, he threw himself at her feet and began to speak to her in the most passionate manner. This sudden declaration seemed ridiculous to Madame de Montesson; she preferred to laugh about it rather than get angry with a friend whom she respected. She was holding a fan and playfully tapped M. de Pont's face with it; but the little hook by which the handle of the fan was attached to the cardboard came off and caught M. de Pont's nose, so that the fan was stuck to his face like a mask, for Madame de Montesson had let it slip from her hand amidst peals of laughter. At that moment, someone entered the room; Madame de Montesson laughed even harder, and M. de Pont, taking advantage of his misfortune, quickly rose to his feet without being seen, since the fan covered his face; he fled and carried it with him, only taking it off in the vestibule. The third party who had interrupted this tête-à-tête had not seen the face of M. de Pont and did not learn his name that day because Madame de Montesson did not want to reveal it; but M. de Pont was betrayed by the deep scratch on his nose which remained for several days. [43]

At first glance, this may seem like a trivial story about a social mishap. There may be more to it. It is curious that in this intimate and vocal society Madame de Montesson was unaware of Depont's feelings "for several years." Was this because it was unthinkable to the marquise that this "new Parisian" could aspire to be her lover? Was Depont's "declaration of love" a calculated move intended—even if it failed—to make the marquise take notice of him and recommend him to the duke and other influential people? Was the move a reflection of Jean-Samuel's self-confidence, a conviction that the marquise and her world were not too good for him? All of these explanations are possible. Montesson's social power and influence were legend. She had a Talleyrand-like talent for survival, later salvaging her entire fortune through her contact with Madame Bonaparte.[44] She commanded the respect of any careerist in Paris after 1760.

The fan incident did not hurt Jean-Samuel. He met his future wife probably in the private theater of Madame de Montesson. An anonymous gossip wrote later in the century that "M. de Pont" became intendant of Metz "because his wife plays on the stage of M. de Montesson," an obvious slander, but not without a grain of truth. [45] Jean-Samuel's wife also played the role of "matchmaker." Madame de Genlis ascribed the "brilliant marriage" of her own daughter to the suggestion of Madame Depont and to the dowry provided by Madame de Montesson. The young groom had been the marquise's lover. [46] Surely this was not the well-regulated world of Jean-Samuel's father; Paul-François could not possibly imagine half of its "sins" or half its corridors. One may doubt the comment of Madame de Genlis that Montesson's salon was "the most brilliant and witty" in all of Paris. [47] Compared to the salons of Mesdames Goeffrin and Lespinasse, the circle of the Duc d'Orléans that emerges from the Genlis mémoires was cynical, sordid, and *intrigant*, and not very intellectual. Yet social assimilation was essential to Jean-Samuel's career. In its own way the Montesson-Orléans circle was a training ground as well.

The tissue of influence that Jean-Samuel had woven was a varied one. At least four distinct coteries of influential people can be identified: the *dévots* with whom Paul-François had corresponded; the Orléans circle which Jean-Samuel had cultivated alone; Escureul de la Touche and other financiers; colleagues in the *corps* of *maîtres des requêtes*. He even gained acceptance from the Lescure-Durfort branch of the family who, although they might snub Paul-François at La Rochelle, were present in force at the wedding of the new intendant of Moulins. [48] The list of wedding invitations had not been assembled at whim. It was a reflection of Jean-Samuel's social and professional ascent. Duc de la Vauguyon, Marquise de Montesson, L'Escureul de la Touche, Jacques Flesselles, and even Duchesse de Durfort, wife of the ambassador to the Two Sicilies had been, in varying degrees, his patrons. For a moment, there was more unity in their world of Paris than their separate functions and social origins would lead us to think.

The marriage contract was signed 11 May 1766. Jean-Samuel's financial problems were over. The dowry of his young wife—she was a minor under the law—totaled 240,000 livres, equal to the dowry of a duke's daughter. Moreover, she was an heiress through whom Depont could one day expect to receive the entire fortune of Escureul de la Touche. In addition, his father in La Rochelle promised him an advance of 180,000 livres on his inheritance. In one ceremonial moment debts on his office were liquidated, 20,000 livres paid in coin by La Touche, and 5 percent annuities from both sides of the new "alliance" made legal obligations of the parents of the couple. That Jean-Samuel needed the money is indicated by his own small capital—public *rentes* yielding only 1,645 livres per annum. He had depended heavily on his father's pension of 8,000, earning only a few thousand livres from his work in the commissions of the *Conseil Privé*. However, his "movables" suggest an ample style of life about which his father's letters had given some hint. He had amassed furnishings, silverware, horses and equipage evaluated at 50,000 livres, over eight times the value of his father's "movables" at La Rochelle. [49] The "house in the country," which had so upset his father, was representative of Jean-Samuel's acquired Parisian tastes and the necessary *mise en scène* for his professional advance.

Although Jean-Samuel was not altogether happy with the arrangement whereby both his father and father-in-law "guaranteed" his income rather than transferred much capital, he could hardly complain about his revenues beginning in 1766 (table 5.2).

Roland Mousnier has argued that the intendants and the *noblesse administrative* in general were a group distinct from other nobilities of robe

Table 5.2. The Income of Jean-Samuel Depont in 1766

		Income	Percent of Total Income
I. Commission of Intendant			
Salary	12,000		
Pension*	4,000		
		16,000	46.2
II. Land, Seigneury of Manderoux in Aunis from father, evaluation, 55,000, leased for		2,756	8.0
III. *Rentes* owned before marriage:			
1. *Aides et Gabelles*, contract 1714	275		
2. *Aides et Gabelles*, 1721	188		
3. 4 contracts on Clergy of France, 1759, 20,000 at 4 percent	800		
4. *Compagnie des Indes*, 1764, 6,000	300		
5. Estates of Brittany, 1759, 1,650	82	1,645	4.8
IV. *Rentes* of father, income "assigned" to son, 1766:			
1. *Tailles* on *Généralité* of Paris, 1717, 6,750	337		
2. *Tailles* on *Généralité* of La Rochelle, 1725–64, 28,001	1,400		
3. on Mouchard, Receiver-General of finances, 1754, 20,013	1,000		
4. on Clergy of France, 9 contracts, 1745–1760, 33,000	1,650		
5. on City of La Rochelle, 1752, 8,000	400		
6. on Chevalier de Coudraye, 1752, 6,000	300		
7. on M. Ferachin, 1752, 8,000	400		
8. on M. Lefebvre, 1748, 1763, 12,000	600		
9. on M. de La Rochebaron, 1752, 3,000	150	6,237	18.0
V. Income guaranteed as a mortgage on all of the property of M. Escureul de la Touche, 1766 (see Fortune, Table 5.1 above)		8,000	23.1
Total income		34,638	100.1

Source: Archives Nationales, Minutier Central, *Etude* 95:302, Contract of Marriage, 11 May 1766; A.N. F¹ 1965, 24 July 1768, 9 Dec. 1770.

*Intendants usually received a pension of 4,000 after three years' service and 6,000 after seven years' service. By 1770, Depont received a combined salary and pension of 18,000 livres.

or sword. One aspect of that distinctness was their source of income. "The essential part of their resources came from their *gages*, pensions, and indemnities, that is, from remuneration from the king for their services to the State, above all, remuneration for their fidelity."[50] There is no question that Depont's *traitement* was no perfunctory *gage*, similar to the almost symbolic remuneration of a parlementary magistrate. It represented 46 percent of his income in 1766. But it would be too easy to conclude from this that the royal government had "bought" Jean-Samuel's loyalty. His years of training as a *maître des requêtes* had surely been a more powerful influence in shaping his attitudes and loyalties. A professional administrator was in the making.

If one considers the fortune as a whole, it may well be a result, more than a cause, of Jean-Samuel's outlook. Like many wealthy Parisians, the intendant was master of a fortune composed of constituted *rentes*, public *rentes*, treasury notes, and shares in the tax farms. Land and seigneurial rights were almost absent. A moment's reflection is enough to see why a Parisian would prefer such assets; they were readily transferable and divisible and, above all, easily managed, requiring none of the administrative skills the land demanded.[51] Fortunately, Jean-Samuel had a father and older brother who could manage his land in Aunis and even collect his *rentes* from private parties "out there." It was not by accident that Paul-François gave Jean-Samuel most of the public *rentes*, which, like La Touche's treasury notes, were most easily collected in the capital. Only the *grande noblesse* with titled ancestral lands at their disposal placed status above convenience of administration and even above rate of return—at least until landed rents began to rise rapidly in the 1770s.[52]

In other words, a portfolio of diversified loans, easily managed, was the main feature of a Parisian fortune; land was the largest component of a provincial one. Perhaps this difference—and it was never quite this stark a contrast—was not only a question of practicality and a rationing of time, but also a matter of temperament. Was there some relationship between Jean-Samuel's frenetic pace of life from Council of State to drawing room and his convenient package of loan contracts? As he approached the threshold of his professional career in Paris, Jean-Samuel did not want to be tied down to rural property. A generation later, he would have reason to appreciate the land more.

Twenty years in Paris had made Jean-Samuel over in more ways than one. He had not only divorced himself from provincial mores and religious asceticism; he had developed a new set of values and skills of his own. Without the direct evidence of personal letters, one cannot be so precise and certain as in the case of his father. But we can go beyond stereotypes. Rubrics such as "noble" and "bourgeois" are not helpful here. It would be entirely misleading, for example, to characterize the deportment and outlook of Jean-Samuel Depont as "noble." Nor can he be placed neatly into categories, such as "robe" or "sword," with either the magistrates of the parlements or the old lineage nobles.[53] Of course, he knew and used these families; he assumed the outer trappings of their social behavior, copied their dress and demeanor, but this did not mean that he shared a common outlook with them.

Two major influences had played on Jean-Samuel in these years in the capital. First, he had learned to be a royal administrator at the highest echelon. As a *maître des requêtes* he had been carefully trained as a professional who understood the business of government, the range and complexity of its functons, and the responsibilities of power. More than a parlementary magistrate, local *trésorier*, or municipal official, a future intendant and councilor of state had to take the "larger view" of public service. Second, Jean-Samuel had learned to negotiate the social corridors of Paris. This meant adapting to a fluid, complex high society that is not easily understood by modern schemes of social classification. The group that gathered for the Depont–La Touche wedding was a social amalgam. Jean-Samuel had to come to terms with a wide variety of "social types" ranging from salon lionesses and haughty dukes to royal procurement officers and quasi-public financiers. If all were not parvenus by social origin, all shared some of the traits of the parvenu—improvisation, quick-wittedness, charm, a capacity to manipulate others' interests, and perhaps, above all, resilience, a thick skin in the face of a hundred slights, real or imagined.

In this society that gave no quarter—indeed gave nothing without the promise of something in return—what did Jean-Samuel offer to a Montesson or a La Vauguyon? La Vauguyon and the *dévots* might well have considered whatever service they rendered as a favor to Jean-Samuel's father, an obligation among "brothers in the faith." But why the Marquise de Montesson and her circle would have an interest in furthering the career of a man well in his thirties is harder to surmise. Montesson had a sufficient number of friends in high places already. Again, this points to the sheer charm of the man. Here was a "society" where women played a major role. Jean-Samuel had learned his skills as a confidant from scratch, and much more besides. In modern terms, he had become an "outer-directed" man. He was at home in "society."

The agility and adaptation he exhibited in the drawing room was also reflected in his attitude toward novel means of accumulating wealth. Jean-Samuel had learned something about the importance—even public usefulness—of the tax farmer and creditor of the state. As an administrator-in-training, he had appreciated the role of the bankers of the crown; as a friend and kinsman of L'Escureul de la Touche, he must have learned its risks and perhaps its excitement as well. Public finance, like administration, was a technical profession. One historian argues that it was the very "scientific" aspect of public administration that most angered the magistrates of the parlements who only dimly understood high finance and public administration. [54] In any event there was nothing incompatible between the professional expertise of Depont and that of La Touche. Their alliance reflects a wider community of interests than simply shared ambition.

In the final analysis Jean-Samuel Depont was a professional administrator with a respect for the levers of power and for the "experts"—financiers, intendants, councilors of state, court nobles, and salon hostesses—who helped make the "machine" work. Despite certain activities that appeared frivolous and wasteful to his father, Jean-Samuel was not an undirected person. The gambling, the house in the country, the *équipage*, the extra louis for the king's signature on the marriage contract—these were not idle self-indulgences; they were the necessary means of social ascent in the capital. But the goal was not an idle existence. Jean-Samuel had become an agent of the Crown of France. Any appraisal of his outlook and deportment must begin here.

CHAPTER SIX

Intendant of Moulins and Metz

In 1765 what were the problems of a new intendant? It has been recently argued that after 1750 royal power began to weaken. Contrary to Tocqueville's thesis of increasing centralization of power, the intendants became the victims of governmental policy in two respects—their freedom of action was increasingly circumscribed, and support from Paris was less sustained. Here too, the Seven Years' War marks a subtle turning point. The controller-general, Bertin, after an abortive effort to pursue Machault's policy to tax the privileged, was disgraced in 1763. He was followed by François de L'Averdy, previous member of the Parlement of Paris, and thought to be partial to its views on financial matters. He seemed inclined to reduce the powers of the intendants, and his edicts on municipal reform of 1764-65 can be seen in this light. In retrospect, royal experiments in local initiative only increased the obstacles to "reform from above," the main instruments of which were the royal intendants.[1]

But if the central direction of the royal administration seemed to flag, the actual apparatus expanded as if by laws of its own. Whether or not under the influence of a particular "school" of physiocrats or economists, the government turned its attention increasingly toward communication, productivity, education, public health, and the plight of the poor. A new vocabulary invaded the intendants' reports—"state of the harvest," artificial meadows, inoculation, midwives, and *ateliers de charité*. In the mid-1760s Bertin launched his project of clearings as Turgot, then intendant of Limoges, began his campaign to end the *corvée*. The debate over the grain trade dominated the decade. No wonder the ministries sprouted new branches, the *petits ministères* such as Bridges and Roads, Water and Forests, Mines, Agriculture, and Manufactures. An enormous expansion of administrative correspondence took place, as Bertin (1762), L'Averdy (1764), and Terray (1772) each launched national statistical surveys to determine the precise resources, human and material,[2] of the kingdom. Thus, at the same moment the royal intendants found themselves challenged by local estates and parlements, the duties of the post expanded into the entire area of public welfare. It was no longer enough to be the guardian of law and order in the provinces; an intendant was expected to be an active public improver.

Jean-Samuel Depont's new assignment must have been disappointing. However long the seventeen years in Paris may have seemed, the thirteen in Moulins were equally interminable. Baron de Frénilly may have remembered that in his youth an intendancy was the finest post a man could desire, but even so dedicated an intendant as Turgot considered his first assignment at Limoges a "misfortune," pulling him away from the "philosophic life" in Paris he loved so much.[3] Jean-Samuel was no *philosophe*—his father's fears on this account were much exaggerated—but the two days' coach ride from the comfortable Marais quarter across the Beauce and along the upper Loire to Nevers and finally to Moulins brought him to a remote rural world that made La Rochelle and Aunis seem "advanced" and prosperous by comparison.[4]

Even by the standards of the time, Moulins was a backward *généralité*. A *pays de petite culture,* it consisted of 1,178 parishes and 49 *villes,* though only Moulins, the capital, with some twelve thousand inhabitants could properly be called a "town," followed by Nevers, Montluçon, and the spas at Bourbon-Archambault and, more recently, Vichy, frequented in summer by the court nobility. The intendancy was coterminous with the old province of Bourbonnais, a region of gravelly soil useful for road-building but not much else. Like Auvergne to the south and Limousin to the southwest, the Bourbonnais produced more rye and buckwheat (*blé noir*) than high quality wheat (*froment*) for the market, and in any case plots were too small and yields too low to produce a grain surplus of any importance.[5] In fact, chronic food shortage was the problem, and the early 1770s would be particularly hard on a peasantry who understandably had a reputation for lethargy which sometimes passed for *douceur.*[6] There were only two main royal roads, in constant need of repair, one from Clermont to the south and the other from Lyon to the southeast, which met at Moulins to form a single route north to Paris. The road from Clermont became a seasonal highway for bands of "vagabonds" out of the Massif Central. The Auvergnat peddlers and "disguised beggars," known for their heavy drinking and aggressiveness, presented a special problem for any local administrator. Many of these *misérables* never got beyond the *hôpital* at Moulins on their way to Paris, swelling the intendant's list of mendicants, vagrants, and *gens sans aveu.*[7] There were few alternative occupations to subsistence farming; a few wood merchants floated logs down the Allier, Nièvre, and beyond; there was the usual range of semirural crafts, but almost no mines, forges, or textile mills, not even an exportable wine or brandy.[8] Probably the most lucrative trade was in smuggled salt, for the *gabelle* (salt tax) in the Bourbonnais was considerably less than in neighboring Auvergne.[9] Otherwise, the toll houses at Vichy, Gannat, and Montluçon did their best to discourage any exports of merchandise from Auvergne,[10] so that the Bourbonnais had little transit trade either. There was ample opportunity for Intendant Depont to be a "public improver" in the Bourbonnais.

If this *généralité* did not carry the prestige or amenities of those of Brittany, Bordeaux, or Dijon, much less Paris, it had some institutional advantages for a new intendant. There was no parlement, no provincial estates, no military governor. There was not even a cathedral chapter or a university. There was only a presidial court and a *bureau des finances;* in this respect it resembled La Rochelle. It was a *pays d'éléction* where the central administration had the fewest institutional challenges to its directives. Moreover, even the poverty of the province had some advantages. The resident nobility was reasonably docile; there were no powerful mercantile interests and not too many lawyers. This may have been one of the reasons why Moulins was designed as a beginner's post. Between 1636 and 1790, there were forty-two intendants, or about one every four years who "passed through" the *généralité*.[11] If Depont's thirteen years (1765–78) suggest that he was not among the most favored intendants, one must not forget that Turgot spent an equal time (1761–74) in Limoges, not the economic or cultural center of the realm either. Moreover, it required a decade of continuous administration to have some lasting impact on the local area.[12]

The town of Moulins was a sleepy provincial capital. It was still "a poor, ill-built town" when Arthur Young passed through in 1789; on that occasion the English traveler made one of his usual comments on French "provincial culture." "This capital of Bourbonnais, on the great post-road to Italy, has not an inn equal to the little village of Chavanne ... as to a newspaper, I might as well demand an elephant."[13] Instead of a parlementary square as at Rennes or a palace for the estates as at Dijon, or even a cathedral as at Autun, Moulins had a *caserne,* a military barracks. The very architecture suggests *ennui,* and one is not surprised to read how bored Madame des Escherolles was as a girl, when her father was garrisoned at Moulins, spending her days in interminable *visites* among the local notables.[14]

The official residence of the intendant was the Hôtel d'Ansac on the rue Sainte-Claire. It was in such poor condition that Depont tried to find a new building. The limitations of the public budget, however, forced him to settle for minor renovations, extending a wall here and adding a room there, but apparently with little permanent success.[15] Jean-Samuel kept his *hôtel* in the Marais; indeed much of his correspondence with the controller-general is posted from Paris.[16] His long sojourns in Paris were one aspect of his style of administration.

Like all intendants, Depont had a very small paid staff. Consequently, he had to depend on a few key men for routine work and was obliged to work with other institutions and even independent entrepreneurs for larger projects such as road-building. His subdelegate-general at Moulins, Faulconnier, handled much of the correspondence; the engineer of the *Ponts et Chaussées,* Desvaux, and his assistants were indispensable for the execution of public works; the local receiver-general had to be willing to transfer tax funds to him on convenient terms; and local suppliers of army provisions or entrepreneurs of spinning mills often contributed raw materials or talent necessary to the operation of the public workhouses.[17] Perhaps contracting to entrepreneurs was more convenient than economical, for Depont was criticized later in his career by the new provincial assembly at Metz for not obtaining the best price for army supplies.[18] There was no hint of graft, but rather the suggestion that Depont preferred the easiest way, which was to procure private services.

Depont was chronically late in sending his reports to Paris. Albert, intendant of commerce, and *commis* (chief clerk) of the controller-general, reprimanded Jean-Samuel on more than one occasion. In the spring of 1772 he wrote: "The controller-general [Terray] asked you in a letter of 9 November, 1771 to send your plans for the public works [*travaux de charité*] before the end of December. They have not arrived yet and I am afraid the poor will suffer from this delay. I will not conceal from you the fact that you are the *only one* of all the intendants who have similar projects to execute in their *généralités* who has not yet taken care of this."[19]

The intendant always had an excuse. On this occasion he blamed the slow payment schedule of the receiver-general and the weather. "Yes, I should have sent my *état* in December. But this does not mean that I would have received my money any sooner, since the receiver-general was to pay it in six installments, beginning March 10. One installment would not have been enough to begin my twenty-five *ateliers*. Besides, work begun when it is still cold would not be very solid anyway."[20]

Depont did better with his "paper work" in 1774 and 1775, only to be reprimanded again for tardiness in 1776. This time it was the fault of the engineers. "The difficulty in assembling all the expense accounts as well as the diverse reports of the engineers and the assistant engineers of my department has made me late. I hope that in the future the charity accounts will arrive at the date specified by the minister."[21] When Depont moved on to Metz in 1778, his replacement at Moulins, M. Reverseaux, referred to the "unfinished business" (*tâches arriérées*) from 1777 and 1778, especially the roads in progress. He then turned to the accounts in his letter to Paris. "I take the liberty to reply that the previous accounts will be difficult to straighten out."[22]

It appears that Jean-Samuel was much more effective dealing with administrative problems by face-to-face relationships. Everything points to his charm and affability. He surely knew what he was about when he went to see the intendant of finance, d'Ormesson, personally about more money for public works. "I would have made my complaint earlier, Monsieur, but since I was coming [to Paris] anyway, I thought it preferable to treat the matter orally."[23]

While Intendant de Pont could hardly be called a meticulous administrator, which was infuriating no doubt for "undersecretaries" like d'Ormesson[24] who were painstaking in these matters, he knew his prerogatives and would brook no jurisdictional incursions. With the local *Bureau des Finances* he was firm and on occasion peremptory. Jean-Samuel may have been the son and brother of *trésoriers de France,* but first and foremost he was "the king's man." He may well have read the latest mémoire by Moreau de Beaumont, councilor of state, on the tax powers of the intendants. The key lines were: "the intendant is *to preside at and have principal voice in* the meetings of the Bureau of Finances which receives the royal orders for the levy of the taille."[25] Whether or not he had read Moreau's *mémoire,* Depont treated the *trésoriers* as his subordinates. His letters had the unmistakable tone of authority. "In addition, Messieurs, I had assumed the second *brevet* [letters patent] containing the taxes for the military for 1768 had been deposited at your office immediately after reaching *my departments,* but since I see that it has not been delivered, I am giving my *Bureaux* the necessary orders to assure its delivery."[26] In fact, his failure to supply the *trésoriers* at Moulins with the requisite tax information from Paris may not have been accidental. The previous year, Depont had bypassed the *trésoriers* completely in the task of assessing royal taxes. The Bureau had protested and the controller-general was obliged to intervene. But instead of chastising Depont, he defended his actions against the *trésoriers.*[27] Perhaps L'Averdy was not the thoroughgoing traitor to royal centralization his critics have made of him.[28]

Jean-Samuel did not stop at treating the *trésoriers* as subordinate tax officials; he even tried to tax them. In 1773 he extended the *capitation* to the *trésoriers.* Again, they protested to Paris and received a word of caution from one of their colleagues, M. de Villantroys: " . . . the supplement to the capitation tax was imposed by M. l'Intendant who has included you, Messieurs, in the category of 'privileged.' Until now that rubric has not been used in this way in any other *généralité.* You must appeal to M. l'Intendant, but with considerable circumspection and without losing sight of the authority of the intendants. Their work is always well regarded by the Council [of State] and they can never do wrong."[29] Apparently, Depont enforced the new *vingtième* taxes of 1772 as well. His tax roll reads: "tax to be levied on all property ... owned by nobles, ecclesiastics, *officiers* exempt and privileged [i.e., the *trésoriers*], bourgeois and inhabitants *taillables et non-taillables*."[30]

But surely the most humiliating blow to the Bureau was the matter of recruitment into their "company." Depont was very officious when called upon to arbitrate in a dispute: "The Guardian of the Seals orders me to inform you that you can do nothing better than to admit Sieur de Fontenay into your ranks. Your refusal is all the more baseless since he is educated, is of proper birth [*il est d'une naissance*], and enjoys a fortune respectable enough [*assez honnête*] to hold his office with honor. Therefore, Messieurs, I am assuming that his admission [to your ranks] will encounter no [further] difficulty from you."[31] Talent, Birth, and Fortune should be rewarded, by administrative fiat if necessary.

The *officiers* of Moulins should never forget that Depont was "Intendant of Justice, Police, and Finances." Backed by the royal council, he consolidated his control over municipal finances. In a series of *arrêts* (judgments) by the Council of State between 1765 and 1772, both the *Chambre des Comptes* at Paris and the *Bureau des Finances* at Moulins were prevented from sharing power to audit the accounts of the communities in the *généralité*. Not one new *octroi* (toll) could be levied at the town gates and not one *sou* spent from the proceeds of a communal wood without the intendant's approval. In 1769, for example, Depont's authorization was required before Nevers could build a bridge, a town hall, and barracks.[32] Some intendants, Etigny at Auch for instance, were not very successful in establishing an exclusive control (*tutelle*) over the finances of the local communities, but Depont was not one of them. Bourbonnais, like Bourgogne, witnessed no weakening of royal power over the villages and towns in the last half of the century.[33]

Unlike the tireless Turgot at Limoges, Depont demonstrated only a perfunctory interest in the promotion of agriculture and manufactures. Nor did he advance any general theories of economic growth based on physiocratic principles. If one judges by existing administrative correspondence, horses and silk production were the extent of Jean-Samuel's enthusiasm for "growth." He made a tour of the royal stud farms in the province and assured Bertin, now in charge of procurement for the royal cavalry, that he would identify the best horses. He also had twelve thousand mulberry trees planted and solicited a government bounty of three thousand livres to encourage two small silk establishments at Moulins. One of the entrepreneurs was Edme Joseph Jacquesson de L'Herbut, tax agent for the *vingtièmes* as well as chief steward for the Prince de Condé. He had laid out a series of projects before Depont, including a plan to manufacture chairs, screens, and cotton cloth.[34] But Depont's main preoccupation was the employment of beggars and foundlings. The minister in Paris concurred: "I agree with your own strong conviction that the bounty be used to reward those female spinners who spin the finest thread."[35]

With regard to the grain trade, Depont was not a promoter of "free trade." When it came to finding the necessary food for a chronically undersupplied province, the "free market" held no great attractions. Depont was too close to the rigidities of the market and shared none of Turgot's grim determination to press a principle like free trade to the bitter end.[36] For example, in October 1775, as *grain* prices happily began to fall, Depont was concerned that the price of *bread* drop at the same rate. To his subordinates at Moulins he wrote: "As soon, Messieurs, as the fall in the price of grains begins to be perceptible, the people must receive the same reduction in the price of bread. ... If the bakers' guild [*jurande*] becomes an obstacle to this, please inform me."[37]

Depont had no inhibitions about selling government grain at a loss when hard times required it. In 1771, a very bad year, he wrote:

I have made the greatest effort to alleviate the conditions of the people and to relieve the destitute in particular. I have obtained grain from the neighboring provinces at considerable expense. ... I have had to use considerable sums for these purchases, on which *there is bound to be a loss.* I have also spent money on alms which I have distributed by the municipal officials in the towns and by the curés in the countryside. The suffering [*mal*], however, continues. This *généralité* has been reduced to a terrible state and deserves all the help it can get.[38]

Depont felt that it was incumbent upon him to distribute a very scarce commodity as equitably as possible. Bread was too precious to be left to the free market. Here, as elsewhere, Jean-Samuel was a thoroughgoing pragmatist, and aware of the limits of economic theory.

In 1775, after he had become controller-general, Turgot proposed that the *corvée* be commuted and road construction paid for by special taxes. He consulted all the intendants on the matter. Depont replied enthusiastically that he had already persuaded the village communities to "repurchase" their obligations for labor services on the royal roads. He even insisted that in the assessment of the new road tax, "no one be exempt," specifying the Church, the Privileged, the Princes of the Blood, the Royal Domain—all property owners, "in proportion to their landed revenue."[39] Depont appeared as a more committed "fiscal egalitarian" than the other intendants who replied to Turgot's circular letter.[40] Most of the intendants simply proposed a supplement to the *vingtième,* thus avoiding any new attempt to tax the "privileged" by means of a reassessment of revenues—the dreaded new *cadastre.*

Two years later, the progress made in road-building in the province earned Depont high praise from the controller-general. "I must praise your administration for the thoroughness with which you have executed the directives of the Council concerning the construction of the *grandes routes* without *corvées* in 1776. The minister is equally satisfied with the construction accomplished in 1774 and 1775 to facilitate communication on the secondary roads."[41] Depont was also careful to compensate the proprietors dispossessed by the new royal roads from a special tax imposed for this purpose.[42]

The most original aspect of the government's policy of public works in the 1770s was the new use of the *ateliers de charité* for poor relief. The idea of State-financed enterprises to put the poor to work was not new in 1770, but Turgot's experiments with them in Limoges encouraged the central administration to extend the projects throughout the kingdom. The *atelier* scheme was intended to reach beyond the chronic beggar and vagabond to offer a supplementary income to the seasonally unemployed, especially to women and children whose ordinary day-wages were so pitifully low. The *ateliers* were not intended to be permanent, nor were they to replace other more traditional forms of Church and private charity, but it is easy to understand how they quickly exhausted the public funds allotted to them.[43] The bad harvest years of 1769–72 placed an especially heavy burden on the *ateliers*.

Jean-Samuel Depont had special reasons to welcome any new effort to help the poor; in addition to his own *misérables*, he had to deal with those Auvergnats who flooded north in the dead season. In mid-December of 1770, a "bad year," he wrote to d'Ormesson, undersecretary in charge of public welfare: "Here we are, Monsieur, in the hardest days of winter. Public works have been halted almost everywhere and the first frost will end them for good. There is not a moment to lose in preparing the relief measures the minister intends for the people."[44] He asked permission to use all the funds granted to his *généralité* from the *taille* for direct charity (*aumônes*) to the poor and destitute. He had spent the grant of the previous year in this way and said it had saved "many lives" even though the formal instructions from Paris had earmarked sixty thousand livres for tax reduction and the remaining twenty-five thousand for public works (*travaux de charité*).[45] Depont explained that, although the proprietors and tenant farmers (*fermiers*) would not receive the tax relief His Majesty had intended, direct charity would help them as well since they would not have to feed the poor. Jean-Samuel never seemed to take the "letter" of the regulations too seriously. But d'Ormesson in Paris did. "However honorable your motives in deviating from the rules prescribed by His Majesty, I cannot approve of the fact that you have taken it upon yourself not to conform to them. Regretfully, I must tell you that I will be very unhappy if such a thing were to happen again. I am convinced, however, that I shall not have another occasion to reproach you in this way. I shall forget this episode in order to cooperate with you for the good of the généralité."[46]

Rebuked by his superior, Depont pleaded that at least the allotment for public works be increased to forty thousand livres, an absolute minimum in his opinion. He did not favor direct tax rebates to the landowners who did not necessarily use these sums to feed their sharecroppers and farmhands, much less to make charitable contributions to the bureaux de charité. On the contrary, observed Depont, in hard times the landowners, large and small, were apt to dismiss their bordiers and valets.[47] "As for the ateliers, as long as that is what you insist on, it is impossible to do the slightest bit of good with less than 40,000. As for the rest of the grant (45,000) it will be used according to your orders. But I must tell you that this is the first time I have been criticized in the six years I have administered this province. The infinite gratitude of a mass of unfortunates [malheureux] whom I have helped by deviating a little from the rules would console me if I did not wish, above everything else, to merit your approval."[48] In fact, Depont had not been the only intendant to "deviate from the rules" that year. Turgot at Limoges apologized for the "considerable deficit," largely due to relief measures, but pleaded that the public service rendered "might merit some approval."[49]

By 1771, Depont's reports on the ateliers began to arrive in Paris. One has an impression of large quantities of earth and gravel being moved about in baskets, stone replacing wood as canal linings, drainage improved, even garbage hauled away from the churchyards. Each of seventeen projects of that year contains an estimate of work days required and the daily cost at 12 sous per man, 10 per woman, and 8 per child. Depont estimated the total cost for 1771 at 40,220 livres, "which would employ 1,941 men for two months." Given a provincial population of about 500,000, such relief was clearly inadequate.[50]

Aside from enlisting the help of the engineers from the Ponts et Chaussées and procuring the minimum of tools and baskets, the main problem was obtaining the money from Paris. Even when the sum was authorized, payment via the local receiver-general of taxes was not immediately forthcoming. One of them wrote to the minister as if the collected taxes were not really public funds. ". . . it is clear that the intendants think they can draw on the receivers-general without any advance planning as if this service were easily performed and as if they had these sums readily at hand, which is very unfair. No doubt that in hard times like these, everyone is prepared to sacrifice his own interest, but such requests must be limited to what is possible and not considered an obligation."[51] The letter would be inexplicable if we did not know that as a financier, the receiver-general "placed" the public funds in short-term loans (six months) and could not raise the capital on very short notice. Jean-Samuel was well aware of these operations—his father-in-law profited from them—but as intendant he did not hesitate to press the receivers for payment.[52]

This was a particularly bad year. The word "desperate" appears three times in Depont's letters in early 1771 to d'Ormesson.[53] By November the bands of poor from the south had inflated the numbers on the roads so that they constituted a menace to security. A petition from the canton of Bourbon asked Depont "to prohibit 'squatting' and building huts along the main road by people who are in extreme misery and who frighten regular travelers."[54] It was a nationwide phenomenon. Throughout the 1770s and 1780s, writes Olwen Hufton, there was a "rising tide of vagrant bands" intimidating the countryside.[55]

The royal government never intended that the *ateliers* be paid entirely from public funds. Since the roads benefited the larger landowners who would use them, the government argued, plausibly, that these people should contribute to their construction. Initially, Depont had some difficulty getting private individuals to pay anything, and the controller-general's office had still another occasion to criticize him. "I notice with distress the indifference of the clergy and of the seigneurs of the parishes of your *généralité*. The comparisons I have made between a number of other *généralités* and yours lead me to believe that the importance of His Majesty's charity has not been sufficiently understood. More zeal in seconding his beneficent views should be demonstrated and I urge you to renew your efforts with those persons in a position to contribute to this relief work."[56] The polite use of the passive form could not disguise the reprimand.

Although Depont was able to enlist the help of a few *gentilshomes* and *bourgeois aisés* at Montluçon to form a "Bureau of Alms,"[57] his superiors complained again the following spring. "It appears that your efforts to make the rich proprietors contribute [to the *ateliers*] have been no more successful than last year. At least I presume that you have done everything possible to stimulate their zeal. Your *généralité* is the only one where there is so much indifference."[58]

By 1773, however, Depont began to report participation by local notables. On a brand new form Depont began to list these contributors—sums of 300 to 600 livres from a dozen resident *gentilshommes-campagnards* and a few churchmen.[59] At the end of the year, Depont handed in his accounts for 1773 and projects for 1774—apparently on time—and received a compliment. His superior was "edified by the zeal of the seigneurs and rich proprietors" which Depont had done so much to stimulate.[60]

Jean-Samuel had suffered from invidious comparison with other inten-
dants regarding his late reports and his lack of zeal in prodding private
contributions to charity. He also had complaints from the local nobility.
In a letter sent directly to d'Ormesson in Paris, one Comtesse de Saint-
Georges began by describing the misery on her estate in the remote Haute
Marche, claiming that "people by the hundreds" came to her gate every
night. "The intendant of Limousin [Turgot] does things for the cantons.
M. Depont, our intendant, sends only the modest sum of two thousand
livres into the small towns of this province. Only the poor of the towns are
admitted to these *ateliers;* the poor of the countryside groan and starve to
death. Yet they are the ones who keep us alive by their hard work. . . . If
we do not help them, the land will not be tilled this year. The seigneurs are
doing what they can for their vassals, but since the harvest was ruined,
they do not have anything either."[61] Albert, d'Ormesson's *commis,* forwarded this letter to Depont with the subtle recommendation: "I notice
that you place almost all your *ateliers* in the towns, but I presume that the
poor inhabitants of the countryside are admitted there as well. Otherwise,
the intentions of his Majesty would not be fulfilled."[62] Again, Depont was
not following the rules to the letter, but in this instance the ministry
seemed more tolerant. With only about forty thousand livres to spend, Depont had to pick his locations carefully. Although he did establish some of
his twenty-five *ateliers* in the least accessible districts such as Combrailles,
he concentrated most of them on the main highway north and south of
Moulins in the eastern half of the province.[63] This was the route by which
the dreaded Auvergnats would arrive after the harvest season. The intendant of Auvergne at Clermont had also concentrated his *ateliers* in the
towns, claiming that his seventy-five thousand livres were simply not
enough to do anything for the countryside.[64]

In the eyes of the central administration Jean-Samuel's performance as
intendant of Moulins was not altogether exemplary. True, he had consolidated the fiscal powers of his office at the expense of such local rivals
as the Bureau of Finances, and increased his *tutelle* over the villages. His
road building was praised, at least by 1777. But his handling of poor relief
not only failed to conform to bureaucratic routine in the submission of
reports, but also deviated from policy directives. Depont first favored
direct charity instead of the *ateliers,* then spent the entire annual welfare
budget on the *ateliers* instead of earmarking a large part for tax relief,
then failed to enlist any private contributions, and finally failed to move
the *ateliers* about the countryside. Perhaps it was this kind of "independence" that kept him thirteen years at Moulins.

It would be futile to argue that Jean-Samuel was a model intendant.
There was an element of carelessness in his behavior that did not make for
bonne administration, at least as a d'Ormesson or a Turgot understood it.

When the minister praised "zeal," he usually meant "exactitude" in following the directives of the office of the controller-general. Jean-Samuel Depont was not made this way. Having spent the first forty years of his life resisting the admonitions of his father, the prescriptions of his church, the mores of his provincial origins, why should he slavishly follow the orders of a d'Ormesson or even a Turgot? Moreover, there was more to it than "carelessness" or "independence." Depont had his own ideas about how to treat the poor, and these ideas differed from the official position adopted by Turgot, controller-general, 1774–76.

Turgot had written that "the *bureaux* of charity must never lose sight of the fact that public aid for real poverty must never serve as an encouragement to idleness." Except for the sick and the aged, Turgot opposed direct aid to the poor, and emphasized employment of the able-bodied in public works. He also preferred that poor families be paid in food, "since wages were too often dissipated in the *cabarets*."[65] As intendant at Limoges, for example, Turgot paid poor persons who worked in the *ateliers* 3 sous and 1.5 pounds of bread daily.[66] Depont, on the other hand, never referred to the laziness (*fainéantise*) or drunkenness of the poor. He paid them in coin—12 sous per day for men, 10 for women. He gave up direct charity, one recalls, only under administrative pressure. When the central office wanted his reports to measure in actual paving stone the work accomplished, he replied that "the accomplishment cannot be measured in *toises* [cubic feet]."[67]

But most important, Depont did not regard the *ateliers* as crisis or temporary relief, but potentially, it seems, as a permanent source of ancillary income for a part of the population that would always be *misérable*. In one of his letters to d'Ormesson, after mentioning the new roads and the grain they could now handle, he wrote:

The *ateliers* have another, even greater advantage. They have permitted a portion of the people to live during the hardest months of the year. It is that portion which *can never be well enough off* and whom we call *locataires* or *journaliers* in the countryside and the children of winegrowers, *jardiniers*, and other types in the towns. This is a charity which does not degrade one's spirits and makes for respectable citizens. If the ministry wishes to continue this successful project, there is every reason to believe that in the next ten years the whole province will be transformed.[68]

Unrealistic though the statement may have been, it was a tribute to Jean-Samuel's more generous inclinations—inclinations that were not widely shared by his colleagues in Paris or his forebears in La Rochelle.[69]

In December, 1774, Jean-Samuel was made *maître des requêtes honoraire*, giving him "rank, presence, voice, and opinion" in the Parlement of Paris. He must have reflected as he read the lines of the royal *brevet:* "Desiring to recompense the services that he has rendered Us for more than twenty-four consecutive years ... and the example of his ancestors who have distinguished themselves in important posts conferred on them by Our Predecessors. ..." Among the distinguished ancestors was his grandfather, "president of the Chamber of Commerce at La Rochelle."[70] His father, Paul-François, had died the previous June. Jean-Samuel himself was approaching fifty. Was this the end of a long climb from commercial and provincial horizons to honorable status as intendant of one of the more mediocre *généralités* of the kingdom?

Although he lived at Moulins only part of the year, he made efforts to improve his provincial surroundings. His colleague and friend, Jacques Flesselles, the previous intendant, had built a bridge across the Allier[71] and also contributed money to the restoration of the old Jesuit *collège.* One of Depont's first gestures on behalf of his "capital" was a gift of 1,200 livres for an iron gate for the *collège* with the appropriate inscription: *Collegium Restauratum.*[72] During his thirteen years, Depont's urban improvements ranged from such relatively minor embellishments as repairing the clocktower and building public fountains to constructing new streets and sewage canals. The filthy sludge from the town's tanneries that flowed down an open stream into the Allier River was channeled through a covered aqueduct. The intendant also built new boulevards,[73] provided street lamps, and was the first to mark the street names on plaques and number the houses. He also planted linden trees along the boulevards. The quays along the river were enlarged to house a depot for wine and foodstuffs and another for lumber. He drained the marshes which encircled the town's prisons. Much of this work was done over the protests of the Bureau of Finances, which objected to the cost. In addition, the large quantities of wood used for construction made Moulins susceptible to fire, one of which ravaged the entire town in 1755, while another burned down the faubourg Chaveau in 1778.[74]

From what we know about Jean-Samuel's father-in-law—*intendant des menus plaisirs du Roy*—and his social life in Paris, we can assume that he must have been particularly adept at organizing the town *fêtes,* especially on the occasion of the passage through Moulins by members of the court *noblesse*—Conti, Bourbon-Lamballe, the Italian brides of the king's brothers, Provence and Artois—on their way to take the waters at Bourbon or Vichy. Paul-François may have taken a dim view of Intendant Le Peletier's celebrations at La Rochelle, but as royal intendant Jean-Samuel organized and enjoyed concerts, illuminations, and fireworks. He was equally proficient at arranging ceremonies for the "great events" of the reign—public prayers on the death of the Dauphin (1766), Maria Leczinska (1768), and Louis XV (1774), as well as the more festive celebration of the coronation of Louis XVI. An unexpected ceremonial occasion was created by the death of the archbishop of Cambrai, Monseigneur de Choiseul-Stainville, who died suddenly while visiting Depont at the intendance in 1774. It was characteristic of the intendant's relations with the Bureau of Finances that they should quarrel over the quality of the musicians at the concerts and complain of the cost of the local Academy of Music of which Depont was president. In 1777 the Bureau criticized certain "abuses" recently introduced into the concerts, such as dancing.[75] Moulins would never be Paris.

In 1778 Jean-Samuel was named intendant of Metz, a much more important post. A few weeks before his departure from Moulins, the municipality decided to establish a monument at the entrance to the new "covered market" in Depont's honor. The deliberation of the town council included these lines: ". . . to perpetuate the memory of the beneficence and the generosity that have marked the administration of M. Depont and to express the recognition that our fellow citizens will always have for all the useful and imporant projects that he has accomplished in this city, for its embellishment as well as for the purety and salubrity of its air."[76] Due allowance made for the ceremonial imperatives of the occasion, the municipality had reason to be thankful to Jean-Samuel. In the province at large, Depont had his critics—the Bureau of Finances and certain proprietors like Comtesse de Saint-Georges—but perhaps his solicitude for the poor, restrained by slender budgetary allowances from Paris, deserved the greatest praise.

In 1790 Metz had thirty-six thousand people, a number almost equal to Strasbourg or Toulouse, three times the size of Moulins, and twice the size of La Rochelle. It possessed three thousand houses and sixty-one churches and chapels, a high per capita ratio of housing and religious "capacity," and a reputation for good sanitary conditions and a relatively low rate of disease. The city had a parlement, a cathedral and an archbishop, a military governor and a large garrison, in addition to its *bureau des finances* and tax receivers. Although Parisian visitors like Voltaire might have found its fortresslike atmosphere a bit austere, Metz was a real metropolis on the main road from Paris to Strasbourg on the Rhine. Nor was Metz an isolated urban center; the towns of Nancy, Toul, Verdun, Pont-à-Mousson, Lunéville were nearby and distinctly more cosmopolitan than Montluçon or Gannat in remote Bourbonnais. The town hall was an impressive new stone building, as was the parlement, and the intendant's residence was a spacious eighteenth-century town house with inner court and large windows. Although the old court of the dukes of Lorraine was at Nancy, Metz boasted a cultural life with its academy of science, *collèges, patois* literature, theater, and Masonic lodges.

The new theater had nightly performances with a repertoire that included Molière's comedies, Voltaire's tragedies, Marivaux's *Le Jeu de l'Amour* and Beaumarchais's *Le Barbier de Séville*. *Le Bourgeois Gentilhomme* and *L'Avare* were special favorites of the Messins and may have elicited a wry smile from the new intendant who surely attended the theater. The royal academy held weekly meetings and sponsored essay contests on serious subjects of public importance, ranging from agriculture to civil equality. The subject of the competition for 1787 was: *"Est-il des moyens de rendre les juifs plus utiles et plus heureux?"* With a Jewish population of two thousand, the issue was a pressing one at Metz. Among the essays submitted to the secretary of the academy was one by an obscure curé from a village in Lorraine, an abbé Grégoire. His "Mémoire sur les Juifs" won the *concours*, an indication of the liberal tendencies of the local academy, especially its leaders Roederer and Le Payen.[77]

The *généralité* of Trois-Evêchés was one of two carved out of newly annexed Lorraine (1766). If the loyalty of its 350,000 inhabitants was less assured than the passive obedience of those of Moulins, they had a reputation for greater discipline and hard work. Although there were still active Jewish and Protestant communities, the Catholic Reformation had made its mark, not only on church architecture, but especially on education. The region was one of the most literate in the kingdom.[78] By the end of the century, it was also in the process of economic growth. In addition to exports of farm produce, salt, wine, and brandy, Lorraine began to industrialize. With forest covering more than one-quarter of the surface of the *généralité,* there was abundant fuel for new iron forges, glassworks, and paper mills.[79] Metz was clearly a step up from Moulins.

It is not surprising that even the intendant's stationery assumed new dignity. Capped by a simple classic decoration, the printed name "Jean de Pont" now headed each official letter, followed by his full title, functions, and dignities:

Chevalier, Seigneur de Manderoux, Forges, Pindelouat, and other places, Councilor of the King in His Council, Honorary Councilor of the Parlement of Paris, *Maîtres des Requêtes* in His *Hôtel,* INTENDANT of Justice, Police, and Finance in the Department of Metz, Frontier of Champagne, Luxembourg and the Saar.[80]

The "Samuel" had been dropped; the prefix of the surname was detached and his principal seigneury was added. Thus, "Jean-Samuel Depont" became "Jean de Pont de Manderoux." As intendant of a "frontier province," he now reported to the minister of war, the Comte de Saint-Germain.[81] After 1779, his regular residence was given in the *Almanach Royal* as 11, rue des Filles Saint-Thomas. It is not surprising, therefore, that the phrase "in the absence of M. l'Intendant" appears more than once in the administrative correspondence from Metz to Paris.[82]

But though Metz was a more prosperous, urban post, it presented Depont with institutional competition. The Parlement of Metz had been reinstalled in October 1775, with the support of the archbishop, the governor, and even Depont's predecessor, Calonne.[83] It was apparently a popular local institution, especially after its four years of suppression under the "Maupeou Reforms." Consequently, much local administration, especially with regard to the grain trade, the local guilds, and religious questions had to be shared with the parlement. In 1787 the provincial assemblies were created, and assumed extensive local power over tax assessment and public works. Although the intendant presided at the sessions of the assembly at Metz, his policy-making power was substantially reduced.[84] It appears that Depont adapted to this new situation. His respect for the parlement is indicated by the fact that he placed his son in the "company" in 1784 when the young man was seventeen years old.[85] The Parlement of Metz was a testing ground for young magistrates and known for its many newcomers launching their careers in the high administration.[86] As for the new provincial assembly, Depont apparently met Mgr. de Fontanges, the bishop of Nancy, who presided over the assembly there. Depont's daughter was to marry a Fontanges in 1788.[87]

In other ways, Depont's style of administration had not changed. He still overspent his budget and delayed filing his reports with the intendant of finance at Paris. Depont's predecessor, Calonne, showed a small surplus on the budget for provincial stud farms. But soon after Jean-Samuel's arrival, the deficits began to accumulate. Although his *états* were as neat and complete as Calonne's, Depont was full of new proposals "for the complete overhaul of this establishment" with "the small means at my disposal."[88] He complained about the small salaries of the "service employees" but stressed that "by economizing" he hoped to improve the "race" of horses with several new "mares of distinguished breeding." He also mentioned in a postscript that he was looking for an Arab horse for the minister.[89]

In a *mémoire* to the war office in 1780, Depont stressed the progress already made and the need to sustain it with more funds. "Last year I made a complete tour of my *généralité* with a cavalry officer who knows his horses and we were astonished at the progress made. The horses at Longwy, Etaing, Verdun, Carignan, and Saarlouis sell at 10 to 15 louis [240 to 360 livres]. M. Calonne received 5,000 livres over his regular budget. ... We need 8 to 10,000 to replace the stud horses. M. le Prince de Montbarey [minister of war] might look at what they are spending in Lorraine and Alsace. ... We are infinitely more advanced [than they] in this matter."[90]

Depont revealed a certain expertise on the subject of pasturage, an issue that had implications for French agriculture as a whole. He mentioned that he had reviewed Calonne's correspondence on the horse farms and personally visited those parts of the *généralité* watered by the Moselle River. He condemned local communal practices of pasturage (*vaine pâture* and *parcours*) which "degraded" the meadows. He supported the right to enclose the land and encouraged the planting of artificial meadows. But aside from endorsing legislation such as Bertin's edict of 1768 "permitting enclosure," he did not make any proposals for spreading modern agricultural techniques by means of model farms, for example. As Arthur Young had so often said, the royal administration knew about artificial meadows, but was unable to persuade either gentry or peasants to plant them.[91]

Depont was always generous with his staff, including bonuses in his budget for his subdelegates and other employees. But after the establishment of the provincial assembly at Metz in 1787, the annual budget of the *généralité* was audited by a committee of that body of thirty-two notables.[92] In July 1788, the committee claimed that Depont's budget of 52,650 livres could be reduced to 45,147 livres. "Circumstances do not permit this extra expense," they informed the controller-general in Paris. Depont had asked not only for bonuses for the subdelegates and the veterinarians treating the cattle plague, but also for "relief to those whose homes were burned down and other individuals stricken with misfortune."[93] The committee of the provincial assembly wanted to use the entire sum for the travel and personal expenses of the deputies during the sessions.[94]

On another occasion the finance committee objected to Depont's buying wood for the army from a single supplier. "Such a contract," read the minutes, "provides the entrepreneur with an opportunity to create a monopoly of the wood supply . . . giving him control of the price. . . . It is calculated from the average price of wood in the capital of the province, which is always well above prices in the local areas. Here the entrepreneur finds subcontractors on whom he makes a very large profit, and they in turn make theirs." The assembly advised the intendant to deal directly with local wood merchants in the future. Depont had accumulated a debt to the wood entrepreneur of almost 140,000 livres in three years.[95] There is no direct evidence that Depont was profiting personally from army-supply contracts, though arrangements such as this gave him an excellent opportunity to do so. On the other hand, convenience always counted for something with Jean-Samuel; competitive bidding required close "on-the-spot" supervision.

Letters were sent by the permanent committee of the new provincial assembly directly to the controller-general in Paris, most of them necessarily relating to the work of the intendant. It must have irritated Depont to have this new body corresponding with Paris, though outwardly at least he maintained a discreet and even patronizing attitude. Referring to one of the assembly's reports forwarded to him by the controller-general, he commented: "I notice nothing in this report that does not conform to the principles of moderation and equity, which they would be well advised not to ignore." Jean-Samuel had mastered the innocuous formulas of public administration. In addition, he knew that the Calonne experiment in provincial assemblies was a new, and perhaps temporary one, which should not be allowed to degenerate into "tumult," a common fear of the central administration. How appropriate that the intendant of Metz should stress "moderation."[96]

In a "frontier province" it was normal that much of an intendant's energies be devoted to raising cavalry horses and gathering army supplies for a large garrison.[97] But there were other problems as well. Despite the relative dynamism of the province, it had its poor and destitute. Although there is no information on the *ateliers de charité* at Metz, there is some regarding the *dépôt de mendicité*. Here Depont's lack of "exactitude" and his budgetary deficits suggested a genuine sympathy for the *misérables*, as it had at Moulins.

Poor relief throughout the kingdom was reorganized by the L'Averdy commission in 1764. The commission proposed the establishment of two or three poorhouses (*dépôts de mendicité*) in each *généralité* in which all "beggars" would be confined. It also attempted to draw distinctions between "beggars" and "vagabonds," between the permanently destitute and the seasonally unemployed, and between the able-bodied and the sick, insane, orphaned, or aged. Unlike the *hôpitaux* and other private charitable organizations, the new *dépôts* were placed under the intendant as agent of the State. It marked a major advance for exclusively *public* welfare in France. Unfortunately, the State had few funds and the need was enormous. Consequently the treatment of the poor became increasingly subject to budgetary considerations, and the various efforts at classification and selection were intended to weed out the "less deserving" and put the able-bodied of the inmates to work, converting parts of the *dépôts* into shops or mills.[98] The "work ethic" also conditioned the attitudes of administrators. The controller-general and *intendants des finances* like Turgot or d'Ormesson cautioned the intendants about opening the *dépôts* to everyone who claimed to be destitute. Fraud and laziness would not be condoned or encouraged. Nor would public begging.

Like so many of his colleagues, Jean-Samuel was severely hampered by lack of funds. The *dépôt de mendicité* at Metz when he arrived was pitifully underequipped for the task at hand. It consisted of twenty rooms (one *infirmerie*), a chapel with one room for the almoner, eighty-eight camp cots, a few wooden tables, and six chamberpots. Each room had about ten beds, each with one blanket, placed against the walls with a table in the middle. The straw mattresses, bedding, and clothing, including 32 coats, 32 *culottes*, 145 skirts, 32 pairs of socks, and 32 *sabots*, were all characterized as *"très mauvaises"* and *"usés"* in 1776.[99] In fact, there was talk of closing the *dépôt* in 1776, but Calonne argued for its continued use, especially in order to keep diseased prostitutes away from the garrison "until they are cured." He suggested that the *dépôt* be renamed a *"renfermerie,"* as indeed he might, since every inmate was threatened by venereal disease.[100]

No wonder that the central government was concerned about the types of people placed in the *dépôts* of the kingdom. In 1780 it was disclosed that the Bertrand family, *Bourgeois de Metz*, was using the *dépôt* to discipline a wayward son, in the same manner that Vincennes was used to keep the younger Mirabeau out of trouble. The *lettre de cachet* was addressed to the intendant asking him "to give orders that Pierre Bertrand, their son, age thirty-five, at present in detention in the *dépôt de mendicité* of this city, be kept there until he has given proof of good conduct." The parents offered to pay 120 livres for room and board, which no doubt tempted the administration to comply.[101]

The *dépôt* was also used to imprison authentic criminals. In 1779 the intendant of Châlons reported that his mounted police (*maréchaussée*) had arrested "a very suspicious beggar without a passport," "scar on his right temple," age twenty-two, now in prison in Reims. He asked Depont if this individual had escaped from the *dépôt* at Metz.[102] Ten years later there were two criminals in the *dépôt* sent by the intendant of Nancy on the excuse that they were born in Metz.[103] The ministry hoped to have the expenses for these men paid by their parents, a budgetary optimism that Depont could not share. As criminals, he said, they are outside of "society"; their parents do not have to support them. In addition, they have been "whipped and branded" for their theft, and are therefore not in condition to work.[104] Yet "the presence of these criminals makes a very bad impression on the morale of the other inmates." At least Jean-Samuel was capable of grasping the human situation beyond the bureaucratic formulas.

The winter and spring of 1789 were as horrendous at Metz as everywhere else in France. The Moselle River froze and all the grain mills stopped, depriving the region of badly needed flour. Thanks to the bishop, the Benedictines, the town notables, and even the army, the city's poor did not starve; there were no food riots that spring.[105] But budgetary restrictions were worse than ever. Depont asked for raises in salary for the personnel at the *dépôt* only to have the *intendant des finances* at Paris ask him to lower salaries and reduce the staff. The physician, the apothecary, and the second guard (*porte-clef*) would have to go; the remaining surgeon was compensated for his extra work load with a raise in salary—to four hundred livres, about twice the wage of a day laborer.[106]

In April 1789 Depont submitted a report on the *dépôt*. Far from having placed everyone in the prescribed classifications and removed those whose presence was unauthorized, Depont drew a picture of a *dépôt* that resembles the Soho society of Bertolt Brecht. There were criminals, beggars, prostitutes, pregnant women, children of all ages, and the insane. Depont argued that they should be kept on even if their terms had expired. In the spring of 1789, it was better to be in a somber *dépôt* than on the road. His report touched each of the cases—the orphans kept "by pity" (*commisération*), the sick retained as "kinds of servants" since they were not well enough to support themselves, the pregnant women or those who had just given birth to be cared for so they could nurse the babies properly, the prostitutes infected with venereal disease retained until cured, and so on. He promised to remove those (male or female) who had "unnatural sentiments," but in general he was reluctant to "release" anyone. He was particularly eloquent in his defense of the insane: "If it is absolutely necessary I will expel these unfortunate human beings, deprived of their reason, incapable of sustaining themselves—a few cannot even speak—but the mounted police will bring them back immediately after they have left."[107]

The reply of the secretary, La Millière, was somewhat less sympathetic. He gave grudging approval to the extension of "terms of detention," warning Depont to follow the *règlements* in the future. He agreed that "the debauched girls" with *maladie vénérienne* should not be released and that the women have their babies in the *dépôt*. However, he advised that the babies be put out to wet-nurses in the countryside and kept there permanently. It was less costly and "children raised in the countryside will acquire a taste for hard work and develop healthy and robust constitutions." Like many Parisians, La Millière apparently believed the myth of the healthy countryside.[108]

Three months later the number of beggars and vagabonds had increased everywhere and Depont no doubt found his small staff inadequate.[109] In July 1789, he abandoned direct administration of the *dépôt* and contracted with an entrepreneur to employ the able-bodied in the manufacture of linen and woolen cloth. Monsieur Maubougard agreed "to employ without interruption all the able-bodied inmates (*renfermés valides*) of both sexes confined in the *dépôt de mendicité* in the city of Metz." He supplied the raw wool and flax as well as the tools—spindles, spinning wheels, brakes, nails—and promised to pay so much for a prescribed measurement of spun cloth. The proceeds would be distributed each week in the following proportions: to the inmates (33 percent), to the manager (*régisseur*) (25 percent), and to the entrepreneur (42 percent). The poorhouse had become a workhouse, an *atelier*.[110]

But there could not have been a worse year for cloth sales. Added to the "change of administration" as it was called by more sanguine contemporaries, the conditions of 1789 assured a business failure. Instead of solving the problem of chronic deficits, the debts for supplies of food accumulated rapidly. A year later, as the secretary in Paris tried to sort out the accounts, Depont urged him to grant the manager an indemnity for his losses. There was no money for "indemnities" in the spring of 1790. The best Depont could do was to provide a new kettle for the soup kitchen.[111]

At sixty-five years of age, Jean-Samuel resigned his post of intendant with dignity, carrying on certain administrative tasks after his official termination in January 1790, until the new administration was in place in June.[112] In March 1790, he responded to a national appeal for a census of the poor from the new committee of the National Assembly on mendicity with more than his usual dispatch. "This will not be easy to do right away. The mounted police, for example, has been arresting vagabonds and vagrants but has not kept records on the parish beggars. I will have to contact each of the parish *curés*. It is difficult enough to account for the resident beggars. Each week the poor of one parish move all over the neighboring parishes. ... I shall send you a report in one month at the latest."[113]

In January 1790, the municipality made Jean-Samuel honorary citizen of Metz. The Moniteur in Paris carried this notice:

The Municipal Committee [of Metz] wishing to give M. de Pont, intendant of the province, a sincere testimony to his administration, which has always been active, mild, and enlightened, charitable in bad times, always wise and moderate in the most difficult circumstances, and wishing also to preserve our relations with this magistrate who will always be cherished by this city, ... and even if, because of a new order of things, M. de Pont must relinquish his duties and leave us, we have unanimously decreed to award him HONORARY CITIZENSHIP of the City of Metz.[114]

One should not make too much of such deliberations. There is no evidence that peasants left their plows or artisans their benches to "salute" their intendant of the past twelve years. The early years of the Revolution were replete with such rhetorical flourishes of national solidarity, usually climaxing with an enormous patriotic banquet at the townhall. A better testimony to Depont's success as an administrator was in a letter of the new city government, regarding the *dépôt de mendicité*. It said they knew that "this service had been well run under the previous administration."[115]

One is tempted to defend Jean-Samuel Depont, not as an exemplary, meticulous administrator, but as a humane one. One could make a case for his "independence" permitting a certain generosity to staff, colleagues, and associates as well as to the mass of *malheureux* of Moulins and Metz. Yet on balance, Zoltan Harsany's evaluation of the intendant of Metz seems more accurate. "Well-liked at Metz, [Depont] was satisfied with informing the government about the economic activities of the region and expediting tax collection, [but] his name cannot be associated with any reform or social innovation, and he seemed satisfied *not* to have attracted any public hostility"[116] (italics mine). Surely he was a likable person, but his amiability was apparently earned negatively, by avoiding controversial projects, by leaving major reforms to others. He was no innovator, no Turgot, which is not to say he was indifferent to his *administrés* or incompetent in the performance of routine duties. Perhaps the historian is not obliged to explain why the run-of-the-mill administrator is what he is. The exceptional calls for explanation.

It seems obvious, however, that somewhere in the 1770s Jean-Samuel's career lost its momentum. He spent his forties, his best years, in Moulins, which, if not the "Siberia" of the kingdom, was something very close to it. Why did he not move on sooner? Did his patrons in Paris, so carefully cultivated and assiduously nurtured, desert him? Had he placed too much stock in his undeniable talent for sociability and personal relations and not enough in professional application? The Old Regime, as Jean-Samuel's father had recognized, was not built exclusively on birth, patronage, and social savoir-faire; in administration, constant application and zeal counted too. The social imperatives of Parisian society had exacted their toll.

How did Depont compare with other intendants of his age and background? If we compare him to his four colleagues in the "class of 1760-65"—Flesselles, Le Peletier de Morfontaine, Taboureau des Réaux, or Perrin de Cypierre—they too remained for long periods in one post, but their *généralités* were more prestigious—Lyon, Soissons, Valenciennes, and Orléans.[117] The other four "new Parisians" were sent to Grenoble, Bordeaux, Alençon, and Orléans, also a cut above Moulins, though perhaps not above Metz. Superficially, Depont's career most closely paralleled those of Chazerat at Riom (1771–90), Depré de Saint-Maur at Bourges (1764–76), and La Bourdonnaye de Blossac at Poitiers (1751–84).[118] But such sketchy career profiles tell us little, except to suggest that "new blood" does not guarantee top performance. The price of social adaptation may, in some subtle way, be paid for in professional drive.

The explanation in Depont's case may be simple. The capital may have crippled him for further adaptation. He was obviously very much tied to Paris from the start of his career. He kept his residence in the capital and in 1773 even bought a larger *hôtel* in the Marais quarter. He conducted much of his administration from Paris, visiting d'Ormesson and other ministers in their *hôtels*, but at the cost of inspection tours of his *généralité*.[119] His residence at Moulins seems like an outpost, one that he was never able to repair fully and where certainly his wife rarely stayed. Even his priorities in administering public works might be seen as a reflection of a myopic urbanity. Depont planted linden trees and named the streets near his townhouse in Moulins; he did not place the *ateliers de charité* in the rural cantons. His tight Parisian world opened on a rural horizon that seemed less familiar and more distasteful to him the closer he came to it. Like his father, *notable* of La Rochelle, Jean-Samuel in turn became a prisoner of his own milieu—Paris.

CHAPTER SEVEN

Douceur de Vivre

The four-day coach ride from the Marais quarter of Paris to the rue du Palais at La Rochelle separated two quite different worlds. Paris—brillant capital of a great world power, where ministers of State amassed reports from the most remote provinces, where venerable magistrates, like Roman senators, handed down solemn decisions on constitutional law, where agile-minded financiers raised millions for the insatiable royal coffers, and where salons sparkled with the latest in science, politics, art, and *agrément*. La Rochelle—provincial port, already past its prime as the magnetic pole of a triangular trade with Africa and the West Indies, as the old Huguenot *armateurs* placed more of their diminishing "real profits" from the slave and sugar trade into vineyards, drained meadowland, and salt marshes in the hinterland. An increasingly quiet town with a growing component of *officiers* and *rentiers*, La Rochelle in 1780 remained dominated by a tight circle of Protestant families whose Calvinist austerity did little to stimulate local intellectual speculation and cultural effervescence. Surely Jean-Samuel Depont was reluctant to visit his older brother at La Rochelle. The intendant of Metz had left La Rochelle for a career in law and public administration at Paris in the mid-1740s. What attraction could that Protestant port hold for him now, more than a generation later? What had become of Paul-Charles Depont, *trésorier de France*, local *propriétaire-seigneur*, in these forty years?

Whatever their differences in style of life, values, and attitudes, the Depont brothers were essential to their clan, complementary components of a successful family. Jean-Samuel represented the socially mobile, professionally active, urbane and mimetic personality who made his public career a vehicle for family advancement. Paul-Charles, much like his father, performed the more mundane role of providing the economic base for family survival. A less "remarkable" and flamboyant personality no doubt, Paul-Charles stood guard over the account books, managed the land and *rentes*, and kept an eye open for new investment opportunities in solid assets. When the crisis of the Revolution came, Jean-Samuel's world of intendancies and parlements, of financial speculations and Parisian salons, was shaken to its foundations. By contrast, Paul-Charles's provincial world was far less vulnerable to social and institutional innovation. By 1800, Depont, intendant of Metz, had disappeared, but his brother, *propriétaire* in Aunis, had survived. The skills required in government service and provincial landholding were in the end complementary. The Deponts of Paris and of La Rochelle had learned to diversify their talents, adapt to the many worlds around them. They had learned, no doubt unconsciously and over a century of experience, the chemistry of amalgamation, the meaning of being "notables," and what the French elite of the future had to be in order to endure.

The last decade of the Old Regime brought good years for the Depont des Granges. Approaching his fifty-sixth year in 1780, Paul-Charles, head of the family, was a respectable notable of La Rochelle, a candidate for mayor, a veritable Consul Buddenbrook from all outward appearances. [1] More, Paul-Charles had replaced his father as *Trésorier de France,* and by becoming the second generation in the same office, converted his father's *noblesse personnelle* into hereditary nobility for the branch of the family at La Rochelle. In 1773, a year before his father's death, Paul-Charles was confirmed in his noble privileges. In 1783 he was made a *chevalier de Saint-Louis.* The cross was attached to his lapel by the daughter of Comte de la Tour du Pin, commander of the province, who recited a quatrain for the occasion. Paul-Charles's father probably—his grandfather surely—would have found such phrases as *"marque d'honneur," "recompense du courage," "rang des chevaliers"* somewhat foreign to the family's role at La Rochelle. But no doubt Paul-Charles wore his badge of social arrival with ease. In 1789 his name appeared on the voting list for the Second Estate as *noblesse d'ancienne extraction.* [2]

Every year the family *chargé d'affaires,* M. Bonnet, reported an increase in revenues from the farms, *cabanes,* and salt marshes. Added to the *rentes,* the landed income, including the seigneurial rights, was close to thirty thousand livres in 1789, a sum near the apex of the revenue scale at La Rochelle, not discounting the Protestant shipowners whose "fabulous profits" rarely reached this sum annually. [3] In fact, thirty thousand livres was a respectable income anywhere in provincial France at the end of the eighteenth century. Paul-Charles's daughters, Pauline-Marie and Elizabeth-Louise-Henriette, were married, one to a naval lieutenant from a noble family of Rochefort and the other to an army officer from a Poitevin landed family. The dowries were fixed at sixty-thousand livres each, well within Paul-Charles's means and with flexible provisions for payment. His eldest son, Paul-François, Chevalier de Virson, had obtained a military commission in the French Guards, despite the warnings of his grandfather, deceased since 1774. His youngest son, Charles-Louis-Marie, was at a *collège* in Paris, also against the advice of his cantankerous grandfather who lamented the general decline of morals to his dying day.[4] Charles-Louis would soon marry Marie-Louise-Clémentine Carré de Sainte-Gemme from a local family of *officiers* and landowners like his own. The Deponts of La Rochelle were not only "living nobly"; their children, by marriage and profession, were assuming traditional "noble" functions as officers in the army and navy, and as landlords and seigneurs.

With rents rising ever more rapidly since the late 1770s, the *Président-Trésorier* could afford some conspicious expenditure, beginning with the renovation of the family town house on the rue du Palais. The work began in 1785 and was completed in 1790 at a total cost of about forty thousand livres, more than a year's income and a sum his father would never have spent in such a manner.[5] Not that the refurbished Depont *hôtel* was pretentious, at least not from the outside. It had none of the exterior embellishments of the town houses along the rue des Armateurs, where the *trésoriers* Rodrigue and Goguet or the shipowners Poupet and Garesché lived.[6] Unlike them, Depont did not have a double inner court or sumptuous carriage gate. The *hôtel* Depont reminds one of a very diminutive Strozzi bank in its simplicity with small rectangular windows on the second floor and a main entrance that opens directly on the arcades of the rue du Palais. To be sure, the rear entrance on the rue de Juiverie has a modest carriage gate and a small inner court, but nothing to compare, for example, with the Maison Poupet, the present *préfecture* with its handsome façade facing a square.[7] Indeed most of the town houses in the old city had very modest and austere exteriors, often hidden by high walls and bordering very narrow streets or *ruelles.* La Rochelle had nothing to compare with the Allées Tourny at Bordeaux or even with the Cours Mirabeau at Aix to impart light, space, and *largesse.* The covered arcades and the slitlike windows above the ground level add to an impression of *fermeture,* especially in the evening when the bustle near the wharves dies down. In this respect, the rue du Palais must have been little different in 1780.

Depont lavished his money on the interior of the town house. The bills of masons, carpenters, and ironmasters indicate that only the exterior walls were left untouched. A new roof was built, floors were torn up, interior walls were knocked down to make room for a circular staircase with columns mounted in the center of each step. The main drawing room was completely redecorated with particular attention to the ceiling, wall sculptures, and a marble fireplace. Floors were laid, windows pierced, and a new entrance or foyer installed. Monsieur Bonnet's office was not forgotten. In this well-appointed *cabinet* one can picture Paul-Charles reviewing the accounts with his *chargé d'affaires* and dictating correspondence across the new filigreed desk. [8]

The rooms were well furnished, though not extravagantly or sumptuously, especially when compared to the interior decoration of Jean-Samuel's *hôtel* in Paris. There was the usual array of gilded andirons, canopied beds, bronzed consoles, pier glass, tapestries, and the inevitable profusion of mirrors, armchairs, and backgammon tables. One gains the impression that, in the provinces at least, a *bonne maison* was judged by the number of chairs and end tables of various sizes and shapes a family could squeeze into the salon. In our eyes the rooms would seem cluttered and broken up into countless circles and alcoves. The *armoires* were stocked with an unusually large quantity of linens— 109 tablecloths and sheets, towels and other linen valued at 1,600 livres. With a stock like this, no wonder the Deponts had only one chambermaid among seven servants; it would take months before any household linens had to be washed. The small stable on the rue de Juiverie housed a cabriolet, very practical on the narrow streets of La Rochelle, and a bright yellow coach, which must have made the *vignerons* along the road to Aigrefeuille take notice as Paul-Charles and Bonnet made their way to the manor house. The inventory makes no mention of the wine cellar, though there must have been bottles of Cognac, a main source of Depont's income, and an assortment of Bordeaux and Burgundies besides. And where was the silverware old Paul-François had promised to divide equally between his two sons in 1766? No doubt it was hidden during the Revolution when the inventory was made, along with some of the thirty thousand livres *in silver* Paul-Charles produced in 1797 to buy back his land from the government. [9]

In 1789 the household staff counted seven, not including a second governess and a full-time gardener for the manor house at Virson. Although about 9 percent of the population of the port (1,288 in a total population of 15,340 in 1767) were *domestiques,* very few families had

Table 7.1. *The Household Staff of Paul-Charles Depont in 1789*

Function	Salary
Cook	350 livres
Lackey	200
Coachman	150
Valet	120
Governess	100
Chambermaid	90
Cleaning Girl	60

Source: Archives Départementales, E-489. "Gages des domestiques, 1764-1792."

seven servants. The richest *armateurs* had four to six. [10] Even by Parisian standards, seven is a good number. [11] Although their salaries did not change much in thirty years, Depont's servants received food and lodging, and of course "borrowed prestige." During the early years of the Revolution at least, they remained loyal to the family. In early 1793 on the eve of the Terror, Paul-Charles's cook, his most highly paid servant, was able to place a *tête de veau* on the Depont table, the veal no doubt carted from one of the *cabanes* near Rochefort. [12]

The manor house at Virson in the vineyard country east of the port was less imposing than the town house and could only be called a château by a considerable stretch of the imagination. Les Granges had neither the medieval pretension of Tremoïlle's Taillebourg or De Poix's Jonzac to the east and south of the province, nor the Renaissance allure of La Rochecourbon or Crazanne closer by. Nor could it claim the classic beauty of Buzay with its charming *allées* and gardens built only a few miles from Virson by the Harouard family, *anoblis* like the Deponts in the early years of the century. [13] Nevertheless, Les Granges was more than a simple Breton *gentilhommière*. The main structure consisted of a single-story lateral axis or corridor with pavillions on each end. Between this axis and the gate was an enclosed court flanked on one side by a chapel and the quarters of the tenant and on the other by a line of low buildings housing the servants, the carriage and horses, the grain lofts, the wine press, and the brandy cellars. The horseshoe design is characteristic of many *maisons de campagne* in Aunis and Lower Poitou. When a new tenant family moved in on Saint-Michael's Day (28 September), their household belongings were stacked unceremoniously in the courtyard only a few meters from the main entrance to the manor house, creating the image of a working *ferme*, not the setting for bucolic leisure. [14] Nevertheless, for all its modesty and utility, Les Granges had an extensive park. Attached to the manor house were fifteen acres of avenues and gardens, twelve acres of meadow, and thirty-two acres of wood, much of it ornamental, including oaks, elms, plane trees, and Italian poplars. Paul Depont at the end of the seventeenth century had already evinced an interest in the park. His grandson, Paul-Charles, employed a gardener at one hundred livres per year to keep the avenues open, plane trees pruned, and gardens trim. In 1796 the Revolutionary government estimated the wood to be worth more than the manor house. Given the fact that 1795 had been one of the worst winters in recent French history, it is not surprising that firewood was worth more than masonry. The manor house had value in that year only as a place to store brandy and grain. [15] As for the "movables," they were estimated at only ten thousand livres; they were adequate but undistinguished. The inventory of the *office* (pantry) included a tin-plated lamp, two bottles and five small glasses, and two balance scales. Perhaps it was in this dimly lit room that Faurie, Depont's *procureur fiscal,* met with the *fermiers* to discuss lease terms.

Despite a respectable income from the land and *rentes*, Paul-Charles was unable to meet all of his obligations in the 1780s without borrowing. The costs of the town house, the dowries of his daughters, and his son's commission all required ready capital. Remember too that these were the years when the *feudiste* from Lorraine completed a new *terrier* for Aigrefeuille at no small expense. Depont also purchased two small houses at La Rochelle for another 12,000 livres, possibly for his two daughters. [16] In any case, Paul-Charles needed money.

He contacted the mercantile community of the city, borrowing from some of the same Protestant families with whom his grandfather had shipping partnerships sixty years before. Who else had liquid capital in La Rochelle? Paul-Charles evinced none of the scruples of his father in the matter of "usury." He signed notes with time limits for sums which almost certainly included the interest charge. For example, he borrowed 2,100 livres from Mlle. Carayon, 2,104 livres from Madame Belin, and 21,000 from M. Audry, all "payable in one year" and all clearly suggesting that a 5-percent interest charge was included in the capital borrowed. In one case the evidence is conclusive. Bonnet's private account book reads: "On 19 January 1785, M. des Granges borrowed from M. Moule, merchant of the Grand' Rue, 6,000 livres by his note of 6,300 livres payable in one year, *prix fixe.* " [17] There is every reason to believe that the other sums were handled in the same manner. Paul-Charles's portfolio of loans indicates a continued reliance on constituted *rentes* as approved by the Sorbonne, but when he needed capital quickly, he did not hesitate to borrow from his Protestant friends with the obligation to repay the capital with interest.

The older Depont had accumulated enough *rentes* in his lifetime to live on the income after he transferred all the land to his two sons. At the time of his death in 1774, the income from these *rentes* totaled 12,000 livres; 8,000 from constituted *rentes* on individuals at 5 percent, and 4,000 in perpetual *rentes* on various public institutions, local and national, from 1 to 8 percent. [18] To be sure, the interest (or *rente*) was not always promptly paid, and back in the 1760s Paul-François had often been obliged to cajole or threaten individual debtors to pay, even though he had no legal right to demand repayment of the capital. The *Hôtel de Ville* was also tardy in its disbursements. [19] Nevertheless, Paul-François rarely borrowed, and when he did, it was always by constituting a *rente.* Paul-Charles, on the other hand, borrowed more extensively than his father, so that by 1787 his interest obligations approached

8,000 livres, over a quarter of his total income. His own *rentes* were no longer enough to cover these charges and he was obliged to draw on his landed income. But more important, since 1775 individual debtors were repaying capital sums more frequently than Paul-Charles was making new revenue-producing placements, a sign that he was spending his capital. *Il mangeait ses capitaux,* to employ the apt French phrase.[20] Bonnet, the *chargé d'affaires,* raised the warning signals by the mid-1780s. He might have to sell land!

Then in 1788 the family at La Rochelle received a windfall from an unexpected quarter. The Lescure branch of the clan, which had done its best to disassociate itself from Paul-François in the 1760s, left an inheritance of 340,000 livres. Upon receiving the news, Bonnet wrote with an enthusiasm uncommon in a man of his *métier*. His choice of words suggests a curious blend of impersonal professionalism and family loyalty: "... the administration will now have adequate means, not only to reimburse all of the notes [*billets*], but also to amortize the *rentes* and not be obliged to sell any domains [*sic*]. ... It [the administration] owes you the most generous thanks. If we can touch a portion of this sum in coin soon, we can reimburse the notes due in March and April."[21]

Bonnet's optimism quickly receded, however, when he learned more about the Lescure inheritance. The first news in such matters was likely to stress the maximum capital evaluation without taking account of the debts, often concealed during the lifetime of the family head, and the creditors, heirs and potential legatees, who have a way of appearing *en masse* at such moments. Unfortunately, the inheritance had to cover the debts of the Clisson family before a distribution to the Deponts in the collateral branch would be made. This was ominous, when we recall that the dowry of a Depont daughter had saved the Comte de Clisson from near bankruptcy in 1753. Since then the Clissons, Vendean *noblesse,* had assumed the risks of living in Paris. When Bonnet learned that the Clisson cousins had contracted debts of about 80,000 livres, he could only throw up his hands in disappointment. "That is really a great deal of money!" he wrote in May 1788.[22]

Nevertheless, from a strictly financial perspective, the next two years went well for Paul-Charles. By the spring of 1790, as Revolutionary *fêtes* and municipal banquets enlivened the Place d'Armes only a few blocks from the Hôtel Depont, the family accounts showed a marked improvement. The outflow of interest and capital was slowed, the *rente* income increased, and the landed revenues were freed from all charges. On a slip of paper left in the leaves of a ledger Paul-Charles jotted down the annual (anticipated?) returns from all the *fermes*. The total was exactly 24,150 livres. The lease-year at the top was 1790–91.[23]

Paul-François Depont has left us private letters; Jean-Samuel has left administrative correspondence and a brief travelogue; Paul-Charles has left little more than accounts and estate correspondence. It may be irresponsible to deduce attitudes and personality traits in each case, given the uneven quality of this evidence. For the old *trésorier de France*, much can be inferred; for the intendant of Metz, less; for Paul-Charles, little can be said with assurance beyond the bare facts of his material existence and his behavior toward land agents, tenants, and the poor. There is little doubt, of course, that Paul-Charles spent much of his time managing the family properties. Although the appointment of Bonnet represented a certain elaboration in the administration that old Paul-François would have considered unnecessary, it also suggests that the task had become more complex. The employment of the *feudiste* supports this suspicion. In any case, Seigneur Depont was an attentive landlord, assiduous in rent collection and enforcement of his "rights," and also alert to new investments, especially in the salt marshes on the islands of Ré and Oleron, and elsewhere.

In many ways, Paul-Charles resembled his father. He did not travel widely; he attended the local Society of Agriculture for a time, but had no desire to become mayor when the opportunity arose. There is some evidence that his wife (and cousin) Marie-Henriette Sonnet d'Auzon, was sickly, which would limit his public activities, though at La Rochelle the range would have been restricted in any case. The office of *Trésorier*, though not totally moribund, was surely less demanding in 1780 than it had been even a generation before. In short, one has the image of a local notable who stayed at home a great deal. Jean-Samuel and Marie-Madeleine Escureul had only two children, born in the first two years after their marriage in 1765; Paul-Charles and Marie-Henriette Sonnet had seven, although only four were still alive in 1795, at least two having died young. The number and spacing of these children suggests that the Deponts of La Rochelle did not practice birth-control and indeed may have considered it the duty of their branch to assure the family a progeny. [24] Did Paul-Charles enjoy family reunions with his children, perhaps with a *déjeuner* at Virson after a family mass in the chapel? Did he read? Did he spend long hours peering down the rue du Palais through those narrow windows, hearing the cries of the hawkers and the barrel-boys and reflecting on the "fortress" he had built against the uncertainties of the future? His father might well have said something about "uncertainties" when he had reminisced about the long wait for the sugar ships on the return from Saint-Domingue in the 1730s.

Yet in some ways he was different from his father, who must have been commanding and even oppressive at close range. [25] In later life Paul-Charles seemed less compulsive, able to enjoy some of the fruits of thrift and discipline, inclined to indulge in some creature comforts in the form of a new town house, an ample table, an array of servants, along with a trip to Rochefort or the Vendée to visit relatives occasionally. But while Paul-Charles could live with "usury," we would hardly expect him to be urbane and cosmopolitan. La Rochelle did not even have a theater. Perhaps the absence of personal testimony should not be ascribed exclusively to the hazards of documentary survival, or even to the fact that Paul-Charles did not separate himself from his family for long periods. He might well have had a provincial distrust of words. Paul-Charles Depont des Granges surely placed greater stock in vineyards and salt marshes, in contracts honored in solid silver, than in the fancy formulas and fine manners of a Parisian *arriviste*.

In the 1760s Paul-François Depont expressed a very low opinion of his grandson at La Rochelle. Young Virson, then barely in his teens, was undisciplined and self-indulgent, incapable of sustained application. *"Il se promène toujours,"* captured much of Depont's opinion of Virson. As for the boy's future, he could never aspire to the "high robe" or an intendancy, and if he attempted the military service, he would "crumble at the first shot of a cannon."[26] In 1788, twenty years later, Paul-François de Pont, chevalier de Virson, signed his cousin's marriage contract in a bold hand surrounded by a very distinguished gathering in the Marais quarter of Paris. He was dressed in the uniform of an officer of the French Guards, a very presentable representative of the La Rochelle branch of the Depont family. Jean-Samuel, his uncle, was marrying his only daughter into an old noble family from Auvergne and no effort to display family *éclat* was spared.[27]

Marriage between robe and sword, even between commerce and sword, was not new to the family. After all, one of Paul-François's sisters at La Rochelle had married a Clisson, and both of the daughters of Paul-Charles had married into local noble families. But the Fontanges were a cut above the common run of provincial noblesse. Without bearing one of the great names of the kingdom, Louis-Marie, Marquis de Fontanges, *maréchal de camp,* was from an old Auvergnat family, seigneur of five domains near Auriac valued at about 200,000 livres. The family château at Velzic was no longer habitable, proof of a certain venerability. The family had purchased a town house in Auriac in the 1750s. In 1765 the marshall married Jeanne-Françoise de Barral-Rochechinard, daughter of a councilor at the Parlement of Dauphiné. The wedding mass was celebrated by the prince bishop of Grenoble. The Barrals were also a clan of ecclesiastics, including a bishop, a coadjutor and vicar-general of Troyes, an archbishop of Bourges, and a number of abbés, two of them at the abbey of Auriac. In short, by the end of the century, the

Fontanges had distinguished representation in sword, robe, and church. The marshall and his wife from Grenoble had two sons: the eldest, Louis, became an abbé, and the second, Justin, became an officer in the royal infantry and Jean-Samuel's new son-in-law. [28]

By pedigree, status, and connection, the Fontanges were in the first rank of the provincial nobility, although the family fortune—about ten thousand livres income—hardly permitted them to live in the capital. They were an excellent complement to the Paris branch of the Depont family. Here was an alliance that would join Parisian robe and finance with unchallenged representation of the First and Second Estates. What a felicitous blend of *capacité* and birth, the very essence of *mérite*, as that word was understood in 1788.

Jean-Samuel might well smile with satisfaction as he surveyed the assembled dignitaries who signed the marriage contract. Of course, he would pay the extra fee to have the King, Queen, and Princes of the Blood sign first. His father's objections to this frill had been forgotten long ago. The array of ecclesiastics from the Barral side must have been a splendid sight. The miters and crosses of the bishops and the more somber habit of the middling clergy were a brillant complement to the braided uniforms of the military and the lace jabots of the magistrates. Two figures must have held Jean-Samuel's attention: Justin, Marquis de Fontanges, captain in the infantry, his new son-in-law, and Charles-Jean-François, councilor at the Parlement of Paris, his son, each just twenty-one years old. But the key personage, in all likelihood the marriage broker, was Monseigneur Louis-Joseph de Montmorency-Laval, Prince of the Empire, Grand Almoner of France, Commander of the Order of the Holy Spirit, Bishop of Metz, and "mutual friend of the future spouses." The intendant and the bishop of Metz were not strangers. How fitting that a Montmorency-Laval—*grande noblesse*—would add his blessing to the Depont-Fontanges union.

Apart from two domains and some *rentes foncières,* most of the Fontanges property in Auvergne was reserved for the abbé, the groom's elder brother, and his widowed mother. The dowager's wedding gift was her late husband's royal pension of 500 livres, an indication of the meager resources the Fontanges family could muster for the occasion. One had to pass on to article four of the marriage contract to uncover something more substantial. Here the script became decidedly bolder: "Mond. S. De La Touche in the name of Mond. S. Depont hereby gives and constitutes as the dowry to Mademoiselle his daughter the sum of 250,000 livres." [29] The articles that follow are replete with five- and six-digit figures, including a somewhat inflated evaluation of Jean-Samuel's assets which were to provide the basis for payment of 12,500 livres interest (*rente*) on the dowry. The Paris town house, which cost 165,000 in 1773, was estimated at 300,000 in 1788, an increase not entirely justified by the rate of inflation it would seem. Jean-Samuel's land and *rentes* at La Rochelle were evaluated at 420,000 livres, also inflated by at least 100,000. On the other hand, these capital sums did not include the La Touche-Cromot fortune which would one day be Jean-Samuel's or his children's. In fact, La Touche *père* gave the couple a taste of that inheritance in the form of a gift of 50,000 livres or 2,500 livres *rente* per annum.

That both Depont and La Touche could raise large capital sums is indicated by their promise to raise 150,000 livres in eighteen months "in the event the future spouses find some real property [*bien fonds*] to purchase at an advantageous price," with the consent of the father of the bride, to be sure.[30] In the spring of 1788 land was without question the safest of investments, bearing what a modern stockbroker would call "enormous growth potential." Paul-Charles Depont's rent rolls were there to prove it. Thus a six-digit dowry was mobilized, in part at least, to buy land. The unusual provision for the young couple to live with Jean-Samuel in his town house in the Marais reflected more, perhaps, than the "minority" of the bride and the "mutual attachment" of father and daughter.[31] Having had only two children in twenty-one years of marriage, Depont, it would seem, left nothing to chance in property matters. Jean-Samuel would supervise his son-in-law's investment of Depont money.

How did Jean-Samuel spend his income? In the absence of an annual balance sheet, one cannot produce a precise accounting. However, it is clear that there was ample capital for handsome dowries of 250,000 livres for each of the intendant's two children and enough remaining to provide an affluent style of life for Jean-Samuel and his immediate family. His travel journal gives us some idea of his consumption habits and tastes. Jean-Samuel's death inventory in 1806 permits us to look back on forty years of accumulation of this world's goods.[32]

In May 1773, just before his father's death and while he was still intendant of Moulins, Jean-Samuel purchased a large town house at 11 rue des Filles Saint-Thomas in the Marais quarter of Paris. The town house cost 165,000 livres and is one more indication that Jean-Samuel intended to live most of the time in Paris, "near the Minister," as he put it. The description of the rooms and furnishings of this house suggests not only affluence, but a certain cultivated taste as well. There is nothing in the furnishings to suggest vulgarity, brashness, or any other stereotype of the parvenu. The wine cellars were well stocked with five hundred bottles of Burgundy and Chablis and smaller lots of Bordeaux, Champagne, Muscat, Malaga, and Cyprus wines; the kitchen contained three large stoves and a spit with cordage and chain, plus the inevitable "battery" of pots and pans; the pantries of the *maître d'hôtel* contained fourteen large tablecloths, eleven dozen napkins, ten dozen aprons, and a complete stock of linen, glassware and porcelain tableware. The salons and bedrooms, invariably connected by ante-chambers, alcoves, and wide staircases, usually overlooked the inner court or the garden. These rooms must have been especially cheerful and elegant. The furnishings include *tric-trac* tables of acajou wood, Aubusson tapestries and rugs, *pots pourris* and large vases of Oriental porcelain, "ornamented in gilded copper," chandeliers, andirons, Alsatian stoves, marble shepherdesses, large mirrors, and salons over-flowing with chairs of all kinds—of straw and of cane, straight backs and armchairs, many covered in damask, striped in blue or green and accompanied by those countless little tables, inlaid, filigreed and orna-mented in great complexity.

Other items give us a closer look at Jean-Samuel's interests and tastes. Papers and money were well cared for, as indicated by the wallet kept in the bedroom: "black leather decorated in silver, inserted in a leather case." Although the "little room" on the top floor contained an oaken strongbox, there were no silver *écus* or golden louis in it in 1806. Jean-Samuel had 1,100 francs in a bedroom drawer, however, 500 representing a draft (*billet*) on the Bank of France and the rest in coins of various regimes—francs, livres, *liards*—not an excessive liquidity. The silverware was valued at 2,600 francs, again respectable but neither inordinately pretentious nor a hoard or cache of precious metal. Re-member that Jean-Samuel liked to keep his capital moving.

As for the library, notaries are more interested in the market value of bindings and papers than in the titles of books. Jean-Samuel had almost two hundred volumes in the "little room" on the top floor, including "a treatise on sheep raising, the customary law and other works on law and jurisprudence." This is not much more detailed than Depont's own brief comment on the library of Intendant de la Galaisière at the château of Chaumont during his tour of 1779. On that occasion, Jean-Samuel was more impressed by the ventilation system to prevent dampness than he was by book titles. I suspect that Jean-Samuel's precocious son knew the contents of the law books much better than his father.

But Depont's choice of paintings reveals a more genuine artistic taste and an awareness of the contemporary art world, a connoisseur-ship he shared perhaps with his wife and his intellectual son. Occasionally, the notaries forgot the price of each ornamented frame long enough to describe a painting, however summarily, and even mentioned a painter. In addition to a prodigious number of objets d'art, the main salon contained seventeen *tableaux*, the dining room ten, and the study four, making a total of thirty-one in all, not counting the thirteen family portraits in the apartment of Depont's daughter. Jean-Samuel apparently had a weakness for Flemish genre paintings—pastoral settings with waterfalls and lots of animals or military scenes filled with tents, troops, and horses. These motifs were interspersed with an occasional basket of fruit, a *maître d'école*, the Holy Family, or some naiads or river figures, one painted in a wax medium (*en caustique*), "after Raphael." The Flemish genre paintings, like the copies of Raphael, were common collector's items in eighteenth-century France. The Flemish painters Barend Gael and Cingelaar are mentioned, the former more than once. Less expected are Jean-Baptiste Pater and Philippe-Jacques de Louther-bourg, painters whose reputation stands decidedly above the common run. Pater was a disciple of Watteau who reached his prime before 1730, and therefore could be considered established and respectable by the time Jean-Samuel procured the painting. Loutherbourg, however, began his career in the 1760s, a decade before Jean-Samuel bought his town house in Paris. Here at least Intendant Depont was up-to-date, if not avant-garde. [33]

Jean-Samuel's style of life was fully commensurate with his official function and social standing in Parisian society. His town house was different from his brother's at La Rochelle in more ways than capital evaluation. In fact, if he revealed any discernible trace of his provincial origins, it was the pervasive lack of discrimination and the absence of any touch of eccentricity in his personal possessions and physical sur-roundings. Somehow, one does not expect to find a Loutherbourg seascape peering down on the clusters of damask-covered armchairs, *tric-trac* tables, marble shepherdesses, and Aubusson rugs. It is as if his father's and grandfather's cargoes of sugar and slaves were still dimly present in the intendant's Parisian drawing room at number 11 rue des Filles Saint-Thomas.

In 1779 Jean-Samuel Depont made three trips, the first from Paris to Metz to take up his new post as the Intendant of Trois-Évêchés, and two more later in the year, inspection tours of his new *généralité*. He kept a short journal of these trips and in the absence of extensive personal correspondence the journal gives us a closer view of the man as well as the administrator. [34] Since he served for thirteen years as Intendant of Moulins, it is not surprising that Jean-Samuel was trained to make observations on administrative and military installations, on the grain supply, the local manufactures, the state of the roads, and public works generally. Less expected are his comments on other aspects of provincial life, reflecting his own personal attitudes and priorities. Jean-Samuel devoted a relatively large amount of space in his journal to housing, not the modest dwellings of villagers or ordinary townspeople, but the *hôtels* and châteaux of the elites and especially the residences of the royal administrators.

The *hôtel* of the intendant of Strasbourg necessitated two tightly packed pages, so precise that one can recreate the entire plan of the building, floor by floor, room by room. Recall Jean-Samuel's attention to his residence at Moulins and to his town house in the Marais quarter in Paris. But in this instance Depont's interest goes beyond creature comforts and suggests what he deemed the essential *mise en scène* of an intendant. He stressed the arrangement of rooms, utility and function mixed with generosity of floor plan. "On the left a very large *salon d'audience,* followed by a large office; after this office a small ante-chamber which led into a bedroom arranged in a way so that it is inde-pendent of the large apartment" (p. 172). He suggested that the office on the ground floor should be separated from the living quarters on the second floor.

In what was ostensibly an inspection tour of the provinces, Jean-Samuel went into considerable detail. "The first apartment is of great distinction, of considerable height and with a view of the countryside. There are beautiful mirrors everywhere and superb decorations above the doorways" (p. 173). He went on to describe the wallpaper design which matched the armchairs. He only criticized the lack of better stoves in the large salons and pointed to the need for a more elaborate staircase. The third floor with its long hall and adjacent bedrooms housed the children, the servants, and the kitchen help. The kitchens themselves were "very large and very well lit," possessing an enormous spit that required neither ropes or weights for it to rotate. Depont then turned to the "superb courtyard," noting that it could be improved by piercing the wall with an iron gate so that on entering one could see the splendid façade of the main house. Depont also noted the large building across the court serving the intendant's secretaries and their clerks.

For Jean-Samuel, the intendance of Alsace was a perfect blend of elegance and utility, an imposing ensemble of stone masonry that would impress the local elite as well as the ordinary *administrés.* The intendant's presence was evident at the Strasbourg *opéra comique* as well as at the *Palais de l'Intendance.* Depont noted that the intendant's box was directly opposite the loge of the *Commandant* and that both had a sentinel (p. 175). The *mise en scène,* the trappings of power, were as important as the administrative activity itself.

Apart from the state of the roads (*superbes et plantés*) or country inns (*abominables*), Jean-Samuel had little to say about the countryside.

So unlike his contemporary, Arthur Young, he never mentioned a farm or a vineyard. Measuring the distance between towns by coach time, he left little doubt as to his urban preference. On entering a provincial town—Sedan, Longwy, Verdun, Nancy—Depont began with a short description of the site and then passed quickly to the best families of the "society." At Sedan, M. de la Blauche, "in trade," had a fortune of at least 700,000 francs, a fine town house and château with "an immense garden of great elegance and with a flavor of Marly" and "four beautiful ponds and countless charming avenues" (p. 108). Among other assets, M. Poupard, another merchant, had a daughter who was "*la plus jolie femme de Sedan*" (p. 109). Longwy had a beautiful tree-lined promenade along the ramparts and a "superb wall." Although small, the town had its "society." "Mademoiselle de la Martinière is a most distinguished woman; she has a sister who lives with Madame la Comtesse de Barbantanne at Paris" (p. 113).

But Depont was especially impressed by Verdun. "This town is very well peopled [*habitée*]. The tone is very good, the women are very presentable [*bien mises*] and in large number. I have seen more than fifty of them on Sunday at the bishop's outing where there were thirty games of cards [*parties de jeu*]" (p. 109). He proceeded to describe the twelve most prominent women of Verdun in some detail. For example, "Madame Perin is a very beautiful woman who can be favorably compared with the two [ladies] described above. All her features are very well cut and could not be more regular." As for Madame de Mausse, wife of the lieutenant-colonel of the Dauphine regiment, she too was "*fort bien.*" "She is a blonde with blue eyes, superb skin, beautiful teeth, and has a very respectable air about her." Concluding that "the society of the town is altogether very *agréable,*" Depont then turned without transition to a description of the Cathedral choir (pp. 109–10).

It would be easy, of course, to suggest that Jean-Samuel's checklist of beautiful women in the towns of Lorraine was the sign of a repressed childhood and an act of rebellion against the Catholic puritanism of Depont *père* and the cramped social world of La Rochelle. Perhaps he simply liked beautiful women. Surely it was a tribute to the enormously important social role women played in provincial France, even in towns as small as Longwy, Sedan, or Phalsbourg. It may even have been a simple mnemonic device for remembering the important people in each town. When discussing other local elites—the military, for example—Jean-Samuel also included the male members of prominent families, though in less physical detail, to be sure.

All the same, there were traces of puritanism beneath the sophisticated exterior the new intendant of Metz had cultivated so well. At the entrance to the Cathedral of Verdun, Jean-Samuel was struck by the nudity of the statues of Adam and Eve. "The bishop showed them to me in his garden. Eve carried a cloak on her arm, but in a manner that is no less indecent" (p. 110). At the Abbey of Châtillon a few months later, he expressed similar shock. "All the stalls are ornamented with women, completely nude, and in every possible posture" (p. 113).

What are we to make of these two incidents? It appears that Jean-Samuel, who had no apparent difficulty describing the physical attributes of the women of "society," was shocked by female nudity in a religious context. Recall that his mother died at his birth. Perhaps the absence of a mother should not be ignored here. Was the "Eve" of the bishop's garden a maternal substitute who required special respect? If so, we can be sure that Jean-Samuel never acknowledged it. A more mundane explanation might describe his concern about female nudity as a "lapse" in worldly urbanity, one of those rough edges not yet entirely smoothed out like his misspelling of "Sèvres" as "Sêves" (p. 171). Indeed, in almost every other way, the fifty-four-year-old intendant appeared as an accomplished man of the world, bred to the role from birth.

At Nancy, Jean-Samuel focused attention on the shops of two cloth merchants, Solomon-Moyse Lévy and Beer-Isaac Beer. Here too, he went into considerable detail, intended presumably for his wife's eyes and not for those of his administrative superiors. "I have found satin gowns, *brodées des Indes,* far superior to those I have seen in Paris, possessing, among other qualities, a white background with blue stripes and embroidered flowers done with delicious taste and selling for twelve louis, twelve yards to the roll. ... This gown is probably the only one of its kind. Madame la Marquise de Clermont tells me that one like it was sent to the Queen" (pp. 167–68). Depont went on for a full page on the comparative merits of various kinds of finished cloth and embroidered gowns, including the cost per yard and the choices made by the wives of other notables of the region. He concluded the passage with a reference to a purchase of a *"robe de perse à médaillon"* for Madame Depont. But this was only a small part of the shopping venture. The pursuit of luxury apparel was both a fine art and a pleasurable recreation. If the rue Saint-Georges at Nancy could not compare with the rue Saint-Honoré at Paris, to frequent such shops was a mark of status all the same.

In fact, Depont's interest in the consumption of goods seemed irrepressible. He loved shops, especially luxury shops and retailers of all sorts of specialities. He visited Herr Dürr, the best-known fish merchant of Strasbourg. "The celebrated Rhine carp come from Lindre pond in my *généralité*," he wrote. He made a special arrangement with a reputable caterer to have several boxes of goose-liver pâtés shipped to

Metz in lots to accommodate thirty table settings at a time. He also bought a costly fur muff from a prominent furrier and spoke with M. Schröter, the royal gardener, about the purchase of some shrubbery for his own garden (p. 176).

We must not conclude that because of his serious attention to Persian gowns and goose-liver pâtés Jean-Samuel was fundamentally frivolous. After all, these were cultivated consumption habits, social graces that were marks of the social position a younger son of a Rochelais *anobli* had won for himself. Jean-Samuel was not born to these habits; they were another sign of his remarkable adaptation to high administration and a cosmopolitan milieu.

Jean-Samuel's obvious mastery of *le superflu si nécessaire* often merged with a concern for utility and even public administration. His interest in luxury manufacture seemed no less "studied" than his taste for the finished product. He observed that M. La Blauche's elegant garden near Sedan had a stream that propelled a fulling mill. "I notice that the sound of water, which also turns the mill wheel, muffles the hammer blows to produce a pleasant effect which is rare and perhaps unique, bringing together the useful and the *agréable*. That one can find such an establishment in a spot designed for pure luxury does honor to M.M. de La Blauche and reveals their modesty" (pp. 108–9). A "machine in the garden"?[35] As a practical man, an administrator concerned with the development of his country's resources, yet also a devotee of gracious living, Jean-Samuel is pleased to see this rococo "middle landscape" in which art and nature exist in harmony.

At Saint-Quirin on the road from Nancy or Strasbourg, Jean-Samuel examined local glassmaking. He demonstrated considerable expertise in the matter, noting the juxtaposition of both water and wood, comparing the manufacturing process here with that employed at Saint-Gobain and even assessing comparative prices. "I was surprised, after examining this glass, which is really very beautiful, to discover that there is a difference of only about 10 percent in the price" (p. 170). At Niderviller, a few miles farther east, Depont visited the porcelain factory of Comte de Custine which he compared favorably to that at Sèvres. "The *Vénus Sortant du Bain* I saw there is superior to any I have seen at Sèvres. The figure is charming and perfectly designed, [but] it cost ten louis (230 livres). I am surprised that this manufacturer can survive with such high prices" (p. 171). In this matter Depont indicated a greater awareness of price competition than many French entrepreneurs.

Not that he limited his professional interests to luxury manufacture, though his aesthetic inclinations probably did increase his attention span. His observations about the cannon factory at Strasbourg are brief, though not devoid of expertise (p. 175). He made a special detour over poor roads to inspect the salt beds at Dieuz, comparing the process of salt-making employed by two entrepreneurs, and observing that one process yielded an attractive scent of violet (p. 177). Jean-Samuel also referred to the evaporation method used in salt marshes no doubt familiar to him from his own family properties in Aunis.

Depont showed professional competence in dealing with military installations in what was a frontier province. At Verdun, after a detailed description of the town's female "society" and the "indecent" Eve in the bishop's garden, Jean-Samuel inspected the military barracks, the officer's quarters, and the engineering school headed by M. de Rugi, a military engineer and artillery specialist whom Depont recognized as a veritable local Vauban (p. 111). But he could also be critical, proof that his observations were not merely perfunctory. He wrote a long passage on ways of improving the garrison's water supply, removing the "fecal matter from the latrines" which threatened the drinking water, and improving the sanitary conditions of the installation generally (p. 110). His observations on the *gendarmerie* at Lunéville and the military hospital at Phalsbourg were especially thorough. Depont suggested construction of a warehouse for wood, but with special attention to fire prevention (pp. 169, 171).

Competence rather than excessive "zeal" emerges from the journal. Depont also exhibits a certain tolerance for religious minorities, numerous in Alsace and Lorraine. From the tone of the journal, it appears to be a tolerance based on indifference as much as on principle, but the result is a certain open-mindedness all the same. Crossing the northeastern corner of Lorraine between Faulquemont and Morhange, Depont encountered German-speaking villages and his reference to them represents almost his only allusion to rural conditions in the journal. He was impressed by the number and quality of stud farms for the royal cavalry. "The most beautiful colts are in possession of the Anabaptists, who are all well-to-do people, and the best tenant farmers [*fermiers*] of M. le Comte d'Helmstadt. They all wear long beards and have peculiarly shaped heads; they are very honest people, very orderly and very religious. They have no churches and worship God at home without gathering publicly" (p. 165).

Although the bishop of Metz wanted to banish all Anabaptists from the diocese, it is quite clear that Intendant Depont considered them ideal citizens. The Lutherans of Alsace may have seemed rather odd to him, but he showed no sign of intolerance toward them either. At Strasbourg Jean-Samuel was struck by the "seclusion and silence of their churches compared to ours." "The altar in this kind of church has neither paintings nor chandeliers. The singing in these churches is noble and majestic and always accompanied by an organ." He appeared to regret that Baron Wurmser, the notable who had the finest town house in Strasbourg, could not be awarded the highest military honors because he was a Lutheran (pp. 175–76). Depont said less about the Jews, also numerous in this province, but he referred to the Jewish cloth merchants at Nancy with respect (pp. 167–68).

Not that Depont was always well disposed toward Lorrainers. He characterized the German villagers who had delayed construction of a new road near Thionville as motivated by an *"esprit tracassier,"* a cliché for blind opposition to public works (p. 118). On the other hand, he sympathized with the humble country people near Longwy who suffered from the claims of the local seigneur. "M. le Marquis de Mézières has obtained a right that is very onerous for the inhabitants, that is, carrying his wood to Longwy by forced labor [*corvée*]. Recently, by *arrêt* of the Royal Council, he has converted this *corvée* into a perpetual rent of six hundred livres levied on the country people around Longwy. This kind of right is even worse than the first because now they do not even have the hope that the descendants of M. de Mézières will not live in Longwy [and not need any *corvée* of wood]" (p. 113). Depont ended this passage by stating that Mézières as local military commander had a larger per diem ration of forage than he did, suggesting a certain competition for public perquisites. The marquis obviously lacked a sense of honor and *largesse*. In this instance, Depont indicated no remedy for such seigneural burdens.

Of course, a journal is neither a philosophical tract nor a personal confession. Jean-Samuel reveals himself only partially and indirectly. But the evidence here does substantiate and complement the personality traits we have seen already. Jean-Samuel was not a zealous reformer or a man with a vision like his contemporary Baron Turgot. He was an administrator who had assimilated the attributes of his office, and if he observed the forms a bit better than the substance of his function, this was probably because he had spent so much of his early years in Paris consciously learning a style of behavior that was not native to him. The success of his career is a triumph of human plasticity and adaptation, not independence, innovation, and leadership. "New men" do not necessarily infuse rejuvenating lifeblood into a governing elite, which is not to say they do not help keep it going. Above all, Depont's case suggests that the administrative apparatus of the Old Regime had considerable absorptive power and co-optive capacity.

In one generation Jean-Samuel had rejected—not always consciously—the mercantile, provincial, and religious rules of behavior of his immediate forebears. He had literally made himself over to fit the image required in the capital. In the process he had spread himself thin and forfeited a certain integrity, following only too faithfully the role models he saw around him. His very vocabulary reflects a curious mixture of salon commonplace and administrative phraseology. Jean-Samuel's choice of adjectives is inordinately repetitious; certain expressions seem ready-made. Courtyards, roads, and public works are always "superb"; gardens and operas are always "charming"; châteaux are "elegant," their salons "magnificent"; the best town houses are *"recherchées en tout"* or *"fort jolies"*; and "society," female-dominated society, is *"fort agréable."* This cliché-laden prose appears especially superficial when it treats people. Female notables are *"bien mises"* or of *"bon maintien"* and occasionally possess *"beaucoup d'esprit et d'agrément."* Males are given a certain occupational differentiation. Noble military officers are usually *"fort galant"* a cardinal can be "brillant," a technician *"éclairé"*, a war contractor *"très vif,"* though "living in bad company," specialty retail merchants are *"bien assortis"* or even *"fameux,"* almost like their wares, and secretaries and Anabaptists, like an Alsatian stove, are *"fort honnêtes."* Commonplace as this vocabulary was in Depont's social milieu, it nonetheless places him distinctly below a Turgot, a Calonne, or a Roederer, as an original thinker or leader of men.

The few glimpses we have of Jean-Samuel from contemporaries confirm this impression. Baron Roederer, famous Revolutionary publicist, active member of the National Assembly, and councilor of the Parlement of Metz before 1790, wrote enough political tracts, letters and memoirs to fill eight published volumes. He had regular correspondence with many notables of Metz—the military and Church establishments, members of the Parlement, and municipal officials. Yet he mentions Intendant Depont only once, in the context of a gathering at the home of the First President of the Parlement of Metz just before the Revolution. The encounter was as banal as it was brief. "M. l'Intendant ... approaches me. 'You are well, Sir? I am charmed to see you again. I received and read with great interest the little book which you were good enough to send me.'"[36] Obviously, their relationship did not go much beyond the minimal social courtesies. Jean-Samuel, despite his important position in Metz, was not active in reformist circles where Roederer was so prominent. Their reactions to the Revolution at Metz would be different.

In this decade before the Revolution there is little doubt that Depont enjoyed the emoluments of his successful social metamorphosis. These included an open invitation to the best houses in the province, thirty servings of *pâté de foie* at the *Intendance,* and a sentinel at the opera box. Less palpable, but no less real was the privilege of building roads, inspecting glass works, protecting religious minorities, managing the poor, and even expressing disapproval of old military nobles like Mézières who enforced burdensome *corvées* on the king's subjects. Whatever his limitations as a man of principle or a person of introspection and depth, by the standards of his *état* and milieu, Jean De Pont, Intendant of Metz, had "arrived."

Jean-Samuel's career in government had been facilitated by many people in high places, connections he had cultivated with the help of a charming young wife. Among many contacts both at Paris and Metz, one of the most valuable was Madame de Genlis, novelist, educator, and governess of the five children of the Duc de Chartres, one of whom was the future Louis-Philippe. The "fan incident" with Madame de Montesson, which Jean-Samuel had little reason to relish, was a small price to pay for the generation-long friendship with a key member of the Orléans circle.[37] Jean-Samuel's wife, Marie-Madeleine L'Escureul de la Touche, remained a close friend of Madame de Genlis until her untimely death in 1787. They had performed many services for each other. Madame Depont had helped arrange the marriage of one of Genlis's daughters, and it appears that Genlis provided the setting at least for the marriage to Jean-Samuel.[38] In 1785 Madame de Genlis introduced Jean-Samuel to one of her friends in England, indicating how important his wife's role had been. "M. de Pont, Intendant of Metz, is a man of intelligence and merit, and a respected magistrate . . . . He has asked me to give him a letter of introduction to you, but he would have asked in vain if I were not his wife's friend, for I would not wish to importune you."[39]

The visit of Jean-Samuel and his eighteen-year-old son, Charles-François, to London in the fall of 1785 was not altogether felicitous. The sojourn was not improved by the fact that their host's brother was entrusted with entertaining the pair in the City, a task he obviously did not enjoy. The brief report of the day at the Guildhall ending at the Lord Mayor's dinner and ball records *maladresse,* awkward incomprehension, and acute discomfort on all sides.

As a royal intendant and a Parisian, Jean-Samuel was accustomed not only to all the French formulas of respect and politesse, but also to a modicum of order and discipline in public places. The London Guildhall, situated in the densely packed City not far from the Tower, had little of the dignity and calm of the Intendance of Metz. Jean-Samuel was ill prepared for the London of the recent Gordon Riots or even for the London of the "school of thieves."[40] The streets were crowded and the coach was forced to make detours before the three men reached the Guildhall. The host for the day, one Richard Burke, calmly describes the atmosphere along Lud Lane, "little incommoded by the crowd who sometimes however was in motion and clamorous," a *tumulte* that obviously unnerved the Deponts. After meeting the Lord Mayor and Lady Mayoress, the two French visitors encountered Lord Sydney, the dukes of Leeds and Richmond, and finally William Pitt himself, no group of petty officials. Again, Burke described the scene as if it were an everyday occurrence. "The last two [Richmond and Pitt] came together, and the mob saluted them with a shower of stones. The Duke showed his arm to the Recorder, marked by a stone. The Recorder assured him that it was not meant for him, but that it was a consequence of keeping bad company. Pitt was, I think, badly vexed, for he came in laughing very heartily."[41] Apart from the incongruity of the "hearty laughter," Jean-Samuel must have raised an eyebrow about the virtues and efficiency of local English administration. The City was simply not well policed. Five years later, Intendant Depont had reasons to recall the stone-throwing incident, as a French crowd broke into his *hôtel* in Metz. At the Guildhall, the worst was yet to come.

In the middle of dinner at the Lord Mayor's hustings, Jean-Samuel discovered that his wallet had been stolen. Richard Burke described the incident with something less than complete sympathy for the plight of his foreign guests. "At last the father got something on his plate, and searching in his pocket (for his knife, I suppose), he gave a great start and exclaimed, *'par Dieu, on m'a volé.' 'Quoi,'* said the son? *'On m'a piqué le poaket,'* replies the father. 'Oh Sir,' I said, *'ce n'est qu'une mouchoir.' 'Oh mon Dieu, Monsieur, j'ai perdu mon porte-feuille.'"*[42] This exchange, added to Jean-Samuel's constant refrain of *"encore de pic poakets"* every time he entered a crowd, left a lasting impression on both Richard Burke and his brother, Edmund. Four years later, Edmund Burke referred to Jean-Samuel's son, then a councilor at the Parlement of Paris, as "young Picky-Poky."[43]

The balance of the evening at the Guildhall was hardly more success-ful. Richard Burke admitted that the dinner was poor, the wine "exe-crable," and the women less than elegant. He referred to the Mayoress as "a little old hag." Young Depont declined an invitation to dance. Completing his "commission" to his brother, Richard left the Deponts for another "assembly" in St. Alban's Street where *his* pocket was picked "after the manner of such Assemblys, as De Ponts was after the manner of that at the Guildhall"—an everyday occurrence it seemed.

Jean-Samuel must have felt more than the normal frustrations of an uninitiated visitor in a foreign land. His acquired skills of charm and persuasion were tied not only to a firm command of the French language and the requisite forms of *politesse*, but also to a special setting which facilitated either pronunciamentos—in the *salon d'audience* of the intendance, for example—or *causeries*, highly stylized verbal exchanges in a drawing-room atmosphere. Richard Burke regarded Jean-Samuel's formulas of politesse—those "mille remerciements and cent mille pardons given and asked" as a waste of time and slightly comical. Needless to add, the London Guildhall and its immediate street surroundings were not a setting conducive to charm of any kind. Yet if Jean-Samuel was totally out of his depth in London, his son was willing and able to listen and learn from the Burkes at Beaconsfield. At sixty, the intendant of Metz could not be expected to appreciate English manners and customs. But at eighteen, an *avocat-général* at the Parlement of Metz might overlook the stumbling blocks of social intercourse. Charles-François Depont would soon join the parlementary opposition at home. [44] He was fast becoming an ardent Anglophile.

IV
Revolution and Survival

L'âge des passions et des talens est l'époque de tous les succès. A cet âge seul on peut inspirer l'enthousiasme et exciter un tendre intérêt. Il faut mourir jeune, comme Alexandre et Germanicus, pour laisser une mémoire chère, un nom éclatant, un souvenir agréable. Quand on se figure Mithridate avec une longue barbe, on convient froidement de ses talens et de son courage.

On aime à contempler l'homme dans toute sa force et dans le moment d'énergie des passions. Les idées de dégradation et de foiblesse diminuent de l'admiration. Une belle femme enlevée à la fleur de son âge, ne présente à la postérité que l'idée des agrémens et des charmes qui faisoient sa célébrité. Ninon qui a été belle et qui a vieilli jusqu'à la caducité, offre l'image d'une vieille femme spirituelle et philosophe, tandis que Madame de Montbazon ne rappelle que l'idée de la beauté.

Il est pour chacun un âge pour mourir.

—Sénac de Meilhan
"Du Penchant de l'Homme à Admirer Tous les Genres de Puissance"

CHAPTER EIGHT

A Young French Gentleman in Paris

On the morning of 4 May 1788 the august halls of the Parlement of Paris were invaded not by the habitual claque of parlementary supporters but by portions of the general public. Guy-Marie Sallier, then a young councilor at the Parlement, described the scene: "... a crowd of lackeys and idlers from the dregs of the populace halted at the doorway of the *Grand' Chambre.* ... At a signal from the ushers, they rushed noisily into the hall. ... The mob applauded, not for what had been read, which it did not understand, but to register its own importance at being asked to serve as auxiliaries. In this distressing situation, natural curiosity made me glance over the ranks of my colleagues where I saw on all faces the embarrassment and confusion I myself felt."[1] But whatever second thoughts the magistrates had about such "public" support, these were heady days, when resistance to "ministerial despotism" elicited the finest rhetoric and bold assertions of "individual liberty" and "fundamental law."

Among many eloquent orators in the chambers of the Parlement, none was so effective as Duval d'Esprémesnil. Henri Carré has labeled Duval "an unconscious precursor of the Revolution"—unconscious indeed, since he quickly joined the conservative royalists after June 1789. But in 1787 he was the recognized leader of the parlementary opposition.[2] Known for his nervous temper, penetrating eyes, strong voice, theatrical gestures, and a capacity to speak for hours without apparent fatigue, Duval was especially effective with the young councilors in the subordinate chambers, the *Requêtes* and *Enquêtes.*[3] He was surely their hero during those days of May 1788, which culminated in his arrest and that of his young colleague

Goislard de Montsabert by a special emissary of the king, though not before the whole hall had risen as a man to shout: "We are all Messieurs Duval and Goislard. You have to arrest all of us!"[4]

The older magistrates had reason to suspect the "vivacity" and "turbulence" of their younger colleagues because of a temperamental difference that reached back at least to the early 1780s between the upper and lower chambers and reflected not only a marked disparity of age but also a festering resentment over the distribution of litigation fees, the *épices* and *vacations*.[5] As early as March 1783, the Parisian bookseller S. P. Hardy referred to the "very great division between the magistrates of the *Grand' Chambre* and those of the three chambers of *Enquêtes*,"[6] who were demanding reform of legal fees, not an unpopular issue with litigants either. As magistrates of merit, the senior members of the *Grand' Chambre* left much to be desired. Even Etienne Denis Pasquier, whose later career under Napoleon and Louis XVIII hardly suggests a man partial to radical change, admitted that the *grand banc* provided "laudable virtues" but "no eminent merit, and above all, no talent for speaking," of which there was such an abundance among the younger parlementarians.[7] Pasquier remembers how the young men, lacking any models among the senior magistrates, looked elsewhere for guidance.

The young had suffered from the control of their elders. Placed on their own, and attracted by new ideas, they did produce men of talent, some even eloquent, but almost all of them were dominated by the ardor of their imaginations. Without other guides, is it strange that these young people were seduced by some of the greatest names of France, the La Rochefoucauld, Harcourt, Luynes, Aumont, Luxembourg, Praslin, and many others? ... Among 150 magistrates, at most half belonged to families long committed to the magistracy. The other half had more recent origins in the second rank of magistrates and high finance.[8]

Pasquier proceeds to explore this unlikely alliance between an important part of the old blood nobility and the young robe nobles of recent vintage. He recalls his own seduction by the peerage.

I shall never forget how powerful was the appeal of such peers on the minds of young magistrates. Suddenly they saw themselves linked by party with these great names and their style of life; one knows how party spirit brings together, fuses even, people of different ranks [*conditions*]. Such a seductive and uncommon relationship easily turned heads; it did not take much to win us over: a kind word, the willingness to take notice of our opinions, submerged any difficulties. Then, when we returned home, our minds were full of the exchange in the assemblies of the Chambers. After these meetings, about twenty of us would regularly eat together, usually at the home of our colleague, M. de Trudaine.[9]

If Pasquier saw the young magistrates of the *Enquêtes* as auxiliaries of the liberal aristocrats—La Rochefoucauld, Noailles, Aiguillon, Talleyrand-Périgord, Lafayette—Councilor Sallier considered them equally "seduced" by the gallery, by the hundreds of barristers, attorneys, bailiffs, and clerks who made up the *basoche*, mixed with unemployed lawyers, law students, and other *oisifs* who crowded the corridors outside the *Grand' Chambre* waiting for the latest news of the debates within. Far from obeying the oath of secrecy, wrote Sallier, "the young magistrates reported the debates to the public and were greeted with acclamation and applause. Flattered by this, they made it a point of honor not to exercise moderation."[10] Translated into oratory, claimed Barentin, Keeper of the Seals, youthful rashness swamped mature judgment in the halls of Parlement. Convinced that the young magistrates were responsible for the "doubling of the Third" in the approaching meeting of the Estates-General, Barentin reflected on 1788 in Burkean prose. "Reason was sometimes submerged by the brilliant flashes of elocution and the strong imagination of a few young magistrates; they silenced the experience and sound reasoning of the old senators."[11]

Yet it would be wrong to attribute the "innovative spirit" of the reformist magistrates exclusively to the enthusiasm of youth, to resentment against their senior colleagues, to the manipulation of liberal peers, to a puerile desire for popularity, or even to public pressure pure and simple. Even Sallier and Pasquier, who would soon regret their youthful idealism, remembered that they too were brimming over with a spirit of generosity and moral earnestness in those fast-moving months before the spring of '89. "I am far from absolving myself . . . of having shared in the impetuosity of a new outlook, proud of our independence and purity."[12] Pasquier was even more lyrical and less apologetic. "From the moment when our interest was clearly at issue, we saw nothing more beautiful than to sacrifice it to what we regarded as the public welfare. Generous feelings seized us and there was no holding us back."[13] Barentin, to be sure, indicated no appreciation for such moments of euphoria. For him, the disastrous sequence of events leading to the calling of the Estates-General was brought about by "seditious assemblies" of "frondeurs, *philosophes,* and preachers of ephemeral philosophies [*systèmes du jour*], who drew up various plans for the destruction of legitimate power."[14] Barentin was fifty-one in early 1789; Sallier and Pasquier were in their late twenties; and a young councilor in the *Deuxième Chambre des Enquêtes*, Charles-Jean-François DePont, was only twenty-one.

Young DePont's political education began as early as 1787, when he was still *avocat-général* at the Parlement of Metz. In August 1787, at the age of twenty, Charles-François wanted to be included in the "exile" of the Paris parlement to Troyes. He had been overlooked in the distribution of *lettres de cachet.* To baron de Breteuil, the minister, he wrote: "I request that you forward my *lettre* to Troyes," where he was going to join his colleagues. [15] Here was genuine solidarity with his colleagues of the *Enquêtes.*

Political ferment was not limited in these years to the chambers behind the *grille* on the Ile de la Cité. Public political life in France was literally born between 1787 and 1789. [16] By 1788, "seditious assemblies," as Barentin put it, took place in private homes and other unofficial places. Since the first meeting of the Assembly of Notables in February 1787, Paris was alive with private societies, dinner clubs, and politicized salons, all of which focused attention on the financial crisis now fully exposed by the government for the first time. "From the halls of the Parlement the agitation spread to the clubs," wrote Sallier. "Public opinion sallied forth in the theaters, on the boulevards, the usual sign of great excitement." [17] Again, in these unofficial settings, the young robe magistrates were the most active and the most vocal.

Less eloquent, but also less mercurial than Duval d'Eprémesnil, the spellbinder of the *Enquêtes,* was the twenty-eight-year-old councilor Adrien-Jean-François Duport. [18] Jean Egret does not hesitate to call Duport a "formidable party leader" at a time when political groupings in France were only beginning to expand their organization beyond coteries of families linked by institutional or "corporate" ties or drawn together by some salon oracle or Parisian hostess. Duport's circle started very modestly as a dinner group of only twelve people who met at his town house on the rue du Grand Chantier. By late autumn of 1788 it began to grow rapidly until it gained a reputation as the most famous political club in Paris, the "Committee of Thirty." [19] Barentin, the Keeper of the Seals, saw it as a den of "*sectateurs,*" where the "frondeurs" of the Parlement of Paris plotted such subversive measures as the doubling of the Third Estate. And indeed, the parlementary *arrêt* of December 1788 amended the famous September ruling that the meeting of the Estates-General would follow the constitutional forms of 1614. According to Barentin and other conservative royalists, the new ruling opened the way to the destruction of the Old Regime. "This act can be regarded as the product of seditious meetings that took place at M. Duport's. These meetings were made up of magistrates, most of whom were young and very ardent"— and, by implication, wrongheaded at best. Barentin identified thirty-one members. [20] Twenty-three were magistrates, and fifteen of these were councilors in the *Deuxième Chambre des Enquêtes.* Mirabeau called them a "reserve corps of *parlementaires.*" [21]

Magistrates in the Committee of Thirty* (December 1788)

From the *Grand'Chambre*:
Le Peletier de Saint-Fargeau, *président à mortier* (28)
Barillon de Morangis, honorary councilor
Robert de Saint-Vincent, councilor
Fréteau, councilor
Clément de Verneuil, councilor
Abbé Sabatier de Cabre, councilor
Abbé Lecoigneux, councilor
Abbé Mauperché de Fontenay, councilor

From the *Enquêtes*:
Duval d'Esprémesnil, councilor (42)
Robert de Lierville, councilor (30)
Bourré de Coberon, councilor (32)
La Bletonnière d'Ygé, councilor (30)
Rubat, councilor (45)
Abbé Perrotin de Barmond, councilor
Trudaine de Montigny, councilor (24)
Trudaine de la Sablière, councilor (22)
Huguet de Sémonville, councilor (34)
Clément de Givry, councilor (42)
Morel de Vondé, councilor (29)
Geoffrey de Charnois, councilor (27)
Abbé Louis de Barmond, councilor
Charles-Jean-François Depont, councilor (21)
Adrien-Jean-François Duport, councilor (29), chairman

*Ages, where known, are given in parenthesis.

The Keeper of the Seals, himself a veteran of thirty years in the Paris Parlement, spoke regretfully of the remaining eight members of the Committee of Thirty. "A few persons of quality have abandoned honor to be admitted there; they have learned at this 'school' how to censor the king and his ministers. The police should have kept a close watch on these meetings and the authorities should have proscribed them."[22]

Luynes, duc de
Montmorency-Luxembourg, duc de
Aumont, duc d'
Béthune-Charost, duc de

Aiguillon, duc d'
La Rochefoucauld, duc de
Condorcet, marquis de
Lafayette, marquis de

Conservatives like Barentin and his successors in the nineteenth century will always regard the Committee of Thirty as a conspiratorial group, to be associated with Cochin's or Tocqueville's bearers of "abstract" and "utopian" ideas that launched the French nation on an uncharted and ultimately disastrous voyage. Historians of a Marxist bent, on the other hand, see the Committee of Thirty as a vanguard of the "rising bourgeoisie." It seems to me that it was neither as conspiratorial nor as omnipotent as the conservative, anti-Revolutionary historians would have it. Nor were its ideas and legislative proposals "utopian," unless due process of law and representative government were utopian in France in 1789. The Committee was profoundly legalistic; its overwhelming majority of magistrates made this almost a certainty from the outset. The composition of the membership also makes it difficult to label it "bourgeois" or even "aristocratic" without oversimplifying and distorting the actual situation beyond recognition. In a formal sense, all thirty-one members were nobles, but this does not mean that they were part of an "aristocratic reaction" any more than they were spokesmen for "bourgeois capitalism." As Elizabeth Eisenstein has put it, the Committee of Thirty was "a loose political coalition based on an informal grouping of *like-minded notables.*"[23] This is not to say, of course, that the ideas discussed and the organization for political leadership provided by the Committee were not important at this stage of the pre-revolution.[24]

Adrien Duport was an organizer of the first order. He carried on a prodigious correspondence, increased the membership, and published many of the famous Parisian pamphlets. By the time of the meeting of the Estates-General in May 1789 the Committee of Thirty was able to distill the key issues, distribute model cahiers, prepare for the elections, devise parliamentary strategies, mobilize votes, and eventually establish corresponding and affiliated societies throughout France.[25] Equally important, Duport made a conscious effort to expand the earlier alliance between the robe magistrates and the liberal aristocrats by bringing together like-minded men from all the elites, nobles and non-nobles, bankers and magistrates, lawyers and physicians, journalists and men of letters, in what was to become the largest and probably most influential political club of the French Revolution, the "Society of Friends of the Constitution," later known simply as the Jacobin Club.[26] It was to this nascent national or "patriotic" party, led by an elite of all talents, that Duport first proposed the doubling of the Third Estate and made it seem natural among such equals of "merit" and dedication to public service to envisage the union of "Orders" and even voting "by head" in the Estates-General. Barentin and the conservative royalists were correct in their appraisal of Duport's position on this vital issue, a position he had held as early as 1787.

Historians have always stressed the importance of the Committee of Thirty in the "preparation" of the French Revolution, especially in its organization of a legislative program that went far beyond fiscal reform.[27]

But whatever the Committee's precise impact on Revolutionary events—an influence almost impossible to measure—there can be no doubt that the frequent meetings at Duport's town house were an intense political education for the participants. We do not know if Charles-François De-Pont actually designed a model cahier, but he surely read them; he may not have written any of the eleven articles of the Committee's "declaration of rights,"[28] but he knew them well; he may not have spoken himself about a new national constitution, but it must have been discussed in his presence, and no doubt with vigor, given the professional and age composition of the Committee of Thirty.

"Meetings were held Sundays, Tuesdays, and Wednesdays, from five to ten in the evening, and one would be admitted only by unanimous consent of the society, which initially numbered only twelve. We chose a chairman, who sat at the head of the table, announced the issues to be discussed, controlled the discussion, took the vote . . . , gave the sense of the meeting, and announced the next session."[29] We can rather easily imagine a rather short and stocky twenty-one-year-old listening intently as Duval d'Esprémesnil discussed "due process" and Duport explained the English jury system to the dukes of La Rochefoucauld and d'Aiguillon, or as Marquis de Lafayette invoked America and introduced such provocative phrases as "National Assembly."[30]

Charles-François DePont had been a follower of Adrien Duport from the very beginning as his younger colleague in the *Enquêtes* and as a charter member of the Committee of Thirty. He was the youngest in a very young group of magistrates and surely impressed by the distinguished company around him. He was not elected to the Estates-General, nor did he leave evidence of a speech, except one given in November 1789, before the National Assembly, apologizing for his former colleagues at the Parlement of Metz who had resisted the abolition of the parlements.[31] But his correspondence with a well-known Englishman indicates how close his political ideas were to those of Adrien Duport and to the new National Party in 1789 and 1790.

Only with our advantage of hindsight do we know that the programs and policies of the National Party would be short-lived. By the end of 1790, after eighteen momentous months of political activity, the "Society of Friends of the Constitution" had become a thriving organization with its own publications, a dozen permanent committees, affiliated clubs throughout France representing perhaps 20,000 members and foreign correspondents throughout the continent and in England.[32] In December 1790 the Society published its first complete list of 1,102 members, and a very distinguished group it was. In addition to the famous triumvirate—Duport, Lameth, and Barnave—there were contingents from all the nation's elites, a mass of lawyers, magistrates and physicians, a large sprinkling of men of letters, journalists, and eminent scientists, a lesser number of financiers, *négociants*, ironmasters, and agriculturalists, and a few nobles and clergy. It very closely matches Alfred Cobban's occupational breakdown of the National Assembly,[33] although it shows a greater density of distinction. Among scientists, one sees Cabanis, Monge, Lecépède; among artists and poets Vernet, David, Talma, Fabre d'Eglantine, Sabatier, and Chénier; among writers Sedaine, Mercier, Moreau de Saint-Méry, Carra, and Laclos; and among journalists Maréchal, Noël, Le Hodey, Saint-Aubin, Fréron, and Jourdan. To be sure, one also detects some future *Conventionnels* such as Billaud-Varenne, Rabaud Saint-Etienne, Reubell, Tallien, and the Robespierre brothers, but more frequent are those less notorious men who survived the Revolution and reappear as administrators or deputies to the legislatures of the Directory or as barons of the Empire. In short, the membership was what Adrien Duport hoped it would be—a notability of talent and wealth from all *états*, though, by late 1790, it lacked the great names of the high nobility.[34] Among the "D"s we see "Depont, rue des Filles Saint-Thomas, no. 11," without any other notation.[35]

No doubt young DePont heard the speech of Abbé Monnier at the Society's meeting of 25 December 1790, in which the abbé spoke of the latest action of "a desperate aristocracy" trying to undermine "all that our legislators have done for the stability of the French Empire." He referred to the establishment of a rival club called the *Constitution Monarchique* "as if our club were not concerned with founding a constitutional monarchy, but a legal monarchy, a monarchy based on the laws, and whose goal is the welfare of the nation."[36] Indeed the speeches of the Society would reiterate again and again the theme of legal monarchy. In May 1791 another speech referred to the sacred motto on the doors of the Jacobin Club: *la Nation, la Loi, le Roi.*[37]

In 1790 there was confidence in the National Party and pride of accomplishment. In the very first months of debate, the *Monarchiens* with their proposals for a hereditary upper house and an absolute veto for the king had been decisively voted down. "Aristocractic privileges," from tax exemptions to venality of office were ended, "*féodalité*" abolished, and the financial crisis alleviated by the nationalization of Church property and the creation of paper money. The entire governmental structure was being rebuilt from top to bottom. And perhaps dearest of all to a reformist councilor of the former *Chambre des Enquêtes* was the plan for a complete overhaul of the judiciary, abolishing judicial torture and instituting trial by jury. This project was the fruit of a long study by Duport, including an investigation of the English system of justice.[38] Surely DePont had good reason to anticipate the approval of his English friends for legislation of this kind. Two years of intense political experience provided the setting for young DePont's correspondence with the oracle of European conservatism, Edmund Burke.

Turning to the English side of the Channel, recall a few circumstances shaping Burke's perspective on French affairs. Burke did not know French society well. He had only visited Paris once in 1773 and even then he had been alarmed by the salon talk of the *philosophes*. Their religious skepticism and irreverent tone he characterized as "the confederacy of the powers of darkness" undermining the "props of good government."[39] What little contact he had with France came to him through French visitors to Beaconsfield and by correspondence. Although Burke exchanged some letters with reformists such as Adrien Duport and even with a Revolutionary enthusiast like Jean-Baptiste Cloots,[40] he had many more regular correspondents among political conservatives such as Lally-Tollendal, Pierre-Gaëton Dupont (not Charles-François DePont), François de Menonville, and Calonne, the former controller-general. Once the Revolution began, these correspondents reinforced Burke's hostility and even employed the same lurid vocabulary, effectively masking any nuances of difference among the revolutionaries.

Menonville, surely not the most violent of Burke's French royalist friends, expressed himself in these words in November 1790: "You cannot be acquainted, Sir, with the despicable Productions of the crawling, desperate, foolish, but altogether too much popular Scriblers, who daily pester this unhappy country with their firebrands,—perhaps you don't know they receive direct encouragement from this ignorant, ravenous, sophistical, atheist, mobbish Assembly of the Jacobins."[41] Menonville might not fully agree with Burke that the National Assembly resembled "a gang of Assassins" but he more than met him halfway. This epithet he said, "exactly fitted to the majority of the Assembly, I must confess,"[42] though there was a minority of moderates left. Menonville even suggested to Burke that these moderate influences in the Assembly were being weakened by the emigration of such men as Lally-Tollendal and Mounier, and that "they were looked upon as Deserters from the patriotic Party."[43] Burke replied that "those who consider Mounier and Lally as deserters must be themselves considered murderers and traitors, because what have they deserted if not crime and treason?"[44]

As if his own prose were not dramatic enough in evoking the passage of the royal couple from Versailles to Paris in the "October Days" of 1789, Burke chose to print an extract in French from his friend Lally-Tollendal in the *Reflections*, as "an eye-witness" to substantiate this day of infamy. After an allusion to the "guilt" of the city of Paris and of the National Assembly, and his own failing health, Lally wrote: "... it is beyond my strength to stand any longer the horror of this blood—these heads—this queen *almost with her throat cut*—this king—led *as a slave*—entering Paris, in the middle of these assassins, and preceded by the heads of the unfortunate guards. These perfidious Janissaries, these assassins, these cannibalistic women, this cry of 'Hang all the Bishops' at the very moment the king was entering his capital with two bishops of the royal Council in his coach ....'' [45] For Lally, as for Burke, the humiliation of the Crown was even worse than the violence of the crowd.

Burke's idealization of the French court and the royal couple in particular owed something to his son's presentation to the Queen at Versailles before the Revolution in 1785. Wrote Richard to his mother, on that occasion: "The King asking quel est M. Burke, the Queen asking où est M. B. ... in short, there is no end of inquiries about me. ... What court is there higher and more brillant than that of France? What court where one could more desire to be distinguished treated and caressed?"[46] No doubt Richard responded willingly when his father asked him to visit the émigré court at Koblenz in July 1791.[47] As Ernest Barker points out, the whole cast of Burke's mind was aristocratic and religious much before 1785.[48] But his idealization of the Queen would seem to require a special inspiration. "I saw her just above the horizon, decorating and cheering the elevated sphere ... glittering like the morning star, full of life, splendor, and joy. Oh, what a revolution!"[49]

As for Burke's view of the French nobility—"men of a high spirit and a delicate sense of honor ... well-bred, very officious, humane, and hospitable"[50]—he may well have been thinking about his friend, Lally-Tollendal. He described Lally as "one of the most honest, intelligent, and eloquent members of the National Assembly, one of the most active and zealous reformers of the State," and obliged to secede from the Assembly and become a voluntary exile.[51] Lally's fight for bicameralism and an absolute royal veto was one with which Burke could sympathize.[52] Most important, Lally was a spokesman for the *Monarchiens*, the Anglophile Party in the National Assembly which believed there was an unwritten French constitution to which the Nation should "return." Would-be disciples of Montesquieu, the *Monarchiens*—Mounier, Clermont-Tonnerre, Malouet, Bergasse, Virieu—employed a parliamentary discourse Burke could appreciate. Proclaimed Clermont-Tonnerre from the rostrum: "There are two public opinions, one precipitous, ephemeral and fleeting, born of prejudice and passion; another is slow, stable, and irresistible, born of time and reason."[53]

Indeed from almost every point of view, Lally would seem to be the most appropriate French recipient of Burke's *Reflections*. Yet he chose Charles-François DePont, a magistrate whose noble pedigree barely embraced three generations.

It is curious that, despite the great attention given to Edmund Burke by historians, relatively little has been written about Burke's correspondent in France. For years, most commentators have considered the "very young gentleman at Paris, who did him the honor of desiring his opinion"[54] on recent events in France to be a literary fiction devised by Burke in 1790, while others have confused the name DePont with Dupont, who later translated the *Reflections* into French. Only in 1936 was the real correspondent identified by the discovery in England of four DePont letters among the Fitzwilliam papers. The actual French texts appeared in 1951. The last of these four letters, written by DePont in December 1790, was translated into English in 1791 and published in England under the title *Answer to the Reflections of the Right Hon. Edmund Burke, by M. Depont with the Original Notes* (London: Debrett, Picadilly, 1791). It is possible that young DePont sent a copy of his letter to one of Burke's political opponents, perhaps to Thomas Paine. The authorship of the "Notes" is somewhat problematical, but it is my opinion that they were written by DePont himself. For some reason, historians, English and American in particular, have evinced little interest in this reply to Burke, perhaps considering it only one among so many English radical brochures of the year 1791.[55]

The four letters written between January 1786 and December 1790 reflect DePont's growing excitement about the French Revolution and a desire to elicit Burke's comment and approval. Initially, DePont indicated a great respect and admiration for the English statesman, considering him an oracle of "Liberty," an inspiration and an example. DePont's youthful enthusiasm, together with political developments in England, moved Burke to comment on the Revolution and eventually led him to elaborate his views in the famous *Reflections*. DePont's letters serve to underline how different the political thinking of French liberals was from Burke's, and how inappropriate this "young gentleman" was as a sympathetic recipient of Burke's philosophical tract. The letters reveal the Frenchman's growing incomprehension, an increasingly frantic effort to convince Burke, and finally a recognition, albeit regretful, of the abyss that separated the two men's thinking about "Liberty," institutional change, and the meaning of the French Revolution.

Shortly after the visit of the DePonts, father and son, to London in 1785, Charles-François thanked Burke profusely for his hospitality in extremely deferential terms, praising his mind, his generosity, and even his "Nation," "*la plus estimable de l'univers.*" "It seems to me that the three days I have spent with you have given my soul new strength and that, in short, I am better for them. Would that I could pass more time with you, have the pleasure of listening to you, of profiting from your enlightenment [*vos lumières*] and your gentle and informing knowledge, and finally bring myself to deserve your friendship. What a joy for me if I have been able to inspire you with a little interest in me, and if you sometimes think of a young Frenchman who overwhelmed you with questions!"[56] Making adequate allowance for the forms of *politesse,* and the "vivacity" of a youth not yet twenty years of age, DePont's letter was surely sincere and deeply felt.

Almost four years later, in November 1789, Charles-François resumed correspondence with Burke. Reminding his former host of the days at Beaconsfield and apologizing for his failure to write sooner, DePont supplicated: "Be assured [this young Frenchman] will never forget that his heart beat for the first time at the name of Liberty when he heard you speak of it. Do not doubt the interest with which he has followed in the public press the various motions you have made in Parliament."[57] DePont proposed that he inform Burke regularly about events in France. Above all, he solicited a reaction from the English statesman whom he yearned to see again face to face in the halls of Parliament, evoking his desire "to hear this great man speak again, this man who makes ministers tremble and encourages young men who are lovers of liberty."[58] DePont was convinced that Burke would approve the momentous events of 1789. Were they not the application of principles Burke himself had proclaimed? "I cannot leave France to see you now; public affairs hold me here. ... I have heard the great principles of government proclaimed in our own National Assembly; I learned them from talking to you ... and I have come to feel for my own new *patrie* those sentiments of which you were the first to speak, but which I could not then grasp in their full meaning."

Surely, the English stateman, DePont's political mentor, would approve—indeed bless—the Revolution of 1789. "If you will deign to assure him that the French are worthy of being free, that they know how to distinguish liberty from license, and legitimate government from a despotic power—if you will deign also to assure him that the Revolution now begun will succeed—proud in your support, he will never be cast down by the discouragement that often follows hope."[59]

Burke's first reaction to DePont's plea to resume contact was expressed in a letter to his son Richard.

I enclose [for] you the letter I had this morning from young Picky Pokey [of Nov. 4]. You see he correctly remembers every good point of our attention to him, which gives one a good opinion of his heart. He is in the very focus of the flame of French Liberty. I am not sorry to have one Frenchman give some account of their proceedings. There really is some appearance, as if the Nation was more united than one would have imagined; and that *they will be able to accomplish their ruin in the Establishment of what they call a constitution.* You see that Dumpling hangs back. All that are firm against the Parisians are obliged to fly. Lally,[60] it seems, is one of the fugitives. All of this looks as if no part of France offers a residence for the dissentients.[61]

This short passage reveals a number of things. First, it indicates that by November 1789 Burke had already made up his mind about the French Revolution, that he had no faith in the new constitution and in the "flame of french Liberty," which he suggested was a kind of illness or fever. The "Parisians," presumably both the majority in the National Assembly and the "street mob," were forcing "statesmen" like Lally to flee the country. He could only have formed this idea from his conservative royalist correspondents, possibly from Lally himself. In November 1789, the French government was not "forcing" anyone to "flee." In fact, emigration was a growing problem for the new government, as the émigrés gathered outside of France, especially at Turin and Koblenz, and made active efforts to solicit foreign intervention in French affairs. But Burke apparently never understood how the counterrevolution affected the actions of the revolutionaries and how his own work—his lurid characterizations more than his philosophy—would contribute to the counterrevolution. Carl Cone, in his standard work on Burke, states the issue well: "The constitution of 1791, whose provisions Burke scorned, never received a fair test, and the counterrevolution that finally caused its death was caused by Burke himself."[62] Finally, Burke's unguarded allusion to "young Picky Pokey" and "Dumpling" indicates at best a condescending attitude toward his French disciple and at worst a mocking, even xenophobic one. The brief exchange of letters between Burke and DePont could hardly be expected to take on the flavor of a "Great Debate" among equals. But one might have expected a more open-minded, tolerant attitude toward a young man who was obviously sincere in his political convictions and full of good will toward Burke. Perhaps Burke's coolness toward the young magistrate in this passage was a reflection of the growing passion, even "alarm" he felt for DePont's "Revolution."

Burke replied to DePont a month later in a letter that fills twelve pages of his correspondence.[63] It was his first important "reflection" on the French Revolution, written a full year before the publication of the famous pamphlet. Burke hesitated to send the letter when he had finished it and, given its contents, one can see why. Knowing in retrospect Burke's political philosophy, we are not surprised by his skepticism toward "constitution-making" in France. And knowing something about the young councilor at the Paris Parlement and his family background, we can well imagine the growing consternation on DePont's face as he assimilated Burke's English prose. Burke begins by explaining that he has delayed writing not only because he might say something "disagreeable to your formed opinions" but also because he fears that the French government is censoring all letters and that his criticisms of France might be transferred, as he puts it, "from the guilty Writer to the innocent Receiver." Burke's mistaken belief that censorship prevailed in France at a time when freedom of the press had just been established sets the tone of his letter. Despite his disclaimer to any expertise on the "political Map of which I must be very imperfectly acquainted," Burke nevertheless refers to "the scene now displayed in France," where rapid changes defy "all speculation" and where "equitable judgments" and "deliberate resolutions" on the part of the "Power prevalent at the time" are undermined by the "inconclusive logick of the Passions." Indeed, for Burke, rapid political change has to be the result of the "logic of the Passions" and therefore a dangerous game, like a child playing with fire. Surely, Burke looked upon his "French gentleman" as on an innocent child—"in the very focus of the flame of french Liberty"—who must be warned.

He begins with "Liberty," a very complex abstraction: "You hope, Sir, that I think the French deserving of Liberty? I certainly do. I certainly think that all Men who desire it, deserve it. It is not the Reward of our Merit or the acquisition of our Industry. It is our Inheritance. It is the birthright of our Species." We can only imagine how these words were translated into French and what they signified for a man who knew so well the remonstrances of the French parlements against "despotism," remonstrances which by 1788 were based as much on "natural right and the law of reason" as on an "ancient constitution." [64] Was this the "sentiment" of which Burke was the first to speak?

A paragraph later Burke assumes a more didactic tone.

You kindly said, that You began to love Freedom from your intercourse with Me. This is the more necessary because of all the loose Terms in the world Liberty is the most indefinite. Permit me then to continue our conversation, and to tell you what the freedom is that I love and that to which I think all men entitled. It is not solitary, unconnected, individual, selfish Liberty, as if every Man was to regulate the whole of his Conduct by his own will. The Liberty I mean is *social* freedom. [Italics Burke's.]

There is no need to review in detail all the elements of Burke's political philosophy; but the *Reflections* are clearly announced here in this long letter to young DePont. Characteristically, Burke treats the actual institutional changes in France in an almost casual manner, as if the precise facts could make little difference in the ultimate outcome, unless they were guided by the proper "spirit" and "principles." "But if neither your great Assemblies, nor your Judicatures nor your Municipalities act and forbear to act in the particulars, upon the principles, and in the spirit that I have stated, I must delay my congratulations on your acquisition of Liberty. You may have made a Revolution, but not a Reformation. You may have subverted Monarchy, but not recover'd freedom." The "spirit" is characterized by those Burkean terms we know so well—Prudence, Moderation, Prescriptive Right, Individual Property, all properly elaborated and understood. "If a Constitution is settled in France upon those principles and calculated for those ends, I believe there is no Man in this Country whose heart and Voice would not go along with You." One line in this long letter might have given DePont the key to the fundamental difference between himself and Burke. In a disarming sentence, Burke writes: "You will however be so good as to receive my very few hints with your usual indulgence, tho' some of them I confess are not in the taste of this enlighten'd age, and indeed are no better than the ripe fruit of *mere experience*." (Italics mine.)

In this same month of November 1789, Charles-Jean-François DePont, councilor at the Parlement of Paris, was addressing the National Assembly as representative of the city of Metz. Recall that his father, Jean-Samuel De Pont, had been intendant at Metz since 1778, and that he himself had been *avocat-général* at the Parlement of Metz since 1784. Charles-François, therefore, had close relations with the robe magistracy there. [65] On this occasion in Paris, he offered the apologies of his "*anciens confrères*" for their mistaken action in resisting the decrees of the National Assembly "suspending" the parlements of France. It should be added that Charles-François had been elected two months before to the *Comité patriotique* of Metz, a "patriotic" political organization that put him in good standing with the National Assembly. [66]

Adrien Duquesnoy, a representative of the Third Estate from Bar-le-Duc, was present in the National Assembly on that November day. Duquesnoy was struck by young DePont's political idealism and his respect for the work of the Assembly, even when it appeared to undermine his own place and status in French society.

It was a spectacle worthy of attention to see at the bar of the Assembly the son of an intendant (an *intendant*!), solicitor-general of the Parlement of Metz, councilor of the Parlement of Paris, deputy of the Commune of Metz, thanking the Assembly for pardoning a parlement! Add to this the fact that he is a noble, that this is an Assembly that has destroyed the noblesse, the intendants, and the parlements about which this deputy is speaking. And he is tendering his respects and obedience to this Assembly! These spectacles continue without end, and they never cease to astonish me every time they occur. [67]

DePont's words before the Assembly make clear how far he was ideologically from Edmund Burke. The magistrates at Metz, he said, had been temporarily seduced "by false and dangerous principles," but these fortunately had no influence on public opinion, so that "they cannot hinder the happy effects of a Revolution which all Frenchmen will soon be ashamed to have hindered in any way." There is no reason to doubt young DePont's loyalty to the National Assembly and his conviction that his country was on the threshold of a new era. "For many months,

Messeigneurs, you have been giving birth to new sentiments in our hearts that are impossible to express."[68] DePont gained clemency from the Assembly for his former colleagues of the parlement of Metz and for the past "errors" of the Commune of Metz.

In late December 1789, DePont replied to Burke's first reaction to the French Revolution. His letter conveys a tone of perplexity rather than bitter disappointment. He still retains a very large measure of deference toward his senior correspondent. He even agrees with Burke that the issue of freedom has not yet been resolved in France. "I earnestly desire we should be free, I hope we shall be so—but it is for the foreign observer without passions and without prejudices in this respect to determine whether we are using the best methods to arrive at liberty"[69] (p. 366). DePont proceeds to plead with Burke to understand the French situation. True, the new constitution has defects, "and some passages in your letter make me feel that you find terrible ones in it." "But does it not establish in the most precise manner the distinction between the powers and the rights of the nation?" Yes, there still is some "anarchy" here, but "is it not astonishing that this anarchy is not greater in an old, corrupt, and formerly servile nation, suddenly enlightened as to its rights, and that at the instant when all judicial and executive authority was annihilated? We have felt some violent shocks—but were they not naturally to be expected at the moment of attacking the formidable bodies of the nobility and the clergy, and of reforming the abuses under which the people groaned?" The next line contains the conclusion of DePont's argument, which Burke could not concede. "Ah, tell me, you to whom I look as a guide and master, tell me that the events that have taken place have been the necessary consequences of *a change which circumstances rendered indispensable!*" (p. 367, italics mine).

Throughout this letter, DePont stresses the differences between England and France. "I am of the opinion that we require stronger means than you do to maintain [our personal freedom] and that local and national differences (*l'esprit de notre nation*) oblige us to adopt precautions on our part that with you are unnecessary. That single consideration perhaps has determined us to institute only one assembly and to give to the king only a suspensive veto." Here again, Burke seems to have no grasp of the apprehension felt by men like DePont and other constitutional monarchists toward the counterrevolution.[70] This fear makes it easier to understand why young DePont, who, after all, owed much to birth and privilege, regarded "nobility" as a danger to "liberty" and dissociated himself from it. Moreover, his own self-image was changing. Charles-Jean-François DePont, magistrate, "constitutionalist," municipal leader, colleague of Duport and Lafayette, and charter member of the Committee of Thirty, did not need the trappings of noble status to gain recognition, or so it seemed. His Anglophilia was apparently undeterred by Burke's circumlocutions about Liberty. He promised to learn English, though "politics have made me neglectful of it." He still hoped that he would be able to meet Burke again at his "charming house at Beacons-field."

> We shall again examine the different details of your farm. We shall renew those in-
> teresting walks from which I used to derive so much pleasure and instruction, and
> we shall talk of politics and reason together. It will be curious indeed to see one of
> the greatest men in England condescend to reason with a young Frenchman of
> twenty-three. That Frenchman has inspired some interest in Monsieur Burke; that
> Frenchman does not claim to be a philosopher, but he feels deeply about Liberty
> and Equality. Therefore he is worthy of your conversation. (pp. 367–68.)

These lines were written on 29 December 1789, after what can only be called the most spectacular six months of institutional change in French history. Burke must have winced at the last lines of DePont's letter, which associated him with the enterprise.

It was a full year before Burke replied. If 1790 was an eventful year for DePont from his vantage point in the Society of Friends of the Constitution in Paris, it was an equally important year for Burke. According to Carl Cone, this was the time when Burke's political philosophy matured under the traumatic impact of real political events that forced him to bring together previously scattered writings and ideas on constitutional change and the sacrosanct nature of institutions. More than by the "October Days" and other "acts of violence" in France, Burke was shocked by the legislation of the National Assembly concerning the Church, especially when Dr. Richard Price, the eminent Dissenting minister, praised the Revolution and proposed the disestablishment of the Anglican Church and parliamentary reform. Price's sermon in November was followed by DePont's reference in his letter of December 1789 to the "authority" of the London "Revolution Society," which had also approved of the French Revolution. This excited Burke even further. The contagion of the French Levellers had crossed the Channel.[71]

Then, in February 1790, the London Chronicle advertised a "letter" to be published "soon" by the Hon. Edmund Burke on affairs in France. The "letter" grew into a 350-page book and was finally published under the title: *Reflections on the Revolution in France and on the Proceedings of Certain Societies in London Relative to That Event in a Letter Intended to Have Been Sent to a Gentleman in Paris.* In short, the book was intended for more than one audience, and DePont's allusion to the London "Revolution Society," a correspondent of his own Society of Friends of the Constitution, was an important catalyst for its composition.[72]

Burke's *Reflections on the French Revolution* has been the source of an enormous literature and commentary down to the present. It seems inappropriate, even presumptuous, to discuss the political ideas of a relatively unknown French magistrate as if they were of comparable significance and importance. It is certainly not my intention to add another footnote to the already prodigious corpus of Burkeana, not to say Burkomania. Burke was, of course, much more than a political thinker. He has been praised as a great moralist, Romantic, aesthete, English nationalist, philosopher of history, Whig politician, parliamentary orator, and expert in the common law. And of course he was a very effective writer, a stylist of the first order. What may seem to us today a florid and overly ornate prose was very attractive in its own day, and many passages in the *Reflections* still cast a certain spell even in less romantic and style-conscious times. Given this formidable array of assets, those who chose to respond to Burke's *Reflections* by marshaling the empirical evidence and arguing in the lean, prosaic style a Cartesian logic imposes were at a distinct disadvantage. Even where the weight of the evidence and the cogency of the argument seemed compelling, the critic often emerged as a literal-minded pedant who failed to grasp the depth and the grandeur of the master's thought. Respectable commentators today do not claim that Burke knew much about French society, but by implication, even for them, "facts" and "events" are such poor things, ultimately irrelevant and tedious, beside such an Olympian vision.

If this be true in our own time, how difficult it must have been for a twenty-two-year-old French magistrate, whose English was far from perfect, and who considered the elderly English statesman his "guide and master," to criticize a book of 350 pages that had been dedicated to himself. That is why DePont's letter of 6 December 1790 retains a deferential tone, even though disappointment, not to say disillusionment, is now apparent. [73] On the other hand, DePont attempts, once again, to explain the peculiarities of the French situation without directly attacking Burke's overall philosophy of change. He agrees with Burke that certain acts of violence are reprehensible, but points out that they must be weighed against the enormous benefits of the Revolution. For Burke, of course, it was almost an a priori truth that revolutions could not have "benefits," the very mode of change condemning this possibility from the start. Burke, as we know, was more impressed by the dangers of radical change and precipitous action than by the "abuses" of the Old Regime.

DePont was concerned that those abuses, only recently eradicated, might return and that Burke's book might be welcomed and used by the counterrevolutionary forces, which constituted a real danger in his eyes. "Yes, Monsieur, your kind, sensitive heart has been so deeply moved by the sorrows accompanying our Revolution that you must surely shrink from bringing more terrible suffering on us by *involuntarily supporting* the party that actually wishes for a Counterrevolution"[74] (italics mine). DePont not only enumerates the abuses of the Old Regime and stresses the inability of the old institutions to change them, but also attempts to answer Burke's criticisms of specific policies and acts of the new regime point by point in order to build a case for the necessity and the achievements of the Revolutionary cause. The overall impression is one of a lawyer's brief, organized into rather distinct sections, grounded in specific facts, punctuated with certain rhetorical devices, especially alliteration, and appealing to the reason and impartiality of the reader. At the same time, DePont conveys the sense of an enormous national effort grappling with complex and difficult problems. He appeals to Burke's patience and also assures him that, given time, "the new political machine" will function "without difficulty." (p. 373). The letter is not a manifesto of liberty and equality comparable to an oration by Mirabeau, Barnave, or Brissot—DePont was no orator—but it is, on balance, a coolly reasoned piece with a decided overtone of earnest pleading and friendly persuasion. It is not a vindictive tract, certainly not hostile to Burke personally, and indeed it encourages a further exchange of views, perhaps face to face at Beaconsfield.

Yet behind a courteous and even deferential façade, there are indications of a deep disagreement that DePont only dimly perceived. There is at times a perplexity in his reaction that reveals a profound difference in two men's assumptions about man, reason, and progress. "I am strongly reassured, Monsieur, by the progress of the Enlightenment[75] that you have so cruelly attacked. I am reassured by the freedom of the press of which you do not speak at all, and I am convinced that these economists, these philanthropists, these philosophers whom you so harshly insult, by their writings will contribute as much to the maintenance of freedom and to the reestablishment of order as those brave paladins, those knights errant whose loss you so bitterly deplore" (p. 373).

DePont obviously had no understanding of Burke's complex notion of "prejudice" and "untaught feelings." He said little about religion, except that it had not functioned to temper despotism in France. Indeed he felt that religion was part of the "ignorance, fanaticism, and superstition" of the past (p. 370). Good Voltairean slogans these, but hardly refined semantic tools for dissecting Burke's "grand prejudice," Christianity. For the English Whig, religion and the awe it inspired were fundamental to the English constitution. DePont had no grasp of this kind of constitution; for him a constitution was a rational, written, legal instrument assigning and limiting the public powers. Consequently, he could not understand Burke's strong aversion to the nationalization of Church property and especially the new "Constitution of the Clergy." "I cannot see how religion is attacked and atheism established," wrote DePont, "because the salaries of public officials in the service of religion are not high enough" (p. 372). The phrase *"fonctionnaires publics destinés au service du culte"* clearly suggests that DePont had accepted the new Church-State arrangement.

Like Paine, DePont also wondered whether Burke had mistaken "the plumage for the bird" in his adulation of the French nobility. On this issue, DePont had more to say. A magistrate and the son of an intendant, he did not consider himself a nobleman. By December 1790 he identified "nobles" with "abuse" and "counterrevolution."

> You say, Monsieur, that it would have been better to reform and perfect it [the government] without making any innovations. But why should the firm, courageous man who has always been the most strenuous opponent of abuses in his own country suddenly adopt the clever language of Frenchmen [nobles] who, having been ignominiously beaten down from the ramparts of despotism, have sought refuge in a so-called Constitution that offers them, in the monstrous division of Orders and with four vetoes (adding the king's), a second line of defense where they hope to defend step by step all the vices of the Old Regime. [76] (pp. 370-71.)

DePont proceeds to explain why the National Assembly voted against a second Chamber, "somewhat similar to the one that exists today in your country." "We need not retrace," he writes, "the special circumstances that made the people fear that the *noblesse*, which had kept it out of every public employ, should manage to usurp the same privileges [*avantages*] in another form" (p. 371).

It may seem strange that the scion of a family that had succeeded in gaining its own "noblesse" by "public employ" should subscribe to the thesis of an aristocratic blockage of office. Perhaps DePont believed that his own family's mobility was the exception or that there should be more DePonts and fewer d'Ormessons or d'Aligres in high office. But the passage may also suggest that DePont, like Burke, lived by his own rhetoric, not a total delusion to be sure, but a set of assumptions that brooked little deviation, even in the face of empirical facts. "Nobility" had come to mean "abuse and privilege," and France must eradicate both before it could be considered "worthy of freedom." DePont did not think that *aristocratie* was always and everywhere an abuse, an evil. Somewhat reluctantly, he conceded that "an inhabitant of the canton of Berne, or an Englishman, may be free and happy *in spite of the aristocratic element in his government*" (p. 373, italics mine).

For Burke, of course, the word had quite different connotations. In November 1791 he wrote to Earl Fitzwilliam: "I will not enter into the baseness and depravity of the System they adopt, but one thing I will remark, that its great Object is not ... the destruction of all absolute Monarchies, but totally to root out that thing called *Aristocrate* or Nobleman and Gentleman. This they do not profess; but in France they profess it and do it." [77] As Burke said in his essay "On Nobility": "The Nobility are not only the natural councillors of the Crown, but they are the natural guardians of the people. ... Be assured that those who talk or practice any other principle are the true friends of despotism." [78] DePont and Burke could not have been further apart in their respective conceptions of "aristocracy," regardless of the "objective facts" concerning noble behavior in either country.

Given these fundamental differences of outlook, one wonders how the two men had got on as long as they did. DePont, to be sure, was no longer asking Burke if he considered the French "worthy to be free" (see letter of 4 Nov. 1789), for he must have realized at last that he and Burke did not use the word "Liberty" in the same way. Yet he still wished to convey the notion that his "love of liberty had not been weakened by the temporary oppression of a few individuals ... and that the fault you see in Dr. Price, of mistaking the deviation from principles for the principles themselves, must not be attributed to me" (p. 371). DePont admitted that the internal divisions within the National Assembly were not always dignified, and that the oratory was occasionally excessive, but "how can anyone who is only divided from us by a few miles maintain that the Assembly is not free?" As for the reorganization of the judiciary, no doubt it had its faults, "but I am consoled by the ease with which they can be rectified, and by the great advantages we have acquired in the institution of juries, of which you do not say a word" (p. 372).

Burke had taken the violence of the October Days, which, like other "events" of the year 1789, had been dramatized by his ultraroyalist friends in Paris, as the central message of the Revolution. DePont saw these events differently. He had celebrated his first Bastille Day only a few months earlier. "It was during the twelfth and thirteenth of July, 1789, that the battle was joined between the oppression of the past and the dawning of liberty. It was then that the French nation expressed its will [*volonté*] with the greatest of energy, and won the most complete victory" (p. 369). Burke had a strong appreciation of the providential and the messianic in history. His correspondent's verve and youthful exuberance must have reinforced his fears that Europe was entering a "time of troubles." What he called the "democratic species of tyranny under the name of rights of man" was on the march. [79]

Taken as a whole, DePont's "reply" to Burke does not constitute a complete political philosophy comparable, for example, to that of his Feuillant leader, Joseph Barnave. There are, however, elements of Barnave's stages of liberty and his general view of the Revolution in DePont's letter. DePont sees a connection between social conditions and political events, between environment and ideas. He depicts a clergy and an aristocracy that are retrograde, if not historically bankrupt, relics of a past age of "superstition and fanaticism." While he does not refer to a "bourgeoisie" as representatives of newer forms of commercial wealth and "movable property" as Barnave did, he clearly discerns a new nation emerging, a groundswell of "democratic" energies that must one day triumph over "aristocracy" and "anarchy," the twin threats to the Revolution and the march of history. And like Barnave, DePont sees this new Nation of ultimately "sovereign people" completed by a constitution placing legislative power into the hands of the people's "trustees," a political elite of families experienced in law and governance, capped by a monarch limited by law. As Harold Laski has said, in Barnave's speeches one will find "the essence of French liberalism after the Restoration." DePont shared this view with Barnave. [80]

As far as we know, Burke never replied to DePont's letter of December 1790. [81] The French translator of the *Reflections,* Pierre-Gaëton Dupont, a conservative royalist, referred to Charles-François DePont in a letter he wrote to Burke a week later. "As for de Pons [sic], he has received his [copy]. Actually that is too much honor for him. Dreadful things are said about him. He is accused of having gone over to Democracy." [82] Again in February 1791 the translator alluded to the publication of DePont's letter in England. "I will not speak about DePont's letter. He is a young man who will have difficulty realizing that he needs instruction." [83] Quite obviously Dupont was speaking as a royalist who made no distinction between moderate constitutional monarchists and Jacobin republicans. "*Démocratie,*" like "*aristocrate,*" had become a party slogan, a rhetorical flourish, devoid of precision. [84] Pierre-Gaëton Dupont ended a letter to Burke of May 1791 expressing the hope that the rest of Europe would intervene, "a generous and powerful coalition . . . to reestablish the King on the throne and to chase from the heart of Europe a band of *factieux* who have overthrown everything, destroyed everything." [85] Apparently Burke had decided to use Pierre-Gaëton Dupont rather than Charles-François DePont as his informant for political events in France. [86]

From the spring of 1791 to April 1792, we know almost nothing about the activities of young DePont. He was a member of the Feuillant Club, which had separated from the Jacobins after the flight of the king in June 1791, indicating that he remained loyal to Duport, Lameth, and Barnave, and to the constitutional monarchy. [87] The Feuillant position was becoming increasingly difficult to maintain, however, as the republicans increased their converts both inside and outside the Legislative Assembly. With each passing month the Feuillants became more vocal in their attachment to the constitution and to their motto—Nation, Law, and King—as the only barrier against the "émigré peril" on one side and the "Jacobin peril" on the other. In December 1791 Duport and Barnave, now close advisers to the Crown, drew up a policy statement that was intended to calm anxieties in foreign capitals and persuade Emperor Leopold to disperse the émigrés gathered at Trier and Koblenz. Between the émigrés and the republicans, the memorandum read, are the majority of French citizens who want peace, order, and freedom. "This is the class of people the king must unite behind him. They form the backbone of the nation; they furnish its wealth and strength, they are strongly attached to the monarchy. The king must gain the confidence of this middle class [*classe mitoyenne*], while remaining loyal to the Constitution, maintaining security, and defending property."[88]

The confidence of the National Party that seemed so firmly grounded in late 1790 had largely eroded by late 1791. The party leaders began to regret the stridency of their declarations only a year before; they spoke less now of "groaning under the yoke" of ancient tyrannies and more about the "incendiary news sheets of Marat, Carra, Audouin, and Desmoulins."[89] Liberty was not to be license.

In April 1791, when the Jacobin Club was still firmly in constitutional monarchist hands, the diplomatic committee of the club, led by Barnave, Fréteau, and Menou, had protested to the foreign minister, Montmorin, for having made his ambassadorial appointments among the members of the *Club Monarchique*, selecting men of the Old Regime like Clermont-Tonnerre and Gouvernet rather than "patriots" of the Jacobin Club.[90] A year later, a new foreign minister, General Dumouriez, committed to the removal of counterrevolutionaries and to financial retrenchment in the foreign office, replaced those whose loyalty was suspect with new men, some from the lower ranks of the service. Among them were two men who had been members of the Jacobin Club the year before. Villars was appointed minister plenipotentiary to Mainz, and Charles-François DePont, minister plenipotentiary to Cologne.[91] With respect to new appointments for the minor courts, the diplomatic corps appeared to be one year behind political developments in Paris, or so Dumouriez would have us believe. On closer inspection, however, Dumouriez's own appointment and those of Clavière and Roland at the ministries of finance and interior, indicated that republicans of the Brissotin persuasion had replaced the Feuillant ministers. In fact, Dumouriez completely overhauled the six central *bureaux* of the foreign office, placing republican sympathizers in all key positions. DePont's division head for Germany was Jean-François Noël, former professor, journalist, "new" Jacobin, and friend of Robespierre. The foreign service, at least at Paris, was ideologically prepared for the declaration of war on Austria on 20 April 1792.[92]

Citizen DePont arrived at his post on 9 May. Dumouriez had recommended the twenty-four-year-old diplomat to the king for his "zeal and inviolable attachment to the Constitution," a characterization surely more applicable to DePont than to Dumouriez and his republican friends. Charles-François found himself in a part of the Rhineland that was rapidly being infiltrated by émigrés from France and by troops from Austria and Prussia. His correspondence with the home office over the next three months provides a great deal of insight not only into the young diplomat's desperate efforts to prevent the Elector of Cologne from joining the enemy coalition but, even more revealing, into his increasing difficulty maintaining a political position independent of both "counterrevolutionary émigrés" in Cologne and Jacobin "anarchists" in Paris. [93]

"There is a general gathering of émigrés in Cologne," he wrote in his first dispatch to Paris. "They think that the counterrevolution is already accomplished. When they heard of my arrival, they threatened the local innkeepers, asking them not to let me in; otherwise they would move out" (9 May 1792). DePont's dislike of the émigrés extended to the outward signs of their royalism, their uniforms, cockades, and ribbons, which, he said rather naively, "have been outlawed by the Constitution" (18 June). He was acutely embarrassed by his awkward position in a small principality where he might meet those "fifty or sixty French families" presented at court every day "in their large white cockades" (9 June). After all, it was *his* task as the official French representative to present French subjects to the Elector.

Among well-known émigrés, DePont noted that Calonne had rented an apartment in Frankfurt in order to attend the coronation of the new Hapsburg emperor, Francis II. "Let us hope he will have no more influence on the new emperor than he has had on his two predecessors, Joseph and Leopold" (28 June). Calonne had been very actively urging military intervention on behalf of the émigrés; in fact he acted as a kind of prime minister for the princes in exile. [94] Unfortunately for the new French regime, Francis II needed little prodding from Calonne. [95] DePont also reported that Mallet du Pan, the intellectual of the emigration, had passed through Cologne. Obviously he was unaware that Mallet was on an important secret mission for the king to the princes at Koblenz. Louis XVI had his secret diplomacy parallel to official channels. [96] DePont also found it diplomatically embarrassing that his predecessor, Colbert de Maulevrier, had remained in nearby Bonn despite his recall by Dumouriez, and that he entertained such counterrevolutionaries as Abbé de Maury. Conservative clerical deputy to the Estates-General, Maury had violently opposed the Constitution of the Clergy and emigrated early. DePont said that the abbé was now telling the Elector, himself a prince of the Church, that there was a "system of subversion threatening all Europe"—shades of the "contagion" so dreaded by Burke and Mallet du Pan (13 May, 17 June). [97]

Far from implementing any "system of subversion" or issuing any manifesto about the liberation of foreign states, DePont informed Paris that "it is very important we assure the Elector that we do not intend to attack him" (22 May). Moreover, he did not believe the German states were ready for revolution.

The German peasants are in general too unenlightened to have the slightest idea about the rights of nations. The opposition that exists in a few diets of the Empire at the sufferance of the prince is purely aristocratic and can be compared to the resistance of the old estates of our provinces at the sufferance of our kings. However, it is no less true that we can take advantage of this resistance to prevent the princes from obtaining new taxes. ... But I think we must begin by making every effort to reassure the clergy and the nobles (who alone, or almost alone, are represented) of the preservation of their privileges so that they will not see any advantage in uniting with their princes against us. (17 June.)

In this letter, young DePont reveals a keenness of observation and a tactical acumen that would have pleased his father. He warned his government against Brissotin bravado; and he was convinced that the peoples of Central Europe were not awaiting a "liberation" to be brought by the armies of France. "There is nothing to hope for from desertion or insurrection of peoples. The different states of the Empire enjoy a form of government incomparably better than the one destroyed in France by the General Will of the Nation" (7 July). DePont had a capacity, not uncommon among diplomats, to separate political idealism at home from political realism in foreign affairs. In any case, multiplying France's enemies might well unseat the delicate equilibrium of power at home and abroad.[98]

DePont was constantly forced to look over his shoulder at events in Paris. If he had praised freedom of the press to Burke in 1789, he was concerned about the responsibilities of the press in foreign affairs in the spring of 1792. He was distressed to see the *Mercure de France* reporting that the Elector of Cologne had obtained the necessary money to fulfill his quota of troops for the coalition. DePont said that this news had not been confirmed and that in any case it was premature. "Of course, the newspapermen must retain the widest possible freedom of opinion, but they must not oblige me to deny the false news they have reported in their papers" (12 June). As the eventful month of June passed, DePont exhibited increased anxiety. "Austrian and Prussian troops are pouring through Cologne. The émigrés are so encouraged that my position here becomes more difficult by the hour." DePont would stay on if the minister insisted, "but I must admit to you, Monsieur, that useless courage has always seemed unnatural to me" (9 June). A few days later he repeated that the post "required more courage than service in the field" (18 June), very hard on a man who is "sensitive [*délicat*], concerned about his integrity [*honnête*], and excessively desirous of performing his task with dignity" (9 June). He yearned to resign his post and retire to his country house at Mantes-sur-Seine, forty kilometers from Paris. "I have the greatest desire to return to France and to rejoin that imposing mass of the Nation which will defend to the death the Constitution, the different powers created by it, and the sacred person of His Majesty" (12 June). On more than one occasion, DePont invoked the Constitution of 1791 as an institutional bulwark against a growing disorder that threatened more than just the outward rhythm of his political and professional life.

On 15 June, Dumouriez was forced to resign in what turned out to be the last effort of the king to stem the tide of republicanism. Duport, Lameth, and the Feuillants regained the ministries, but their hold was precarious, even in the eyes of contemporaries. [99] DePont seized the occasion to write to the new foreign minister, Scipion Chambonas, a member of his own Feuillant Party. "If you will permit a Frenchman who has devoted his life and his very existence to the defense of Liberty to express his personal opinion, I confess to you that the security of the Assembly in the face of powerful movements united against us does not seem very strong" (22 June). Worse news arrived a few days later. On 20 June the royal palace was invaded by Parisians from the east-side wards, and the king narrowly escaped with his life. [100] The effects of this incident abroad were "deplorable." All embassies complained that after this "atrocity" their task of reassuring foreigners that the French loved their king had become immeasurably more difficult. [101]

DePont clung ever more tenaciously to the legal façade of the Constitution, but with receding confidence. "My father and my friends [in the Feuillant Party?] must have begged you, Monsieur, to grant me leave if you cannot accept my resignation. ... My motives must not be misrepresented by those who have not followed my political career from the beginning of the Revolution. ... If political fortunes change once again and you are forced to leave office, please tender my resignation along with yours to the King, to whom I hope to prove during the course of my life my respect for the Constitution and my devotion to His person" (28 June). The plea has the mark of a career nearing its end.

DePont then outlines the qualities his replacement should possess in words reflecting his own political beliefs. "The new secretary ... should be strongly attached to constitutional principles and exhibit a conduct worthy of esteem and general confidence. He must be penetrated with those great truths that have inspired our Constitution and remain the foundation of our National Sovereignty. But he must no less maintain a deep respect for the established governments of our neighbors and refrain from interfering in their domestic affairs." Moving abruptly from general principles to immediate and practical considerations, he explains his efforts to counteract émigré propaganda, which stressed the bad treatment of the king and queen at the Tuileries. "I have replied with skill [*art*], but without affectation, to various versions of this event, about which I have heard through the newspapers or from private letters. This kind of effort [counter-propaganda] should have been made much earlier. Long ago we should have shown foreigners the difference between the Constitutional Party and the anarchic faction [a distinction] that the French counter-revolutionaries have tried so hard to blur" (28 June). Two years earlier, DePont had tried in vain to make this distinction clear to Edmund Burke. Did he believe it possible to "educate" the German princes in this matter when he had failed with an eminent English political philosopher?

DePont was still at his post in July 1792. No doubt he received news in the *Mercure* of Lafayette's dramatic speech before the Assembly in Paris, demanding the immediate dissolution of the Jacobin clubs and punishment for those responsible for acts of violence at the Tuileries on 20 June. [102] Almost in the words of Lafayette, DePont called the "events" of 20 June "illegal," an attack on the constitution never to be repeated. "The moment has finally come, Monsieur, when all men who have risen with strength and courage against despotism and aristocracy must unite and raise their voices against the *factieux*" (6 July). Like most adherents to the Feuillant Party in these weeks immediately before the invasion of France and the end of the monarchy, DePont turned to Lafayette, last hope of the "*constitutionnels.*" [103] He intended to visit the military camp at Maubeuge on his return to France, just as the general had stopped at Cologne to see him earlier. DePont's words are even more laden with adulation than those of his first letters to Burke, also a "friend of freedom," or so it had seemed. "I shall never miss an occasion to see again this brave friend of liberty, my hero, my master, my friend" (6 July). Perhaps there was a touch of desperation as well.

This letter was written on the day France declared war on Prussia and as the armies of the first coalition began advancing toward the French frontier. In fact, the inaction of Lafayette's army at Maubeuge proved to the republicans that he was more concerned with the "*factieux*" at home than with the preparations of the enemy in the Rhineland. [104] Lafayette's popularity in the street had also considerably eroded since the halcyon days of 1789 when he was commander of the National Guard of Paris. [105] DePont's last days in Cologne were spent reporting Prussian troop movements and the arrival of the Duke of Brunswick in the Rhineland. The camp near Koblenz was said to contain fifty-two thousand troops (4 July); DePont also reported an important meeting of the kings of Bohemia and Prussia, the German electors, and the French émigré princes, which was expected to produce a "manifesto" (17 July). On 24

July, DePont sent a coded letter to Paris, stating that he was sure the Allies would attack on the first days of August. The next day, the Elector of Cologne asked DePont to leave for Paris.

It hardly needs emphasizing that young DePont was a political moderate, at least in the spectrum of French parties and beliefs in the first five years of the Revolution. Perhaps less obvious was his identification of a peculiar set of institutional arrangements with his idea of France. He often used the word "constitution" interchangeably with the French "nation." He wrote, for example, that Prussian troops will not be used "against our constitution, since our constitution does not threaten the tranquillity of their States" (6 June). Or, again, "we must break up the formidable alliance against our constitution" (8 June). He refused a solemn reception as French envoy, "in accordance with the principles of simplicity of our constitution" (13 May). The Constitution of 1791 was not, he felt, universally applicable: it was peculiarly French. The earlier words of DePont's reply to Burke make his position clear. "I do not wish to exalt myself to the character of a reformer of mankind or a missionary of the new French institutions ... but I will always defend the constitution *of my country*." [106] On this point, DePont did not change since his days in the *Chambre des Enquêtes*.

For DePont, the émigrés were not only aliens to the constitution, but a people without a country. They were no longer "French." He described them in Cologne as adapting their dress and their mores to whatever country seemed to share their cause for the moment. "They have almost entirely abandoned their English dress to adopt Prussian styles. They have exchanged little tight-fitting boots for big heavy ones; they cut their hair very short; they wear big Swiss-style hats, ... and they always carry long pipes with them. The old Prussian officers laugh through their whiskers at this sudden metamorphosis, which surely would have amused Frederick the Great" (6 July). If there was always something slightly ridiculous about the émigrés, the menace of the Jacobin "anarchists" was only too serious. But both seditious factions—"*aristocrate*" and "*anarchiste*"— had blasphemed the sacred motto of the old Jacobin Club: *la Nation, la Loi, le Roi.* [107]

For Charles-François DePont, the fall of the monarchy in August 1792 must have been more than the triumph of "tumult" and "illegality"; it was the end, at least temporarily, of the "France" he had spent his early twenties building anew. Yet the words of his reply to Burke in 1790 still held true: "... your charge against Dr. Price, of taking the deviation from principles for the principles themselves, is not applicable to me." And surely he agreed with—if indeed he did not write it himself—a note appended to the English publication of his *Answer to the Reflections*: [108] "It is by a similar error in reasoning that the Revolution is confounded with events ... such as those of October, those of Nancy, [and those of August 1792?] ... These are perhaps calamities inseparable from every great Revolution; these are not, it cannot be too often repeated, *the work of the nation.* [109]

In all of his references to politics, whether in his reply to Burke or in his diplomatic correspondence with Paris, DePont used the political vocabulary of the leaders of the Feuillant Party. When he spoke of the "Constitution," he reiterated the judicial phraseology of Adrien Duport and his colleagues from the former Parlement of Paris; when he referred to the "King," he appeared to be following Lafayette and Lameth, who were increasingly concerned about political "order"; and when he spoke of the "Nation," he seemed close to Sieyès, even to the point of adopting the abbé's rather mystical notion of a "will" inherent in the Nation. [110]

As a touchstone to a political philosophy, or even as an appealing political program, these "three principles" were failing to hold together. King and constitution were both being undermined by a newly organized democratic nationalism. Keith Baker has recently argued that the tension between the rights of man and the rights of the nation was not created by the Jacobin Party nor by the Declaration of the Rights of Man and of the Citizen in 1789, but was latent in much of the thinking of the Enlightenment. [111] But by 1792, new political issues and a new political awareness made it impossible to paper over a fundamental incompatibility of goals. On a personal level, DePont experienced these tensions.

With the dispatch of 25 July 1792 the diplomatic correspondence of Charles-François DePont comes to an end, and with it any further opportunity to explore the man's thinking. A police report in 1795 refers to him living *"dans ses terres"* near Mantes-sur-Seine. Apparently, he found his country retreat after retirement from the foreign service and survived the year of the Terror in the quiet wheat fields of the Beauce. [112] In this he fared better than the leaders of the Feuillant Party. Adrien Duport and Théodore Lameth emigrated to England, Lafayette and Alexandre Lameth were imprisoned by the Prussians after fleeing from the French Army, and Joseph Barnave was arrested and executed in November 1793. [113] In 1796 DePont married Avoye-Marie Michel de Grilleau, possibly from a non-noble family. [114] The couple had a son who would never see his father.

In September 1797, at the age of thirty, Charles-François DePont blew out his brains. [115] One can only speculate on the reasons for this unexpected and early death. The precipitating event, according to Théodore de Lameth, was the refusal by Madame de Castellane of his gift of some partridges, a trivial incident that strongly suggests that Charles-François was overwrought, if not clinically insane at the time of his suicide. No doubt the meteoric career of this young man and its sudden end with the fall of the monarchy, his father's arrest, and the loss of his colleagues and leaders in the Feuillant Party had placed him under considerable stress. He had pleaded in a dispatch to the minister (9 June 1792) that he was *un homme délicat*, sensitive to the treatment he was receiving at the hands of the emigrés at Cologne. He obviously abhorred popular violence and explicitly denied any claim to physical courage. In 1785 Richard Burke, Edmund's brother, had already described him as socially rather awkward,[116] and Edmund did not refer to him as "Dumpling" without some cause, however mean the metaphor. In short, although the evidence is rather slim, there were some signs of a disturbed personality. Despite his apparent competence as a lawyer, as a diplomat, and as a political thinker whose "reply" to Edmund Burke was printed in London, it is possible that he suffered from a sense of inadequacy. Had he been given too much responsibility too early in life? His obvious dependency on "guides" and "masters," terms he applied to both Burke and Lafayette, together with the fact that he seems to have reversed roles with his father earlier than most young people,[117] suggests someone who needed authority and yet had spent his youth and early manhood in the pursuit of "liberty" and the fight against "tyranny" and "privilege." He must have placed enormous stock in that "Constitution" and in being "worthy of liberty." His "world" had indeed collapsed by 1797.

Little could he know in those difficult years of the Directory that a new social amalgam was in the making in France, one in which professional competence, national consciousness, and political moderation, pruned of any "fanaticism" of the past, would join those older "qualities" of birth, fortune, and connection. Had he lived, Charles-François DePont would have made an ideal "notable" of the early nineteenth century.[118]

CHAPTER NINE

Survival: Metz, La Rochelle, and Paris

The municipal revolution at Metz was a relatively peaceful affair. The nearness of the city to the Rhine frontier, facilitating importation of badly needed grain and wood, the relative flexibility of the local elite, and the fact that the Parlement of Metz had opposed "ministerial despotism" in the recent past, all helped make the transition to a new political order a nonviolent one. The worst effects of the economic crisis of the spring of 1789, especially the shortage of bread, were blunted by the prompt and coordinated efforts of the local authorities. The bishop of Metz, Montmorency-Laval, began weekly distribution of bread to the poor in January; the military commander, Marquis de Bouillé, opened the garrison's grain stores (sufficient for 30,000 troops) to the public; the Parlement halted all exports of grain or flour from the *généralité*, prohibited the use of grain in the manufacture of beer or starch, and made an inventory of all local supplies.[1] Intendant Depont promptly executed a series of royal ordinances between November 1788 and August 1789, encouraging imports of grain from all European ports and offering subsidies for purchases even from North America.[2] He also proposed that additional *ateliers de charité* and a municipal charity fund be established for the poor. Officers of the garrison invited the hungry to eat at their mess; the wealthier citizens advanced money without interest for the city to stock *magasins d'abondance*, and bread, beans, and rice were imported from the Rhineland, the Palatinate, Poland, and from North America via the Rhine and Moselle rivers.

Although the problem of subsistence remained critical throughout 1789, prices did not reach the exorbitant levels experienced at Paris and elsewhere and even declined slightly in August. Equally important, consumers had the clear impression that prompt action was being taken and that even the wealthier Messin families were making some sacrifices or at least did not profit from the food shortage. The municipal government could indulge in self-congratulations in mid-August 1789: "It is well known that Metz is one of those [few] cities in the kingdom which has least felt the calamity of the time. It owes this to the cooperation which exists among the Parlement, M. le Marquis de Bouillé, the commissioners of the *Trois Ordres* [the old town council], and the municipal officials for the large quantity of wheat bought and shipped from abroad."[3]

In the countryside of Lorraine around Metz there was no "Great Fear," no agrarian revolt or château-burning as took place further south in Franche-Comté and the Mâconnais. Arthur Young witnessed the destruction and pillaging of the town hall in Strasbourg that same summer of 1789, and Nancy, only fifty kilometers to the south of Metz, would explode with a mutiny of the garrison a year later.[4] But Marquis de Bouillé could rightly claim that at Metz under his command (1789–91), there had not been a single "murder," not a single château burned, and not a single seigneur or *propriétaire* exposed to the "*fureur du peuple.*"[5]

If economic distress at Metz was limited by the coordinated efforts of the local elite, the political impact of the Revolution was also assimilated with a minimum of social tension, at least until early 1791. As in most towns of comparable size, a "Patriotic Committee" was formed in the early spring at the time of the elections to the Estates-General, and immediately challenged the established municipal oligarchy.[6] The Patriotic Committee was not only ably led by a councilor of parlement, Jean-Louis Roederer, but also gained early recognition from both the minister of war and the National Assembly at Paris.[7] The Committee claimed credit for the many public and voluntary efforts of charity and the distribution of food in the city and surrounding villages. Again, as elsewhere in the kingdom, the Committee learned how to use the local press—the *Affiches des Evêchés et Lorraine* in the case of Metz—to mobilize public opinion. On 20 July the news of the fall of the Bastille was welcomed throughout this city of thirty-six thousand by the sound of churchbells, the singing of the *Te Deum,* and displays of fireworks in the evening—a joyous and peaceful *fête* at Metz.

If the Patriotic Committee had replaced the old municipal government by summer, the National Assembly at Paris moved quickly to regularize, institutionalize—some would say "control"—the local committee at Metz. By a ministerial letter in September 1789, the old committee was transformed into a "Municipal Committee" to be composed of eighty members elected by the guilds and parishes, substantially by the same procedures used in the national elections the previous spring.[8] It was a large body, even larger than the original Patriotic Committee of fifty-one. The elections tool place without the slighest murmur in the streets. The Clergy elected mostly local canons and priors, and the bishop of Metz was conspicuously absent among the twenty representatives of the First Estate. The forty members of the Third Estate included eleven lawyers and magistrats, eleven officials, two military officers, one physician, one architect, one *rentier*, two *négociants*, and, most novel, eleven master artisans. There had been only one artisan, a master clockmaker, on the former committee.[9] The twenty representatives of the Nobility were divided almost equally between robe and sword—eight military officers and eight magistrates of the Parlement of Metz, three other *officiers*, and Depont *fils*, councilor of the Parlement of Paris, former *avocat-général* of the Parlement of Metz. It was in his capacity as a representative of the new Municipal Committee, not as a member of the parlement, that Charles-François went before the National Assembly in November 1789.[10]

Thus began the second phase in the life of the new municipal government at Metz. Its performance in treating the subsistence crisis, given the means at its disposal, was exemplary. Next came the issue of organizing the local militia, repository of civic loyalty, shield of "the new order of things." This proved a special problem since Metz had a large military garrison—perhaps twenty thousand troops of the line—under an active commander, Marquis de Bouillé, whose opposition to Revolutionary changes was becoming more apparent each day. Willing as he had been to help the needy by distributing the garrison's food supply, Bouillé was of quite a different mind when it came to handing out muskets to a maverick "National Guard." He considered it his duty to keep his own troops isolated from the "contagion" of "insurrection and licentiousness," to use his own words.[11] There had been precious little of either at Metz up to this time.

The marquis recalled later in life that he had never been on good terms with the *peuple* of the city and that he had refused to take the oath to "what they called the constitution," until he was forced to do so by order of the minister of war, La Tour du Pin.[12] "The principal crime laid to my charge was that I opposed the fraternization of the National Guard with the troops of the line. This, as I have said, was one of the chief means employed to corrupt the soldiers. I endeavored, on the contrary, to keep them separated from each other and to maintain a certain rivalry between them. In addition, I continued to refuse to deliver to the people of the towns and country the great quantity of arms which they demanded of me daily."[13] In October, a month to alarm even moderate royalists, Bouillé, apparently in an effort to cleanse the ranks, dispatched four hundred of his troops to Toul and prepared to replace them with Swiss and German mercenaries. This action led to an attack on the town hall by a crowd of journeymen and "*jeunes gens*" who removed some seventy-five muskets from the *salle des armes*.[14]

Until this moment, Intendant Depont had been extremely circumspect about the recent events. In May 1789 he had expressed the popular view that the bread shortage was caused, or at least aggravated, by the "cupidity and avarice" of grain speculators who were holding back supplies, a statement that Bouillé would regard as inflammatory coming from a high government official.[15] As always, Jean-Samuel aimed to please his *administrés*. "A realist," writes Harsany, historian of Metz, "the intendant ... played a discreet role which earned him a certain sympathy from the people of Metz and [even] their protection during critical moments of the Revolution."[16] Moreover, he was sixty-five years old and had no military force under his own command to challenge either Bouillé's garrison or the new National Guard. But now on the occasion of Bouillé's dispatch of the four hundred troops to Toul, Depont reacted strongly in a letter to the minister of war in Paris:

Monseigneur, we are charged by the Commune of Metz to inform you of its views and we ask you to transmit these requests to the King. We have witnessed with deep dismay the departure of four hundred men from the Saintonge regiment whom M. le Marquis de Bouillé thought it necessary to send to Toul. We beg you to order them back promptly to Metz so that the six hundred others making up the regiment will remain here. We also ask, Monseigneur, that no foreign regiments, other than those composing the present garrison, be sent here. The difference in language would prevent them from establishing the kind of confraternity that must exist between soldiers and citizens. One final request, Monseigneur: The national colors [*cocarde nationale*] must be worn by all regiments in garrison in this city, especially since the King himself has deigned to wear these colors.[17]

Written with the "October Days" clearly in mind, and no doubt encouraged by his son on the new Municipal Committee, Jean-Samuel chose to accommodate to the municipal revolution at Metz. Surely he had doubts about the wisdom of the *peuple*. But were *tumultes* and *attroupements* avoided by adopting Bouillé's tactics of relying exclusively on the old professional army, that "*noyau de fidelité*," as Bouillé's son put it?[18] Here the difference between commander and intendant reflected a wider division between the two elites at Metz, the military and the Parlement, which had not first appeared in 1789. Twenty years before, Depont's predecessor, Calonne, had complained about how difficult it was to please both "*le militaire*" and "*la robe*," a latent rivalry accentuated by special conditions at Metz.[19] The military garrison was an important one (30,000 at full strength), but staffed by officers who were underpaid and politically unsophisticated.[20] Arthur Young dined with seven officers of the Metz garrison on 13 July 1789, on his way to Strasbourg. He lamented their banal conversation at a time when all of France was being politicized. "Out of whose mouths," he wrote, "not one word issued for which I would give a straw, nor a subject touched of more importance than a coat or a puppy dog. At these tables de hôtes of officers you have a voluble garniture of bawdry or nonsense."[21] What a contrast to the well-to-do councilors of the local parlement, Roederer, Emméry, Depont *fils,* among them.[22] These magistrates delivered daily orations on constitutional law, fought the Lamoignon "reforms," dominated the local academy of sciences. Among French parlements, Metz was considered progressive, open to new ideas; while the magistrates of Toulouse were still living under the shadow of the Calas Affair, those of Metz were discussing the possibilities of Jewish emancipation.[23]

One would not expect Intendant Depont to break openly with the local military establishment before 1789; his place was that of royal agent and his role to conciliate the rival elites of Metz. But his cultural and intellectual ties were much closer to the magistrates. His son had been *avocat-général,* his first secretary, Le Payen, was an active member of the academy and an advocate of citizenship for Jews,[24] and even his one documented encounter with Roederer involved a book. When the Revolution came to Metz, Jean-Samuel, though judicious and diplomatic as always, gradually distanced himself from Marquis de Bouillé. If he harbored some reservations about his son's election to the Municipal Committee, he could sympathize even less with the son of Bouillé. In October 1789, when even the king wore the national colors, young Bouillé rode alone through the province proudly wearing the white Bourbon *cocarde,* undeterred by the musket shots of villagers fired over his head.[25] No, surely Jean-Samuel could not understand that mentality.

In December 1789 the National Assembly completed the administrative reorganization of France. Municipal governments assumed their final form. At Metz the eighty-man Municipal Committee, based on election by Order, was replaced by a mayor, fourteen "municipal officers" and thirty "notables," all elected by the "active citizens," who represented about 35 percent of the total adult male population of the city. The municipal election produced a more socially homogeneous city government than either of the previous committees. Among the forty-five members of the new "administration"—the term seems more appropriate than "committee" or "assembly"—there were only four military nobles, including the mayor, Baron de Poutet, and one canon, representing the clergy. On the other end of the social scale, there were only four artisans instead of eleven on the previous committee. The elimination of guilds and orders with corporate voting rights placed local political power in the hands of 3,260 "active citizens" of whom 2,366 voted in February 1790. They preferred lawyers and previous officeholders:[26]

Lawyers and Magistrates	23	*Négociants*	4
Officeholders	4	Military	4
Other Professions	4	Clergy	1
Rentiers	1	Artisans	4
		Total	45

Depont *fils* was not elected this time. His support had come from his colleagues in the Parlement of Metz. Nor was he elected to any of the new district or departmental offices.

Well might Intendant Depont choose this moment to retire gracefully from public service. Parlements and intendancies had been abolished. At the end of January 1790, Jean-Samuel was made Honorary Citizen of Metz.[27] That this was no purely formal recognition of his past services to the city is indicated by the request of the Commune that he remain in his functions a few more months in order to familiarize the new departmental treasurer with his duties. It was fitting that this elected official was Jean Le Payen, Depont's own first secretary of the Intendance, chief administrator of the *Dépôt de Mendicité*, and perpetual secretary of the academy of sciences. A few months later, Jean-Samuel placed an advertisement in the local newspaper, announcing the sale of his wine cellar—*de très bon vins étrangers, de Bourgogne, Champagne, Bordeaux, vin de lignes en Malaga, Madère, Perpignan, Muscat, Tokay, Grec*— a complete line of choice bottles. He was preparing for a dignified retirement in Paris.[28]

One unfortunate episode marred his last months at Metz. In August 1790 part of the local garrison rioted, a foretaste of the much more important army mutiny at Nancy a few weeks later. The troops had not been paid and they sought out Depont as royal paymaster. The six pages of legal argument Depont needed to explain the military budget to the government in Paris did not satisfy the *mutins* who proceeded to break into his town house, haul him down to the *hôtel-de ville*, and force the reluctant treasurer to pay them. The subsequent report of the episode refers to "armed" *soldats provinciaux* mixing with *bas peuple* in a large crowd, threatening Depont with "atrocious" retribution. "Led along the streets [of Metz] by the crowd and surrounded by aroused people [*hommes furieux*] who threatened him with the most barbarous treatment if he tricked them, M. de Pont was fortunate enought to meet a colonel of the National Guard who came to his rescue."[29]

In fact, Jean-Samuel was saved by Marquis de Bouillé's son who distracted the crowd, exchanged his white *cocarde* for the tricolor, and helped the aging intendant escape through the back entrance of the town hall. Young Bouillé made fun of Depont's fright, an indication that their personal relations were strained. But Jean-Samuel had reason to be frightened.[30] The clamor of the crowd, the hail of stones, the narrow streets leading to the town hall must have reminded him of his day at the London Guildhall five years before. More terrible still, he was only a year away from 14 July 1789 when his old friend and colleague, Jacques de Flesselles, Intendant of Lyon and then chief municipal officer of Paris, was killed on the place de Grève and his head stuck on the end of a pike.[31] It was time to seek anonymity in the capital.

The Revolution at La Rochelle at first glance looks very much like the Revolution at Metz. For three years, most energy was focused on reorganizing the administration, forming the militia, electing new officials, and preparing for countless patriotic banquets, parades, and speeches climaxed by the mammouth *Fête de la Fédération* each 14 July. As at Metz, the institutions of the Old Regime, the *Intendance* and the *Bureau des Finances,* were quietly dismantled, their papers transferred to the new departmental *chef-lieu* at Saintes. The first mayor of La Rochelle under the new regime was the *armateur* Goguet, followed by Daniel Garesché in November 1791, both from the merchant elite of the port. The District Directory counted one *avocat,* one *propriétaire,* one ex–ship captain, one officer in the *gendarmerie,* and one former *trésorier de France,* Martin de Chassiron, a colleague of Paul-Charles Depont. The Departmental Directory of nine had the same social complexion—four *avocats,* two *propriétaires,* one *officier,* one administrator, and one mayor. The social change was minimal; the political adjustment peaceful, almost prosaic.[32]

The minutes of the Departmental Directory at Saintes make very uninteresting reading before September 1792, except for readers taken by such topics as the design of buttons on the new uniforms of the National Guard, the annual budget for the department, the funeral ceremony to commemorate the "events at Nancy," and the like. True, in October 1790 the minutes record the first serious instance of a rural revolt. In the village of Varaize deep in the Saintonge some sixteen hundred people protested the arrest of one Sieur Leplance (a lawyer?) and attempted to march on the prison at Saint-Jean D'Angély. The report does not make the deeper motives of the *attroupement* clear, but emphasizes the need to maintain order with a strong display of force by the National Guard. The flight of the king in June 1791 provoked no official comment from the Directory at Saintes. The *séances* seemed absorbed in the preparations for the *Fête de la Fédération.*

Perhaps the resignation of Martin de Chassiron from the La Rochelle Directory that same month, on rather flimsy grounds, was an indication of changes to come.[33]

The summer of 1792 witnessed the first explicit protests against the seigneurial dues, again in the back country near Saint-Jean d'Angély. The Directory responded with shock at the villagers' refusal to pay their dues, a "violation of the sacred law of property."[34] By July the departmental executive body was denouncing "diverse acts of rebellion against payment of the *droits féodaux*" throughout the department and it identified a number of "agitators" who were preaching sedition in the parishes. Young Fauché, a rural weaver, was supposed to have jumped on a tomb at the exit of the parish church after mass and to have told a gathering of eight hundred citizens not to pay their *agriers* and to pounce on anyone who did with their rakes and flails. One Gabriel Chaillou, a member of the village assembly, performed a ritual of protest increasingly typical of the area. He removed a tree from the village cemetery, shaped it into a gibbet, and replanted it on the main road between Pons and Saujon, only twenty kilometers south of Saintes. There he harangued the assembled group of fifty villagers with the words: "Liberty or Death! Those who pay the *droits féodaux* will be hung!"[35] The report of these events presented before the departmental authorities stressed that this "license and anarchy" was infecting even the *bons citoyens* in the countryside and that the local *juges de paix* were too isolated to enforce the law. The department responded by sending twenty-five horsemen of the regular army and thirty troops of the National Guard to arrest the troublemakers and "put an end to the disorders which are arousing people in all corners of the department."[36]

Two months later, however, the tone of the departmental minutes would begin to change. With the creation of the Republic in Paris in September came new elections and a complete turnover of the local administration. Citizen Depy, an *épicier,* replaced Garesché, the *armateur,* and five shopkeepers entered the Municipal Council of La Rochelle. With one exception, the nine-member departmental Directory was completely new.[37] There are no further references in the departmental minutes to the payment of seigneurial rights. A new political vocabulary increasingly took hold. By October, "non-juring priests" were being detained, the sale of "émigré property" begun, and special taxes levied on the families of émigrés. Long memoranda outlined the new procedures for drawing up inventories, the "fixing of seals," appointing commissioners, and other formalities for dealing with the "traitors within." In November, the new impost on the families of émigrés contained a long rhetorical preface. The increasing number of émigrés from the region—naval officers from Rochefort, or country

gentlemen from the interior who made their way to England or Spain—
were referred to as "that horde of armed barbarians intent on bleeding
the fatherland."[38] In January 1793 the Directory addressed the citizens
of the department in the following words: "The Nation has just rendered
justice to the last of its tyrants. His criminal head has fallen under the
sword of the law. . . . We are Republicans. Let us possess their virtues!"[39]

Yet the execution of these laws did not meet the promise of the
rhetoric of the council room at Saintes or the prodigious printing costs
of public bulletins.[40] Grass-roots enthusiasm for the new Republic,
especially at La Rochelle, seemed "lukewarm," as the Jacobins at Paris
said it was.[41] The port may have spawned Billaud-Varenne, member
of the Committee of Public Safety, but he seemed to have had few local
followers. A "Society of Friends of Liberty and Equality" at Marennes
was able to auction off the furnishings of the château of Réals de
Mornac in 1792, but sales of émigré property moved slowly.[42] A group
of Rochelais finally formed a sans-culotte "popular society" in November
1794, but with Robespierre gone its days were numbered. The election
campaign of Billaud-Varennes's father for *procureur-syndic* of the city
aroused only three hundred voters among three thousand eligible
electors.[43] A complete history of the Revolution at La Rochelle has
yet to be written, but it is doubtful that the chapter on "popular democracy" will be a long one.

Much of the time and energy of the departmental administration
in 1793 and 1794 was absorbed by the civil war against the Vendean
rebels and by the defense of the coast against an expected English
attack. In March 1793 the rhetoric at Saintes reflected genuine alarm:
"The brigands are at the gates"; "the *aristocrates* are in criminal
correspondence with them"; a vast "conspiracy has just been exposed
in the departments of Vendée and Loire-Inférieure whose tentacles
reach back to London, Vienna, and Madrid"; "No, Citizens, the time
for indulgence and temporizing has passed."[44] The law that followed
was indeed harsh on the relatives of émigrés, requiring that "fathers,
brothers, and male children over fourteen" of émigrés be transported
(to the citadel of Brouage) and all "mothers, sisters, wives, and daughters" return to their domiciles. However, with only thirty-six permanent
administrators at the district and departmental levels, delay was inevitable until a sufficient number of "commissioners" could be recruited
and trained for their tasks. Most of the sessions at Saintes were now
concerned with military matters as La Rochelle became a major supply
base for operations into the Vendée. The minutes for 1793 are filled
with decisions about recruitment, fortifications, mobilization of support
forces, contracting for uniforms, procurement of gunpowder, and other
measures to pacify the rebellious departments to the north.[45] After

all, Fontenay-le-Comte, taken by the Vendeans in May 1793, was only fifty kilometers from La Rochelle. Military operations took first priority.

All of which does not mean that the old local establishment escaped unscathed. Donald Greer's statistics on the incidence of the Terror and of emigration in the department indicate that both were much greater than at Metz, though the 107 death sentences seem minor compared to those at Lyon and the Vendée in 1793–94.[46] In fact it was after the Terror that nonjuring clergy and émigré families began to feel the sting of the Revolution in the region. The landing of the émigré army under English auspices in Brittany in July 1795 revealed a large number of nobles from Saintonge among those 750 captured and shot by General Hoche on the beaches near Carnac. The relatives of émigrés began to fill the half-deserted, marsh-encircled town of Brouage which served as a prison, just as the islands of Ré and Oleron off the coast were used as staging areas for almost a thousand nonjuring priests on their way to Guyana. The Thermidoreans in Paris hated "aristocrats" just as much as "democrats," especially when they were caught with arms in their hands fighting the Republic.[47]

Paul-Charles Depont, *président-trésorier de France* at La Rochelle, was sixty-five years old when the Estates-General convened in Versailles in May 1789. He witnessed the change in local administration, no doubt reassured by the familiar names in the new regime—Goguet, mayor; Martin de Chassiron, district director; Delacoste, *avocat* of La Rochelle, president of the Departmental Directory. He could see the banners of the National Guard moving up the rue du Palais to the giant banquets on the Place des Armes, hear the cannonades, and see the firework displays in the evening.[48] The city itself presented Paul-Charles with no special anxiety that spring and summer, although the death of his wife in June, after thirty-eight years of marriage, must have been a heavy personal loss.

The news from the domains in the country was scarcely less benign. The cahiers complained about royal taxes, *aides, gabelles, traites,* tailles, and the condition of the roads, grievances Depont could share with "his villagers." At Aigrefeuille, the cahier of the Third Estate protested the *banalité* of the oven and the *corvée,* but even these mild complaints were prefaced by the conciliatory phrase, "without abandoning the submission due to the seigneur." When these two rights were abolished, read the cahier, "we will become new men and ... the parish will flourish with the love of work and submission." Faurie, Depont's agent and attorney, was among the half-dozen local *syndics* who signed the cahier. Similarly at Virson, the cahier referred to the "cruel yoke of the *aides,*" but said nothing about seigneurial rights. It followed the same format used at La Jarne and other neighboring parishes. In fact, "model" printed cahiers were common in the region, suggesting that they were drawn up in the larger *bourgs*—Saintes, St. Jean d'Angély, Rochefort, even La Rochelle—and distributed to the village assemblies for cursory approval under the supervision of responsible attorneys like Faurie.[49] The cahier of Saint-Pierre-près-de-Surgères, close to the Depont's land, even proposed that day laborers be taxed at the rate of twenty sous per year "in order to maintain emulation and love of work." With some naiveté the cahier estimated that such a tax would raise millions in public revenues. That was for the city administrators to read. The local village inhabitants probably wanted to keep labor immobile and limit vagabondage.[50]

Six months later the news from the country was much more unsettling. The winter of 1789 had taken a terrible toll in a region that specialized in brandy-making at the expense of grain-growing. Faurie at Aigrefeuille presented a grim picture of the situation there.

My heart is filled with icy fear as I have just been informed that Widow Giraud's house will be the object of the fury of a crowd of *malheureux* without bread who have threatened action against different houses, not excluding that of the *curé* of Virson [100 yards from the Château des Granges]. ... He has not stopped baking bread for them since Christmas [three days before]. ...

I have no power. We are no longer in a time where my authority alone would have intimidated the most furious of men. ... We are in great danger. The *curé* ... gave a half-loaf of bread to a woman whose family had not eaten for four days. ...

You have the power, Monsieur, to increase your charity in this parish. Give your orders, Monsieur, I beg you. The time has come. We must have bread ... We can no longer retreat. The combustible pile [*bûcher*] is ready. Only a match [*étincelle*] is needed to ignite it. I am doing what I can for this suffering humanity. ... I shall open a subscription among the best houses of Aigrefeuille for twelve livres a month for the *curé* to distribute.

Monsieur, send your orders to give what you have promised the *curé*. Please increase your charity in the parish and with public works we can avoid the worst. I swear to you, Monsieur, I no longer feel safe in my house and do not sleep easily.[51]

Conditions on Oleron, where Depont had salt beds, were also desperate. Already in the spring of 1789 Chauvet, Depont's agent on the island, wrote to Bonnet at La Rochelle, telling him that his salt-makers could not obtain a pound of bread on credit and that their only resource was Paul-Charles's "*sainte main.*"[52] By November the municipal officials at Saint-Georges on Oleron were putting that "saintly hand" to the test. They asked the *ci-devant trésorier,* along with other seigneurs and larger proprietors on the island, for money to stave off famine and prevent "the destruction of your property, the first victim of the fury of the people."[53] Petty officials though they were, they knew how to appeal to reticent landowners. It appears that conditions were no better a year later, however. Depont was not extending credit even to his own salt-makers. Chauvet wrote again to the rue du Palais. "As you know, you have prohibited me from giving any money [*arjent*] to those who are in debt. I cannot pay them anything since most of them will not have enough salt in their shares to pay the advances I have already made to them in past years."[54] There was nothing new in this pattern of perpetual indebtedness, but the year had been especially hard. Even Chauvet, apparently a semiliterate, tough *maître-saunier* who "terrorized his men," was weakening in the face of famine on the island.

Paul-Charles did not give up his seigneurial justice easily. In July 1790, a full year after seigneurial justice had been abolished by the National Assembly, he insisted that his "jurisdiction" be respected by the local inhabitants. Two citizens from Virson had taken their cases to the lower court at La Rochelle, and Depont intervened. He said that Virson was "in the *châtellenie* of Les Granges de Virson which has a judge, a *procureur,* and other officers and where regular court sessions are held." "The said Sieur Depont wishes to conserve the rights of jurisdiction of his *châtellenie* of Les Granges de Virson and to require those who are "*justiciable*" to plead there, even in their own interest since it is the only way to avoid expense and fraud."[55] Is it possible that Depont, a magistrate after all, was not aware of the law? If he chose to ignore the legislation of August 1789, he could hardly avoid the consequences of the law of June 1790, abolishing hereditary nobility.[56] Or were seigneurial rights distinct from honorific and hereditary titles for him?

The previous April, some four hundred peasants had set fire to the manor house of Marquis de Bellegarde as well as the house of the local notary where the archives were stored.[57] Faurie must have shuddered too. Paul-Charles surely agreed with the observations of the *Journal Patriotique de Saintonge* about local government in the countryside east of La Rochelle.

The Constituent Assembly, by decreeing the new municipal code, has honored the great principle of equality. It is a sublime theory, but has not the experience of the last two years proven that in practice it has serious disadvantages? Before everything else, the class of country people [*habitants de la campagne*] must be enlightened enough to understand the nature of the duties a patriarchal magistrature [*magistrature patriarcale*] demands of them. It is clear that most village officials cannot even read, and that many of them, far from respecting the law, are the first to undermine it.[58]

Seigneurial justice brought no net income. To be sure, Paul-Charles gained a certain status from it. But it is also possible that he sincerely believed in its patriarchal function, a mixture of social control and mutual convenience.

In 1791 Paul-Charles left La Rochelle to stay with his younger daughter's family near Saumur on the Loire. He remained there for about two years, leaving Bonnet to manage his property at La Rochelle.[59] He apparently returned before the outbreak of the Vendean revolt, though the fact that he had relatives so close to the rebel heartland could cause him trouble with the Republican government. It is even possible that the Deponts were related to the same Lescure who commanded part of the Vendean army, although there is no direct evidence of this.[60]

As elsewhere in the region, it was not until 1792 that resistance to the collection of seigneurial dues occurred on Depont's properties. In June, a peasant from Aigrefeuille paid Bonnet 92 livres to "liberate" 1.6 acres from the *terrage,* a produce rent of one-eighth, and from the *lods et ventes,* a mutation fee of one-twenty-fourth the price of sale. Under the law of 1789, dues of this kind were *"rachetables,"* that is, they could be terminated if compensation was paid the seigneur at prescribed rates, usually twenty-five times the value of the rent. Bonnet gave a receipt that explicitly reserved "all the other and more important dues" in the jurisdiction. The payment was made in assignats.[61]

Already in 1791 the tenants (*fermiers*) had begun to pay their rents in assignats. In 1792 many of Depont's debtors began to liquidate their *rente* arrears and repay the capital, also in paper. Some of Depont's debtors had emigrated, and Bonnet had to write off that income entirely. The *"rentes* on the *Tailles"* and on other public institutions of the Old Regime were not paid after 1792, though the obligation was not repudiated by the "Nation," which inscribed the capital on the so-called Great Book of the Public Debt, pending a final administrative decision.[62] On the other hand, Paul-Charles was able to liquidate his own debts in assignats, largely offsetting the loss of revenues from his *rentes.* By 1793, his interest charges fell to less than six hundred livres, excluding interest due on unpaid dowries.[63]

The final abolition of seigneurial dues without compensation took place in July 1793. Depont's tenants, who collected these dues from the winegrowers and other small holders, whose rents were fixed by the leases with Depont, were the first to suffer. At Aigrefeuille, La Brande, Chagnées, and Chaumeau, combined revenues fell from over 12,500 livres to less than 2,000, an indication of the importance of the *terrage* on wine as a source of revenue on four of Depont's five seigneuries in Aunis.[64] By 1796, three years later, the tenants were making some headway in the courts toward gaining compensation for their losses.[65]

There is no reason to doubt Paul-Charles's claim to the government that his *métairie* in the Vendée had been "ravaged by brigands," the Republican term for the Vendean peasant army. Only the salt marshes on the islands and the *cabanes* near Rochefort seemed to be holding up. Largely removed from the threat of rural unrest and run without heavy reliance on seigneurial dues, these properties continued to return rents based on sales of salt, grain, and livestock. Chauvet made a good sale of the year's salt harvest in 1793 on Oleron, grossing over 7,000 livres. Depont had even transformed the *dîme,* a 10-percent seigneurial right, into a supplementary rent, and continued to collect the extra salt as before the Revolution. No wonder he and his brother were looking for more salt beds to buy in the middle of the Revolution. It was one of the few safe, high-yield investments still available.[66]

As a result of all these developments, net family income in 1793 was near 12,000 livres. This was down from over 30,000 in 1788 but still sufficient to maintain the town house and keep two sons at Paris. To read the accounts of Paul-Charles's younger son, the abbé Charles-Louis-Marie, during the years 1790–93 would lead one to think that nothing had changed in the everyday life of the capital. In August 1791 the boy noted his gambling losses of a few livres per day. Throughout 1792 and 1793, when inflation began to devastate the ordinary Parisian family, young Charles was buying butter, cheese, wine, coffee, cake, chocolate, and ice cream, luxury foods for the most part, as well as wigs, sword canes, suits, shoes and hats, sometimes "with a *cocarde*" as was the fashion. His allowance of 1,200 livres, paid in assignats after 1791, would seem to have kept him adequately clothed and fed.[67]

Taxes now fell more heavily on the *ci-devant* seigneur of Les Granges. In 1790 he had paid 72 livres *capitation* and 2,350 livres for the two *vingtièmes* on all of his landed property. By 1792 he was paying 1,600 livres *contribution foncière* for Les Granges alone, and 500 more for the salt beds on Oleron, now baptized "Island of Liberty." If his property taxes were assessed at this same rate on all his land as prescribed by law, he paid about 4,000 livres (francs) in land taxes, about one-third of his income in 1792. In addition, Paul-Charles had to meet special "voluntary" levies that anyone whose loyalty was suspect would shun at his own risk. For Depont they were:

1792: Patriotic Contribution	822 fr.
1793: The fourth (Gift)	2,428
1794: Forced Loan	5,031
Total	8,281 fr.

The receipts from these "voluntary contributions" to the Republican cause indicate that Citizen Depont paid promptly, perhaps in the hope that the local Revolutionary government would hesitate to disturb a good source of public revenue.[68]

Depont returned to La Rochelle sometime in 1793 with a "certificate of residence" that testified he had lived in France continuously since October 1792. He passed the year of the Terror without incident. But before the local Committee of Revolutionary Surveillance had been disbanded, a member of the "club" denounced him as "a relative of an émigré" and a defender of "uncivic principles." His accuser claimed that Citizen Depont "had often traveled, supposedly to the interior, but at no time has he proven by his actions that he is a Republican." "Patriotic contributions" were not enough. What had he done in Saumur? Was he a royalist working with the Vendeans? Dechézeaux, a Girondist, had been executed at Rochefort in January 1794 for less. The surveillance committee, by a unanimous vote, ordered that Depont be placed under arrest and that the "seals" be attached to his papers.[69]

But time was now on the side of Paul-Charles. Two months later, in October 1794, the Thermidoreans at Paris were beginning to make their new policies felt in the provinces. Even the popular society at Rochefort, which only a few months before had supported Billaud-Varenne against the local *"fédéralistes,"* now announced that the "tribunal of blood" had ended. The Committee of General Security at Paris ordered Depont's release, though he did not immediately regain complete possession of his property. In early 1795, Billaud, the department's most well-known Jacobin, was denounced, condemned, and sentenced to Guyana by the end of the year. The 679 Vendean prisoners jailed at La Rochelle were released, at least those who had survived the prison epidemic.[70]

Well aware that events were moving in a favorable direction, Paul-Charles reminded the local authorities that the Parisian Committee of General Security had already ordered the *main levée* on his property. "I believed that from that moment [October 1794] having regained my liberty, inestimable blessing of the happy Revolution of Thermidor, I would enjoy the full disposition of all my property." He then summoned his legal talents of persuasion. "Am I responsible for the emigration of my son-in-law and his wife? The Law of 17 Frimaire, Year II, has its exceptions. How could I prevent my daughter Equille from emigrating when I have not seen her since 1789? She has not been under my parental power for seventeen years. Can I be punished for a crime I could not prevent?" Paul-Charles ended with a sentimental appeal to the district directors. "It is with confidence that an unfortunate old man of seventy years, broken by illness and grief, still hopes to enjoy a few more days of peace and quiet in the bosom of the Republic."[71]

The appeal appears to have procured Depont an allowance of 12,500 francs, but not the return of the family lands. In the fall of 1795 he tried again, claiming that since assignats were almost worthless and no longer accepted by the grain merchants at La Rochelle, his allowance from the government was a pure illusion.[72] He then argued that the current food shortage was due to the neglect of agriculture caused by government seizure of private property such as his. Paul-Charles then turned political economist.

These reflections apply not only to grain but to all kinds of farm production. The vineyards on the domain of Les Granges, without cultivation for two years, have scarcely produced a quarter of the yield of neighboring vineyards. ... All of my properties are in the same condition. My salt beds on Oleron require urgent repairs. My basins have not produced a grain of salt despite a favorable year. It is proven by reason and experience that all these seizures are ruining domains and proprietors. Thus the Republic is losing an incalculable product, which is always the result of the care and affection each owner gives to his property.[73]

This time the petition was successful. The District Directory accorded Citizen Depont "provisional use" of his land on condition he submit regular accounts of the revenues and expenses. In March 1796 Depont was again collecting his own rents—in kind, of course, given the rapid devaluation of paper money. One of the accounts reads, "Receipt of 4,315 pounds of beans." In July Depont regained direct control over his salt beds and in August Maître Chauvet was reporting the sales of salt as usual. Depont claimed his share of two-thirds plus a supplementary rent of 10 percent, no doubt still called the *dîme* by the poor salt-makers on the island.[74]

There were other signs in 1796 of a return to normalcy or at least a tidying up of the last debris of the Revolution. At Aigrefeuille the seigneurial rights were gone forever, and Paul-Charles requested that the administration adjust the taxes downward to reflect the loss of revenues. A few acres of his meadow had been taken by the villagers and converted into commons during the Terror, and Depont claimed it back. In November the canton of Ciré received a letter from Jean-Samuel Depont, claiming that his land near Forges had been damaged by marauders. He informed the local administrators that he and his brother were hiring a *garde-champêtre* to protect the property in the future. Not quite a seigneurial *prévôt,* but perhaps the next best thing.[75]

All the *rentes* "on the Nation" were not lost. In March 1795, even before Paul-Charles had regained his land, the National Treasury sent him 250 livres *rente,* representing his interest on the "Voluntary Loan" of 1793, a sum he surely never expected to receive. In the course of 1795, the Treasury liquidated part of the national debt and Depont received 7,000 francs, albeit in depreciated paper. On the other hand, Paul-Charles could pay his taxes with this scrip until February 1797 when the national government insisted on hard currency. More important, until November 1796 one could buy émigré property with paper money.[76] Although there are no bills of sale to pinpoint the time of purchase, it is worth noting that between May 1795, just before he received his indemnity, and March 1797, Depont increased his holdings of salt beds on Oleron from 54 to 96 *livres,* or an expansion of approximately 90 acres. This represented an increase in income of about 1,500 francs and an investment of perhaps 60,000 francs in 1796. It seems that Jean-Samuel, who had the larger share of his father's public bonds, also received compensation and joined his brother in La Rochelle in a joint investment. They probably bought the salt basins that once belonged to émigré robe nobles from Bordeaux. Paul-Charles had kept his eye out for good buys since 1789. In March 1792 he told Chauvet that 1,500 livres per *livre* was too high, but by 1796 he had probably changed his mind.[77]

In late 1796, Paul-Charles had reason to regret his fine words about the "happy Revolution of Thermidor." The local authorities discovered that Depont's son-in-law had landed with the émigré army at Quiberon a year before.[78] The government of the Directory did not dally over Depont's personal responsibility for Equille's act of treason. The local directors simply enforced the new law dividing the property of the families of émigrés. In early 1797 the government assessed all of Depont's assets at La Rochelle.

The Fortune of Paul-Charles Depont in 1797

Assets:	Domains in Aunis and Oleron,	
	Town house in La Rochelle	272,326 fr.
	Mortgage Loans	46,955
	Credit on the "Nation"	32,779
	Private Loans	3,435
	Movables (furnishings, livestock,	
	tools)	28,220
	Total Assets	383,715 fr.
Liabilities:	Capital due four individuals	18,666 fr.
	Net Assets	365,049 fr.

Source: Archives Départementales, Q-250, Partage des Biens des Emigrés, Depont des Granges, 28 March 1797.

Under the new law, the Nation took the place of the condemned émigré and ordered equal division of the property among all survivors. That is, Paul-Charles and his three children in La Rochelle retained four shares and the government confiscated the fifth share of his émigré daughter. After deducting an exemption of 20,000 francs, the government's portion was assessed at 69,009 francs, subsequently reduced to 60,850. The portion included the town house, most of the remaining land at La Brande and Chaumeau (about 200 acres), a number of small lots less than an acre each, and 8,000 in "*rentes* on the Nation." The last item was a light loss, since at least partial repudiation of the public debt was almost certain anyway, but the loss of about one-sixth of the land and the town house was a heavy blow. At least the balance of the fortune was now unconditionally restored to Depont's ownership without any more surveillance by the local authorities.[79]

This final division of the Depont property was concluded on 28 March 1797. Three days later the entire portion of the Nation was sold to the highest bidder for 60,930 francs. The purchaser was none other than Paul-Charles himself, who had to pay half this sum in hard money. He was not even obliged to vacate the town house. The Treasury was increasingly desperate for hard money by 1797 and less interested in redistributing the land of the émigré families. In fact, the whole transaction amounted to a heavy cash penalty rather than a confiscation of property. The rapid repurchase not only indicated Depont's determination to keep all his assets but also demonstrated his capacity to pay—in silver. There must have been some strong boxes in the hôtel where the accumulated rents had been kept since 1791, the year the *fermiers* began to pay in assignats. Twenty years later during the Restoration, Paul-Charles's survivors, including his émigré daughter, Madame Froger d'Equille, made application for indemnification for the sum their father had paid to regain the family property in 1797. The final outcome is not certain, but there is every reason to believe from the evidence available that they received at least partial compensation, under Villèle's famous indemnity bill of 1825.[80]

Paul-Charles Depont des Granges died in December 1800, the year of Marengo and of the consolidation of the new Napoleonic regime. The last decade of his life had not been easy, filled as it was with chronic threats to his property and even his life. As a local *officier* he was less obtrusive, less a target for Jacobin animosity and suspicion than a *ci-devant* intendant of Metz. He clearly saw no need to "please" his *administrés,* if that is what his agents, tenants, salt-makers, and *"justiciables"* can be called. There is no evidence that he became less stern as a landlord during the decade of Revolution. On the contrary, he fought for his "rights" every step of the way from the retention of seigneurial justice at Virson in 1791 to the restoration of his property in 1795 and 1797. His tenacity in the face of adversity is clear. By 1800 he emerged from the ordeal with his 1,400 acres intact, though the losses of seigneurial rights and public *rentes* reduced his income from thirty thousand in 1789 to about fifteen thousand in 1800.

Ironically, these losses made Paul-Charles more than ever a *propriétaire*, to employ the fiscal vocabulary of the new regime. Like Martin de Chassiron, his colleague who returned to his estate in 1791 and took up "English farming" or Pierre Harouard, the landlord of La Jarne who wrote *mémoires* on agriculture in the first years of the new century, Paul-Charles Depont viewed the land as a reliable source of revenue, to be sure, but also as something of a style of life. Chassiron propagated the "precious criticisms" of Arthur Young, Harouard evoked the *"douces jouissances"* of the countryside, and Depont linked farm productivity to "the care and affection each owner gives to his property."[81] This is not to make Paul-Charles an agricultural pioneer or a benign, paternal landlord; he was neither. But clearly he accommodated to a modified provincial elite of landed families, who had been sobered and also defined more clearly by the Revolution, as seigneurial trappings disappeared and property rights became more simple and precise. I doubt that the Deponts were sentimental about the land, as Harouard was, but it is obvious that they were increasingly concerned about the market for salt, grain, and livestock in a Napoleonic France that prohibited seigneurial rights and prevented the export of cognac. La Rochelle would never again recapture the dynamism of the sugar and slave trade, and the "romance" of the Islands would gradually be restricted to the exotic artifacts of a salon on the rue des Armateurs. But in a quieter way, the reign of the local notables had already begun.

We know little about Jean-Samuel Depont after 4 August 1790, the day his life was threatened by mutinous troops at Metz. Apparently he made his way back to Paris and remained there in relative obscurity. Then some time in 1794, at the height of the Terror, he was ferreted out by the local *section*, Guillaume Tell, and placed under house arrest as a *ci-devant* intendant. The laconic police report states that Depont, seventy-two years of age, was living with his divorced daughter, former wife of "Fontanges émigré" and also had a son in the country near Mantes-sur-Seine.[82] Needless to say, Charles-François's diplomatic services to the Revolution at Cologne in early 1792 were insufficient to compensate for the political sins of the Fontanges of Auvergne. Following a rural revolt on their land at Velzic in March 1792, the dowager marquise and her two sons left Auvergne for Lyon. The marquise was tried before the Revolutionary Tribunal at Paris for her actions during the Federalist Revolt at Lyon, and barely escaped conviction, thanks to Thermidor. Justin, Jean-Samuel's son-in-law, had escaped from Lyon and joined the émigré army of Condé at Koblenz, the same army his son as minister to Cologne in 1792 had tried so hard to neutralize.[83] Alliances with old military nobility from Poitou and Auvergne had suddenly become liabilities. Like Bouillé at Metz, the Fontanges and Froger d'Equille could hardly be considered flexible in political matters. Their first loyalty was to a king unfettered by "constitutions"; emigration was a duty of their *métier* and milieu.

This was not Jean-Samuel's way. He would not suffer from rigid political principles. Giving his age as seventy-two instead of sixty-nine, and declaring a revenue of only 4,983 francs, he convinced the Parisian police that he had few friends and liaisons of any kind, that he was, in short, politically innocuous. Although the report observed that Citizen Depont was not "a known friend of the National Assembly," it concluded that he had complied with the transfer of power at Metz, and that, given his advanced age, police surveillance was unwarranted.[84] It did not end, however, until September 1795, shortly after Paul-Charles's son-in-law was discovered on the coast of Brittany with the émigré army. Fortunately for the Deponts in Paris, the police of the 1790s had no rapid way to cross-check their files on all branches of the family.

The ci-devant intendant of Metz was indeed no threat to the Republic. Nor was he quite the helpless, impoverished septuagenarian the report suggested. To begin with, Jean-Samuel was not economically destitute. The financial aspects of his existence during the Revolutionary decade, sketchy as they are, suggest that his political and psychological uncertainties were not always matched by financial ones. Throughout the 1790s, Jean-Samuel kept a meticulous account of each contract, title, and receipt in his study, claiming, if not always collecting, his *rentes* from individuals and the State. In June 1791, Depont had sufficient liquidity to lend the Villedou family 6,000 livres at 5 percent. The subsequent emigration of this noble family apparently hindered regular interest payments, and Depont filed a claim for the arrears nine years later. In July 1793, not many months before Jean-Samuel himself was arrested, he and his brother brought fifty-four *livres* of salt marsh south of La Rochelle for 66,666 livres, two-thirds of them for himself for 45,000 livres. The entire sum was made payable, presumably in assignats, by Sr. Valles de Valleneuve, Treasurer of the City of Paris.

Where did the Depont brothers get this much capital? It appears that their claims on the City of Paris, carefully recorded in the "*Grand Livre*" were not a total loss, after all. At least, the transactions marked in Depont's death inventory suggest that he was paid a round sum in compensation for his earlier investments in government bonds. If this be so, how many other government bondholders were able to convert their claims on the government of the Old Regime (*rentes* on the *Hôtel de Ville,* for example) into solid land during the Revolution? The sellers of the salt marshes appear to have been three small owners from the *bourgs* of Saint-Georges and Marennes; hence it was a case of large owners buying out small ones. From the estate correspondence it appears that the Depont brothers were turning more attention to salt production throughout the 1780s and 1790s. With brandy exports halted by the war with England, salt, forage, and livestock were about the only marketable commodities left in Aunis. The land was one of the few remaining assets in 1800. La Rochelle and its hinterland appeared more and more as a haven of security for Jean-Samuel.

Financial difficulties in Paris were signaled by the necessity to default on payments for his daughter's dowry. Recall that Jean-Samuel had paid a great deal of money to make his daughter a marquise in 1788. In practice, many handsome dowries were considerably reduced by the deduction of previous payments or by the stipulation of a low rate of interest on the balance due. But in the case of Depont's daughter, the entire dowry of a quarter-million livres was to be paid at a full 5 percent, that is, 12,500 livres annually, a very heavy charge even by Parisian standards. The Marquise de Fontanges received this sum regularly until 1797 when payments fell below 5,000 livres. In 1798, the marquise, having "divorced" her husband in February 1793, was living in her father's town house in the Marais quarter with her eight-year-old daughter, and agreed to accept 6,000 livres per annum. The marquise had apparently been "reasonable," which was not always the case in other families at this time. Two years before, Charles-Jean-François had married Thérèse-Avoye-Marie Michel, a commoner and possibly a merchant's daughter. Despite this "misalliance," Jean-Samuel promised to pay his son a portion equal to the dowry of his daughter. However, earlier payments for the office of councilor were deducted and the balance paid at only 4 percent. Was Jean-Samuel estranged from his son at this time or was he bowing to financial necessity? In any case, he had to sell a *cabane* near La Rochelle to meet his obligations to his son. Financially, the years 1796 to 1798 were difficult ones for Jean-Samuel, now in his seventy-first year.[85]

Nevertheless, by the spring of 1798 the old resiliency had returned. Jean-Samuel bought thirty-three shares of stock worth about forty thousand francs. Had he economized on his daughter's dowry in order to accumulate capital for fresh investments? So it appears. And what was this stock, about which the inventory comments only too briefly: "with all of the rights and advantages detailed in the prospectus"? Jean-Samuel also established closer contact with his brother at La Rochelle. He took a direct hand in the administration of his land at Forges and Manderoux in Aunis, probably for the first time. Writing from Paris in 1798, he seemed surprised by the "miserable rent of 1,100 francs" from his tenant at Forges, unaware, it seems, of the loss of seigneurial rents. He was suspicious of his new estate manager, whom he regarded as a walking account book, devoid of spontaneity. "When one has a machine for an *homme d'affaires,* it is impossible to know what he is doing." Jean-Samuel exhibited the irritability of an absentee landlord who does not trust his paper controls. No provincial agent or tenant could cheat a wily Parisian. "One must not proceed too quickly and fall into the hands of people who want something for nothing," he wrote, in words that his father might have used back in the 1760s. In matters of the land, Jean-Samuel meant it when he said he had confidence in the "wise and prudent" management of his elder brother.[86] With his brother's experience in the provinces and his father-in-law's skills in Paris, all was not over. Moreover, with the tragic loss of his son in September 1797, Jean-Samuel had another reason to return to the family.

The first years of the nineteenth century saw the septuagenarian as active as ever in financial ventures in Paris. Between 1801 and 1803 Jean-Samuel began to lease "apartments" in his town house for very good rents. Among the new tenants were Jean-François Baucheron La Vauverte, who rented a third-floor apartment for 1,500 francs; the Crépin brothers who rented a whole "front" along the rue Vivienne for 2,200 francs; François-Gabriel La Hoult, owner of a cotton-spinning mill at Versailles, an apartment on the second floor for 2,400 francs; and Albert Jakovsky, a shop in one of the buildings adjoining the town house at an unspecified rent. Altogether, Jean-Samuel rented out seven apartments, at least one of which was used as a shop. His rents from the town house brought a minimum of 6,600 francs, more than double the return on his estate of Manderoux near La Rochelle. Urban real estate paid well in these years.

Equally interesting was Jean-Samuel's willingness to finance these high rents by lending his tenants short-term capital. In the same two years his seven tenants borrowed a total of 13,750 francs from the former intendant in thirty-six separate drafts with time limits from four to five years. There seems little doubt that these tenants—Doazen, Jakovsky, Senety, La Vauverte, La Hoult, and the Crépin brothers— were merchants and shopkeepers and that Depont was willing to finance their enterprises, rent them apartments, and even convert parts of his town house to commercial use.[87]

Commercial loans and urban rentals, especially when they included whole wings of a town house rented to merchants, may have lacked the distinction of a dovecote in Aunis, but it was much more profitable and kept the capital moving. No doubt the presence of a half-dozen "merchants" in a Parisian town house that symbolized the summit of the Depont family's social ascent must have given Jean-Samuel pause. Where was his world of yesteryear—the salon of Marquise de Montesson, the friendship of Jacques Flesselles, the brocade gown of Madame l'Intendante, the élan of a young parlementaire of Metz? But Jean-Samuel was hardly the sort to look back over his shoulder. One must move on. After all, had not the Duc d'Orléans rented the ground floor of the Palais Royal to Parisian shopkeepers almost a century earlier with equal financial success? Yet, aware as we are of Jean-Samuel's adaptability, we are not quite prepared to see his name on the list of "600 most heavily taxed" citizens in the Department of the Seine (Paris) in 1803.[88]

Quite possibly Jean-Samuel inherited the Touche fortune at the turn of the century. The "brillant Madame de Fontanges" of Restoration Paris did not live on five thousand francs per annum.[89] Still, Depont did not survive the 1790s by chance alone. To the end, he combined a certain flamboyance with calculation and *bon sens.* In early 1798 when he learned that the public debt had been largely repudiated, he exclaimed to his brother, "We are all ruined!" But he quickly followed this hyperbole with another example of his personal resilience, rather remarkable in a man of seventy-three years: "My *pis aller* will be to live with others. Among the bankers here there are people who have money to throw out of the window. I have no hesitation about living off them. Citizen Veith is one of these bankers. The other night he invited Noailles, Aiguillon, and Lameth. One will go to the home of the Devil if there is food and dancing. I was also invited. I waited until midnight, but dinner was not served until one in the morning! Adieu, dear brother."[90]

The passage captures a familiar stereotype of Paris during the Directory—high living among the parvenu bankers and war contractors as inflation devastated those living on *rentes* or wages. The presence of Noailles and Aiguillon, the "great nobles" of the Night of August 4 who renounced their seigneurial rights in a moment of grand gesture, could not have gone unnoticed by Paul-Charles, *ci-devant* seigneur in Aunis. And Lameth, one of the famous "triumvirate" of the Constituent Assembly, was once admired by a young correspondent of Edmund Burke. What did this bizarre assembly talk about in the spring of 1798—the "liquidation" of the public debt, the proclamation of the Roman Republic, the price of cognac?

La Rochelle reasserted its claims on Jean-Samuel. In a letter from Paris dated 18 Brumaire, but without the year, the aging *ci-devant* royal intendant wrote these words: "All that you have told me about the property does not surprise me. It is everyone's story. But when we shall have peace again, the land will remain."[91]

Thirteen Portraits

In 1806 Madame de Fontanges, daughter of the recently deceased Jean-Samuel Depont, passed through the large bedchamber on the second floor of her father's town house on the rue des Filles Saint-Thomas. She asked the notaries who were making the inventory of family effects to reserve a row of portraits for her own keeping.[1] Whether these thirteen portraits were carted off to her husband's modest town house in Auriac or kept in a Paris apartment, we do not know. Nor are we told whom they represented. But in the light of what we do know about the Depont family, let us speculate about who these thirteen people must have been.

Surely there was a Fontanges contingent—a bishop of Troyes or Laval—and perhaps the old marshal himself, Madeleine-Pauline's father-in-law, in military attire with a touch of Auvergnat rusticity. Just as surely there was representation from the Escureul de la Touche family—Jean-Samuel's father-in-law, the former Intendant des Menus Plaisirs, with the flamboyance and self-assurance of a Parisian man of affairs. Beside him, Pierrette de Cromot, fashionably dressed to befit the daughter of a well-known royal financier. If we turn to the main branch of the family, Paul-François Depont, trésorier de France, would have commanded a prominent place. One imagines a creation of the Dutch School of the previous century, shades of Van Dyke, a stern, sober, tight-lipped man in black with a decided touch of the self-righteous. Close by, Paul-Charles, Jean-Samuel's elder brother, a rural seigneur and local notable, also sober and taciturn, perhaps a little sad, dressed in the modest riding coat of a *gentilhomme* from Aunis. Next, Sara Bernon, Jean-Samuel's grandmother, a strong, willful, self-contained person, the family matriarch, unashamed of her Protestant faith and mercantile origins, a physical contrast to Marie-Henriette Sonnet, the wife of Paul-Charles, a thin, fragile, and worried woman in poor health. Their children might follow—Charles-Louis, much like his father; Virson, young musketeer trying to look military; Pauline with her husband, Froger de l'Equille, the naval officer from Rochefort, both of them flaunting a stubborn ultraroyalism that would end in tragedy on the beaches at Quiberon.

Somewhere in the Depont phalanx would appear the eager, youthful, yet anxious face—collared in ermine, capped with mortarboard—of a young magistrate of the Parlement of Paris. Charles-Jean-François De-Pont had political and diplomatic talent, undeniably a "young gentle-man" of promise. Not far from her son's portrait would be Madame L'In-tendante. Marie-Madeleine-Sophie L'Escureul de la Touche, not yet forty, must have been striking in pompadour, *mouches*, and brocade gown, cultivated in the art of conversation and equally at ease at salon soirée and official reception. Finally, Jean-Samuel himself, resplendent, official, a trifle pompous, wrapped in his intendant's sash and clutching a sheaf of royal dispatches. Among the portraits on display in the Marais *hôtel* surely this Depont looked most satisfied.

Making due allowance for the normal distribution of individual talent and mediocrity, of conditioning circumstance, of good fortune and bad, the Deponts had done rather better than survive a century of change and challenge. They had learned that success in their society required con-stant adaptation and the mobilization of a whole gamut of resources—material, professional, and psychological. By one avenue or another, they had entered all the elites, established footholds in all hierarchies—land, law, office, finance, high administration, Parisian society, in addition to alliances to old nobility and upper clergy.

With few exceptions the family had amassed those skills and attributes that Sénac de Meilhan, a former intendant of La Rochelle, expressed so well as he looked back on the Old Regime in 1795. "Favor, rank, *esprit, agrément,* wealth, and talent were equally respected. These diverse prin-ciples of esteem appear to have abolished the differences among in-dividuals."[2] Sénac was not alluding to *all* individuals of course. He was referring to an emerging French notability, a new social amalgam that would survive more than one revolution in the years ahead. The long reign of the *"capacités"* had barely begun.

Notes

Preface

1. John Higham, *History: Professional Scholarship in America* (New York, 1965), p. 143.
2. Lawrence Stone, "History and the Social Sciences in the 20th Century," in *Symposium on the Future of History,* ed. Charles Delzell (Vanderbilt, 1975), p. 39. "It may be that the time has come for the historian to reassert the importance of the concrete, the particular, and the circumstantial, as well as the general theoretical model and procedural insight."
3. Clifford Geertz, *The Interpretation of Cultures* (New York, 1973), p. 23. Writing as an anthropologist, Geertz proposes "fine-combed field study in confined contexts" so that the "mega-concepts with which contemporary social science is afflicted . . . can be given the sort of sensible actuality that makes it possible to think not only realistically and concretely *about them,* but what is more important, creatively and imaginatively *with them.*" Italics in the original text.

Chapter One

1. Henri Robert, *Les Trafics coloniaux du port de la Rochelle au XVIIIe siècle,* Mémoires de la Société des Antiquaires de l'Ouest (Poitiers, 1960), p. 33. See also Marcel Delafosse and Etienne Trocmé, *Le Commerce rochelais de la fin du XVe siècle au début du XVIIe* (Paris, 1952), ch. 1 and passim. I wish to thank John G. Clark of the University of Kansas for permitting me to read his unpublished manuscript, "La Rochelle and the Atlantic World during the Eighteenth Century," an archival study of the merchant community.
2. Robert, *Les Trafics coloniaux,* p. 105; Louis Pérouas, *Le Diocèse de la Rochelle de 1648 à 1724: sociologie et pastorale* (Paris, 1964), pp. 90-91 and passim.
3. Le Père Arcère, *Histoire de la ville de la Rochelle et du pays d'Aulnis,* 2 vols. (La Rochelle, 1756-57). There is need of a general history of La Rochelle. For local artifacts in a town that has not been "modernized," at least at its center, see Marcel Delafosse, *La Rochelle, ville océane* (La Rochelle, 1953); Delafosse, *La Rochelle et la côte Charentaise* (La Rochelle, 1960); René Crozet, *Aunis-Saintonge* (Paris, 1953), pp. 4-15; François de Vaux de Foletier, *Charentes,* Les Albums des Guides Blues (Paris, 1957) for excellent photographs of the "Old Port," the Chamber of Commerce, rue du Palais, etc.
4. Ambroise-Marie Arnould, *De la Balance du commerce extérieur de la France dans toutes les parties du globe,* 2 vols. (Paris, 1791); François Crouzet, "L'Angleterre et la France au XVIIIe siècle: Essai d'analyse comparée de deux croissances économiques," *Annales: E.S.C.* 21 (1966): 254-91; Fernand Braudel and C-E. Labrousse, eds., *Histoire économique et sociale de la France, vol. 2, 1650-1780* (Paris, 1970). All general economic histories of France in the eighteenth century treat overseas trade as the most dynamic and, implicitly, most profitable sector of the economy.

5. Henri Robert refers to profits of 18 percent per shipping venture to West Africa and Saint-Domingue. He admits, however, that complete balance sheets are very rare. Robert, *Les Trafics coloniaux*, pp. 40, 47n. When Léon Vignols described "the extraordinary success" of the slaver, the *Perle*, he did not give the profits of the voyage because he did not find the expenses of "disarming" the ship (*compte de désarmement*). Léon Vignols, "La Campagne négrière de *la Perle* (1755–1757) et sa réussite extraordinaire," *Revue historique* 163 (1930): 51–78. For an excellent bibliography on French overseas trade see Jean Tarrade, *Le Commerce colonial de la France à la fin de l'ancien régime* (Paris, 1972), 2: 814–49.

6. Robert, *Les Trafics coloniaux*, pp 1–2.

7. Tarrade, *Le Commerce colonial*, 1: 136–44; Jean Meyer, *L'Armement nantais dans la deuxième moitié du XVIIIe siècle* (Paris, 1969), pp. 205–48. See also F. Crouzet's long chapter in F. G. Pariset, *Bordeaux au XVIIIe siècle* (Bordeaux, 1968). The older works of Gaston Martin (Nantes), Henri Sée (Saint-Malo), and Pierre Dardel (Le Havre) made little effort to measure the profits of the trade. Even the English slavers with the benefit of a powerful navy never registered average profits of more than 10 percent. Roger Anstey, *The Atlantic Slave Trade and British Abolition, 1760–1810* (London and New York, 1975). It is beginning to appear that contemporary abolitionists who argued the unprofitability of the slave trade were not far wrong in their "theoretical calculations." See *Ephémerides du Citoyen ou bibliothèque raisonnée des sciences morales et politiques* (1771), vol. 11, pt. 2, pp. 51–56, reprinted in Robert Forster and Elborg Forster eds., *European Society in the Eighteenth Century* (New York, 1969), pp. 177–81.

8. Archives Départementales, Charente-Maritime (hereafter cited as A.D.), E-483, "Livre concernant les rentes et intérêts des vaisseaux," 1723–67. The French *livre* in 1780 was very roughly equivalent to $2.00 (U.S.) in 1980. Of course, the components of the cost-of-living were very different. Food for example was quite "cheap" by our standards, while all manufactured goods seem very "dear." An income of 10,000 livres in the provinces would be considered comfortable, while one needed at least 50,000 livres per annum to "cut a good figure" in Paris. Day-labor (male) was paid one livre per day maximum. Comparison of revenues at the lower end of the income scale has little meaning since day-labor was paid partly in bread; moreover, the miserable diet and living conditions of a French day-laborer in 1780 are unimaginable by the standards of a wageearner in the Western world today. The ratio of revenue between a well-to-do provincial landlord and a day-laborer was at least thirty to one, between an overseas merchant and an artisan, perhaps fifty to one, and between a Versailles duke and a provincial magistrate about ten to one.

9. Ibid.

10. Robert, *Les Trafics coloniaux*, pp. 38–40.

11. A subsequent expedition of indigo was evaluated at 39,873 livres. This probably represents part of this debt. If the balance remained unpaid, which seems likely, there was a net loss on the voyage of about 30,000 livres for the six partners. A.D., E-486.

12. Robert, *Les Trafics coloniaux*, pp. 35, 43. John G. Clark has made an in-depth study of the twenty-six "leading" families of La Rochelle. See "La Rochelle and The Atlantic World," ch. 3 and passim.

13. A.D., E-486, "La Fortune," 23 Nov. 1733, "La Victoire," 3 Feb. 1740; A.D., E-483, "La Perle," February 1730.

14. Pérouas, *Le Diocèse de La Rochelle*, p. 103n. Paul Depont's father, Samuel Depont, had been engaged in overseas trade before him. Samuel Depont leased ships to other *armateurs* and served as banker and sugar refiner, especially in the twenty years after 1660. M. Delafosse, "La Rochelle et les Iles au XVIIe siècle," *Revue d'histoire des colonies* 36 (1949): 273–74 and passim.

15. A.D., E-483, 1723–34.

16. A.D., E-482, "Journal," no. 1, 6 Mar. 1721.

17. Ibid., entries of 20 August 1719, 26 July 1721, 30 Dec. 1722.

18. M. Delafosse. "Planteurs de Saint-Domingue et négociants de La Rochelle au temps de Law," *Revue d'histoire des colonies* 41 (1962): 14-21.

19. A.D., E-486, "Compte général de toutes les avances faites . . . pour Ms. de La Compagnie des Indes," 14 Feb. 1722.

20. Emile Garnault, *Le Commerce rochelais au XVIIIe siècle* (Paris and La Rochelle, 1888-1900), 1: 23.

21. A.D., "Inventaire," B-344, July 1730.

22. Robert, *Les Trafics coloniaux,* p. 125; J. Meyer, "Le Commerce négrier nantais (1774-1792)," *Annales: E.S.C.* 15 (1960): 127 for a comparative table of slave "deliveries" by the French ports. See also Clark, "La Rochelle."

23. A.D., E-486, "Comptes d'armement;" Robert, *Les Trafics coloniaux,* pp. 80-81. The mortality rate of slaves on the "middle passage" is a subject of debate. Gaston-Martin estimated these losses at 23.2 percent of the "cargoes" of Nantes slavers in the period 1727-40. For this and a general criticism of mortality statistics, see Jean-Claude Nardin, "Encore des chiffres: La traite négrière française pendant la première moitié du XVIIIe siècle," *Revue française d'histoire d'outre mer* 57 (1970): 434 and passim. Philip Curtin's mortality figures, based on 465 Nantes slavers over the longer period, 1748-92, average 15.2 percent, but reach 19.4 percent for the years 1748-51. Philip D. Curtin, *The Atlantic Slave Trade: A Census* (Madison, 1969), p. 279. A mortality rate of about 20 percent for the first half of the century for slavers out of French ports is probably not wide of the mark.

24. Robert, *Les Trafics coloniaux,* pp. 76-79.

25. Garnault, *Le Commerce rochelais,* 3: 45; Tarrade, *Le Commerce colonial,* 1: 102-10 and ch. 3, passim.

26. Robert, *Les Trafics coloniaux,* p. 127.

27. Ibid., 52-53; Garnault, *Le Commerce rochelais, 3: 170-72.* Garnault presents a list of the ships taken by the English before the formal declaration of war.

28. Ibid., 3: 107, quoted in Robert, *Les Trafics coloniaux,* p. 137.

29. Tarrade, *Le Commerce colonial,* 1: 143. Italics mine. See also Robert, *Les Trafics coloniaux,* p. 133: "The year 1744 certainly does not mark the last great days of the colonial trade at La Rochelle, but surely in an irrevocable way it marks the end of a period when events had been particularly favorable to the trade." For a general survey of French trade policy during the twenty years before 1743, see Arthur M. C. Wilson, *French Foreign Policy during the Administration of Cardinal Fleury, 1726-1743* (Cambridge, Mass., 1936).

30. Robert, *Les Trafics coloniaux,* p. 131.

31. A.D., E-483 "Livres concernant . . . des vaisseaux," 1727-43.

32. Ibid, "Etats," 22 June 1744; 2 Nov. 1746.

33. Robert, *Les Trafics coloniaux,* pp. 84, 150.

34. Ibid., p. 146.

35. A.D., E-487, Paul-François to Jean-Samuel Depont, 24 May 1766.

36. Pérouas, *Le Diocèse de la Rochelle,* p. 103n.

37. See chapter 4 below.

38. A.D., E-486 "Compte général . . . Compagnie des Indes," 1721-22; Robert, *Les Trafics coloniaux,* vii; Garnault, *Le Commerce rochelais,* 1: 78-79.

39. Arcère, *Histoire de la ville de La Rochelle et du Pays d'Aulnis* (La Rochelle, 1757), 2: 554. See also A.D., E-106, "Brevet Royal, 23 Nov. 1743," transferring the office to Paul-Charles Depont, son of Paul-François.

40. Jean-Paul Charmeil, *Les Trésoriers de France à l'époque de la Fronde. Contribution à l'histoire de l'administration financière sous l'Ancien Régime* (Paris, 1964), p. 18. There were 592 *trésoriers* in the entire kingdom in 1788 and 530 in 1635.

41. Marcel Marion, *Dictionnaire des institutions de la France sous l'Ancien Régime*

(Paris, 1969), pp. 60-62; Roland Mousnier, *Etat et société en France aux XVIIe et XVIIIe siècles* (Paris, Les cours de Sorbonne, 1970), 1: 77, 111; Charmeil, *Trésoriers*, pp. 156, 375.

42. François Bluche et Pierre Durye, *L'Anoblissement par charges avant 1789* (Paris, Les cahiers nobles, 1962) 1: 9; Charmeil, *Trésoriers*, pp. 72-73. Charmeil claims that by the mid-eighteenth century a father would buy the office just before his death and pass it on to his son, thus assuring the family of hereditary nobility in a little more than twenty years. This explains the advanced age of many *trésoriers* at the end of the Old Regime.

43. On the question of ennobling office and social mobility see David Bien, "La Réaction aristocratique avant 1789: aristocratie et anoblissement au XVIIIe siècle," *Annales: E.S.C.* 29 (1974): 23-43; 505-32. Between 1774 and 1789, 1,417 commoners entered the nobility via the offices of *trésorier de France* (539) and *secrétaire du roi* (878). On the requirements for admission, see Charmeil, *Trésoriers*, ch. 2. It is not certain that a law degree was required (ibid., p. 24). Paul-François attended law school and went to Paris in 1722 to pay his "reception fee" of 5,000 livres for the office: A.D., E-482, "Journal," fols. 47, 49, 51.

44. *Archives historiques de la Saintonge et de l'Aunis* (Paris and Saintes, 1879), 6: 223, 215-221; Pérouas, *Le Diocèse de La Rochelle.* pp. 86-93, 102ff.

45. A.D., E-476, "Etats des emprunts," 1783-85. The thesis that *rentes* served as a source of social solidarity is presented by Ralph Giesey, "National Stability and the Hereditary Transmission of Political and Economic Power," p. 16 and passim. Paper presented at the "XIVth International Congress of Historical Sciences" (San Francisco, 22-29 Aug. 1975).

46. Mousnier, *Etat et société,* 1: 81. One can place Amiens, Angoulême, Bayeux, Beauvais, Châteaudun, Orléans, among others, in the same category with La Rochelle in this respect. See R. Mousnier, *Les Institutions de la France sous la monarchie absolue,* (Paris, 1974) 1: 178-79 and ch. 5, passim.

47. On social mobility in Boston in the late nineteenth century, see Stephan Thernstrom, "Religion and Occupational Mobility in Boston, 1880-1963" in *The Dimensions of Quantitative Research in History,* W. O. Aydelotte et al. eds. (Princeton, 1972).

48. A.D., E-487, Paul François to Jean-Samuel Depont, 6 July 1765.

49. Mousnier, *Etat et société,* 1: 77-82; Mousnier, "Les Concepts d'Ordres, d'Etats, de fidélité et de monarchie absolue en France de la fin du XVe siècle à la fin du XVIIIe," *Revue historique* 247 (1972): 289-312.

50. Unfortunately, the only glimpse we have of Paul-François's library is from his correspondence to his son. Of Paul Depont's reading habits, we know nothing. However, if the libraries of Marseilles merchant families are any indication, an *armateur* seemed to limit himself to account books and law manuals. Even Jacques Savary's *Parfait Negociant* (Paris, 1675) was rare in Marseilles. See Charles Carrière, *Négociants marseillais au XVIIIe siècle,* 2 vols. (Paris, 1974).

51. Mousnier, *Les Institutions,* 1: 178 and ch. 5, passim.

52. A.D., E-472, Will of 8 Nov. 1712.

53. Ibid., "Obligation," 4 June 1717.

54. Ibid., Codicil of 13 Mar. 1743. Paul Depont drew up at least nine codicils to his will, an indication of many changes of mind.

55. Ibid., Codicil of 1 July 1723.

56. A.D., E-473, Will of 9 May 1753.

57. In 1714 a Lescure married a Green de Saint-Marsault, one of the most important noble families at La Rochelle. See E. H. E. Beauchet-Filleau, *Dictionnaire historique et généalogique des familles de Poitou,* 4 vols. (Poitiers, 1891-1912).

58. A.D., E-473, Will of 9 May 1753.

59. A.D., E-487, Paul-François Depont to Madame de Lescure, 24 May 1765. The bride's mother was a lady-in-waiting of the queen.

60. A.D., E-473, Will of 9 May 1753. In this context "bourgeoise" suggests simplicity rather than "non-noble."

61. A.D., E-473, Act of Marriage, 7 Jan. 1710; Charmeil, *Trésoriers*, pp. 21-22.

62. A.D., B-344, "Sommaire." See Robert, *Les Trafics coloniaux*, p. 187. The complete statement reveals a certain skepticism among local Catholics toward the "newly converted." The children of Paul Depont were considered exceptional in their acts of piety.

63. Pérouas, *Le Diocèse de La Rochelle;* Dominique Julia, "La Réforme posttridentine en France d'après les procès-verbaux de visites pastorales: ordre et résistance," *La Società religiosa nell'età moderna* (Naples, 1973), p. 350 and passim. See also Jean Delumeau, *Le Catholicisme entre Luther et Voltaire* (Paris, 1971) and John Bossy, "The Counter-Reformation and the People of Catholic Europe," *Past and Present* 47 (May 1970): 51-70.

64. Pérouas, *Le Diocèse de La Rochelle,* pp. 334-36.

65. Ibid., pp. 348, 414, 414n.

66. Ibid., pp. 378, 384.

67. A.D., E-487, Paul-François to Jean-Samuel Depont, 17 Apr. 1764.

68. Ibid., 28 Dec. 1765.

69. A.D., E-474, "Etat des fondations de M. Depont," 1751-71.

70. Ibid., "Assemblée d'Aigrefeuille," 23 June 1754; "Plan des bâtiments," 1754-59; Letter of Widow Depont, 30 Aug. 1752; Receipt of Pension, December 1792; "Procès-verbal," 30 Mar. 1814; "Project pour les hospices de communauté d'Aigrefeuille," 1840.

71. Pérouas, *Le Diocèse de La Rochelle,* pp. 169, 169n.

72. A.D., E-474, "Concession de banc," 16 Dec. 1753. The pew cost 120 livres entrance fee and 10 livres per annum rental. They were apparently leased to the highest bidder.

73. A.D., E-487, Paul-François Depont to Madame la Comtesse de Lescure, 7 Jan. 1766.

74. The history of usury has produced a large literature. For the French case, see R. J. Pothier, "Traité du contrat de constitution de rentes," in *Oeuvres* (Paris, 1861), 3: 435ff. and Bernard Schnapper, *Les Rentes au XVIe siècle* (Paris, 1958). For the actual practice of usury and enforcement of the usury laws see Turgot's comments on moneylending in Angoulême in A. R. J. Turgot, *Oeuvres,* ed. Eugène Daire (Paris, 1844) 1: 106ff., 114-16. reprinted in Forster and Forster, *European Society in the Eighteenth Century,* pp. 148-51. See also Giesey, "National Stability," pp. 8-11.

75. A.D., E-483, "Etat," 2 Nov. 1746.

Chapter Two

1. A.D., E-483, "Livre concernant les rentes et intérêts des vaisseaux," 1723-67; E-484, "Livre concernant mes rentes et prix des fermes," 1757-1804.

2. The *Hôtel Depont* on the rue du Palais seems more modest than many of the town houses of the *armateurs*. The *Hôtel Poupet,* for example, which serves as the prefecture today, is much more distinguished, at least from the outside. Depont's town house was a bank in 1962 when the author was there.

3. A.D., E-487. See, for example, Paul-François to Jean-Samuel Depont, 1 Apr. 1758.

4. I have examined sixty-six of these letters in some detail; the remaining letters (about thirty) I found redundant. All of the private letters of Paul-François Depont are found in E-487.

5. L. de La Morinérie, *La Noblesse de l'Aunis et de Saintonge aux Etats Généraux de 1789* (Paris, 1861), pp. 283-84.

6. See Colin Lucas's review of Alan Forrest, *Society and Politics in Revolutionary*

Bordeaux (Oxford, 1975) in the *Times Literary Supplement* 30 Jan. 1976, p. 422. Lucas discusses what Anglo-American scholars can most effectively contribute to the social history of Old-Regime France. I agree with him.

7. A.D., E-487, Paul-François to Jean-Samuel, 23 Oct. 1758. Hereafter, all letters can be assumed to have been written by Paul-François to Jean-Samuel unless otherwise noted. Where substantial passages are quoted, the date will be in the text.

8. Paul-François employed the term *"tourbillon de Paris"* often; he used it almost interchangeably with "continual dissipation." Psychologists might detect a sexual overtone, especially when paired with another favorite word, "engulfed" (*englouti*). I do not intend to pursue this, but it is quite clear that, for Depont *père*, Paris was the maelstrom that consumed, indeed devoured, everyone in its path.

9. See Jean Delumeau, *Le Catholicisme entre Luther et Voltaire* (Paris: Nouvelle Clio, 1971) and especially his review of Michel Vovelle's work in the *Revue d'histoire moderne et contemporaine* 22 (January–March 1975). Delumeau raises the possibility of a religious revival, alongside of a decline of respect for certain outward forms of Catholicism, in the course of the eighteenth century.

10. See letters of 3 Jan. 1758 and 17 June 1758.

11. See Douglas Dakin, *Turgot and the Ancien Régime in France* (New York, 1972), pp. 13–19 and passim. Turgot was made *maître des requêtes* in 1753 (Depont in 1755); he was made intendant in 1761 (Depont in 1765). But after this, Turgot rose rapidly to become controller-general in 1774. Turgot visited La Rochelle in the 1750s on an inspection tour of trade and manufacturers.

12. The phrase *voleurs d'argent* surely extended beyond thieves in the narrow sense.

13. It is not altogether clear what "raising children" meant for a mother in this social milieu in the eighteenth century. Madame des Granges, Depont's daughter-in-law at La Rochelle, had a household staff of nine servants, including a governess. See E-489, "Gages de domestiques depuis 1764 à 1792."

14. This may well have been the Harouard de Beignon family at La Rochelle. Paul-François could only approve of the daughter of Etienne-Henri Harouard de Beignon, *sécretaire du roi,* wealthy *armateur,* director of the chamber of commerce, and seigneur de La Jarne, a domain close to Depont's in Aunis. Here was a family with whom the Deponts could feel comfortable. La Morinérie, *La Noblesse d'Aunis,* p. 258. See also Erik Dahl, "Le Château de Buzay," *Congrès archéologique de France, CXIV^e Session* (La Rochelle, 1956), pp. 21–24.

15. Intendant Bégon, like Baville at Toulouse or Tourny at Bordeaux, was La Rochelle's most well-known intendant, at least before Sénac de Meilhan. He was especially remembered for his pious foundations and charities at the end of the seventeenth century, ably seconding the work of Bishop Champflour. See Michel Bégon, "Mémoire sur la généralité de La Rochelle, 1699" in *Archives historiques de Saintonge et de l'Aunis* (Paris and Saintes, 1875):2: 17–174.

16. To Madame de Lescure, 8 June 1765; to Madame la Princesse d'Armagnac, 4 June 1765.

17. To Madame des Granges, 15 July 1765; 19 June 1765.

18. To M. Depont de Virson, 26 Aug. 1769.

19. To M. Depont de Virson, 26 Aug. 1770.

20. Paul-François ended his letter by expressing gratification over his grandson's recent recovery from smallpox. (To Virson, 26 Aug. 1769. See also Paul-François to Jean-Samuel, May 1769.)

21. 18 June 1765.

22. To Virson, 26 Aug. 1769.

23. To Madame de Lescure, 24 May 1765.

24. To Mlles. Virson and Aigrefeuille, 17 Oct. 1763. Paul-François attached the name of

one of the family properties to each child's proper name; thus Pauline Depont de Virson and Elisabeth Depont d'Aigrefeuille. This seemed common practice even among merchant families who owned land.

25. There are no books listed in the "Inventory of Movables" drawn up by the Republican government in 1797. See A.D., Q-250, "Biens des émigrés, Partages: Depont des Granges." I have not been able to find the *inventaire après décès* of Paul-François, if there was one.

26. 25 Jan. 1766. See A. Monod, *De Pascal à Chateaubriand: les défenseurs français du christianisme de 1620 à 1802* (Paris, 1916), pp. 99–141.

27. This is not to say that other "literatures" were not available at La Rochelle at this time. Robert Darnton has identified at least one bookseller, Mathieu, who found a market for a whole range of pornographic works smuggled in from the eastern frontiers of the kingdom. Needless to say, Paul-François was not one of his clients. I wish to thank my friend Robert Darnton for this information.

28. Archives Nationales, O^1-2810, "Mémoire. Fonctions des Intendants des Menus," n.d. For more information on Jean-Samuel's wife, see chapter 5.

29. 28 June 1766.

30. 23 Oct. 1758.

31. May 1769.

32. Ibid.

33. Carré de Candé became a *trésorier* in 1754, Martin de Chassiron in 1733. M. Arcère, *Histoire de la ville de La Rochelle et du Pays d'Aulnis* (La Rochelle, 1757), 2: 554. Children entered *collège* at twelve, according to Etienne Pasquier. Chancellier E. Pasquier, *Mémoires*, trans. C. E. Roche (New York, 1893), 1: 5–6.

34. Emile Garnault, *Le Commerce rochelais au XVIIIe siècle* (Paris and La Rochelle, 1888–1900), 1: 88–89, 121, 223; Arcère, *Histoire de la ville*, 2: 554.

35. La Morinérie, *La Noblesse de l'Aunis*, "Election de La Rochelle."

36. Garnault, *Le Commerce rochelais*, 1: 148–49.

37. 26 Sept. 1758; 23 Oct. 1758.

38. To Madame de Lescure, 7 Jan. 1766. Depont wrote without further comment, *"On a déjà marqué que M. le Duc de Nivernais remplasserait M. le Duc de La Vauguyon près du Nouveau Dauphin, et qu'il aurait seulement les autres princes."*

39. To *Monseigneur le Duc*, 29 Dec. 1768. Although La Vauguyon owned land in Saint-onge (near Mirambeau), there is no evidence that Depont had used his office to curry favor with the duke. Depont expressed himself strongly against tax concessions to *grands seigneurs*. See below.

40. Court histories and contemporary *mémoires* tell us little about how this network operated. Perhaps a careful reading of Duc de Luynes and Horace Walpole might bring the *dévots* into better light, but the work has still to be done.

41. To M. le Prince de Talmont, 4 April 1758. *"J'ai été charmé que la nouvelle qui s'est répandue sur la nouvelle dignité de Mgr. de La Vauguyon se soit confirmée, ne doutant point que Dieu n'en tire sa Gloire."*

42. 26 Sept. 1758.

43. 1 Apr. 1758.

44. Ibid.

45. To Marquis de Durfort, Marquise de Durfort, and Marquise de Lescure, June 1765. This was also the occasion for the purchase of the wedding gift that would be *honnête*, but costing no more than one thousand livres.

46. To Madame de Lescure, 8 June 1765.

47. To Madame des Granges, 15 July 1765.

48. To Madame la Comtesse de Lescure, 7 Jan. 1766. See chapter 1.

49. To Madame des Granges, 19 June 1765. At this moment did Depont scowl or smile? He was not the sort to smile often.

50. Jean-Samuel's colleague, Jacques de Flesselles, was to become intendant of Lyon from 1768 to 1784. He was very popular at Lyon; in 1783 the city notables petitioned that he not be transferred to Paris. See Maurice Garden, *Lyon et les Lyonnais au XVIIIe siècle* (Paris, 1974.), p. 494. Flesselles also represented Paul-François Depont at his son's wedding in Paris. See Chapter 5.

51. See Robert Forster, "Seigneurs and Their Agents." in *Vom Ancien Régime zur französischen Revolution, Forschungen und Perspektiven,* ed. Ernst Hinrichs et al. (Göttingen, 1978), pp. 169–87.

52. The whole notion of an "aristocratic reaction," fundamental to the classic interpretation of the French Revolution, has recently come into question. It is increasingly difficult to regard the Second Estate as a cohesive social entity with a common mentality or program. Even the notion of a "temporary alliance" in the late 1780s of "Robe" and "Sword" now seems doubtful. Recent articles in the *Annales* by David Bien, Guy Chaussinand-Nogaret, and François Furet, and by William Doyle and Colin Lucas in *Past and Present* discuss this issue. See also Bailey Stone "Robe against Sword: The Parlement of Paris and the French Aristocracy, 1774–1789," *French Historical Studies* 9, no. 2 (Fall 1975): 278–303. The conception of an "aristocratic reaction" should not be confused with "seigneurial reaction," however. This is a separate problem in my opinion.

53. 25 Jan. 1766. The *pauvre honteux* will be discussed below.

54. Olwen Hufton, *The Poor of Eighteenth-Century France, 1750–1789* (Oxford, 1974), pp. 93, 98–99, 101, 240–41. The Auvergnats had a strong sense of identity, which made them especially hard to handle.

55. A.D., C-122, "Etat de la situation de l'Election de La Rochelle, 1754"; C-121, "Etat des pertes faites sur l'Election de La Rochelle dans les recoltes de 1765." See chapter 4.

56. 16 Apr. 1765.

57. To Intendant Le Peletier, 24 Dec. 1765.

58. A.D., C-121, 1765.

59. Hufton, *The Poor,* pp. 214–16 and passim.

60. A.D., E-472, Codicil of 1 July 1723.

61. I am referring to those historians like Funck-Brentano who cite the case of Mirabeau's imprisonment as evidence that the *lettre de cachet* was relatively innocuous. Young Mirabeau did not think so, nor did many others who were put in prison without "due process." Paul-François's grandson would defend the abolition of the *lettre de cachet* in a letter to Edmund Burke in 1790. See chapter 8.

62. 17 June 1758; 20 July 1758.

63. A Giraud and a Fouchard were both tenants (*fermiers*) on Depont's land. Depont may have applied for the "warrants" in his capacity as *Trésorier de France*.

64. 25 Feb. 1769.

65. A.D., E-472, Codicil of 1 July 1723.

66. A.D., E-489, "Gages de domestiques depuis 1764 à 1792." The household of Paul-Charles Depont had nine servants. Measured by the length of service, the *maître d'hôtel,* the governess, the cook, the maids, the valet, the footman, and the gardener were loyal; only the coachmen seemed hard to retain despite a wage of 150 livres per annum plus food, lodging and livery. Richard Cobb might tell us why. The accounts even itemize laundry costs, which were deducted from the servants' wages. The servants made some of their own clothes from the cloth purchased from the household budget.

67. Robert, *Les Trafics coloniaux,* p. 192n. In 1767 there were 1,288 domestics in a total population of 15,340 at La Rochelle. The *armateurs* had between four and six servants per household.

68. A.D., E-487 passim. For endless passages on chronic illnesses see R. M. Myers, ed., *Children of Pride* (New Haven and London, 1972). Why do families love to discuss their

ailments ad nauseam? Apart from a few medical tips, how much material has the social historian lost because of this digression of self-indulgence? See also R. Forster, "Family Biography" in *Biographie und Geschichtswissenschaft: Wiener Beiträge zur Geschichte der Neuzeit,* Band 6 (Vienna, 1979), pp. 111–26.

69. 13 Dec. 1763; 20 July 1758. Perhaps these were silhouettes. This is probably the closest one comes in the eighteenth century to family photographs at Christmas time.

70. 1 Apr. 1758.

71. Why did Paul-François attempt to prevent the nomination of Paul-Charles as mayor of La Rochelle? "That will not suit him from any point of view," he wrote, 2 Mar. 1765.

72. Father and son always addressed each other, of course, as "vous." Jean-Samuel addressed his brother as "tu," at least in 1798 when both men were in their seventies. They had been through a great deal by then.

Chapter Three

1. A.D., E-482, "Journal," 1720–91, fols. 174, 195, 197, 199; Archives Nationales, Minutier Central (hereafter cited as A.N., M.C. followed by the *Etude*), *Etude* 66: 628, Partage Depont, 27 June 1776; ibid. *Etude* 95: 302, "Contrat de mariage," Depont-L'Escureul de la Touche, 11 May 1766.

2. A.D. E-487, Paul-François to Jean-Samuel, 20 July 1758 (hereafter cited by date only). Italics mine: *"mes terres qui sont mon ppal bien ..."* Jean-Samuel sold the domain of *La Babotieux* for forty-two thousand livres, a price his father considered much too low. See 1 Apr. 1758.

3. 18 June 1765. Italics mine: *"mais ne vivant que de mes rentes qui sont très mal payées ..."*

4. French historians have been slow to integrate the legal aspects of family inheritances into their social history. See Roland Mousnier, *Les Institutions de la France sous la monarchie absolue* (Paris, 1974), vol. 1, ch. 2; Pierre Bourdieu, "Marriage Strategies as Strategies of Social Reproduction" *Selections from the Annales: E.S.C.,* R. Forster and O. Ranum, eds. (Baltimore, 1976); Robert Forster, *The Nobility of Toulouse in the Eighteenth Century* (Baltimore, 1960), ch. 6. See also note 6 below.

5. A.D., E-473, "Contrat de mariage," 22 Dec. 1710, Depont-Moreau; A.N., M.C., *Etude* 21: 556, "Contrat de mariage," Depont-Fontanges, 26 June 1788; see chapter 7.

6. Ralph E. Giesey, "Rules of Inheritance and Strategies of Mobility in Prerevolutionary France," *American Historical Review* 82 (April 1977): 262–63, 262n. Among other works, Giesey cites Charles Lefebvre, *Les Fortunes anciennes au point de vue juridique* (Paris, 1912); Jean Yver, *Egalité entre héritiers et exclusion des enfants dotés* (Paris, 1966); Jean Brissaud, *A History of French Private Law* (Boston, 1912), a work, he says, that suffers from poor translation. Giesey is preparing a much needed general survey of French inheritance law from the late Middle Ages to the present.

7. *L'Usance de Saintonge entre-mer et Charente par M. Cosme Bechet, avocat au Parlement de Paris et Siège Présidial de Saintes* (Bordeaux, 1701), article 57, par. 108. The customary law of La Rochelle (Aunis) provided even less for the eldest son under "successions nobles;" a preference legacy (*préciput*) consisting of the manor house and park (*préclôture*) and one-fifth of the noble land (*biens nobles*). See M. René Josué Valin, *Nouveau Commentaire sur la Coûtume de La Rochelle et du pays d'Aunis,* 3 vols. (La Rochelle, 1756), 3: 119.

8. Ibid. Burgundy also provided two-thirds of the *propres* for the eldest son. In areas of the *Droit Ecrit*—Toulouse, for example—if there were four children or less, the eldest son had a right to two-thirds; if five or more, one-half of the *propres.* Mousnier, *Les Institutions,*

pp. 63 and 47–69, passim. Ralph Giesey concludes that it was contrary to the principles of the customary law to bequeath the disposable part of the *réserve* to any of the children. "No one can be an heir and a legatee at the same time" was the rule of *coûtumier* succession. However, the *propres* could be reduced so as to minimize the *réserve* to be divided, "Rules of Inheritance," p. 276.

9. That is, in case of *two* children, the elder could add his share (one-half) of the two-thirds "reserved" for all direct heirs to his own one-third (right of the eldest) and thus accumulate two-thirds of the total *propres*. Daughters were rarely "advantaged" except in cases where there were no sons or where a large dowry might assure a particularly *bonne alliance*.

10. Valin, *Nouveau Commentaire*, 2: 487; 3: 27, 59–60. Valin (1695–1765) was *procureur du roi* at the Admiralty Court and a contemporary of Paul-François Depont. In the small world of *officiers*, they must have known each other and sought each other's advice on family matters.

11. "Immovables" included *rentes* and offices as well as land and houses. Giesey, "Rules of Inheritance," p. 273. Commercial assets, as well as specie and personal possessions, were classified as "movables."

12. Forster, *Nobility of Toulouse*, ch. 6. In Roman Law areas such as Toulouse, the head of the family instituted one principal heir, and in his testament charged that heir to distribute legacies to others. Giesey, "Rules of Inheritance," p. 276.

13. For royal legislation on entails, see Mousnier, *Les Institutions* 1: 66–67. The basic work on the law reforms of Chancellor Daguesseau is Henri Regnault, *Les Ordonnances civiles du Chancelier Daguesseau* (Paris, 1929, 1938, 1965).

14. Philippe Ariès in his now classic work on childhood stresses the secular trend toward equal treatment of children. Without denying the century-long development he describes, attention might also be focused on the attitudes of specific social groups, especially such "socially mobile" families as the Depont. One might uncover hesitancies and countercurrents especially in the eighteenth century when notions of family "splendor" and noble *succession* were still strong. The legist Valin wrote in 1756: *"Il n'y a pas de splendeur à maintenir dans les familles roturières,"* which is to say that there *was* "splendor to maintain" in noble—and would-be noble—families. Valin, *Nouveau Commentaire*, 3: 106.

15. A.D., E–472, Codicil of 10 June 1733.

16. Ibid., Codicil of 1 July 1723.

17. Ibid., "Substitution" of 5 Sept. 1727. These *biens* were *acquêts* over which Paul and Sara Depont had complete control or "free disposition."

18. Ibid., Codicil of 2 July 1715. The words are taken from the first entail of 1715, but they are equally applicable to the second of 1727.

19. Ibid., Codicil of 1 July 1723.

20. A.D., E–492, Sale of Aigrefeuille, 12 June 1726.

21. A.D., E–472, Codicil of 12 Jan. 1733, 10 June 1733. The *retrait* gave the seigneur the right of option to buy land in his seigneurial jurisdiction and attach it to his domain, i.e., land held directly by him. It was one technique of "domain-building." See Marc Bloch, *Les Caractères originaux de l'histoire rurale française* (Paris, 1952), 1: 140 and passim.

22. The Cognac country, already an exporter of the famous brandy, was about fifty miles southeast of La Rochelle along the Charente River. The *chais* with their "serpentine" boilers for distilling the brandy can be visited today (1980s) in the villages east of Saintes and Saint-Jean d'Angély.

23. The "most prestigious" property was not necessarily the most remunerative. In 1733, the return on *rentes* (5 percent) was higher than on land (3 to 4 percent). This relation would change in the last third of the century, when land values rose dramatically.

24. These later codicils included enforcement clauses, stating that if any of the children

refused to abide by the testamentary wishes of their parents, they could claim their portions (*légitimes*) under the customary law. That law provided that "in the absence of *propres*" (the Depont case), the *acquêts* would be distributed in the same manner, namely, two-thirds of the property divided equally among all (three) children, and the remaining third and *all* the movables given to the eldest son. Since the "movables" included all the commercial assets and specie, the children would think twice before rejecting the testamentary provisions. And then there were the added legal costs of contesting the will. Valin, *Nouveau Commentaire,* 2: 334; Mousnier, *Les Institutions,* 1: 64.

25. A.D. E-472, Codicil of 11 June 1734.

26. Ibid., "Donation entre vifs" of Widow Bernon, 7 Dec. 1747.

27. Ibid., Codicil of 13 Mar. 1743; "Révocation de Substitution," 14 Mar. 1743.

28. Ibid., "Révocation," 14 Mar. 1743. Italics mine.

29. The Daguesseau Ordinance of 1747 extended the use of entail to *"toutes personnes capables de disposer de leurs biens, de quelque état et condition qu'elles soient."* But it also limited the entail to "two degrees," that is, from grandparents to grandchildren in direct descent. Even before 1747, entails had not been limited to the nobility. The Code Michaud of 1629 had permitted all but *laboureurs* and artisans (*personnes rustiques*) to entail. Mousnier, *Les Institutions,* 1: 66–67.

30. A.D., E-472, "Révocation," 14 Mar. 1743. *"Paul Depont et Sara Bernon ... en bonne santé."*

31. Ibid, "Donation," 7 Dec. 1747.

32. A.D., E-487, 20 July 1758.

33. A.D., E-482, "Journal," fol. 195.

34. A.D., E-487, 6 July 1765. Italics mine.

35. Ibid., 24 May 1766. Paul-François guaranteed Jean-Samuel an annual income of 8,900 livres in his marriage contract a month earlier. A.N., M.C. *Etude* 95, "Procuration" of 29, Apr. 1766. Italics mine.

36. "If Manderoux [Jean-Samuel] insists, I must divide my silver and take some from you. I know this will inconvenience you when you have company." A.D., E-487, Paul-François to Madame des Granges, 19 June 1765.

37. The *rentes* averaged 5 percent; the land 3 to 4 percent. However, the capital value of land was often calculated simply by multiplying landed rents (*fermages*) by a factor of 20 (or 5 percent). Hence, 32,000 livres is a conservative estimate of Depont revenues in 1746.

38. For fortunes of nobles and financiers and what they represent in style of life, see Jean Meyer, *La Noblesse bretonne au XVIIIe siècle* (Paris, 1966); Forster, *Nobility of Toulouse:* "The Noble Wineproducers of the Bordelais in the Eighteenth Century," *Economic History Review* 14, 2d ser. (August 1961): 18–33; *The House of Saulx-Tavanes* (Baltimore, 1971); Yves Durand, *La Maison de Durfort* (Paris, 1975); *Les Fermiers généraux en France au XVIIIe siècle* (Paris, 1971); Guy Chaussinand-Nogaret, *Les Financiers de Languedoc au XVIIIe siècle* (Paris, 1970); Gaston Roupnel, *La Ville et la campagne au XVIIe siècle* (Paris, 1922); Mousnier, *Les Institutions,* 1: 135–53, 172–87; Henri Carré, *La Noblesse de France et l'opinion publique au XVIIIe siècle* (Paris, 1920). Carré demonstrates that a revenue of 50,000 livres was the minimum required to live *"noblement"* at Paris in the late eighteenth century; one could "cut a good figure" on one-fifth of this amount in the provinces.

39. Henri Robert, *Les trafics coloniaux du port de la Rochelle au XVIIIe siècle* (Poitiers, 1960), pp. 192–96. There is still a need for a published work on the fortunes of the merchants of La Rochelle. Robert's book was published posthumously before he had completed all his research. See John G. Clark, "La Rochelle and the Atlantic World during the Eighteenth Century" (unpublished manuscript) and chapter 1 above. I hope Clark's work will soon be published.

40. The word "decapitation" was first used by Henri Hauser, "French Economic History, 1500–1750," *Economic History Review* 4 (1933): 257ff. Cultural values as determinants of French economic growth have been stressed by a whole generation of historians, especially in the United States. See E. Carter, R. Forster, J. Moody, eds., *Enterprise and Entrepreneurs in Nineteenth- and Twentieth-Century France* (Baltimore, 1976), introduction and passim.

41. Robert, *Les Trafics coloniaux,* p. 192. This is based on *inventaires après décès.*

42. A.D., E–473, Will of 9 May 1753; E–487, 4 May 1765.

43. A.D., E–487, Paul-François to Sieur Chanois, *négociant* at La Rochelle, May 1769. See also Robert, *Les Trafics coloniaux,* p. 195, and Clark, "La Rochelle," chs. 6–7, on the difficulties obtaining legal action against the planters.

44. Compare Table 3.1 (fortune in 1746) with Table 3.4 (fortune in 1776) in this chapter.

45. A.D., E–484, "Livre concernant mes rentes et prix de mes fermes," 1757–1804.

46. Ibid.; see Table of *Rentes* (3. 2) and compare Tables 3.1 and 3.4 below.

47. A.D., E–489, "Rentes sur haut et puissant seigneur M. Jacques-Louis-François Gazeau de la Brandanière, chevalier, baron de Champagné près Luçon en Bas-Poitou."

48. A.D., E–487, Paul-François to M. le Marquis de Champagné, 20 May 1758.

49. A.D., E–489, 7 Sept. 1770. Loan of 7,000 livres *"payée et delivrée en bon argent et espèces sonnantes ayant cours ..."* Paul-François never seemed to lack hard specie.

50. A.D., E–484, fol. 18.

51. Ibid., fol. 21.

52. Ibid., fol. 18.

53. Ibid. Marginal notation: *"rente par an* (?); *c'est un aveu."* For a definition of the various kinds of *retrait,* see Marcel Marion, *Dictionnaire des Institutions de la France aux XVIIe et XVIIIe siècles* (Paris 1923, 1969), pp. 488–89.

54. Permission to "repurchase" a *cens,* even at thirty times the annual charge, was a reform proposal even before 1789. See P. F. Boncerf, *Les Inconveniens des droits féodaux* (London, 1776); J. Q. C. Mackrell, *The Attack on Feudalism in Eighteenth-Century France* (London, 1973) ch. 6. The legal confusion between *rentes foncières* and *cens* was used by both landlords and tenants to improve their position during and after the Revolution. See Pierre Massé, "Les Amortissements de rentes foncières en l'an III," *Annales historiques de la Révolution française* 165 (1961): 380 and passim. Massé argues that the tenants gained at the proprietor's expense. For a more pessimistic view, see Albert Soboul, "Persistence of 'Feudalism' in the Rural Society of Nineteenth-Century France," in *Rural Society in France: Selections from the Annales,* ed. R. Forster and O. Ranum (Baltimore, 1977), pp. 50–71.

55. Giesey, "Rules of Inheritance," p. 279; Robert J. Pothier, "Traité du Contract de Constitution de Rente," *Oeuvres* (Paris, 1861), 3: 498, par. 166; Charles Lefebvre, *Observations sur les rentes perpétuelles dans l'ancien droit français* (Paris, 1914), pp. 56–57, and passim for legal aspects of *rentes.*

56. The best work on *rentes* is Bernard Schnapper, *Les Rentes au XVIe siècle: Histoire d'un instrument de crédit* (Paris, 1958). Unfortunately, Earl Hamilton's book on the Law System (and *rentes*) is not yet published. I have adopted the terminology of *credi-renter* and *debi-renter,* used by Ralph Giesey. See note 6 above.

57. A.D., E–484, fols. 21, 62.

58. Montesquieu in the *Persian Letters* (1723).

59. George V. Taylor, "Non-Capitalist Wealth and the Origins of the French Revolution," *American Historical Review* 72 (1967): 469–96; "Types of Capitalism in 18th-Century France," *English Historical Review* 79 (1964): 478–97. I have never understood why Taylor considers *rentes* a "non-capitalist" form of wealth; they seem to conform to most definitions of capitalist investment. See Giesey "Rules of Inheritance," pp. 279–80 on the popularity of *rentes constituées,* reflected in the steady reduction in the stipulated legal rate from 8.3 percent in the 1550s to 6.25 percent after 1665, and to 5.0 percent in the eighteenth century.

60. See Table of *Rentes* (3. 2).

61. For small loans to peasants with an eye on foreclosure, see Pierre Goubert, *Beauvais et le Beauvasis de 1600 à 1730* (Paris, 1960); Roupnel, *Ville et campagne;* Forster, *Nobility of Toulouse;* Pierre de Saint-Jacob, *Les Paysans de la Bourgogne du Nord au dernier siècle de l'Ancien Régime* (Dijon, 1960); Bloch, *Les Caractères originaux.*

62. Fortunately, Virson survived smallpox. A.D., E–487, Paul-François to M. de Virson, 26 Aug. 1769. Both grandchildren defied the life-expectancy tables; Virson died in 1801, Pauline in 1808. Had the Revolution not intervened, the investment of 1762 would have yielded an accumulated interest of 124,800 livres, almost four times the original capital.

63. A.D., E–484, fol. 26. The *rente* was reduced in 1778 to 2,340 livres, still above 7 percent. The 10 percent reduction probably represented the new *vingtième* taxes prompted by still another war with England.

64. Marion, *Dictionnaire des Institutions,* p. 483.

65. A.D., E–484, fols. 84, 90. To be sure, the *rente* was still being paid in 1780, fifty-five years later. Even at 2 percent, the capital had been completely repaid.

66. A.D., E–487, 18 Oct. 1763.

67. Ibid., 17 Apr. 1764. This is the same letter in which Paul-François lamented the loss of the Jesuit tutor and reproached his son for being *"parlementaire,"* a Jansenist sympathizer.

68. Ibid., 2 Mar. 1765.

69. A.N., M.C., *Etude* 95: 302, "Contrat de mariage," 11 May 1766.

70. A.D., E–487, 18 June 1765.

71. A. N., M.C., *Etude* 95: 302, "Procuration," 29 Apr. 1766; "Contrat de mariage," 11 May 1766, article 4, item 4, *"Somme de 1,000 livres 13 au ppl. 20, 013 de livres constituée au Sr. Depont père par M. Mouchard, receveur général des finances par contrat, 1 Octobre 1754."* Depont had other contacts as well, such as MM. Lepelier and Eberto, *banquiers,* who honored his bills of exchange in Paris. A.D., E–487, 28 Apr. 1764.

72. A.D., E–487, 6 July 1765. Turgot observed that the rate of interest was 6 percent in the principal money markets of the kingdom in the 1760s. A. R. Turgot, "Mémoire sur les prêts d'argent," *Oeuvres* (Paris, 1844), 1: 119.

73. A.D., E-482, fol. 177, 5 Apr., 28 Apr. 1748.

74. A.N., M.C., *Etude* 95: 302, 11 May 1766, articles 5, 11.

75. John F. Bosher, *French Finances, 1770–1795* (Cambridge, 1970), pp. 92–110 and passim.

76. A.D., E–484, "Livre de rentes." See Table of *Rentes* (3. 2).

77. A.N., M.C., *Etude* 95: 302, 11 May 1766, article 4.

78. A.D., E–487, Paul-François to M. Charpentreau, 5 Nov. 1768.

79. Ibid., Paul-François to Madame de Coudraye, 6 Dec. 1768; Paul-François to M. le Baron de la Rochebaron, 2 Dec. 1768.

80. Ibid., Paul-François to M. de Chevalier, 17 Dec. 1768.

81. Giesey, "Rules of Inheritance," p. 273.

82. See Table of *Rentes* (3. 2).

83. Goubert, *Beauvais,* pp. 538–40 quoted in Giesey, "Rules of Inheritance," p. 279n. See also Schnapper, *Les Rentes.* Both authors are concerned primarily with the sixteenth and seventeenth centuries, however.

84. As Ralph Giesey puts it: "If *rentes constituées* were unsuitable to an individual's wish to get rich quickly, they were well-suited to a family's hope of getting rich eventually." Giesey, "Rules of Inheritance," p. 280.

85. The rate of capital growth by compounding interest is not readily grasped without a mathematical representation. It is doubtful that Paul-François made this kind of precise calculation, but he no doubt took the long view about capital accumulation.

86. A.N., M.C., 11 May 1766, articles 5, 11. It must have pained Jean-Samuel to see sixty

thousand livres, one-fourth of his wife's dowry, pass directly from his father-in-law to his father's creditors. This provision would require consent of the bride's parents of course. A wife's *propres* could not be "assigned" at her husband's discretion, not before the *Code Napoléon* at least.

87. The notion of a "threshold figure" of 1,000,000 livres' fortune to attain the style of life of a nobleman has been suggested by Guy Chaussinand-Nogaret, "Capital et structure sociale sous l'Ancien Régime," *Annales: E.S.C.* 25 (1970): 463–76. In 1764, there were seventy-one *officiers* and fifty-eight nobles on the *capitation* tax rolls for the Election of La Rochelle. Paul-Charles Depont, eldest son of Paul-François and mayor of the city, was among the five most heavily taxed. True, the *capitation* was only roughly proportional to income, but it is still a good indication of the Depont family's standing at La Rochelle. *Archives historiques de Saintonge et de l'Aunis* (Paris and Saintes, 1879), 6: 215–27; "Le Sieur de Pont," p. 223.

88. A.D., E–487, Paul-François to Madame de Lescure, 5 May 1764.

89. Ibid., 24 May 1765.

Chapter Four

1. A.D., C–198, "Mémoire sur les dessèchements et défrichements," 1780. See André Bourde, *Agronomes et Agronomie au XVIIIe siècle* 3 vols. (Paris, 1967) for a thorough examination of royal policies toward agriculture.

2. P. C. Martin de Chassiron, *Letters sur l'agriculture du district de La Rochelle par un cultivateur* (La Rochelle, 1795), p. 83.

3. Claude Laveau, "Le Monde rochelais de l'Ancien Régime au Consulat," (*thèse de doctorat*, Paris, 1972), pp. 331–32. This eight-hundred page, single-spaced thesis based on the local archives is a mine of information. I venture to say that Claude Laveau knows more about agriculture in this region in the eighteenth century than any living person.

4. A.D., C–172, "Actes d'Assemblée des intéressés des marais des côtes de Saintonge," 17 Aug. 1750.

5. Laveau, "Monde rochelais," pp. 496–500; Bourde, *Agronomes,* 3: 1459.

6. Laveau, "Monde rochelais," pp. 326–27.

7. A.D., C–175, "Marais de Voutron." Marquis de Saint-Georges to M. Barentin, 24 Oct. 1739. See also letters of 13 May and 3 July 1739. I wish to thank M. Camille Gabet for drawing my attention to this correspondence.

8. See Table 4.1.

9. Laveau, "Monde rochelais," p. 329.

10. A.D., C–198, "Mémoire sur les dessèchements," 1780; E–52, "Transaction," 14 Nov. 1766.

11. A.D., C–175, "Marais de Voutron;" A.D., 4-J-1226, "Marais de Rochefort et Ciré, 1756–65."

12. A.D., C–198, "Réponse de la Société d'Agriculture de la généralité de La Rochelle ... pour parvenir à former un Tableau d'Agriculture ...," 1764, p. 30.

13. A.D., C–198, "Réponse," 1764. "Des Bestiaux."

14. Bourde, *Agronomes.* André Bourde is completing a study of Henri Bertin.

15. A.D., C–198, "Mémoire," 28 Nov. 1761.

16. M. Arcère, *Histoire de la ville de La Rochelle et du pays d'Aunis,* 2 vols. (La Rochelle, 1757) 2: 477, 477n.

17. Ibid., 2: 488.

18. A.D., C–198, "Mémoire," 1761.

19. Ibid., "Réponse," 1764.

20. A.D., C-182, "Etat de la population," 1775; "Election de La Rochelle," 1773–82.

21. Ibid., "Election de Marennes," 1763. Many French sailors from this area had been in English prisons for eight years.

22. A.D., C-183, "Renseignements statistiques . . . dans 122 paroisses de la Généralité de La Rochelle par les syndics," 1774.

23. A.D., C-198, "Réponse," 1764.

24. A.D., C-122, "Etat de la situation de l'Election de La Rochelle," 1754.

25. A.D., C-121, "Etat des pertes," 1765.

26. See figure 4 (Wheat Prices at La Rochelle).

27. Laveau, "Monde rochelais," pp. 495–96.

28. A. M., La Rochelle, C-2843, quoted in Laveau, "Monde rochelais," p. 503.

29. Ibid., p. 520. Laveau gives a complete inventory of the *hôpitaux*.

30. See chapter 2 above.

31. Laveau, "Monde rochelais," p. 747; J. Pandin de Lussaudière, ed., "Aigrefeuille, 1623–1792" (Parish Registers), *Archives historiques de la Saintonge et de l'Aunis* (Paris et Saintes, 1910): 40, 113 and passim.

32. "Aigrefeuille, 1623–1792," 206–31.

33. Ibid., pp. 105–6, 113, 209–15, 221, 225, 229, and passim.

34. On the hybird quality of estate agents see Robert Forster, "Seigneurs and Their Agents," in *Vom Ancien Régime zur französischen Revolution, ed. Ernst Hinrichs et al.* (Göttingen, 1978), pp. 169–87.

35. See chapter 3 above.

36. For the holdings of these merchant families, see the *centième denier* rolls recording property transfers and even leases in A.D., Series 2C.

37. A.D., E-494, Seigneurie de Manderoux; E-491, Seigneurie de La Brande; A.D., E-492, Seigneurie d'Aigrefeuille.

38. Recall the twofold nature of a seigneury. The domain consisted of land held directly by the seigneur, while the *mouvances* were semi-independent parcels of land, held usually by peasants, and owing quit-rents (*cens, champarts, rentes*) and other dues and services to the seigneur. In Aunis the *mouvances* of a seigneurial jurisdiction frequently covered many times the area of the domain lands. See A.D., Q-287, Q-288, Petitions Relative to Leases, 1790–96.

39. A.D., E-489, "State of the Domain of Les Granges," 3 Jan. 1714; E-490, Lease of 23 Oct. 1738.

40. A.D., E-490, Lease of 23 Oct. 1738.

41. A.D., E-491, Depont v. DuBuisson, 19 June 1726.

42. A.D., E-475, "Procès Jouriau," 22 July 1790.

43. A.D., E-483, -484, -499, -501. See Table 4.2.

44. A.D., E-490, Sales of 30 Nov. 1777, 2 Nov. 1778, 28 Mar. 1781 (Tétaud), 28 Mar. 1781 (Bevin).

45. A.D., E-490, Sale of 28 Mar. 1781 (Bevin).

46. Ibid., Sale of 28 Feb. 1790.

47. It was seldom necessary. The prospect of paying the legal costs necessitated by the number of local appeal courts usually sufficed. A cahier of the Third Estate from neighboring Saint-Pierre-près-de-Surgères stated: "In our neighborhood there is a jurisdiction called la Gravalle; from la Gravelle one appeals to Ciré; from Ciré one appeals to Surgères; from Surgères one appeals to Benon; from Benon one appeals finally to the Presidial of La Rochelle." The cahier asked that royal justice be made more accessible. A.D., C-267, Cahier of Saint-Pierre-près-de-Surgères.

48. A.D., E-494, "Retrait" of 6 July 1735; A.D., E-495, "Retrait" of 19 June 1730; A.D., E-492, "Retrait" of 25 Apr. 1751; A.D., E-497, "Retrait" of 17 Nov. 1764; A.D.,

E-492 "Retrait" of 26 Jan. 1778. See R.-J. Valin, *Nouveau commentaire sur la coûtume de La Rochelle et du pays d'Aunis,* 3 vols. (La Rochelle, 1756), 1: 112–3, 2: 201–2 for the legal provisions regarding the *retrait.*

49. M.-L. Autexier, *Les Droits Féodaux et les droits seigneuriaux en Poitou de 1559 à 1789* (Fontenaye-le-Comte, n.d.), pp. 150–51; Marcel Marion, *Dictionnaire des Institutions de la France aux XVIIe et XVIIIe siècles* (1923; reprint ed., Paris, 1969), p. 76. See also Valin, *Nouveau commentaire.*

50. A.D., E-490, "Prise de Possession," 2 June 1758.

51. Valin, *Nouveau commentaire,* 1: 80–81.

52. A.D., E-490, "Prises de Possession," 22 Mar. 1775, 29 Mar. 1782, 9 May 1784.

53. A.D., E-490, Judgment of 22 Ventôse, Year V (12 Mar. 1797) by the Civil Tribunal of Charente-Inférieure. This judgment reversed an earlier decision in 1796 awarding the two *cultivateurs* 7.2 acres of the land, twenty-two years' income, interest, and damages. In 1800 it was Depont's turn to sue for damages.

54. A.D., E-489, Q-250 (Depont des Granges).

55. See Table 4.1. The *terrier* of Aigrefeuille gives the precise area. See Laveau, "Monde rochelais," p. 348.

56. A.D., E-492, Faurie to Paul-François, 7 Aug. 1749.

57. A.D., E-500, "Arpentage" of 21 Mar. 1746; "Dossier d'Aigrefeuille," 1756.

58. Laveau, "Monde rochelais," pp. 397–400.

59. Ibid., p. 324. Laveau has used the *matrices* or indexes to the *terrier* which I did not see during my stay in La Rochelle. Bibliothèque Municipale, La Rochelle, MSS 506–9. This is very precious documentation.

60. Ibid., pp. 324–25.

61. "Terrier d'Aigrefeuille," 1788. Special collection.

62. Laveau, "Monde rochelais," p. 398.

63. Ibid., p. 400.

64. See chapter 9.

65. A.D., E-500, "Mémoire," 11 May 1786. Italics mine.

66. See Robert Forster, *The House of Saulx-Tavanes: Versailles and Burgundy, 1700–1830* (Baltimore, 1971), ch. 2, and Forster, "Seigneurs and Their Agents."

67. A.D., E-490, Leases of 17 July 1719, 16 Apr. 1725; A.D., E-489, "Métairie de la Porte de Granges," 23 Oct. 1738.

68. See Table 4.3 and Figure 4.3.

69. A.D., E-490, Lease of 8 July 1731.

70. A.D., E-483, "Livre concernant mes rentes," 1723–67.

71. See Table 4.1. C.-E. Labrousse, *La Crise de l'économie française à la fin de l'Ancien Régime et au début de la Révolution* (Paris, 1944), pp. 260–61; Labrousse, *Esquisse du mouvement des prix et des revenus en France au XVIIIe siècle* (Paris, 1933), 1: 269–72 and passim on rents.

72. Laveau, "Monde rochelais," pp. 339ff.; Pierre d'Harouard, *Lettre à un cultivateur sur les avantages de convertir son vin en Eau-de-vie,* 8 pp. (La Rochelle, 1805). Harouard said that four to one was "extremely rare."

73. Figures 4.1 (by volume) and 2 (ad valorem).

74. Figure 4.3 (rents).

75. Figure 4.4 (grain prices).

76. A.D., E-484, "Livres concernant mes rentes et prix des fermes," 1757–1804.

77. Laveau, "Monde rochelais," pp. 359–65.

78. See Robert Forster, "Obstacles to Agricultural Growth in 18th-Century France," *American Historical Review* 75 (October 1970): 1600–15. In this article I argue for a rehabilitation of the *gros fermier,* one of the few "capitalist entrepreneurs" in the French countryside.

79. Harouard writes: "Distillation requires large expenses and considerable advances of capital which oblige the small *cultivateurs* to sell their wine as soon as it reaches their storage sheds (*chais*)." Harouard, *Lettre sur l'Eau-de-vie,* p. 2.

80. Harouard, *Manuel du cultivateur pour gouverner dans la gestion de sa Borderie* ... (La Rochelle, 1802), pp. 1–2.

81. Harouard alluded to a high population density even in 1808, when *la Grande Armée* must have taken the cream of local youth. "If we diminish farm work, what will become of our numerous population of 1,000 to 1,100 persons per square league?" (about 62 to 69 persons per square kilometer). Harouard, *Différents Modes de cultiver nos domaines dans l'arrondissement de la sous-préfecture de La Rochelle* (La Rochelle, 1808), p. 16.

82. A.D., C–183, "Renseignements statistiques ... 124 paroisses," 1774. The comments on each parish are often more informative than the bare statistics. At Saint-Laurent-de-Barrière, for example, the syndics wrote: "The vines have been ruined by the dogs, chickens, and children of the village; only two or three individuals have enough grain to feed themselves; the others live from hand to mouth by selling their ancestral property bit by bit." This is an extreme case, to be sure, but any *fermier* who worked stills at Aigrefeuille or Virson would have been aware of such conditions. See C–198, "Réponse," 1764, on the day laborer.

83. Harouard writes with a certain mixed feeling: "the *tonneliers* [coopers] of our countryside are our chemists. They follow a routine that has been handed down to them and have made little progress in their *art.*" Harouard, *Lettre sur l'Eau-de-vie.* See also Robert Delemain, *Histoire du Cognac* (Paris, 1935).

84. A.D., E–490, –491, –492, Leases at Les Granges, La Brande, Aigrefeuille.

85. A.D., E–492, Paul-François to Faurie at Aigrefeuille, 28 Apr. 1757.

86. A.D., E–483, –484, –488, Income, 1790–91.

87. A.D., E–483, fol. 222.

88. Ibid., fol. 196.

89. A.D., E–490, "Mémoire" of 21 July 1779; Judgment of the Bourg of Aigrefeuille, 21 Nov. 1782. Depont collected another 2,000 livres in 1795. A.D., E–484, fol. 23.

90. A.D., E–487, Paul-François to Paul-Charles Depont des Granges, 17 May 1769.

91. Ibid., Paul-François to Faurie, 31 May 1769.

92. Ibid., Paul-François to Jean-Samuel, April 1769. Jean-Samuel had been pressing his father for money as usual.

93. Ibid., Paul-François to François Questron, 15 Apr. 1769.

94. Ibid., Paul-François to M. Bonneau, 22 September 1769.

95. Alexis de Tocqueville, *Democracy in America,* trans. H. Reeve (New York, 1951), 2: 186.

96. A.D., E–487, Paul-François to Faurie, 28 Apr. 1757.

97. A.D., E–485, "Grand Livre de Régie de la Terre d'Aigrefeuille—Entretenue de pain."

98. Ibid.

99. A.D., E–488, Procuration of M. Depont de Manderoux to Sr. Bonnet, 11 Apr. 1775.

100. A.D., E–487, –499 (Bonnet correspondence).

101. A.D., E–487, Bonnet to M. d'Auzon, 4 May 1788, 2 Mar. 1788.

102. A.D., E–492, Paul-Charles to Bonnet, 1 July 1789.

103. A.D., E–484, fol. 29 (letter between pages of ledger), Mainguet to M. de Pon des Granges, 11 Dec. 1783. Mainguet's spelling left something to be desired.

104. A.D., E–484, fol. 29, Paul-Charles to Mainguet, 11 Dec. 1783. Curiously, Depont's private account indicates that the higher rent was paid. A.D., E–484 (Chagnées).

105. A.D., E–487, Paul-François to Jean-Samuel, 4 May 1765.

106. Ibid., Paul-François to Jean-Samuel, 3 Dec. 1765.

107. Ibid., Paul-François to M. le Peletier at Paris, 24 Dec. 1765. See the "Terrier

d'Aigrefeuille." Several maps demonstrate how the new royal road to La Rochelle cut a wide path through the vineyard parcels.

108. Harouard, *Différents Modes,* p. 17.

109. A.D., C-122, fol. 129. Subdelegate to Intendant, 20 Feb. 1779. "The parish tax collector is always a person dependent on the seigneur of the parish. . . . He is his "justiciable;" on a thousand occasions he can be hassled [*vexé*] by the seigneur, which he will surely be if he is not docile in waiting for tax payment;" C-70, "Taille," 1733. "The country *gentilshommes* . . . are little tyrants. . . . They threaten, intimidate, and even mistreat the collectors."

110. A.D., C-122, "Vingtièmes," 1779.

111. A.D., C-121, Intendant of La Rochelle to Necker, 21 Mar. 1779. I wish to thank M. Camille Gabet of Rochefort for drawing this letter to my attention.

112. Selling brandy wholesale did not "derogate." Delemain, *Cognac,* 123-24; See Figures 4. 1 and 2. Curiously, the unit price recorded at La Rochelle in 1762 is only 70 livres per cask.

113. A.D., E-492, Inventory of Brandy Sales, 1757-62. These were the very best years for brandy exports since the 1720s. See Figure 4.2 (ad valorem).

114. After 1835, salt-making on the French Atlantic coast went into rapid decline. But between 1780 and 1830 the rise in Western Europe's population increased the demand for salt from all sources—sea water, brine, and rock salt. On the offshore islands of Ré and Oleron, the abolition of the *grande gabelle* in 1790 gave a special incentive to proprietors like Depont, although a salt tax reappeared in 1805. Alert though Paul-Charles and his brother Jean-Samuel were to new investment opportunities, they probably did not know about the new process of converting sodium chloride into sodium carbonate developed by French chemists in 1792, the year the Depont brothers bought more salt beds on Oleron. See M. Delafosse and C. Laveau, *Le Commerce du sel de Brouage aux XVIIe et XVIIIe siècles* (Paris, 1960); Robert P. Multhauf, *Neptune's Gift: A History of Common Salt* (Baltimore, 1978). pp. 14-15, 23-24, 56-61, 73-76, 109; Edmond-René Labande, ed., *Histoire du Poitou, du Limousin, et des Pays Charentais* (Toulouse, 1976), pp. 392-93.

115. Delafosse and Laveau, *Commerce du sel,* pp. 14, 25, 27-31.

116. A.D., C-198, "Mémoires," 19 Apr. 1780; 18 Sept. 1780; A.D., E-501, "Compte de Sauniers," 1783-89; "Etat général des ouvrages aux marais."

117. Delafosse and Laveau, *Commerce du sel,* pp. 24-25, 60-61, 104, 87-88.

118. Ibid., p. 35.

119. A.D., E-501, "Compte de Sauniers," 1783-89; Delafosse and Laveau, *Commerce du sel,* pp. 35-38.

120. Harouard, *Manuel du cultivateur,* pp. 3-5.

121. Robert Forster, "The Survival of the Nobility during the French Revolution," *Past and Present* 37 (July 1967): 71-86.

122. Forster, "Seigneurs and Their Agents." This is a study of the administration of four estates, those of Choiseul-Beaupré, Choiseul-Gouffier, Rosnyvinen de Piré, and Saulx-Tavanes.

Chapter Five

1. A.D., E-487, Paul-François to Jean-Samuel Depont, 24 May 1766.

2. Ibid.

3. For Jacques de Flesselles, see Maurice Garden, *Lyon et les Lyonnais au XVIIIe siècle* (Paris, 1974), p. 494; Contract of proxy [*procuration*] for signing Jean-Samuel's contract of marriage as Paul-François's representative: A.N., M.C. *Etude* 95: 302, 29 Apr. 1766.

4. A.N., M.C., *Etude* 95: 302, "Contrat de mariage entre Me Jean-Samuel Depont et Dlle. Marie-Madeleine-Françoise L'Escureul de la Touche," 4 May 1766. (The ceremony of signing took place on 11 May).

5. Cf. Roland Mousnier, *Les Institutions de la France sous la monarchie absolue* (Paris, 1974), 1: 177. Mousnier feels that this image is false.

6. A.N., M.C., *Etude* 95: 302, "Partage entre Sieur de la Touche et Sieur et Dame Depont, 3 June 1766. This *partage* contains an *observation* on the terms of La Touche's marriage to Pierrette Cromot of 24 June 1745, as well as an "Etat des biens de M. de la Touche provenant de la succession de son père."

7. A.N., O¹-2810, "Maison du Roi," undated memorandum, "Fonctions des Intendants des Menus;" ibid., O¹-2812ᴬ, "Hôtels et Magazines des Menus."

8. Papillon de la Ferté, *Journal intime,* ed. Ernest Boyse (Paris, 1887), p. 232. See also pp. 65, 219, 272, 297.

9. A.N., O¹-2812ᴬ, "Observations de M. de la Ferté."

10. Ibid., "Prêts et mutations des différents effets du magazine en 1769."

11. Guy Chaussinand-Nogaret, *Gens de finance au XVIIIᵉ siècle* (Paris, 1972), pp. 68-69.

12. George V. Taylor, "Types of Capitalism in Eighteenth-Century France," *English Historical Review* 80 (July 1964); "The Paris Bourse on the Eve of the Revolution, 1781-1789," *American Historical Review* 67 (July 1962); Chaussinand-Nogaret, *Gens de finance.*

13. "Partage" of 3 June 1766 (cited in note 6), "Observation" 5.

14. For the Brunet family, see Guy Chaussinand-Nogaret, "Capital et structure sociale sous l'Ancien Régime," *Annales: E. S. C.* 25 (March-April 1970): 474.

15. "Partage" of 3 June 1766, "Observations" after each of the 29 articles.

16. Chaussinand-Nogaret, *Gens de finance,* pp. 52-53; J.-F. Bosher, *French Finances 1770-1795: From Business to Bureaucracy* (Cambridge, 1970).

17. "Partage" of 3 June 1766, article 14.

18. A. Renaudet, *Etudes sur l'histoire intérieure de la France, de 1715 à 1789: la Finance,* (Paris, Les cours de Sorbonne, 1946), pp. 57-58 and passim; Marcel Marion, *Dictionnaire des institutions de la France aux XVIIᵉ et XVIIIᵉ siècles* (Paris, 1923), "Ferme et Ferme Générale."

19. "Partage" of 3 June 1766, articles 18 and 19.

20. Ibid., article 17.

21. Chaussinand-Nogaret, *Les financiers de Languedoc au XVIIIᵉ siècle* (Paris, 1970) and *Gens de Finance;* Bosher, *French Finances.*

22. "Partage" of 3 June 1766.

23. Chaussinand-Nogaret, *Gens de finance,* p. 78.

24. Ibid., pp. 86-88.

25. See Vivian A. Gruder, *The Royal Provincial Intendants* (Ithaca, 1968). This is a study of the social and geographic origins of ninety intendants at the end of the Old Regime.

26. A.N., V-1, 354, "Provision d' office."

27. Etienne Denis Pasquier, *Mémoires du chancelier Pasquier, 1767-1862* (Paris, 1893), première partie, I:17.

28. Gruder, *The Royal Intendants,* p. 89.

29. Marion, *Dictionnaire des institutions,* "Maître des Requêtes"; Michel Antoine, *Le fonds du Conseil d'Etat du Roi aux Archives Nationales* (Paris, 1955), introduction; Roland Mousnier et al., *Le Conseil du Roi de Louis XII à la Révolution* (Paris, 1970), pp. 27ff.; Gustave Schelle, ed., *Les Oeuvres de Turgot, avec biographie et notes,* 4 vols. (Paris, 1913-23) 4: 124-28; Gruder, *The Royal Intendants,* Chs. 3 and 4. See also *Almanach Royal* (Paris: chez le Breton, 1765) under "Bureaux de MM. les Conseillers d'Etat" and "Commissions extraordinaires du Conseil." Gruder (*Royal Intendants*) estimates that 125 men ruled France in the councils of state in the 1760s and 70s.

30. A.N., V⁶-1243, 993. Series V⁶ contains lawcases of all kinds.

31. Alfred Neymark, *Turgot et ses doctrines,* 2 vols. (Paris, 1885), 1: 26-27.

32. A.N., V⁶-1243. The register listing the cases treated during this period by the *Conseil*

mentions the name of the *rapporteur* in the margin. Future intendants such as Taboureau des Réaux, Le Peletier de Cypierre, Perrin de Morfontaine, or Jacques de Flesselles appear somewhat more frequently than Depont. On the other hand, Chaumont de la Galaizière and Trudaine de Montigny appear less frequently. Depont and Turgot handled about the same number of cases. Without claim to statistical precision, we can say that Depont as *maître des requêtes* carried an average workload.

33. Mousnier, *Le Conseil du Roi*, p. 43.

34. *Almanach Royal* (1761–65), passim, especially 1765. pp. 158–61.

35. Ibid., p. 161. Depont served on Bureaux IV, VIII, X, XII, XIV.

36. Gruder, *The Royal Intendants*, p. 41n.

37. Roland Mousnier, *Etat et société* (Paris, 1967), p. 112. See also Paul Ardacheff, *Les Intendants de province sous Louis XVI* (Paris, 1909), pp. 55–56.

38. A.D., E–487, 24 Dec. 1765.

39. Douglas Dakin, *Turgot and the Ancien Régime in France* (1939 reprint ed; New York, 1972), pp. 16–17.

40. Croÿ, duc de, *Journal inédit du duc de Croÿ*, ed. vicomte de Grouchy and P. Cottin, 4 vols. (Paris, 1906) 1: 81.

41. See Dakin, *Turgot*, p. 122 on the *coteries* around the Duc d'Orléans, the Prince de Conti, and the Duc de Chartres.

42. Stéphanie Félicité Ducrest de Saint-Aubin, comtesse de Genlis, *Mémoires de la comtesse de Genlis sur le dix-huitième siècle et la Révolution française, depuis 1756 jusqu'à nos jours*, 10 vols. (Paris, 1825), 1: 374.

43. Ibid., 9: 313–14.

44. Ibid., 5: 110.

45. *L'Espion dévalisé* (London, 1782), p. 217. This polemical work, political as well as personal, has been attributed by Barbier to Baudoin de Guemanduc. *"Depont à Metz est un imbécile à jouer, mais sa femme joue sur le théâtre de M. de Montesson, et Depont a eu une intendance, clef du royaume."*

46. *Mémoires de la comtesse de Genlis*, 3: 324ff.

47. Ibid., 2: 168.

48. Reference in note 4 above.

49. Ibid., article 3. Cf. chapter 3 above, Table 3. 2.

50. Mousnier, *Etat et société*, p. 28.

51. Robert Forster, "Seigneurs and Their Agents," in *Vom Ancien Régime zur französischen Revolution*, ed. Ernst Hinrichs et al. (Göttingen, 1978), pp. 169–87; "The 'World' between Seigneur and Peasant," in *Studies in Eighteenth-Century Culture*, ed. Ronald Rossbottom (Madison, 1976), 5: 104–22; *The Nobility of Toulouse in the Eighteenth Century* (Baltimore, 1960).

52. Robert Forster, *The House of Saulx-Tavanes, Versailles and Burgundy, 1700–1830* (Baltimore, 1971); François Bluche, *Les Magistrats du Parlement de Paris au XVIIIe siècle* (Paris, 1960).

53. Gruder, *Royal Intendants*, 210.

54. Chaussinand-Nogaret, *Gens de finance*, p. 86. "The development of an authentic administration, easily seen as despotic, reduced their role [that of the magistrates of the Parlement of Paris]. Hostility to *finance* was only one aspect of their struggle against the administrative monarchy symbolized by the intendant."

Chapter Six

1. Maurice Bordes, *L'Administration provinciale et municipale en France au XVIIIe siécle* (Paris, 1972); A. Renaudet, *Etudes sur l'histoire intérieure de la France de 1715 à*

1789: La Finance, Les cours de Sorbonne (1946), pp. 60-65; Guy Chaussinand-Nogaret, *Gens de finance au XVIIIe siècle* (Paris, 1972), pp. 88-89.

2. Roland Mousnier, *Les Institutions de la France sous la monarchie absolue* (Paris, 1974), pp. 540-45; Bordes, *L'Administration,* pp. 148-52; Michel Antoine, *Le Conseil du roi sous Louis XV* (Paris, 1978); Antoine, "Les Conseils des Finances sous le règne de Louis XV," *Revue d'histoire moderne et contemporaine* 5 (1958): 161-200; J.-F. Bosher, *French Finances 1770-1795: From Business to Bureaucracy* (Cambridge, 1970); Steven L. Kaplan, *Bread, Politics and Political Economy in the Reign of Louis XV,* 2 vols. (The Hague, 1976); Douglas Dakin, *Turgot and the Ancien Régime in France* (New York, 1939, 1972), ch. 4; André Bourde, *Agronomes et Agronomie en France au XVIIIe siècle,* 3 vols. (Paris, 1968); Alexis de Tocqueville, *The Old Regime and the French Revolution* (New York, 1955); Pierre Goubert, *L'Ancien Régime II: Les Pouvoirs* (Paris, 1973).

3. Baron de Frénilly, *Souvenirs, 1768-1828* (Paris, 1908), p. 227; Dakin, Turgot, p. 21.

4. A.N., M.C., *Etude* 78: 1073, "Inventaire après décès de M. Depont," 13 Jan. 1806. No book titles are mentioned in the inventory; André Leguai, *Histoire du Bourbonnais* (Paris, 1960).

5. Leguai, *Bourbonnais,* pp. 72-84; Arthur Young, *Travels in France, 1787, 1788, 1789* ed. Jeffry Kaplow (Garden City, N.Y., 1969); Abel Poitrineau, *La Vie rurale en Basse-Auvergne au XVIIIe siècle, 1726-1789* (Paris, 1965).

6. "*Mémoire de la Généralité de Moulins*" by Le Vayer, intendant at the end of the seventeenth century, cited in Yves Camus, "Un Intendant de la généralité de Moulins au XVIIIe siècle, Jean de Pont, 1765-1778" (law thesis, University of Paris, 1956), p. 11n. I wish to thank M. Yves Camus for sending me his law thesis. Fortunately for my purposes he quotes generously from the intendant's correspondence at Moulins.

7. Olwen Hufton, *The Poor of Eighteenth-Century France, 1750-1789* (Oxford, 1974), pp. 80-91, 93n.

8. Leguai, *Bourbonnais,* p. 80. By the 1780s, there were a few wood-fueled iron forges, some mills producing chestnut meal and some stocking-making at Montluçon. But altogether these "industries" employed four hundred workers at most.

9. Hufton, *The Poor,* ch. 10 passim; Poitrineau, *La Vie rurale,* p. 370.

10. Poitrineau, *La Vie rurale,* pp. 463-64 on costs of transportation.

11. Leguai, *Le Bourbonnais,* 73.

12. Poitrineau, *La Vie rurale,* p. 696 suggests that Chazerat, intendant at Clermont from 1772 to 1789, was one of the few to stay long enough to see his projects through to completion.

13. Young, *Travels in France.*

14. Alexandrine des Escherolles, *Une Famille noble sous la terreur* (Paris, 1879), 1: 7.

15. Camus, "Un Intendant," pp. 17-20. Jean-Samuel's successor, in 1786, was again obliged to ask Paris for funds to repair the *hôtel de l'intendance:* "une aussi mauvaise maison," he wrote. A.N., H¹-1408, Moulins, 1786.

16. The *Almanach Royal* lists a succession of addresses in the Marais quarter; after 1779, it is 11, rue des filles Saint-Thomas, the residence he occupied with his father-in-law until Jean-Samuel died in 1806.

17. See Camus, "Un Intendant," pp. 21-23, 57, 60, 63; A.N., H¹-1149, Depont to Controller-General, 17 Jan. 1777; also A.D., Moselle, C-858, Contract of 1 July 1789.

18. A.N., H¹-1140, "Mémoire" of 10 July 1788.

19. A.N., H¹-1149, Albert to Depont, 28 Apr. 1772. Italics mine.

20. Ibid., Depont to Albert, 9 May 1772.

21. Ibid., Depont to Controller-General, 16 Jan. 1777.

22. Ibid., Reverseaux to Controller-General, 23 June 1779.

23. Ibid., Depont to Albert, 12 Dec. 1772, "... *faire mes démarches de vive voix.*"

24. Dakin, *Turgot,* pp. 152-53.

25. Jean-Louis Moreau de Beaumont, *Mémoire concernant les impositions et droits en Europe* (Paris, 1787–89), 2: 22–24, quoted in Vivian Gruder, *The Royal Provincial Intendants* (Ithaca, 1968), 6n. The *mémoire* was first published in 1769. Italics mine.

26. A.D., Allier, C–253, 12 Nov. 1768, quoted in Camus, "Un Intendant," pp. 26–37. Italics mine.

27. A.D., Allier, C–244, L'Averdy to *Bureau des Finances de Moulins*, 5 Mar. 1768, quoted in Camus, "Un Intendant," p. 36n.

28. Bordes, *L'Administration*, p. 145; Renaudet, *Etudes*, p. 62.

29. A.D., Allier, C–174, Villantroys to *Bureau des Finances*, 27 Aug. 1773, quoted in Camus, "Un Intendant," p. 39.

30. A.D., Allier, C–102, quoted in Camus, "Un Intendant," p. 41.

31. A.D., Allier, C–241, Depont to Bureau des Finances, 2 Oct. 1775, quoted in Camus, "Un Intendant," p. 30n.

32. Archives Municipales (hereafter A.M.) de Moulins, pp. 155, 244, 333–41, quoted in Camus, "Un Intendant," pp. 49–53, 51n, 52n.

33. Bordes, *L'Administration*, pp. 196–98. Bordes admits that the experience of the intendants on this issue varied greatly from province to province.

34. Camus, "Un Intendant," pp. 54–55, 59–61.

35. A.D., Allier, C–288, Ormesson to Depont, 12 Apr. 1770, quoted in Camus, "Un Intendant," p. 61n.

36. Dakin, *Turgot*, ch. 6; Kaplan, *Bread, Politics*. Kaplan's entire two-volume study treats this struggle between Turgot's new policies and the traditional defenders of grain *police*. In the massive correspondence of the intendants Kaplan has collected, I have found not one letter *from* Depont at Moulins. There are of course examples of instructions *to* Depont and other intendants. See Kaplan, *Bread, Politics*, 2: 495. In 1770 when Terray complained that he was poorly informed about the grain supplies, he rebuked many intendants for their slovenliness. 2: 550.

37. A.M., Moulins, 387, Depont to *Officiers de police* of Moulins, 16 Oct. 1775, quoted in Camus, "Un Intendant," p. 89n.

38. A.N., H¹–1149, 26 Apr. 1771, Depont to Saint-Prest, quoted in Camus, "Un Intendant," p. 90n. Italics mine. No doubt Depont's correspondent was Brochet de Saint-Prest, colleague of the new controller-general, Terray; he made a forture in the administration of grain supplies. See Dakin, *Turgot*, p. 153.

39. Gustave Schelle, ed., *Les Oeuvres de Turgot, avec biographie et notes*, 4 vols. (Paris, 1913–24), 4: 545, Depont to Turgot, n.d.

40. Ibid., pp. 538–47.

41. Controller-General to Depont, 15 March 1777, quoted in Camus, "Un Intendant," p. 72.

42. Camus, "Un Intendant," pp. 41–42, 65.

43. Dakin, *Turgot*, p. 105 and ch. 8 passim; Hufton, *The Poor*, pp. 182ff.

44. A.N., H¹–1149, Depont to d'Ormesson, 14 Dec. 1770.

45. Ibid., Depont to d'Ormesson, 27 Nov. 1770.

46. Ibid., d'Ormesson to Depont, 20 Dec. 1770.

47. Schelle, *Oeuvres de Turgot*, 3: 225.

48. A.N., H¹–1149, Depont to Albert, 28 Dec. 1770.

49. Dakin, *Turgot*, p. 117.

50. A.N., H¹–1149, *Détail des ateliers de charité, 1771*. Turgot at Limoges spent 47,200 livres on poor relief that year (Dakin, *Turgot*, p. 117); 70,000 livres were spent for the same purpose in Auvergne. See Hufton, *The Poor*, pp. 191–93.

51. A.N., H¹–1149, Harvoin to d'Ormesson, 1771.

52. Ibid., Depont to d'Ormesson, 29 Mar. 1771.

53. Ibid., 20 Jan., 29 Mar., 26 Apr., 1771.

54. A.D., Allier, "Inventaire sommaire ..." Series E, supplément (Moulins, 1906) 2, Letter of 26 Nov. 1771. See also Jean-Pierre Gutton, *La Société et les pauvres en Europe, XVIᵉ-XVIIIᵉ siècles* (Paris, 1974), p. 174 on the fear and hatred of rural inhabitants for "itinerant beggars" (*mendiants forains*).

55. Hufton, *The Poor,* p. 243.

56. A.N., H¹-1149, Controller-General Terray to Depont, 21 Sept. 1771.

57. Ibid., Depont to d'Ormesson, 21 Jan. 1771.

58. Ibid., Albert to Depont, 20 May 1772. Italics mine.

59. Ibid., Depont to d'Ormesson, 12 June 1773; "Ateliers de charité," 1773.

60. Ibid., "Ateliers de charité," Moulins, 1774.

61. Ibid., Comtesse de Saint-Georges to d'Ormesson, 16 June 1772.

62. Ibid., Albert to Depont, 3 July 1772.

63. Ibid., Depont to d'Ormesson, 20 Jan. 1771.

64. Hufton, *The Poor,* pp. 191–92.

65. Schelle, *Oeuvres de Turgot,* 3: 213, 217.

66. Dakin, *Turgot,* p. 114.

67. A.N., H¹-1149, "Ateliers de charité," Moulins, 1771.

68. Ibid., Depont to d'Ormesson, 30 Oct. 1771. Italics mine.

69. A.D., E-487, Paul-François Depont to Madame des Granges, 19 June 1765: "Although I am convinced that their misery is great, one must not always believe what they say, because there are many lazy individuals [*fainéants*] who make the hardship look worse than it is." This is not to say that Paul-François was indifferent to the plight of the poor; but he made distinctions among them. See above, chapter 2.

70. A.N., X¹ᴬ 8809, fol. 175, 14 Dec. 1774.

71. The tariff barriers counterbalanced the economic benefits of better transportation for the Auvergnats. Poitrineau, *La Vie rurale,* p. 708.

72. A.D., Allier, "Inventaire sommaire" (Moulins, 1913), 6, "Dons," MM. Flesselles et Depont, 1764. For the *collège,* see Leguai, *Bourbonnais,* p. 76.

73. One of them bore his name until the mid-nineteenth century, when it was renamed Boulevard Ledru Rollin. *Sic transit ...*

74. Camus, "Un Intendant," pp. 96–103, based on the municipal archives. Depont partially indemnified the victims of the second fire.

75. Ibid., pp. 104–7.

76. A.M., Moulins, "Registre" 212, fols. 49–50, Deliberation of 28 May 1778, cited in Camus, "Un Intendant," p. 112.

77. Robert Parisot, *Histoire de Lorraine (duché de Lorraine, duché de Bar, Trois Evêchés)* (Paris, 1922), 2: 188–266 and passim; Jean Schneider, *Histoire de la Lorraine* (Paris, 1951), pp. 83–85; Zoltan-Etienne Harsany, "Metz pendant la Révolution," *Mémoires de l'Académie de Metz,* ser. 5, vol. 5 (1957–59), ch. 1; Thibout de Morembert, "Est-il des moyens de rendre les juifs plus utiles et plus heureux?" *Mémoires de Metz,* ser. 6, vol. 1 (1973); Ruth F. Necheles, *The Abbé Grégoire, 1787–1831* (Westport, Conn., 1971), pp. 16–18.

78. René Taveneaux, "Les Ecoles de campagne en Lorraine au XVIIIᵉ siècle," *Annales de L'Est,* ser. 5, vol. 22 (1970): 164–165 and passim; Taveneaux, *Le Jansenisme en Lorraine, 1640–1789* (Paris, 1960); Alix de Rohan-Chabot, *Les Ecoles de campagne en Lorraine au XVIIIᵉ siècle* (Paris, 1969); M. Fleury and P. Valmary, "Les Progrès de l'instruction élémentaire de Louis XIV à Napoleon III d'après l'enquête de Louis Maggiolo," *Population* 12 (1957): 71–92.

79. *La Lorraine dans l'Europe des Lumières, Actes du Colloque, Université de Nancy, Octobre 24–27, 1966.* (Nancy, 1968). See especially the papers by Pierre Léon and Michel Devèze.

80. A.N., H¹-1140.

81. *Almanach Royal* (1778), *"Départements de MM. les Sécrétaires d'Etat."*

82. For example, A.D., Moselle, C–858, October 1780, March 1789.

83. Justin Worms, *Histoire de la ville de Metz depuis l'établissement de la République jusqu'à la Révolution française,* 2d ed. (Paris and Metz, 1963), p. 268; Parisot, *Lorraine,* 2: 129.

84. Bordes, *L'Administration,* pp. 160–70. This institutional setting might account for the scanty documentation of Depont's intendancy at Metz, even if the Archives of Moselle (the former *Hôtel de l'Intendance*) had not been destroyed by fire in 1870.

85. Jules Villain, *La France moderne* (Montpellier, 1911), 3: 505–7. See genealogy above (before ch. 1).

86. Gruder, *The Royal Intendants,* pp. 38, 128.

87. Parisot, *Lorraine,* 2: 130. See chapter 7.

88. A.N., H–1142, Depont to Prince de Montbarey, Metz, 3 Aug. 1780.

89. Ibid., Depont to Bertin, 8 March 1780.

90. Ibid., "Mémoire sur les haras," 25 June 1780.

91. Young, *Travels in France,* passim; Bourde, *Agronomes.*

92. Parisot, *Lorraine,* 2: 131.

93. A.N., H–1141, Blondel to Controller-General, Metz, 10 July 1788.

94. Ibid., "Frais des Etats," 1787–89.

95. Ibid., "Bureau" of Assembly to Controller-General, 17 Nov. 1788; "Mémoire," 10 July 1788.

96. Ibid., Depont to Controller-General, 17 May 1788.

97. Parisot, *Lorraine,* 2: 189. The garrison at Metz numbered thirty thousand at full strength. It was under the command of Marquis de Bouillé, a fervent royalist, in 1789.

98. Hufton, *The Poor,* pp. 226–44; Gutton, *La Société et les pauvres,* pp. 173–74, stresses the repressive aspect of the *dépôts.* See also Michel Foucault, *Discipline and Punish: The Birth of the Prison* (New York, 1979) and other works.

99. A.D., Moselle, C–858, "Etat des meubles ... du dépôt de mendicité à Metz," 1 Jan. 1776. Cf. Hufton, *The Poor,* pp. 235–36, on the dépôt at Riom.

100. A.D., Moselle, C–858, Calonne to Controller-General. The number of soldiers infected by venereal disease garrisoned at Metz had fallen from 248 in 1773 to 151 in 1774, and to 143 in 1775; the intendant did not want to see the trend reversed. Cf. also Hufton, *The Poor,* pp. 306–9.

101. A.D., Moselle, C–858/2, "Lettre de cachet," 7 Dec. 1774.

102. A.D., Moselle, C–858, Bertin to Depont, 26 May 1779.

103. Ibid., La Millière to Depont, 26 Apr. 1789.

104. Ibid., Depont to La Millière, 10 Apr. 1789, 11 May 1789.

105. Zoltan-Etienne Harsany, "Metz pendant la Révolution," *Mémoires de l'Académie de Metz,* ser. 5, vol. 6 (1959–61), ch. 2, pp. 8–9.

106. A.D., Moselle, C–858/2, Depont to La Millière, 5 July 1789, 18 Nov. 1789.

107. Ibid., Depont to La Millière, 10 Apr. 1789. See Gutton, *Société,* p. 174, on the mounted police and the poor.

108. Ibid., La Millière to Depont, 19 Apr. 1789. In retrospect, we now know that sending poor babies to the countryside was in fact a form of infanticide. Cf. George D. Sussman, "The Wet-Nursing Business in Nineteenth-Century France," *French Historical Studies* 9, no. 2 (Fall 1975): 304–28.

109. Parisot, *Lorraine,* 2: 199, claims that in 1787 this *géneralité* had a greater number of beggars than others.

110. A.D., Moselle, 858/3, La Millière to Depont, 23 June 1790, 4 July 1970.

111. Ibid., 3 Mar. 1790.

112. Harsany, "Metz pendant la Révolution," *Mémoires de l'Académie de Metz,* ser. 5, vol. 7 (1962), ch. 3, pp. 30–31.

113. A.D., Moselle, C-858, Depont to MM. les députés de l'Assemblée Nationale, 29 Mar. 1790.

114. *Moniteur Universel* no. 54, 23 Feb. 1790.

115. A.D., Moselle, C-858/3, MM. les Administrateurs de la Moselle to La Millière, November 1790.

116. Harsany, "Metz pendant la Révolution," *Mémoires de l'Académie de Metz*, ser. 5, vol. 5 (1957–59), ch. 1, p. 13.

117. In three cases these were first posts.

118. See Gruder, *The Royal Intendants*, appendix 4, for a list of intendants with their posts.

119. This is not to suggest that Depont was unique in this respect. Still, most of the intendants did not list Parisian addresses in the *Almanach Royal*.

Chapter Seven

1. A.D., E-487. Paul-François to Jean-Samuel Depont, 2 Mar. 1765. "Let us do our best . . . to prevent your brother [Paul-Charles] from being named mayor. That would not suit us at all."

2. E. Garnault, *Livre d'Or de la Chambre de Commerce de La Rochelle* (La Rochelle, 1902), p. 14; L. de La Morinérie, *La Noblesse de l'Aunis et de Saintonge aux Etats Généraux de 1789* (Paris, 1861), pp. 283–84.

3. A.D., Q-250. *"Biens des Emigrés"* (Depont des Granges). John G. Clark's unpublished manuscript on the merchants of La Rochelle indicates that profits in overseas trade were decidedly lower after 1756; the balance sheets he produces suggest that an *annual* revenue of thirty thousand livres would be exceptional by 1780, except for a handful of merchants such as Garesché, Goguet, Rasteau, and Vivier. See note 1, ch. 1 above.

4. A.D., E-487, Bonnet to M. Rondrale, 7 May 1788; E-487, Bonnet to M. L'Abbé Depont, 6 Dec. 1787.

5. A.D., E-489, "Etat général des payements faits pour la maison" June 1785 to July 1790.

6. Henri Robert, *Les Trafics coloniaux du port de La Rochelle au XVIIIᵉ siècle* (Poitiers, 1960), pp. 190–91. See John G. Clark's study of the merchants of La Rochelle in the eighteenth century. A part of this work appeared in *French Historical Studies* 10, no. 4 (Fall 1978): 572–98.

7. These *hôtels* are still there. The Depont town house is now a bank. It was bought by the bishop of La Rochelle in 1809 for forty-four thousand livres. A.D., E-509, Sale of 5 Aug. 1809. During my stay at La Rochelle I could see the Maison Poupet from the window of the Departemental Archives.

8. A.D., E-489, Receipts and Memoirs, 1786–88.

9. A.D., Q-250, "Biens des Emigrés" (Depont des Granges).

10. Robert, *Les Trafics coloniaux*, pp. 192, 192n.

11. François Bluche, *Les Magistrats du Parlement de Paris au XVIIIᵉ siècle* (Paris, 1960), pp. 341–42. "Fifty parlementaires had only four or five Parisian servants." Great families like the Choiseul-Gouffier or the Saulx-Tavanes had closer to twenty, but they were exceptional. French nobles or *"bourgeois vivant noblement"* did not amass servants like English lords or South Italian princes.

12. A.D. E-489, "Totalle de viande," October 1792 to February 1793.

13. Erik Dahl, *Le Château de Buzay* (La Rochelle, 1956). In 1962 La Rochecourbon was selected for *"Son et Lumière"* because of its extensive park.

14. Thanks to Père B. Coutant, local *curé* and historian, I was able to visit many of the manor houses in the region. The scene just described took place on Saint-Michael's Day,

1962. The *châtelaine*, an imposing woman in tweeds, assured us that the *fermiers* were always drunk.

15. A.D., Q-250, "Biens des Emigrés" (Depont des Granges).

16. A.D., 2C-3367, "Centième denier—achats." The *centième denier* is a transfer tax of 1 percent.

17. A.D., E-476, *"Etat des Emprunts,"* 1783-85. No notarized contract would be so phrased.

18. A.D., E-484, "Livre concernant mes rentes et prix de fermes," 1757-1807.

19. See chapter 3 above.

20. A.D., E-488, "Tableau des charges à payer," 1787; E-484 "Livre concernant mes rentes et prix de fermes."

21. A.D., E-487, Bonnet to M. D'Auzon, 21 Feb. 1788.

22. Ibid., 4 May 1788.

23. A.D., E-488. Income on slip of paper.

24. E. Garnault, *Le Livre d'Or de la Chambre de Commerce de La Rochelle* (La Rochelle, 1902), p. 14; A.D., E-475. Their efforts were in vain, at least through the male line. Of five sons, three died before 1795 without issue. Of the remaining two, Virson died unmarried in 1801 and Charles-Louis had no children. Charles-Louis-Marie was the last of the Deponts of La Rochelle. We catch a glimpse of him the year before his death in 1841. At seventy-two, "M. Depont, *propriétaire,"* stood beside the prefect and parish priest, dedicating a charity to one indigent sick person per annum from Aigrefeuille, an old family property. A.D., E-474, *Projet . . . les hospices de Communauté d'Aigrefeuille.* See chapter 1 above.

25. Recall that he must have lived close to his father, probably in the same town house, for the greater part of fifty years, 1723 to 1774.

26. See chapter 2.

27. A.N., M.C., *Etude* 21: 556., "Contrat de mariage," 24 June 1788.

28. For the information on the Fontange family in Auvergne, I am deeply indebted to M. Yves Leymarie, local historian at Auriac. See A.D., Cantal, series Q for an estimation of the Fontanges property. Their compensation under the Restoration settlement was 188,370 francs.

29. See note 27, article 4.

30. See note 27, articles 6 and 7.

31. A.N., M.C., *Etude* 21: 607, "Pacte de Famille," 12 pluvôse, An II (31 Jan. 1794). The *pacte* states that "at the death of Madame Depont in 1787 no inventory of the property belonging respectively to her estate and to the common property has been made in view of the perfect union and mutual attachment between the father and the two children who are the mother's heirs." One must be skeptical about such formulas, especially given the age of the children in 1787, still legal minors. In fact, only Jean-Samuel knew exactly the dimensions of his wife's fortune.

32. A.N., M.C., *Etude* 78: 1073., "Inventaire après le décès de M. Depont," 13 Jan. 1806.

33. J. Seznec and J. Adhémar, eds., *Diderot Salons* (Oxford, 1960), 2: 165-171 [1765]. Diderot was enthusiastic about Loutherbourg at the Salon of 1765, comparing him favorably to Vernet. I wish to thank my friend Michael Fried for indicating this reference and for identifying Loutherbourg's place in the history of French art in the eighteenth century.

34. Jean-Julien, ed., "Journal des Voyages faits en 1779 par M. Depont, intendant de la généralité de Metz," *Pays Lorrain et Pays Messin* (1912): 105-19; 164-77.

35. See Leo Marx, *The Machine in the Garden: Technology and the Pastoral Ideal in America* (New York, 1964).

36. A. M. Roederer, baron de, ed. *Oeuvres de Roederer, Comte de, pair de France* (Paris, 1853-59), 7: 642.

37. See chapter 5 above. Madame de Montesson was the aunt of Madame (later countess) de Genlis.

38. *Mémoires inédits de Madame la Comtesse de Genlis* (Paris, 1825), 3: 324–25.

39. Holden Ferber and R. J. Marshall, eds., *The Correspondence of Edmund Burke* (Cambridge and Chicago, 1965), 5: 226–27. The Comtesse de Genlis to Edmund Burke, 12 Oct. 1785.

40. See George Rudé, *Paris and London in the Eighteenth Century: Studies in Popular Protest* (New York, 1971), pp. 268–92 and passim. An anonymous informer of 1780 gave this description of the Gordon rioters: "200 house brakers with tools, *550 pick-pockets,* 6,000 of alsorts, and 50 men that gives them orders ..." Rudé, *Paris and London,* p. 298. Italics mine. The "school of thieves," of course, refers to Dickens's *Oliver Twist.*

41. *Burke Correspondence,* 5: 236. Richard Burke, Sr., to Edmund Burke, 10 Nov. 1785.

42. Ibid., p. 237.

43. Alfred Cobban and Robert A. Smith eds., *The Correspondence of Edmund Burke* (Cambridge and Chicago, 1967), 6: 33. Edmund Burke to Richard Burke, 11 Nov. 1789.

44. Charles-François preferred to be known as "DePont" rather than "Depont." I have kept his spelling since it helps distinguish him from other members of the Depont family.

Chapter Eight

1. Guy-Marie Sallier, *Annales françaises, 1774 à 1789,* 2d ed., (Paris, 1813), pp. 147–48.

2. Henri Carré, "Un précurseur inconscient de la Révolution: Le conseiller Duval d'Esprémesnil, 1787–88," *Révolution Française* 33 (1897): 349–73; 405–37. See also Carré, *La Fin des Parlements* (Paris, 1912).

3. Carré, "Un précurseur," p. 352. For a brief description of the chambers, see Jean Egret, *The French Prerevolution, 1787–1788,* trans. W. D. Camp (Chicago and London, 1977), pp. 293–96. See also J. H. Shennan, *The Parlement of Paris* (London, 1968); Bailey Stone, "The Old Regime in Decay: Judicial Reform and the Senior Parlementarians at Paris, 1783–84," *Studies in Burke and His Time* 16, no. 53, (Spring 1975): 245–59; William Doyle, "The Parlements of France and the Breakdown of the Old Regime, 1771–1788," *French Historical Studies* 6 (1970): 415–58.

4. Sallier, *Annales françaises,* p. 151, quoted in Egret, *Prerevolution,* p. 148. On 3 May 1788 the Parlement of Paris refused to register the royal edict establishing the new Plenary Court intended to reduce the competence of the Parlement and prepare the way for tax reform from above. See Marcel Marion, *Le Garde de Sceaux Lamoignon et la réforme judiciaire de 1788* (Paris, 1905).

5. For the age of the councilors, see Egret, *Prerevolution,* p. 90; for conflict over legal fees, see B. Stone, "The Old Regime in Decay," pp. 245–59.

6. Stone, "The Old Regime in Decay," p. 250.

7. Etienne-Denis Pasquier, duc d'Audiffret, *Mémoires du Chancelier Pasquier, 1767–1862,* première partie, vol. 1 (Paris, 1893), p. 24.

8. Pasquier, *Mémoires,* 1: 23.

9. Pasquier, *Mémoires,* 1: 26; Egret, *Prerevolution,* p. 90.

10. Sallier, *Annales françaises,* p. 94.

11. Charles-Louis-François Barentin de Paule, *Mémoire autographe de M. de Barentin, chancelier et garde des sceaux, sur les derniers conseils du Roi Louis XVI,* ed. M. Champion (Paris, 1844), p. 91.

12. Sallier, *Annales françaises,* pp. 94–95.

13. Pasquier, *Mémoires,* 1: 27–28.

14. Barentin, *Mémoire autographe,* p. 88.

15. A.N., 0¹-357 (258). Letter of 15 Aug. 1787 cited in Egret, *Prerevolution,* p. 91.

16. Cf. J. F. Bosher, introduction to translation of Egret's *Prerevolution,* xi.

17. Sallier, *Annales françaises,* p. 95, ca. August 1787.

18. Georges Michon, *Essai sur l'histoire du parti feuillant: Adrien Duport* (Paris, 1924).

19. Egret, *Prerevolution,* p. 192; R. Darnton, "The Gallo-American Society" (M.A. thesis, Saint John's College, Oxford, 1962), appendix.

20. Barentin, *Annales françaises,* p. 87.

21. Louis Gottschalk, *Lafayette between the American and the French Revolutions, 1783–1789* (Chicago, 1950), p. 416.

22. Barentin, *Annales françaises,* pp. 87–88.

23. Elizabeth Eisenstein, "Who Intervened in 1788? A Comment on Georges Lefebvre's Coming of the French Revolution," *American Historical Review* 71 (October 1965): 102, italics added. Eisenstein calls for "some sort of collective biography of these men" as indispensable to any understanding of how the Revolution came about (p. 99). In a small way, this chapter contributes to a collective biography of the Committee of Thirty.

24. See Egret, *Prerevolution,* passim.

25. *"Duport a été par excellence un animateur . . . un homme politique de première place."* Michon, *Histoire du parti feuillant,* pp. 3, 24–39.

26. Ibid., pp. 30–31.

27. Ibid., pp. 24–38; Egret, *Prerevolution,* pp. 192, 330; George Lefebvre, *The Coming of the French Revolution: 1789,* trans. R. R. Palmer (New York, 1960), p. 31, 46, 58.

28. Michon, *Histoire du parti feuillant,* pp. 38–39.

29. *Mémoires* of the duke of Montmorency-Luxembourg, one of the charter members and a very close friend of Duport's. Quoted in Egret, *Prerevolution,* pp. 191, 327.

30. Louis Gottschalk and Margaret Maddox, *Lafayette in the French Revolution: Through the October Days* (Chicago and London, 1969), pp. 8–9; Gottschalk, *Lafayette* (cited in note 21), pp. 314, 412–13, 416, 418.

31. *Procès-Verbal de l'Assemblée Nationale* (Paris, chez Baudouin, 1789) vol. 8, no. 135, pp. 15–18. "Séance du 26 novembre 1789."

32. Alphonse Aulard, *La Société des Jacobins,* 6 vols. (Paris, 1889), 1: 437.

33. Alfred Cobban, *The Myth of the French Revolution* (London, 1955); see also Cobban, *Aspects of the French Revolution* (New York, 1968); *A Social Interpretation of the French Revolution* (Cambridge, 1962).

34. Except the duc d'Aiguillon, the duc de Broglie, and the vicomte de Noailles.

35. Aulard, *Jacobins,* 1: xlv.

36. Ibid., p. 437.

37. Ibid., 2: 416.

38. Michon, *Histoire du parti feuillant,* pp. 135–80; *The Correspondence of Edmund Burke,* vol. 6, ed. A. Cobban and R. A. Smith (Cambridge and Chicago, 1967), pp. 104–9, Burke to Duport, esp. p. 107.

39. Ernest Barker, "Burke on the French Revolution," *Essays on Government* (Oxford, 1945), p. 210.

40. *Burke Correspondence,* 6: 105–6, 109–15.

41. Ibid., pp. 163–64, François de Menonville to Burke, 17 Nov. 1790. The description of the Jacobin Club was especially unfortunate, given its moderate complexion in 1790. The translation also leaves something to be desired.

42. Ibid., p. 166.

43. Ibid., p. 167.

44. Burke, *Réflexions sur la Révolution française* (French ed. of 1791), p. 547, quoted in

Notes to Pages 186–90 / 261

Jacques Godechot, "Une première critique des 'Réflexions sur la Révolution française' de Burke," *Annales historiques de la Révolution française* 27 (July-September 1955): 225n.

45. Edmund Burke, *Reflections on the Revolution in France and on the Proceedings in Certain Societies in London Related to That Event in a Letter Intended to Have Been Sent to a Gentleman in Paris by the Right Hon. Edmund Burke,* (8th ed., Dublin, 1791), p. 109n. Italics Lally's.

46. *Burke Correspondence,* vol. 5. ed. Holden Furber (Cambridge and Chicago, 1965), Richard Burke to Jane Burke, 9 Nov. 1785.

47. See Hans A. Schmitt and John C. Weston, Jr., "Ten Letters to Edmund Burke from the French Translator of the *Reflections on the Revolution in France,*" *Journal of Modern History* 24 (1952): 406-23; 25 (1953): 49-61. Calonne asked Burke to help establish diplomatic relations between the émigré court in exile and England. (*JMH* 24: 412n).

48. Barker, "Burke on the French Revolution," pp. 211-12.

49. Burke, *Reflections* (1791), p. 112. See also Fredrick A. Dreyer, "The Genesis of Burke's *Reflections,*" *Journal of Modern History* 50 (September 1978): 462-79. On the place of the Queen of France in Burke's work, see Isaac Kramnick, *The Rage of Edmund Burke: Portrait of an Ambivalent Conservative* (New York, 1977). Kramnick draws attention to Burke's emphasis on the "nakedness" of Marie-Antoinette as she fled "the lustful, ravaging mob" in October, 1789. "Uncovering and exposing nakedness is, however, essential both for intensifying the sense of sexual violation and as a crucial link to Burke's central ideological argument." Ibid., pp. 152-53 and passim.

50. *Reflections* (1791), p. 202.

51. Ibid., p. 109n; see also *Burke Correspondence,* 6: 33n.

52. Jean Egret, *La Révolution des Notables: Mounier et les Monarchiens 1789* (Paris, 1950).

53. Alphonse Aulard, *Les Orateurs de l'Assemblée Constituante* (Paris, 1882), pp. 326, 342-43, and passim; pp. 323-75 on the *Monarchien* Party. Aulard betrayed his own aversion to flights of rhetoric—especially conservative royalist rhetoric—when he commented on this speech: "*Cette réflexion ingénieuse, trop ingénieuse peut-être . . .*" (p. 343).

54. Preface, 1791 edition.

55. H. V. F. Somerset, "A Burke Discovery," *English* 8 (Spring 1951): 171-78. The French version of these four letters was published in the *Annales historiques de la Révolution française* (1951): 360-73. Thanks to Thomas Copeland, well-known biographer of Burke, I received a copy of the pamphlet, *Answer to the Reflections of the Right Hon. Edmund Burke with the Original Notes* (London, 1791) from the Bodleian Library. See also Jacques Godechot, *The Counterrevolution,* trans. Salvator Attanasio (New York, 1971), pp. 57-58.

56. Paris, 15 Jan. 1786. *Annales historiques de la Révolution française* (1951): 364.

57. Ibid., p. 365 (4 Nov. 1789).

58. Ibid., p. 366.

59. Ibid., pp. 365-66.

60. Lally-Tollendal, a *Monarchien.* emigrated after the October Days. Burke gives the false impression that he was forced to flee. The *Times* (27 Oct. 1789) mentioned Lally's "flight."

61. *Burke Correspondence,* 6: 33, Edmund to Richard Burke, 11 Nov. 1789. Italics mine.

62. Carl B. Cone, *Burke and the Nature of Politics* (Lexington, 1964), 2: 339. Cone does not mean to exclude other influences, of course.

63. *Burke Correspondence,* 6: 39-50, Edmund Burke to Charles-François DePont, November 1789. Cone, *Burke,* 2: 296-99.

64. Keith M. Baker, "French Political Thought at the Ascension of Louis XVI," *Journal of Modern History* 50 (June, 1978): 294-95 and passim. See Robert and Elborg Forster, eds.,

"A Remonstrance of the Parlement of Paris," in *European Society in the Eighteenth Century* (New York, 1969), pp. 377–81. A passage in the Remonstrance of 13 Mar. 1788 reads: "Thus the rights of the human race, the fundamental principles of Society, the most enlightened reason, the most cherished interest of legitimate power, and the most elemental notions of morality and legality all unanimously condemn the use of *lettres de cachet*," ibid., p. 381.

65. E. Michel, *Biographie du Parlement de Metz* (Metz, 1855), p. 427.

66. *Burke Correspondence,* 6: 189n.4.

67. Adrien Duquesnoy, *Journal* (Paris, 1894), 2: 90. Italics his.

68. *Procès-Verbal de l'Assemblée Nationale* (cited in note 31.)

69. 9 Dec. 1789. Published in *Annales historiques de la Révolution française* (1951): 360–73.

70. Cf. Godechot, *The Counterrevolution.*

71. On the importance of Richard Price for the writing of the *Reflections,* see Frederick A. Dreyer, "The Genesis of Burke's *Reflections,"* cited in note 49.

72. Cone, *Burke,* 2: 296–313.

73. See also Adrien Duport's disappointment, *Burke Correspondence,* 6: 104–5 (29 Mar. 1790).

74. *Annales historiques de la Révolution française* (1951): 369. It is not clear how "involuntary" Burke's support was; after all, he was a close friend of Lally-Tollendal and the *Monarchiens,* many of whom had emigrated. He was also a friend of Calonne, the first emigré and chief minister for the émigré court at Koblenz. Cf. Godechot, the *Counterrevolution,* pp. 12–13, 149–51, 156–57.

75. The English translation of 1791 reads, "progress of that enlightened spirit." I think the French words "*le progrès des lumières*" are better translated as "the Enlightenment."

76. For some reason the last half of this passage was omitted from the English translation of 1791.

77. *Burke Correspondence,* 6: 451, Burke to Earl Fitzwilliam, 21 Nov. 1791. ("They" appears to be the English reform societies and their sympathizers in the Whig Party).

78. MS fragment, endorsed "On Nobility." Fitzwilliam MSS (Sheffield) Bks. 27–28, quoted in Robert Smith, "Burke's Crusade against the French Revolution: Principles and Prejudices," *The Burke Newsletter* 7, 3 (Spring 1966): 561.

79. Cone, *Burke,* 2: 304.

80. Harold Laski, *The Rise of European Liberalism* (London, 1936) pp. 231–36, especially p. 231. See also Emanuel Chill, *Power, Property and History: Barnave's "Introduction to the French Revolution" and Other Writings* (New York, 1971). Chill sees Barnave as the "classic embodiment of bourgeois political culture in its heroic period," (p. 64) and a kind of pre-Marxian thinker. Recent historians of the French Revolution have, in retrospect, disparaged such "moderates," considering them captives, as it were, of their own progressive view of history. An exception to this view is R. R. Palmer, *The Age of Democratic Revolution: The Challenge* (Princeton, 1959). After all, Barnave was also a "democrat" in 1789.

81. Cone, *Burke,* 2: 345.

82. Schmitt and Weston, "Ten Letters," cited in n. 47, p. 411. See also *Burke Correspondence,* 6: 189.

83. Schmitt and Weston, "Ten Letters," p. 414 (21 Feb. 1791).

84. Duquesnoy, the deputy from Bar-le-Duc, made this entry in his journal in November 1789: "So the 25th of November has passed and no revolution. Who would believe it? No one, not even my lackey, who told me yesterday that the '*isocrates*' are not strong enough to fight back. He is right." For Duquesnoy and his lackey, the "isocrates" were a political frac-

tion in the National Assembly who opposed the legislative changes of the summer and fall of 1789. In this context they hardly appear as a social class, but rather a group of like-minded (or wrong-headed) people, Duquesnoy, *Journal,* 2: 90.

85. Schmitt and Weston, "Ten Letters," p. 421 (29 May 1791).

86. The last of the ten letters from Dupont to Burke is dated 11 August 1791. Correspondence with Adrien Duport and Baron Cloots had ended in mid-1790.

87. Schmitt and Weston, "Ten Letters," p. 411n. See also Aulard, *La Société des Jacobins,* 3: 33–35.

88. Michon, *Histoire du parti feuillant,* p. 326, quoting from the correspondence among Marie Antoinette, Joseph II, and Leopold II. In this text Duport and Barnave seem to be using the word "class" as a political category, with social overtones perhaps, but primarily signifying *those who support constitutional monarchy.*

89. Aulard, *La Société des Jacobins,* 2: 197, 114 and passim. See also Jack R. Censer, *Prelude to Power: The Parisian Radical Press, 1789–1791* (Baltimore, 1976).

90. Aulard, *La Société des Jacobins,* 2: 281. Montmorin shocked his audience when he replied: "This is not the moment to send those who have declared themselves in favor of the Revolution to foreign embassies."

91. Charles-François-Duperier Dumouriez, *Mémoires du général Dumouriez,* 4 vols. (Paris, 1822), 2: 159–61. "These promotions," wrote Dumouriez in an effort to minimize his own radicalism, "were wise. Most of these men were former diplomats. They were all known to the king. There was only one Jacobin among them, and he was a man of intelligence, wisdom, and prudence."

92. Frédéric Masson, *Le Départment des Affaires Etrangères pendant la Révolution, 1787–1804* (Paris, 1877), pp. 163–64, 170, and 143–81 passim. See also Albert Sorel, *L'Europe et la Révolution française* (Paris, 1921), pp. 409–10, and Albert Mathiez, *The French Revolution,* trans. Catherine Alison Phillips (New York, 1956), pp. 144–47.

93. Archives des Affaires Etrangères, Paris, "Correspondance politique," vol. 112, May 1792–August 1792.

94. Godechot, *The Counterrevolution* (cited in note 55), pp. 149–51, 156–59.

95. Ibid., p. 161; Mathiez, *The French Revolution,* p. 147.

96. Jacques Mallet du Pan, *Mémoires et correspondence pour servir à l'histoire de la Révolution française,* 2 vols., ed. A. Sayous (Paris, 1851), 1: 280–83; Godechot, *The Counterrevolution,* pp. 76–77. Burke's son Richard went to Koblenz at Calonne's instigation in July 1791. See Schmitt and Weston "Ten Letters," cited in note 47, p. 412n.

97. Abbé Maury (1746–1817) became a cardinal in 1795, presumably in exile, and archbishop of Paris under Napoleon. On his love of order see Alphonse Aulard, *Les Orateurs de l'Assemblée Constituante* (Paris, 1882), pp. 213–62.

98. See Dumouriez's instructions to DePont and the ministers to other German courts of 28 April 1792 in Sorel, *L'Europe et la Révolution française,* 2: 416–17, 417n.

99. Mathiez, *The French Revolution,* pp. 152–60.

100. Ibid., p. 153; George Rudé, *The Crowd in the French Revolution* (Oxford, 1959), pp. 98–103 and passim.

101. Sorel, *L'Europe et la Révolution française,* 2: 487ff.

102. Mathiez, *The French Revolution,* pp. 153–54; Michon, *Histoire du parti feuillant,* pp. 405–7.

103. Michon, *Histoire du parti feuillant,* p. 380.

104. Mathiez, *The French Revolution,* p. 154.

105. Gottschalk and Maddox, *Lafayette . . . Through the October Days,* chs. 11–12.

106. *Answer to the Reflections* (cited in note 55), p. 15; Somerset, "A Burke Discovery" (cited in note 55).

107. Aulard, *La Société des Jacobins*, 2: 416.

108. *Answer to the Reflections* (cited in note 55 above), p. 11. See also *AHRF* (cited in note 55), pp. 51–52.

109. *Answer to the Reflections*, p. 25, note 15 in original, italics mine.

110. Glyndon G. Van Deussen, *Sieyès: His Life and His Nationalism* (New York, 1932), pp. 74–76.

111. Keith M. Baker, "French Political Thought at the Ascension of Louis XVI," *Journal of Modern History* 50 (June 1978): 303.

112. A.N., F⁷–4670, DePont.

113. Michon, *Histoire du parti feuillant*, pp. 434–43; Chill, *Power, Property, and History*, p. 16.

114. A.N., M.C., *Etude* 78: 1073, 13 Jan. 1806, "Inventaire après le décès de M. Depont."

115. Théodore de Lameth, *Notes et souvenirs de Théodore de Lameth faisant suite de ses Mémoires*, ed. E. Welvert (Paris, 1914), pp. 6, 113.

116. *Burke Correspondence*, 5: 235–38.

117. Ibid.

118. André-Jean Tudesq, *Les Grands notables en France, 1840–49* (Paris, 1964) 2 vols.; Louis Bergeron, Guy Chaussinand-Nogaret, Robert Forster, "Les Notables du 'Grand Empire' en 1810," *Annales: E.S.C.* 26 (1971): 1052–75.

Chapter Nine

1. Zoltan-Etienne Harsany, "Metz pendant la Révolution," *Mémoires de l'Académie de Metz*, ser. 5, vol. 6 (1959–61) ch. 2, pp. 4–18.

2. A.N., 29 AP 87, "Ordonnances," 23 Nov. 1788, 18 Jan. 1789, 29 Apr. 1789, 28 Aug. 1789. I wish to thank Joseph Mandel of Columbia University for giving me this information, taken from his own work on Jean-Louis Roederer.

3. Harsany, "Metz," ch. 2, pp. 17–18.

4. Arthur Young, *Travels in France during the Years 1787, 1788 and 1789*, ed. Jeffry Kaplow (Garden City, N. Y., 1969), pp. 152–53; Samuel F. Scott, "Problems of Law and Order during 1790, the 'Peaceful' Year of the French Revolution," *American Historical Review* 80, no. 4 (October 1975): 865–71. See also William C. Baldwin, "*L'Affaire de Nancy, 1790*" (Ph.D. dissertation, University of Michigan, 1973).

5. Marquis de Bouillé, *Mémoires* quoted in Harsany, "Metz," ch. 2, p. 18n.

6. On the role of the "Committees" during the municipal revolutions see Lynn A. Hunt, "Committees and Communes: Local Politics and National Revolution in 1789," *Comparative Studies in Society and History* 18, no. 3 (July 1976): 321–46.

7. Harsany, "Metz," ch. 2, p. 19n gives the list of members with occupations.

8. Ibid., p. 24.

9. Ibid., pp. 19n, 25–26; See Hunt, "Committees," pp. 338–41, for the occupational composition of the committees at Montpellier, Reims, and Troyes.

10. See chapter 8 above.

11. François-Claude-Amour, Marquis de Bouillé, *Memoirs Relating to the French Revolution* (London, 1797), p. 140; Louis-Joseph-Amour, Marquis de Bouillé, *Souvenirs et Fragments*, 3 vols. (Paris, 1906), 1: 93, 111–13.

12. Bouillé, *Mémoirs*, p. 99.

13. Ibid., p. 139; Harsany, "Metz," ch. 2, p. 36n.

14. Harsany, "Metz," pp. 32–33.

15. M. L. Klepffel, "La Disette à Metz au moment de la Révolution, 1788-1790," *Mémoires de l'Académie de Metz.* ser. 4, vol. 9ᵉ(1928): 65.

16. Harsany, Metz," *Mémoires de l'Académie de Metz,* ser. 5, vol. 5 (1957-59), ch. 1, p. 14; Harsany, "Metz," ch. 2, p. 20 *"Depont n'était pas homme à prendre des responsabilités et à résister à un mouvement populaire qui avait triomphé à Paris comme ailleurs."*

17. A.M., Metz, ser. D, no. 2, D 9, quoted in Harsany, "Metz," ch. 2, p. 32n.

18. Bouillé, *Souvenirs,* 1: 113.

19. Harsany, "Metz," ch. 1, p. 31n.

20. Ibid., pp. 31-32.

21. Young, *Travels,* p. 145.

22. Harsany, "Metz," ch. 1, pp. 13-14; See also Emmanuel Michel, *Biographie du Parlement de Metz* (Metz, 1855); René Paquet, *Bibliographie analytique de l'histoire de Metz pendant la Révolution,* 2 vols. (Paris, 1926).

23. Thibout de Morembert, "Considérations sur les concours de l'Académie Royale de Metz de 1787 à 1788," *Mémoires de l'Académie de Metz,* ser. 6, vol. 1 (1973): 186-99, 226.

24. Ibid., p. 226. See chapter 7 above.

25. Bouillé, *Souvenirs,* 1: 111-12. In June 1791, Bouillé helped to organize the famous Flight to Varennes which earned him "suspension" of his command from the Commune of Metz. He emigrated the same month. Depont's other "colleague," Montmorency-Laval, bishop of Metz, refused to take the oath to the new Constitution of the Clergy in February 1791. The Commune requested of Paris that he be removed as well. See Harsany, "Metz," *Mémoires.* ser. 5, vol. 7 (1962), ch. 3 pp. 112-14.

26. Harsany, "Metz," ch. 3, pp. 21-26. Metz had 20,035 males in 1790, 3,260 of whom were "electors." If half the males were "adults," then 32.6 percent of them could vote. Given the age structure in 1790, I suspect the percentage of voters was higher than one-third of adult males.

27. See chapter 6.

28. Harsany, "Metz," ch. 3 p. 30n.

29. A.N., AD SVI, carton 53. "Exposé de ce qui s'est passé à Metz le 4 août 1790"; Paquet, *Bibliographie de Metz,* p. 1355.

30. *"M. Depont était encore tellement effrayé et même anéanti, qu'on eût été presque tenté d'en rire."* Bouillé, *Souvenirs,* 1: 151. For the entire episode from Bouillé's perspective, see pp. 148-52. The young marquis was indignant that Depont forgot to mention the rescue in an article in the *Gazette de Nancy,* vaunting his own courage and *gloire* instead.

31. Maurice Garden, *Lyon et les Lyonnais au XVIIIᵉ siècle* (Paris, 1970), 494; Albert Mathiez, *The French Revolution* (New York, 1956), p. 47.

32. "Procès-Verbaux des Actes du Directoire du Département de la Charente-Inférieure," *Archives historiques de la Saintonge et de l'Aunis* (Paris and Saintes, 1906) 36: 31 July, 1790 to 29 April 1792.

33. Ibid., pp. 235-36. For the Varaize affair, see pp. 66-67.

34. Ibid., 39: pp. 31-32, 8 June 1792.

35. Ibid., p. 93, 19 July, 1792.

36. Ibid., pp. 94-96. There are examples of similar protests in the parishes of Loiré (p. 29), Chaniers, Fontcouverte, La Chapelle (pp. 66-67), and Mosnac (p. 97).

37. Claude Laveau, "Le Monde rochelais de l'Ancien Régime au Consulat," (*thèse de doctorat,* Paris, 1972), pp. 553-62.

38. "Procès-Verbaux," 39: p. 142, 1 Nov. 1792. Donald Greer estimates that there were 1,335 émigrés from the department, although he found no information on their social composition. D. Greer, *The Incidence of the Emigration during the French Revolution* (Cambridge, Mass., 1951), pp. 109ff. A large number of the émigrés whose land was sequestered

were military nobles from the hinterland. See A.D., Q-248-50, "Partages des Biens des Emigrés, Years III-VIII."

39. "Procès-Verbaux," 39: p. 183, 30 Jan. 1793.

40. For the budgets of 1791 and 1792, See "Procès-Verbaux," 36: pp. 356-63; 39: pp. 57-59. The *"frais d'impression"* represented between 10 and 18 percent of the annual budget for the department, roughly equal to public expense for welfare (*bienfaisance*).

41. Laveau, "Monde rochelais," p. 557.

42. "Procès-Verbaux," 39: pp. 168-69, 8 Jan. 1793. See A.D., series Q.

43. Laveau, "Monde rochelais," pp. 553-58.

44. "Procès-Verbaux," 39: pp. 245-49, 21 Mar. 1793.

45. Ibid., pp. 189ff. In May 1793 the department was spending thirty thousand francs daily to procure supplies for General Marcé's army of fifteen thousand men who were preparing to march on the Vendée. Ibid., pp. 241-43.

46. Donald Greer, *The Incidence of the Terror during the French Revolution* (Cambridge, Mass., 1935), pp. 145ff. Over half of the death sentences during 1793-94 were pronounced in four departments: Rhône (Lyon), 1,880; the three that touch the Vendée, 7,050. Moselle (Metz), incidentally, had 45 death sentences.

47. Georges Lefebvre, *The Directory,* trans. Robert Baldick (New York, 1964), pp. 6-8, 14, 106-7.

48. "Procès-Verbaux," 36: passim.

49. A.D., C-267, Cahiers of Aigrefeuille, Virson, La Jarne, Thairé.

50. Ibid., Cahier of Saint-Pierre-près-de Surgères. See Olwen Hufton, *The Poor of Eighteenth-Century France, 1750-1789* (Oxford, 1974).

51. A.D., E-479, Faurie to Paul-Charles Depont, 28 Dec. 1789.

52. A.D., E-501, Chauvet to Bonnet, 15 May 1789.

53. A.D., E-479, Phillotine de Fougère to MM. at Saint-Georges, Ile d'Oleron, 5 Nov. 1789.

54. A.D., E-501, Chauvet to Bonnet, 29 Jan. 1791.

55. A.D., E-475, "Procédure," 22 July 1790.

56. D. Massiou, *Histoire politique, civile et religieuse de la Saintonge et de l'Aunis depuis les premiers temps historiques jusqu'à nos jours,* 6 vols. (Paris, 1836-40), 5: 66-80.

57. Ibid., p. 41.

58. *Journal Patriotique . . . de Saintonge et d'Angôumois* (1792), p. 126 quoted in Massiou, *Saintonge,* 5: 160. This history was published in 1840. The passage reflects the "philosophy" of many "notables" of the July Monarchy, especially the need to educate the "poor and ignorant" before giving them the vote.

59. A.D., E-475, Paul-Charles to District of Rochefort, Year III.

60. Recall that the Clisson-Lescure branch of the Depont family came from the heart of the Vendée. See chapter 1.

61. A.D., E-492, "Quittance d'affranchissement," 5 June 1792.

62. A.D., E-484, "Livre conçernant mes rentes." See the account for La Brande and Manderoux for 1791. The history of the French public debt during the French Revolution has not been written. Jacques Godechot, *Les Institutions de la France sous la Révolution et l'Empire* (Paris, 1951), pp. 329-33, 329n; Leo Gershoy, *The French Revolution and Napoleon* (New York, 1964), pp. 321-22. Lefebvre, *Directory,* ch. 11.

63. A.D., E-475, Declaration for the Forced Loan, 17 Dec. 1793.

64. See chapter 4.

65. A.D., E-491, Claims of Mainguet, Year VI (1798); E-492, Claims of Mainguet, undated; E-479, Paul-Charles to Administration of Ciré, 27 Sept. 1796.

66. A.D., E-475, Declaration for the Forced Loan, 17 Dec. 1793; E-501, Chauvet to Bonnet, 11 June 1793.

67. A.D., E-487, Bonnet to M. l'Abbé, 6 Dec. 1787; E-489, Expenses, 1790–93.

68. A.D., E-488, Income 1790-91 (on slip of paper); E-489, "Contribution foncière, Commune de Forges," 1791-93; E-501, Chauvet Accounts, 1796; E-475, Receipt of 7 Apr. 1792; Declaration for the Forced Loan; Receipt of 25 Feb. 1794.

69. A.D., E-475, Certificate of Residence; Extract of the Deliberation of the Committee of Revolutionary Surveillance of La Rochelle, 11 Fructidor, Year II (27 Aug. 1794). Massiou, *Saintonge,* 5: 282-83.

70. Massiou, *Saintonge,* 5: 322, 331; Laveau, *Monde rochelais,* pp. 559-62.

71. A.D., E-475, Paul-Charles to District of Rochefort, Year III.

72. This is no doubt true. The assignat of a hundred livres in 1790, still worth forty in August 1794, fell to twenty-five in January 1795 and to four in August 1795! R. Mousnier and C.-E. Labrousse, *Le XVIIIe siècle (1715-1815), Histoire générale des civilisations* (Paris, 1953), 5: 410. See S. E. Harris, *The Assignats* (Cambridge, Mass., 1930).

73. A.D., E-475, Paul-Charles to District of Rochefort, 15 Fructidor, Year III (1 Sept. 1795).

74. Ibid., Session of 4 Sept. 1795; Receipt of 4,315 pounds of beans, 21 Mar. 1796; Tribunal of Marennes, 25 July 1796; E-501, Chauvet to Bonnet, 17 Aug. 1796. See M. Delafosse and C. Laveau, *Le Commerce du sel de Brouage aux XVIIe et XVIIIe siècles* (Paris, 1960), p. 32 and passim.

75. A.D., E-479, Paul-Charles to Canton of Ciré, 27 Sept. 1796; Q-250, "Biens des Emigrés." See "Ferme des Chaumes"; E-481, Jean-Samuel Depont to Canton of Ciré, 20 Nov. 1796.

76. A.D., E-475, Receipt of 26 Mar. 1795; Liquidation of the Public Debt, 1 June 1795. See Gershoy, *French Revolution,* pp. 321-22; Godechot, *Les Institutions de la France,* pp. 441-44.

77. A.D., E-501, Survey by Chauvet, 30 May 1795; Q-250, "Biens des Emigrés," 28 Mar. 1797; Delafosse, *Commerce du sel,* pp. 14, 28-29. The *livre* varied from 0.5 to 0.9 hectares or 1.2 to 2.2 acres; E-501, Chauvet to Bonnet, 12 Mar. 1792.

78. L. de La Morinérie, *La Noblesse d'Aunis et de Saintonge, 1789* (Paris, 1861), see "Froger d'Equille": *Capitaine de Vaisseau, chevalier de St.-Louis, . . . émigré, périt avec son frère, Michel-Henri, 1795, à la descente de Quiberon."*

79. A.D., Q-250, Depont des Granges.

80. A.D., Q-301, Restitution of Unsold Land, 1814-1825; Marcel Garaud, *Histoire générale du droit privé français* (Paris, 1958) 2: 323 and passim.

81. Bibliothèque Municipale, La Rochelle, P. C. Martin de Chassiron, *Lettres sur l'agriculture du district de La Rochelle par un cultivateur,* 124 pp. (La Rochelle, 1795); René Porak, *Un Village de France* (Paris, 1943), a eulogy to Chassiron at Beauregard; A.M., La Rochelle, MS 312. P. Harouard, *Différents modes de cultiver nos domaines dans l'arrondissement de la sous-préfecture de La Rochelle* (La Rochelle, 1808). For Depont, see note 73 above.

82. A.N., F⁷-4670. The exact date of the arrest is not given. The report refers to the "Law of 4 frimaire" (October 1793?).

83. For information on the Fontanges family during the Revolution, I am deeply indebted to M. Michel Leymarie of Auriac (Cantal).

84. A.N., F⁷-4670. The release is dated 11 Vendémiaire, Year III, September 1795.

85. A.N., M.C., *Etude* 78: 1073, "Inventaire après décès de M. Depont," 13 Jan. 1806; A.N., M.C., *Etude* 21: 607, "Pacte de Famille," 12 Pluvôse, Year II (31 Jan. 1764).

86. A.D., E-479, Jean-Samuel to Paul-Charles, 15 Mar. 1798.

87. A.N., M.C., *Etude* 78: 1073, "Inventaire après décès," 1806.

88. A.N., AF^{IV}-1422 (Depont, Jean-Samuel), Nivôse, Year XI (January 1803). I wish to thank Joseph Mandel of Columbia University for sending me this reference.

89. Baron de Frénilly, *Souvenirs, 1768–1828* (Paris, 1908), pp. 211, 211n, Frénilly refers to the salon of *"la brillante Madame de Fontanges, fille de M. de Pont,"* but that is all.

90. A.D., E-479, Jean-Samuel to Paul-Charles, 15 Mar. 1798. Is "Veith" really "Weis," the well-known Swiss banker of the Directory? Jean-Samuel was not very quick to grasp foreign names.

91. A.D., E-479, Jean-Samuel to Paul-Charles, 18 Brumaire.

Epilogue

1. A.N., M.C., *Etude* 78: 1073. "Inventaire après décès de M. Depont," 13 Jan. 1806.

2. Gabriel Sénac de Meilhan, *Du Governement, des moeurs, et des conditions en France avant la Révolution* (London, 1795), p. 70.

Index

The Johns Hopkins University Press
This book was composed in Compugraphic English Times text and
display type by Action Comp. It was printed on 50-lb. #66 Eggshell
Offset cream stock and bound in Roxite linen cloth by Universal
Lithographers, Inc.